Understanding Authority
in Higher Education

Understanding Authority
in Higher Education

Dean O. Smith

ROWMAN & LITTLEFIELD
Lanham • Boulder • New York • London

Published by Rowman & Littlefield
A wholly owned subsidiary of The Rowman & Littlefield Publishing Group, Inc.
4501 Forbes Boulevard, Suite 200, Lanham, Maryland 20706
www.rowman.com

Unit A, Whitacre Mews, 26-34 Stannary Street, London SE11 4AB

British Library Cataloguing in Publication Information Available

Library of Congress Cataloging-in-Publication Data Available

ISBN 978-1-4422-4177-0 (cloth : alk. paper) -- ISBN 978-1-4422-4178-7 (electronic)

∞™ The paper used in this publication meets the minimum requirements of American National Standard for Information Sciences Permanence of Paper for Printed Library Materials, ANSI/NISO Z39.48-1992.

Printed in the United States of America

Contents

Preface

Within the complex environment of higher education, administrators and faculty members face daunting challenges in their unique domains of institutional governance. Although they may have sound expertise in their academic specialties, many of them come from backgrounds that provide minimal formal preparation for university administration. Furthermore, what training they acquire through occasional specialty workshops may provide fundamental guidelines for specific administrative procedures but may not provide sufficient depth to handle challenging situations where managerial guidelines become blurred.

As I look back on my academic career, I realize that many of the greatest administrative challenges in higher education arose from basic misunderstandings of authority and its limitations by administrators and faculty members alike. These misunderstandings were the primary source of disruptive confusion, mistrust, and mismanagement. Consequently, I have concluded that institutional governance would improve significantly if its personnel clearly understand the fundamental principles of authority. This raises the need for a book on higher-education administration that clarifies issues of authority in an academic context. And that is the motivation for writing *Understanding Authority in Higher Education*.

Throughout, I have introduced basic principles of authority in academic settings and then analyzed their application in court decisions, nonlegal real situations, and anecdotal cases. Pedagogically, the book strives continuously to ascertain whether authority is used properly in an academic setting from a legal perspective, emphasizing the influence of academic cultural norms on legal principles and vice versa. Thus, the legal basis of authority in numerous administrative circumstances is well established. But, *Understanding Authority in Higher Education* goes further than law textbooks by using real and anecdotal case studies to examine aspects of authority that don't appear in court proceedings—those that lie beyond the reach of the law. In these cases, the book explores the anthropology—the behavior and the culture—of authority in the academic environment.

Understanding Authority in Higher Education is designed to be a core or supplemental text in courses on higher-education administration. It provides a concise introduction to fundamental legal and theoretical principles of administration in academia. As a study aid, each chapter concludes with a succinct summary of its key points. Furthermore, extensive citations documenting original sources provide detailed guidance for further in-depth study. In addition, regardless of the audience—administrators, faculty members, or students—the book is a unique resource as a text or reference book for anybody involved in higher education.

The book's twelve chapters sort informally into three groups: definitions and types of authority; selected major areas involving authority; and misuse of authority. Accordingly, the first four chapters characterize authority and its limitations. Chapter 1 defines the several meanings of the word and its cognate subjects, responsibility and accountability. It then explains various modifying influences on authority. The delegation of authority and its distribution into a bureaucratic organization are then examined. In chapter 2, the principles of shared authority are explored further. Specific attention focuses on the consultative nature of shared governance in academic settings. Chapter 3 examines loyalty and how it relates to authority, including the government's authority to require loyalty oaths. The legal aspects of loyalty—the fiduciary duty of loyalty—are then defined. The chapter concludes with an analytical look at conflicting loyalties in several commonplace situations. Chapter 4 describes the fundamental legal limitations on authority. These include constitutional rights such as due process, civil rights, Title IX requirements, and institutional policy obligations. Several forms of immunity from lawsuits are then discussed, including sovereign and qualified immunity.

The subsequent four chapters discuss authority in specific academic settings. Chapter 5 introduces the special features of academic authority, embodied in academic freedom, from the courts' and the faculty members' perspective. This includes a discussion of the legal limitations on the authority to criticize the administration, assign grades, and award degrees. Next, chapter 6 focuses on the authority to admit students. Salient legal parameters are described, such as antidiscrimination laws and affirmative action requirements. The occurrences of legacy preferences, bribery, and personal favors are then analyzed in several unorthodox but common situations. Student affairs are examined in chapter 7. The relationship between the university and its students is defined initially. Then, the university's custodial authority is analyzed in various situations, such as student conduct on and off campus, housing, room searches, and privacy rights. Chapter 8 looks at authority relationships in the hiring process. The constraints imposed by equal employment opportunity and affirmative action laws are presented from a legal perspective. This is followed by a discussion of hiring processes that lie outside the normal limits of authority, such as patronage.

The final four chapters explore various aspects of misused authority. Chapters 9–11 take a look at accidental and deliberate transgressions of the limits of authority. In chapter 9, individual transgressions are considered. It begins by analyzing cases of unintentional and intentional disregard for the limits of authority, primarily in the context of agency law. The impact on institutional governance is examined in context. This includes a discussion of the legal doctrines of promissory estoppel and detrimental reliance. Chapter 10 continues by examining intrusions on authority by external parties. Initial attention concentrates on micromanagement by a superior, particularly during changes in institutional leadership. This is followed by an extensive examination of intrusive management by governing bodies, such as the legislature, the governor, and the governing board. Chapter 11 expands the study of transgressions with an analysis of individuals who resist authority. Various modes of resistance include insubordination, procrastination, incompetence, and delayed decision making. The final chapter, 12, describes various contractual aspects of firing authority, including "for cause" and "at-will" provisions. It concludes with discussions about progressive discipline, constructive discharge, and employees with substance abuse problems.

As in the predecessor to this volume, *Managing the Research University*, I should like to thank numerous mentors throughout my thirty-eight-year career at the University of Wisconsin–Madison, the University of Hawaii, and Texas Tech University. They taught me invaluable skills for managing both routine and more difficult administrative situations. And they thoughtfully pointed out and corrected weaknesses in my managerial approach. It is predominantly their wisdom tempered by my own experiences that I wish to share.

Likewise, I thank my colleagues who provided thoughtful comments on various aspects of this project. I am most appreciative. Also, I extend special thanks to Drs. Karlene Hoo and Judith Inazu. They patiently read and critiqued two draft versions of the entire manuscript, providing expert advice on various topics and constant encouragement. As everybody knows, that kind of support is invaluable. And, finally, I wish to acknowledge my beagle Barney, who faithfully lay at my side for many hours as I worked on this project.

Chapter One

Organizational Authority

AUTHORITY IN ACADEMIA

Over the centuries, universities have evolved into wonderfully complex organizations. The course of evolution has progressed from the medieval self-governing scholastic guilds where "the faculty is the university" to the modern multi-campus systems administered by politically charged governing boards. The distribution of authority within the institutions has co-evolved with the governance structure. As the universities became more complex, bureaucratic organization developed with numerous administrative levels. And, as an inevitable consequence, authority has become distributed downward into the hierarchy.

The complexity of authority distribution within academic institutions has attracted scholars of higher education, organizational behavior, management theory, sociology, and other interests. They have analyzed the impact of governance models on factors such as student graduation rates, research productivity, and levels of public support.[1] In addition, they have examined the intricacies of authority and governance within the academic environment, paying special attention to relationships involving the governing board, the administration, and members of the faculty.[2] Often, an already complex organization becomes even more complicated when viewed with such scrutiny.

In many analyses, the key issues often reduce to questions of who has authority, how is it shared, and what are its limits.[3] Answers to these fundamental questions derive from rudimentary organizational and legal principles. If university administrators and faculty members understand these principles, knowledgeable respect for authority and its limits enables reasonably smooth cooperation. In contrast, if they do not understand them, mistakes and misjudgments of authority can lead to unsettling mistrust. Thus, the best interests of the institution are served when its personnel clearly understand the limits of authority.

However, except in the most unusual cases, even within academic circles, individuals have little inclination to study the extensive scholarship on the meaning and dimensions of authority bestowed upon them. Why should they? They most probably have a working understanding of their authority and what it means from on-the-job training, personal experiences, newspaper accounts, school coursework, and so forth. Furthermore, they are usually operating within a comfort zone, where they are generally indifferent to the nuances of authority.

However, disruptive challenges to this innately relaxed position can arise occasionally. At the highest administrative levels, for example, the governor orders the university provost to close an academic research center; a state legislator asks the university president to hire a close relative; the president recommends admission of a wealthy donor's child into a graduate program. These examples at high administrative levels can be transposed to lower levels throughout the organization. A dean tells a faculty member to stop criticizing university policies; a departmental chair asks a professor to change a student's grade; a shop supervisor instructs employees to vote for a particular presidential candidate or risk being fired.[4] Regardless of the exact context, the dilemma remains the same: "I've been told to do something that I don't agree with. How do I respond to this directive? What are my rights?" If the limits of authority are not understood, each of these situations can cause considerable discomfort, confusion, and fear. Suddenly, control of a specific realm of responsibility seems lost as administrative guidelines become blurred.

Before pondering situations like this that push to the limits of authority, it helps to consider what the word "authority" really means. Indeed, even to frame questions and answers sensibly, the word's meaning and its relationship to two closely related words, responsibility and accountability, merit introductory attention. It is equally important to examine the ground rules for delegating authority. Therefore, initial attention will lay out the essentials of authority and its delegation. Or, stated more colloquially, "who has the power and who doesn't."

AUTHORITY DEFINED

According to the Oxford Dictionary, the word authority has two meanings. The primary definition describes authority as "the power or right to give orders, make decisions, and enforce obedience."[5] As institutionalized power, authority also carries the weight of enforcement. Orders are given, and they must be obeyed. For example, as an elected official, a governor has this kind of authority. However, the dictionary assigns an additional meaning to the word: "the power to influence others, especially because of one's commanding manner or one's recognized knowledge about something." This softer definition says nothing about enforcement or, for that matter, a right to give orders. Authority is limited to influence in this meaning of the word. Orders are given, and they may be obeyed if they convincingly make sense.

"Power or right to give orders . . . and enforce obedience" *versus* "power to influence." These two definitions constitute what scholars call formal and functional—or de facto—authority, respectively. Formal authority derives from a higher source; it is delegated from above. Ultimately, the source may be the electorate via an elected government body such as a legislature or, in a private setting, the articles of incorporation. Alternatively, functional authority is less formal; it is recognized by dint of an individual's skills, knowledge, or craftsmanship. In that sense, it is informal. This difference is expressed adroitly by Mortimer and McConnell: "Formal authority is based on legitimacy . . . and position, whereas functional authority is based on competence and person."[6] In other words, authority is either conferred by a higher source (formal) or acknowledged by a respectful audience (functional). This distinction is also described in terms of executive (formal) and epistemic (functional) authority: "between the authority of those who are 'in authority' (e.g., political leaders, parents, military commanders) and that of those who are 'an authority' (e.g., technical experts, scholars, medical specialists)."[7] Importantly, only formal authority conveys the powers of legal enforcement. The command would be: "Do as I say, or else." The parallel command of functional authority would be "Trust me on this: do as I say."

"Moral authority" is a special case of functional authority. This widely used phrase has an elusive definition. It is used in many different ways. Generally it refers to the right to weigh in on some topic based on personal experience. For example, Senator John McCain's opinions on military imprisonment carry moral authority because of his six years as a prisoner of war. It also refers to authority based on virtue: "The quality or characteristic of being respected for having good character or knowledge, especially as a source of guidance or an exemplar of proper conduct."[8] In either sense, moral authority conforms to the definitions of functional authority.

Both definitions of authority (formal and functional), refer to authority as a "power." In this context, power is defined as "the capacity or ability to direct or influence the behavior of others or the course of events."[9] The intertwined relationship between authority, power, and influence further characterizes the distinction between formal and functional authority. According to Robert Presthus, "Authority can be defined as the capacity to evoke compliance in others on the basis of formal position and of psychological inducements, rewards, or sanctions that may accompany formal position. The capacity to evoke compliance without relying on formal role or the sanctions at its disposal may be called influence. When formal position is not necessarily involved, but when extensive sanctions are available, we are concerned with power."[10] In this definitional scheme, "authority" refers to formal authority, whereas "influence" refers to functional authority; "power" is the ability of an individual to exercise control over another, regardless of formal or functional authority. In either guise authority evolves when power is vested in a particular individual—sometimes called the authority figure. By extension, misuse of authority implies the misuse of power, and these two phrases are often used interchangeably.

Authority confers discretion—the power to decide or to act according to an individual's own judgment. Or, as the dictionary puts it, discretion is "the freedom to decide what should be done in a particular situation."[11] From this perspective, the exercise of discretion and independent judgment implies that an individual has authority to make an independent choice, free from immediate direction or supervision. Thus, discretion is a hallmark attribute of authority. In fact, the terms authority and exercising discretion are also used interchangeably in some contexts.

ACCEPTANCE OF AUTHORITY

Formal authority may be ineffective if it is not accepted by a subordinate. That is, it lies outside the subordinate's zone of indifference and is, therefore, unacceptable. This fundamental concept linking authority and acceptance derives from Chester Barnard: "the decision as to whether an order has authority or not lies with the persons to whom it is addressed, and does not reside in 'persons of authority' or those who issue the orders."[12] For example, a governor has the power to enforce a politically unpopular order, but exercising this power would probably consume an inordinate amount of time and effort because of the public's nonacceptance. In this sense, "the use of authority is a reciprocal process," as Mortimer and McConnell put it.[13]

If authority is accepted, it is considered legitimate and vice versa. According to Richard Sennett, authority is legitimate "when people voluntarily obey their rulers. If they have to be coerced, it is because they don't find their rulers legitimate."[14] By inference, people will not obey willingly if they consider the authority illegitimate. In universities, the use of formal authority by a provost, for example, to handle academic hiring, curricular, or educational policy issues, is not always perceived as legitimate by some faculty members, who consider these matters to fall within their realm of authority. In that context, reliance on legally defined but illegitimate formal authority is perceived as a weakness. Indeed, any academic leader that has to rely consistently on formal authority to get things done generally does not last very long.

Within a university, administrators usually try to generate acceptance of a major decision, which is tantamount to acceptance of authority, by accommodating input from various constituencies, including students, faculty members, administrators, the governing board, alumni, donors, and so on. This quest for acceptance (often called "buy-in") limits an administrator's authority to control the time required to make the ultimate decision. But, it is an important component of academic governance. Furthermore, acceptance must be sought prior to the decision. As seasoned administrators generally realize, gaining buy-in after a decision has been made is nearly impossible.

MODULATION OF AUTHORITY BY EXTERNAL FACTORS

Acceptance of authority goes far beyond subordinates. It may extend to interested third parties capable of challenging authority. These include labor unions, legislatures, public interest groups, alumni, the news media, and accrediting associations. Each of them has the potential to interfere if they disagree with the way formal authority is used—even if it doesn't impact them directly. For example, the Western Association of Schools and Colleges (WASC), one of six regional accrediting associations, expects that an institution has "an independent governing board or similar authority that, consistent with its legal and fiduciary authority, exercises appropriate oversight over institutional integrity policies and ongoing operations."[15] While the accreditors cannot readily dispute a governor's formal authority to order closure of an academic research center on legal grounds, they can declare the institution noncompliant with its accreditation standards because of the governor's interference in university governance, which they would consider an abuse of authority. Certainly, a politically savvy governor would not want to be held responsible for jeopardizing the university's accreditation. Thus, the accreditors, a third party, impose realistic limitations on the governor's authority. Ironically, the university may be impacted adversely if the governor were to ignore this limitation—even though it had done nothing wrong—because it must conform to the accrediting association's standards or risk loss of accreditation.

Stated more formally, by their independent challenges, external parties, such as the accrediting associations, can modulate authority. Modulation means that they exert a controlling influence on the exercise of authority. In the example, the accreditation association modulates—influences in a controlling way—a governor's authority. Although it is an external factor, the accrediting association modulates administrative authority at the highest levels. Therefore, when making decisions neither the governing board nor the administration can ignore the accreditation association's vigilance, any more than a governor can ignore it.

Acceptance and modulation of authority interrelate with each other. The need for acceptance necessarily influences (that is, modulates) the use of authority. An administrator may pause before issuing an order that jeopardizes acceptance of his or her authority by some external modulatory factor, such as an accrediting association. Indeed, he or she may modify the order to ensure continued acceptance of his or her authority, despite any managerial inefficiencies that may occur as a result.

Likewise, government regulators can modulate authority. Government regulations do not alter the limits of an administrator's authority, but they certainly modulate how authority is used within the limits. To state the obvious, administrative actions must comply with local, state, and federal laws. This need for compliance imposes a modulating influence on authority. For example, if a university receives federal funds, including student financial aid, the president's authority to administer the athletic program depends on compliance with the provisions of Title IX, which requires equal opportunities and institutional support for men's and women's sports.[16] The modulation is subtle but powerful: "A college or university is not required to offer particular sports or the same sports for each sex. Also, an institution is not required to offer an equal number of sports for each sex. However, an institution must accommodate to the same degree the athletic interests and abilities of each sex in the selection of sports."[17] That last sentence strongly controls administrative prerogative, in contrast to the permissiveness of the first two sentences. Of course, the university could flout the provisions of Title IX but at the cost of federal funds. Very few institutions are willing to make that sacrifice.

Modulation may involve multiple parties external to an organization. And that's when matters can become far more complicated. In the extreme, the ability to manage breaks down when there are too many variables. According to James D. Thompson, "When interdependence is so diffuse that the local job lacks command over the resources needed to carry out a discretionary commitment, we would expect the individual to evade discretion. This situation is sometimes referred to as 'responsibility in excess of authority.'"[18]

As in a supply chain, where any member can potentially exert power over the others by withholding or reducing orders for a necessary commodity, within academe the governing board's authority is subject to disruption by numerous modulatory external considerations. These include the opinions of parents, alumni, students, donors, the general public, and government officials. Within this structure, each element has the potential to exert power over the others. For example, by raising tuition, the university exerts a controlling influence over financial decisions by students and parents. Conversely, prospective students exert a modulating influence on the governing board's authority to set tuition levels: raise the tuition too high, and they will enroll elsewhere. The consequent loss of tuition revenue thus limits the board's budget options. Also, raising tuition may pressure a legislature into a politically divisive debate about state support for higher education. And on and on, the actions of one of these factors may impact some or all of the others. Indeed, any one of these constituencies has the power to modulate the governing board's authority through protests, withholding monetary support, legislation, and so forth.

Consequently, the efficacy of the board's formal authority depends on favorable interactions with all of these external factors. As James D. Thompson states, they are all interdependent in an open system, thus "permitting the intrusion of variables penetrating the organization from outside."[19] In a sense, the board's authority to manage the university is really the authority to adapt to the uncertainties of a complex, dynamic operating environment.

DELEGATION OF AUTHORITY

In all institutions, formal authority bestowed on a governing board is divided through delegation to subordinates in the organizational structure. Through delegation, "a manager is given the right to plan the activities of a unit, direct the work of subordinate personnel, and make other decisions pertinent to the operations of the organization."[20] Because of this, the choice of individuals to whom authority is delegated becomes a very important managerial task.

Importantly, as a fundamental rule, the governing board may delegate authority, but it always retains the ultimate control. In other words, its principal authority always takes precedence over any delegated authority. This axiom is stated explicitly in some university bylaws, such as the University of Alabama: "Any authority delegated by the Board shall be subject always to the ultimate authority of the Board."[21] Whether documented or not, this is a cardinal rule.

Good examples of delegated authority can be found in academe. Within the microcosm of a university, a founding charter, a state constitution, or legislative act grants formal authority for university administration to the governing board and explicitly allows the board to delegate this authority. Stanford University's founding grant illustrates a typical delegation pathway. It establishes a board of trustees whose powers include the appointment of a president. In turn, the board delegates to the president the authority to "control the educational part of the University to such an extent that he [or she] may be held responsible for the course of study therein and for the good conduct and capacity of the professors and teachers."[22] And, along a pathway documented in university policies, authority flows downhill from the president into the organization.[23]

Constitutional establishment of the University of California provides another example. As stated in the California constitution, "the University of

California shall constitute a public trust, to be administered by the existing corporation known as 'The Regents of the University of California,' with full powers of organization and government."[24] Furthermore, the constitution explicitly allows the regents to "delegate to its committees or to the faculty of the university, or to others, such authority or functions as it may deem wise." Thus, the regents delegate overall system administrative authority to the president. And, conferred with that authority, the president usually further delegates administrative authority at individual campuses to the chancellors, who delegate academic authority to the provosts, and so forth on down the organizational hierarchy.

There may be informal limits to delegation. In principle, when authority over a particular domain of tasks is formally delegated, it may be assumed a priori that the recipient has been granted full authority—that is, all rights—to manage the assignment. However, in reality, the recipient may discover that some aspects of authority have been withheld, despite the formality of full delegation. This situation may manifest itself as micromanagement. In the same sense, delegation may prove to be nominal, not real. The superior, such as the governing board or the president, may have delegated authority but exerts persuasive influence over the recipient's actions. For example, in casual conversations with the provost, a president may express a strong opinion about some action, such as closing a research institute. Although the president has not ordered the closure, the message may hardly be subtle: "Do what I'm saying." What is the provost supposed to do in these cases? The answer is simple: honor the president's opinion if the provost really wants to keep the job. Although authority over academic affairs has been delegated to the provost in this example, the president is nonetheless exerting control over the situation.

Oversight by higher-level superiors may impose informal limits on delegated authority, but it does not necessarily diminish discretion. That is, discretion and independent judgment associated with delegated authority can be exercised even if decisions or recommendations are reviewed at a higher level. Thus, in the context of delegated authority, the terms "discretion and independent judgment" do not require that the decisions being made have to be final or free from review. As stated in Department of Labor guidelines, "the fact that one's decisions may be subject to review and that upon occasion the decisions are revised or reversed after review does not mean that one is not exercising discretion and independent judgment."[25]

There are also formal limits to what can be delegated. A major limitation is that individuals cannot delegate more authority than has been delegated to them by their superiors. Although this point may seem obvious, scenarios of what might be called "over-delegation" can be envisaged. This would occur, for example, if a provost singlehandedly were to close a research institute by assigning a subordinate the authority (and responsibility) to lay off employees, withdraw budgetary support, and so forth. Since the governing board retains the authority to close an academic institute, the provost would have been delegating authority that had not been delegated to him by the board.

A more explicit limitation occurs when an organization's founding charter or policies place limitations on delegating specific aspects of authority. For example, the University of Hawaii Board of Regents' policies state this in general terms: "Authority delegated to the President may at the President's discretion be further delegated unless the Board specifically limits the delegation of authority to the President."[26] In a more specific case, the board delegates the authority to speak for the faculty on academic policy matters to the faculty senate but explicitly prohibits the senate from any further delegation of this authority: "The role of the faculty as set forth herein shall not be delegated to any other entity by the faculty organization [the senate] established pursuant to this policy."[27] In another example, the board may delegate to the president the authority to make negative decisions in tenure cases, but it cannot delegate its authority to award tenure.[28]

As a rule of thumb, authority cannot be delegated unless the institutional charter and policies clearly allow delegation. This has been established in the courts. For example, in *Blanchard v. Lansing Community College*, a faculty member claimed that he had been illegally fired because the governing Board of Trustees had not voted on the matter.[29] The board argued that it had delegated the authority to hire and discharge faculty members to administrators. Citing Michigan statutes, the court noted that "The power to hire or discharge employees was expressly committed to the discretion of the board, and that power . . . could not be delegated." For clarification of the board's delegation authority, the court noted further that "The authorization . . . for the board to appoint an administrator to perform 'such duties as the board may determine' merely permits the board to assign the administrator ministerial duties." So, the court ruled in Blanchard's favor. Stretching the point, another rule of thumb counsels that "the highest official of an organization should retain those functions that cannot be delegated, while others take care of those that can be."[30]

RESCISSION OF DELEGATED AUTHORITY

Now for a critical question: is delegation reversible? To understand what is being asked, consider the following not-so-implausible scenario. In a university setting, the board of trustees appoints the president who, in turn, appoints the provost. *Pari passu*, authority is delegated down this hierarchy. If the board becomes displeased with some aspect of the provost's performance, can it rescind his or her authority to perform that delegated job? Ultimately, the answer is yes; delegated authority may be taken back, although it may require some effort to satisfy procedural requirements.

Fundamentally, the process for rescinding delegated authority generally mirrors the actions setting up the delegation. If the state constitution mandates the governing board to delegate authority for administering the university to the president, for example, then the constitution must be amended to alter that delegation. Likewise, if legislation specifies delegation, then the law must be changed for any rescission. At lower organizational levels, authority is usually delegated according to institutional operating policies or job descriptions, which must be changed prior to un-delegation.

A question might arise: why go to all of this trouble to rescind delegation? For example, why can't the governing board simply pull back authority delegated to the president without taking formal action? After all, formal action requires a publicly posted meeting and probably public discussion, not to mention the demands on the busy board members' time. The answer to this reasonable question is that the governing board may not violate its own rules, procedures, and bylaws. If its rules claim that authority over campus administration is delegated to the president, the board cannot logically (or legally) ignore that rule by simply yanking back the delegation. It has to amend the rule to negate the delegation first.

There is a simpler way to rescind delegated authority on a temporary basis: declare an exception to policy. Often, rescission is targeted to a specific individual who has performed unsatisfactorily. After that person is gone, the intent is to restore the delegation. In these cases, the standard procedure is to declare an exception to established policy. The rationale must be convincingly documented and, to the extent possible, available for public scrutiny. Moreover, requests for these exceptions must occur very rarely. Otherwise, they become de facto policy, which erodes managerial effectiveness and credibility.

RESPONSIBILITY AND ACCOUNTABILITY

Authority has a conjoined twin: responsibility. Technically, responsibility is "a thing that one is required to do as part of a job, role, or legal obligation."[31] Or, as defined in the *Dictionary of Military Terms*, responsibility is the "obligation to carry forward an assigned task to a successful conclusion." Moreover, "with responsibility goes authority to direct and take the necessary action to ensure success."[32]

The coupling of authority and responsibility is a cardinal feature of effective management. Indeed, it is a fundamental rule of effective administration. If an individual is responsible for a job, then he or she must have the authority to get it done. Conversely, if an individual has authority, then he or she must have associated responsibilities. Otherwise, the authority is of no consequence and, in some cases, may be abused. Thus, delegated authority is accompanied by delegated responsibility.

Importantly, however, there are limits to the delegation of responsibility. Managerial authority and responsibility can be delegated. However, the ultimate responsibility for institutional mission, integrity, and financial matters cannot be delegated; the highest authority, such as the governing board, remains responsible for these fundamental aspects of the organization. As stated obversely by the Association of Governing Boards of Universities and Colleges (AGB), "While they cannot delegate their ultimate fiduciary responsibility for the academic quality and fiscal integrity of the institution, boards depend upon the president for institutional leadership, vision, and strategic planning, and they delegate to the president abundant authority to manage the operations of the institution."[33]

In the army, for example, the relationship between authority and responsibility within the organizational structure is particularly well defined. "Commanders subdivide responsibility and authority and assign portions of both to various subordinate commanders and staff members. In this way, a proper degree of responsibility becomes inherent in each command echelon. Commanders delegate sufficient authority to Soldiers in the chain of command to accomplish their assigned duties, and commanders may hold these Soldiers responsible for their actions."[34] Of course, the army and universities differ in many significant ways, but the basic relationship between authority and responsibility transposes from one organization to the other.

Accountability is corollary to responsibility. In its definition of responsibility, the *Oxford Dictionary* incorporates accountability: responsibility is "the state or fact of being accountable or to blame for something."[35] "Accountable" is the key word in this definition. In some lexicons, responsibility and accountability are synonymous. For example, the *Oxford Dictionary* defines accountable as "required or expected to justify actions or decisions; responsible." But there is a subtle functional difference between the two concepts. On the one hand, accountability cannot be delegated. Although the president may delegate authority and responsibility down into the organization, he or she is still held accountable for any deviations from the expected performance. Or, according to a basic maxim of authority, "He who orders or commands is deemed to have done the thing himself." On the other hand, responsibility can be delegated, but, like accountability, the executive who delegates responsibility will still be held responsible for the success or failure of the delegated actions. In military terms, "Commanders who assign responsibility and authority to their subordinates still retain the overall responsibility for the actions of their commands."[36] Former President and Commander-in-Chief Harry S. Truman got it right: "the buck stops here."

CHAIN OF COMMAND

This hierarchical structure of delegated authority and responsibility in many institutional settings closely resembles the paradigmatic military chain of command. This organizational backbone evolved because "A simple and direct chain of command facilitates the transmittal of orders from the highest to the lowest levels in a minimum of time and with the least chance of misinterpretation. The command channel extends upward in the same manner for matters requiring official communication from subordinate to senior."[37] In the military organizational model, authority, and therefore power, flows along an uninterrupted, well-codified delegation pathway from the top brass down into the ranks. Likewise, in traditional business, government, and university organizations, authority and responsibility for a specific assignment are transmitted down a chain of command, from higher- to lower-ranking individuals until they are received by the person expected to perform the task.

Incidentally, the chain of command model for delegated authority was formally tailored for civilian organizations in the mid-twentieth century. In their seminal contributions, sociologists Henri Fayol and Max Weber set this stage for modern university management principles.[38] This hierarchical structure, also known as the scalar chain, became the foundation for modern bureaucracies. In coining the term "bureaucracy," Weber pointed out that efficient management of large corporations requires bureaucratically defined hierarchies of authority and responsibility, consistent with the chain of command principle.[39] As former IBM Chief Executive Officer Louis Gerstner commented, "The word 'bureaucracy' has taken on a negative connotation in most institutions today. The truth is that no large enterprise can work without bureaucracy."[40]

This emphasis on size understates the criteria for bureaucratic organization. A better determinant is complexity. In his discussion of organizational structure, James D. Thompson states that: "an organization need not be large to be complex. Voluntary hospitals and universities tend toward the small end of the size scale, as organizations go, whether we measure size in terms of the number of employees, size of budget, or cost of plant. Yet hospitals and universities are among the most complex of purposive organizations."[41] Although the rigidity of this structure varies considerably between the military, private businesses, and universities, institutions within each of these sectors are generally organized hierarchically. Members of academe usually loathe the notion of working in a bureaucracy, but, in fact, universities are by necessity a richly complex bureaucratic organization.

A fundamental corollary to the chain of command organizational structure is "unity of command." Each individual reports to only one supervisor. This eliminates the potential for conflicting orders from a variety of supervisors and provides the superior with a clear position of authority. Thus, pursuing the ideal military paradigm, personnel give orders only to those directly below them in the chain of command and receive orders only from those directly above them.[42] Indeed, in his classic treatise on business management, Henri Fayol claims that should the unity of command be violated, "authority is undermined, discipline is in jeopardy, order disturbed and stability threatened. This rule seems fundamental to me and so I have given it the rank of principle."[43] In reality, subordinates may communicate information outside the chain of command structure when it is justifiably necessary for efficient operations. But the immediate superior must always be informed, because his or her authority is de facto undermined when this occurs. Indeed, "short-circuiting the official chain of command quickly undermines the position of a by-passed manager. . . . Subordinates may well reason, 'If the boss does not take our supervisor seriously, why should we?'"[44]

Notably, it is important to remember that despite the importance of "unity of command," everybody up the chain of command has authority over a subordinate. In the military, for example, a general has authority to issue orders to a colonel, major, captain, and on down the ranks to the lowliest private. Similarly, the colonel has authority to issue orders to the major, captain, and so forth on down the line of authority. Translated into a university setting, the governing board's sphere of authority extends to the president, the provost, the deans, and on down the hierarchy. In principle, the board could order a dean to remove a particular faculty member from a teaching assignment. And the dean must comply or risk recrimination for insubordination. Indeed, within the chain of command, a subordinate must always follow orders if they are issued by a superior at any level. (Caveat: the order must be within the superior's sphere of authority. For example, a dean could not order a dining hall chef to put catsup on all scrambled egg orders for breakfast.)

ORGANIZATION CHARTS: LINE AND STAFF AUTHORITY

The distribution of authority down into an organization through the chain of command is customarily documented in an organization chart. Well-designed, up-to-date charts summarize the relative ranks of managerial positions, and in that sense, provide a concise overview of organizational structure. Thus, "who has formal authority over whom and what" can be quickly discerned from the chart. Moreover, simplified reporting relationships can be traced quickly. As a byproduct, an individual's prestige (and usually, therefore, power) within an organization depends on the location of his or her box in the chart: the closer to the top, the better. And this prestige is conveyed to anybody associated with the individual. For example, an assistant to the president enjoys greater prestige than an assistant to the provost.

In the organization chart jargon, the authority to direct and control immediate subordinates is called "line authority." As shown in figure 1.1, a sample chart for a university system, the authority for academic programs follows the line from the governing board to system chancellor to campus president to provost to the deans. And, the reporting lines retrace this route back to the top. The deans do not report to the Vice President for Research, and, therefore, the Vice President has no formal line authority over them. Likewise, the campus Vice President for Research does not report to the System Vice Chancellor for Research, despite the higher level of the Vice Chancellor in the organization.

In the jargon, there is also "staff authority." This authority is generally functional authority—it conveys the right and responsibility to provide advice and counsel in the staff specialist's field of expertise to an individual with line authority. In figure 1.1, the general counsel, who possesses staff authority, is shown reporting to the system chancellor, but from the side and not within the academic line. A manager with staff authority may also have line authority over staff members reporting to him or her. For example, the general counsel may have line authority over several other lawyers (deputy counsels) who report directly to him or her. Like their supervisor (the general counsel), these deputy counsels are in staff-authority positions.

Whereas a solid line indicates a formal reporting relationship, a dotted (or dashed) line is used by some organizations to indicate some form of indirect

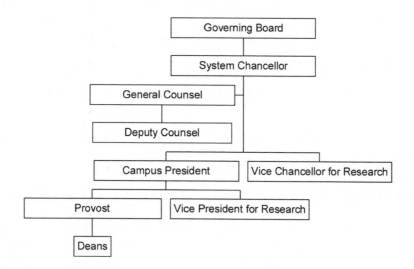

Figure 1.1. Sample Organization Chart

advisory relationship. According to the *Oxford Dictionary*, the dotted line represents "an indirect, informal, or secondary line of responsibility within an organization."[45] The nature of this dotted-line relationship varies from case to case. Although the use of dotted lines conveys information about the organization, it also can become a source of major confusion if it is not understood properly. It should always be made clear that the dotted line does not duplicate or detract from the formal reporting relationship represented by the solid line. As a rule of thumb, it is better not to use dotted lines.

Organization charts can be invaluable administrative tools. As an exercise, preparing a chart clarifies lines of authority and reporting relationships, identifies overlapping responsibilities, and detects gaps in responsibility. When thought out carefully, they serve as a definitive reference for organizational authority, answering questions about who is in charge and, therefore, accountable for specific assignments. As a best practice, administrators at every level of the organization should prepare and maintain an organizational chart for their domain of responsibility (that is, their office). At some institutions, this is a requirement.

Although the organization charts provide a formal summary of organizational authority and reporting relationships, they do not provide information about informal relationships. Commonly, a superior will rely on a staff person to communicate his or her wishes to subordinates in the hierarchy. Since the staff person has staff but not line authority, a subordinate might be tempted to question the legitimacy of a directive delivered in this way. That would generally be a mistake, for the superior implicitly empowers the staff person with his or her full authority to implement an order or decision.

In the sample organization (figure 1.1), the campus vice president for research might be tempted to disregard an instruction from the (system) vice chancellor for research because they are not linked by a formal reporting relationship. However, that would be a costly mistake, for the chancellor implicitly (or even explicitly) empowers the vice chancellor with the requisite authority to implement his or her decisions. Stated reciprocally, the chancellor asserts "when you speak to the vice chancellor, you're speaking to me." And vice versa: "when the vice chancellor speaks to you, I'm speaking to you." Pragmatically, therefore, it is always safe to assume that authority has been transferred implicitly to staff and higher-level line appointments to carry out the boss's wishes.

AUTHORITY IN AGENCY LAW

From a legal perspective, universities conduct their business according to the rules of agency law. This is because most of the university's business is performed by individuals working for the university in what is known as an agency relationship. The individuals are agents, and the university is the principal. In legal terms, the term "agency" refers to "A consensual relationship created by contract or by law where one party, the principal, grants authority for another party, the agent, to act on behalf of and under the control of the principal to deal with a third party."[46] In much simpler terms, agency refers to the relationship when one person has the legal authority to act for another. Importantly, the agent acts under the control and direction of the principal. Thus, an agency relationship is based on the authority granted by an employer, such as a university, to their employees, the principal and the agents, respectively, when dealing with a third party. Conferred with this authority, the agent's actions and words exchanged with a third party bind the principal. That is, the principal becomes responsible for the acts of the agent, and the agent's acts are like those of the principal. Thus, according to the fundamental maxim of agency law, "whoever acts through another does the act himself."

Incidentally, within the university's hierarchy, the governing board is technically the principal. Therefore, members of the governing board are not agents. That would be logically inconsistent. But all other administrators, including the president, are agents. For example, if a dean hires a faculty member, the dean acts as an agent working for the principal (the university). In the opinion of some courts, when faculty members teach a course to students, they act as agents of the university. Thus, the doctrine of agency goes beyond just the university's commercial activities and extends deep into its core academic activities.

In an agency relationship, the authority granted to the agent comes with responsibilities. Generally an agent owes the principal loyalty, obedience, and reasonable care. Loyalty means that the agent must act in the best interest of the principal, avoiding conflicts of interest. Obedience means the agent must obey the principal's instructions. And reasonable care means that the agent must act rationally under the circumstances. In return, the principal must compensate the agent for acts on behalf of the principal, indemnify the agent for any harm that occurred as a result of the agency relationship, and cooperate with the agent in order to accomplish the agent's ultimate task.

The legal system recognizes four distinct forms of authority in agency law: express, implied, inherent, and apparent authority. An agent acting with any of these forms of authority is capable of binding the principal in contract to a third party.

In agency law, express authority is synonymous with formal authority, "that which is found within the plain meaning of a written grant of authority."[47] It defines an agent's power to act on behalf of a principal—that is, an employee's power to act on behalf of the institution. This authority is stated explicitly in an agreement such as a contract between the institution and the employee.

Implied authority stems from the assumption that a written grant of authority cannot always foresee and document the exact limits of express authority. Some undocumented aspect of authority may be inferred because it is necessary to carry out the responsibilities of express authority. Stated differently, it is "authority that is not proved expressly but by inferences and reasonable deductions and that arises out of the language and course of conduct of the principal toward his agent and the agency."[48] It is authority that isn't written down expressly but is presumed necessary for an individual to do a job within the limits of formal authority. As an example, a university may grant a development officer express authority to solicit gifts for the institution. With this express authority, the university also gives the officer the implied authority to telephone prospects on behalf of the university to arrange for a meeting to discuss a potential donation.

Legally, an agreement creating an agency relationship may be express or implied. Thus, in this context, an employee's actual authority is the combination of express and implied authority. Stated differently, actual authority is "an agent's power to act on behalf of a principal, because such power was expressly or impliedly conferred."[49]

Inherent authority refers to the existing authority built into an institution or an employment position. It is, therefore, a form of authority that is not granted explicitly or implicitly by another individual or institution. However, it would be unreasonable not to have that authority. For example, a university president has the inherent authority to maintain law and order on campus. This example derives from *Morris v. Nowotny*, which involved a lawsuit against the University of Texas filed by Chester Morris after he was arrested on campus.[50] The court noted that the statutes establishing the university granted the governing board the authority to "enact such by-laws, rules and regulations as may be necessary for the successful management and government of the University." Continuing, the court stated that these statutes "imply the power and if they do not so imply then that the power is inherent in University officials to maintain proper order and decorum on the premises of the University and to exclude therefrom those who are detrimental to its well-being." The administration was not granted that authority; inherently, it just came with the job.

Apparent authority arises when an agent acts on behalf of the principal despite not having been granted the actual authority to do so. It exists only if the principal's words or conduct would lead a reasonable third party to believe that the agent was authorized to act. For example, the authority to negotiate the terms of a faculty job offer is delegated to department chairs. However, only the governing board has the authority to make the offer. Suppose that during the course of negotiations, a chair makes the job offer via an email. Judging from the chair's authority to negotiate, the candidate reasonably believes that the chair has the authority to make the offer. But in fact, only the board has that authority. In these circumstances, the chair has apparent (but not actual) authority. Thus, apparent authority really isn't authority at all; it is the appearance of authority.

UNIVERSITY TYPE: PRIVATE OR PUBLIC

These defining principles of authority can now be viewed from the perspective of higher education. That perspective is influenced profoundly by an institution's organizational status: private or public. Indeed, at first glance, the legal dimensions of authority in the two institutional types appear sharply different. However, at a closer look, these differences become much less apparent.

Private institutions are generally established by a founding charter based on a donor's bequest, a religious group, private investors, or some other nongovernmental organization. The charter is generally filed with the state government to establish corporate status. Also known as the articles of incorporation, it documents the institution's objectives, organizational structure (such as the composition of the governing board), planned mode of operations, and intended tax status (such as nonprofit). Moreover, as a corporation, the institution is authorized by the state to adopt rules and regulations and to benefit from limited liability for debts and obligations. The articles of incorporation also identify the broad authority of the governing board to act in the interest of the institution as well as any state-imposed limits on that authority. Thus, although an institution may be private, it usually files articles of incorporation with the state government.

Another key corporate document is the bylaws, which outlines how the organization is to be run. Bylaws work in conjunction with the articles of incorporation to form the legal backbone of the institution. These include the number of trustees, the terms of their service, their duties and obligations, and the frequency of their meetings. The institution's personnel structure is also documented in the bylaws, including the various key job titles, such as assistant processor, assistant research professor, assistant clinical professor, adjunct professor, and so forth. Typically, an institution has more detailed operating policies and procedures (separate from the bylaws) that spell out how the elements of the bylaws will be administered.

In private universities, the governing boards' authority is, theoretically, independent of governmental influence. While state legislatures can impose requirements on the formation and operation of private colleges and universities, such as the need to be accredited, states cannot alter their private nature. Although private institutions may be subject to statutory requirements (for example, antidiscrimination laws) if they accept federal assistance, they are not subject to most constitutional mandates that provide protection from the government, such as the Fourteenth Amendment. Instead, they operate according to contractual relationships with students and employees. Whether a private university honors constitutional protections depends voluntarily on the institution's policies.

Public universities are by nature public corporations. Their mission, structure, and governing board authority—their equivalents to a charter or articles of incorporation—are spelled out in their founding document. In that context, there are two fundamental subtypes of public universities, constitutional and legislative, depending on whether they were founded by the state constitution or a legislative act. In either case, the governing board's authority falls directly or, more commonly, indirectly under governmental oversight. And, as state agencies, they must abide by constitutional protections guaranteed to their students and employees, such as the right to due process established in the Fourteenth Amendment. Beyond this, however, the distinction between constitutionally and legislatively established institutions can profoundly affect the governing board's authority.

In constitutional universities, the governing boards have maximal authority (relatively speaking). These occur in a few states (for example, Michigan) where the state constitution establishes the university as an autonomous branch of government, comparable to the other branches, such as the legislature or the judiciary. In those states, the university is not responsible to the legislative or executive branches. Consequently, the governing board has full authority over the direction, administration, and expenditures of the university. Over the years, this autonomy has been protected by the courts. In a notable case from 1896 involving the University of Michigan, *Sterling v. Regents of the University of Michigan*, the court ruled that "The board of regents and the legislature derive their power from the same supreme authority, namely the constitution. . . . By no rule of construction can it be held that either can encroach upon or exercise the powers conferred upon the other."[51] In other words, the legislature and the university are separate and distinct constitutional bodies.

Numerous other states mention the state university in their constitution, but they do not grant full, unconditional autonomy. For example, according to the California constitution, the authority of the governing board (the regents) is "subject only to such legislative control as may be necessary to insure the security of its funds and compliance with the terms of the endowments of the university and such competitive bidding procedures as may be made applicable to the university by statute for the letting of construction contracts, sales of real property, and purchasing of materials, goods, and services."[52] Similarly, the Hawaii constitution grants the university autonomy over its management but leaves open the opportunity for legislative involvement: "The board shall also have exclusive jurisdiction over the internal structure, management, and operation of the university. This section shall not limit the power of the legislature to enact laws of statewide concern. The legislature shall have the exclusive jurisdiction to identify laws of statewide concern."[53] This last sentence accords the legislature carte blanche to assert its authority over the university, for it alone can declare that a particular issue is "of statewide concern." Notably, the legislature has never taken advantage of that power.

The governing boards have less authority, relatively speaking, in legislative universities. These occur in most states, where the public universities have been established by a legislative act. They report either to the legislature directly or via some other government agency that reports to the legislature, such as a state higher education coordinating board or commission. Although the governing board has the authority to administer the university, it must always contend with legislative approval—or disapproval—of its decisions.

Legislatures exert power mainly through their control of the state budget. Some state legislatures grant a lump sum budget for the board to administer, which limits legislative intrusion. But in less permissive states, legislatures provide line-item budgets, which can significantly dilute the governing board's authority. The rationale for tight legislative control over university affairs resides primarily in the legislature's commitment to sound management of taxpayer money.

OBSCURED LIMITS OF AUTHORITY

Against this definitional backdrop, the limits of authority should come into sharp relief. The organizational and legal principles should provide clear guidelines. But do they? Not necessarily; the boundaries can remain quite fuzzy at times. For example, a governor's personal authority to demand an academic program closure becomes less defined as it follows the delegation pathway through the governing board and the president to the provost. Complicating matters, the administration's authority to close a program requires consultation with another responsible group, the faculty senate, whose authority over these matters originated from the governing board. Plus, authority is further checked by the accrediting association, which vigilantly monitors adherence to its standards of university governance. This tangled web obfuscates the exact limits of authority for each player in this scenario. And that kind of obfuscation is not unusual in a complicated organization; it is an inherent trait.

Stated differently, what does authority mean outside a dictionary's dust cover? The answer to that question will help determine the best response to challenging situations, where myriad factors may obscure the limits of authority. Legal instruments such as statutes, judicial opinions, and regulations provide some guidance, but they do not address everything that goes on in the real world. When individual personalities enter the mix, sometimes even the most experienced administrators face vexing challenges determining the limits of authority. Ultimately, however, somebody must be in charge and be held accountable. The remainder of this book explores these interactions in search of an answer to the pivotal question: "who's in charge here?"

SUMMARY

Authority has two definitions: "the power or right to give orders, make decisions, and enforce obedience" and "the power to influence others, especially because of one's commanding manner or one's recognized knowledge about something." They define formal and functional authority, respectively. Formal authority may be ineffective if it is not accepted by a subordinate. If authority is accepted, it is considered legitimate and vice versa. Acceptance of authority may extend to interested third parties, such as accreditation agencies, capable of challenging and modulating authority. Formal authority bestowed on a governing board is distributed through delegation to subordinates in the organizational structure. However, the board always retains the ultimate control. The coupling of authority and responsibility is a cardinal feature of effective management. Authority and responsibility for a specific assignment are transmitted down a chain of command, from higher- to lower-ranking individuals until they are received by the person expected to perform the task. The distribution of authority down into an organization via the chain of command is customarily documented in an organization chart. Distinct forms of authority—express, implied, and apparent—defined under agency law play an important role in academia, because the institution conducts business through its employees. These defining principles of authority are influenced profoundly by an institution's organizational status: private or public. Although private institutions may be subject to statutory requirements if they accept federal assistance, they are not subject to constitutional mandates that provide protection from the government. Public universities are public corporations, and the governing board's authority falls under governmental oversight. And, as state agencies, they must abide by constitutional protections guaranteed to their students and employees. Against this definitional backdrop, the principles and limits of authority will be examined further in academic settings.

NOTES

1. John V. Lombardi et al., *University Organization, Governance, and Competitiveness: The Top American Research Universities* (Tempe, AZ: Center for Measuring University Performance, 2002).

2. Kenneth P. Mortimer and Colleen O'Brien Sathre, *The Art and Politics of Academic Governance* (Westport, CT: Praeger, 2007).

3. Kenneth P. Mortimer and T. R. McConnell, *Sharing Authority Effectively* (San Francisco: Jossey Bass, 1978).

4. Steven Greenhouse, "Here's a Memo from the Boss: Vote This Way," *New York Times*, October 26, 2012, http://www.nytimes.com/2012/10/27/us/politics/bosses-offering-timely-advice-how-to-vote.html?pagewanted=all&_r=0. (Accessed January 17, 2013).

5. "Oxford Dictionaries Online," Oxford University Press, http://oxforddictionaries.com/?attempted=true. (Accessed March 26, 2012).

6. Mortimer and McConnell, *Sharing Authority Effectively*, 19.

7. Bruce Lincoln, *Authority: Construction and Corrosion* (Chicago: University of Chicago Press, 1994), 3–4.

8. Wiktionary, "Moral Authority," http://en.wiktionary.org/wiki/moral_authority.

9. "Oxford Dictionaries Online."

10. Robert V. Presthus, "Authority in Organizations," in *Concepts and Issues in Administrative Behavior*, eds. S. Mailick and E. H. Van Ness (Englewood Cliffs, NJ: Prentice-Hall, 1962), 123.

11. "Oxford Dictionaries Online."

12. Chester Barnard, *The Functions of the Executive* (Cambridge, MA: Harvard University Press, 1938), 163.

13. Mortimer and McConnell, *Sharing Authority Effectively*, 17.

14. Richard Sennett, *Authority* (New York: W. W. Norton, 1980), 22.

15. Western Association of Schools and Colleges, "Organizational Structure and Decision-Making Processes, § 3.9," *Handbook of Accreditation* (2008), 19; https://www.wascsenior.org/findit/files/forms/Handbook_of_Accreditation.pdf. (Accessed March 26, 2012).

16. *Title IX of the Education Amendments of 1972, 20 U.S.C. §§ 1681–1688 (1972).*

17. U.S. Department of Education, "Requirements under Title IX of the Education Amendments of 1972," *ED.gov* (2005), http://www2.ed.gov/about/offices/list/ocr/docs/interath.html. (Accessed August 27, 2012).

18. James D. Thompson, *Organizations in Action* (New York: McGraw-Hill, 1967), 119.

19. Ibid.

20. Justin G. Longenecker, *Principles of Management and Organizational Behavior*, Fourth ed. (Columbus, OH: Charles E. Merrill Publishing, 1964), 242.

21. The Board of Trustees of the University of Alabama, "Primary Functions of the Board," *Board Manual* Article 1, Section 6 (2013).

22. Stanford University, *The Founding Grant with Amendments, Legislation and Court Decrees* (Stanford, CA: Stanford University, 1987).

23. "University Organization," in *Administrative Guide Memo 11* (Stanford, CA: Stanford University, 2008).

24. Article 9 Education, section 9 *California Constitution*. Article 9, §9.

25. U.S. Department of Labor, "Discretion and Independent Judgment," http://www.dol.gov/elaws/esa/flsa/overtime/glossary.htm?wd=discretion_and_judgment. (Accessed July 9, 2014).

26. University of Hawaii Board of Regents, "Duties of the President, Ch. 2 §2-2.E," *Board of Regents Policies* (2011).

27. "Regents Policy on Faculty Involvement in Academic Decision-Making and Academic Policy Development, Ch. 1, §1-10.B.5," *Board of Regents Policies* (2011).

28. *Abramson v. Board of Regents, University of Hawaii*, 548 P.2d 253 (Hawaii Sup. Ct.) (1976).

29. *Blanchard v. Lansing Community College*, 370 N.W. 2d 23 (1985).

30. Rudolph H. Weingartner, *Fitting Form to Function: A Primer on the Organization of Academic Institutions*, 2nd ed. (Lanham, MD: Rowman and Littlefield, 2011), 16.

31. "Oxford Dictionaries Online."

32. Department of Defense, "Dictionary of Military and Associated Terms Joint Publication 1-02," Department of Defense, http://www.dtic.mil/doctrine/new_pubs/jp1_02.pdf. (Accessed March 26, 2012).

33. Association of Governing Boards of Universities and Colleges, "AGB Statement on Board Responsibility for Institutional Governance," (2010), http://agb.org/news/2010-03/statement-board-responsibility-institutional-governance. (Accessed August 1, 2014).

34. Department of the Army, "Chain of Command, Section 2-1," in *Army Command Policy, Army Regulation 600-20* (2008).

35. "Oxford Dictionaries Online."

36. "Chain of Command, Section 2-1."

37. Ibid.

38. Henri Fayol, *General and Industrial Management.* Trans. Constance Storrs (London: Pitman, 1949); Max Weber, *The Theory of Social and Economic Organization.* Trans. A. M. Henderson and T. Parsons (New York: Oxford University Press, 1947).

39. Weber, *The Theory of Social and Economic Organization*, 333.

40. Louis Gerstner Jr., *Who Says Elephants Can't Dance? Leading a Great Enterprise through Dramatic Change* (New York: HarperCollins, 2002), 195.

41. Thompson, *Organizations in Action*, 74.

42. Department of the Army, "Appendix a Roles and Relationships a-14 - a-16, Authority," in *Field Manual 22-100, Army Leadership Be, Know, Do* (Washington, D.C.: 1999).

43. Fayol, *General and Industrial Management.* Trans. Constance Storrs, 24.

44. Longenecker, *Principles of Management and Organizational Behavior*, 227.

45. "Oxford Dictionaries Online."

46. The Free Dictionary, "Agency," *West's Encyclopedia of American Law* (2008), http://legal-dictionary.thefreedictionary.com/agency. (Accessed February 14, 2014).

47. William A. Kaplin and Barbara A. Lee, *The Law of Higher Education*, 5th ed., 2 vols. (San Francisco: Jossey-Bass, 2013), 190.

48. "Merriam Webster Dictionary," Merriam-Webster, Incorporated, http://www.merriam-webster.com/dictionary/. (Accessed January 10, 2013).

49. Legal Information Institute, "Actual Authority," Cornell University Law School, http://www.law.cornell.edu/wex/actual_authority. (Accessed February 11, 2014).

50. *Morris v. Nowotny*, 323 S.W. 2d 301 (Tex.) (1959).

51. *Sterling v. Regents of the University of Michigan*, 110 Mich. 369, 68 N.W. 253 (1896), 17. Cited in Patricia A. Hollander, *Legal Handbook for Educators* (Boulder, CO: Westview Press, 1978), 17.

52. *California Constitution.* Article 9, §9.

53. Article X Education; Section 6 Board of Regents: Powers,*Constitution of the State of Hawaii.* Article X, §6.

Chapter Two

Shared Authority

THE MEANING OF SHARED AUTHORITY

By definition, to share is "to let someone else have or use a part of something that belongs to you."[1] Thus, the term "shared authority" implies that authority over some realm is granted to more than one individual or group. For example, authority over a sovereign land might be parceled out to several princes; they share the authority to govern the sovereignty. In the academic realm, the term implies that the authority to govern a university is distributed to not only the governing board but also some other group, such as the faculty members. In theory, this concept of shared authority sounds appealing, because it empowers various constituents in the governance of their affairs. Managerially, however, it can become a mess; there is no single group or individual to resolve differences of opinion, to make controversial decisions, and, most importantly, to be held accountable if things go wrong. And, of course, there is the root problem: who has the authority to mandate shared authority? Somebody or some group must have the authority to decide what is shared and what isn't.

For those reasons, shared authority doesn't necessarily mean all that its definitional core implies. The theoretical conception of shared authority seldom exists in reality. Realistically, the ultimate authority and accountability are not truly shared; they are vested in one individual or group, such as a sovereign king or the governing board. The princes and faculty members may be consulted by the king and the governing board, respectively, about various issues and even be granted nominal responsibility for decisions concerning them. In that sense, authority is considered to be shared. But, the sharing is limited to influencing the decision-making process through consultation. As in the examples, the authority of the king or the governing board to make a decision always supersedes the recommendations of a constituency. In the vernacular, "the boss is still the boss." Moreover, the supreme authority (the king or the board) can always rescind or modify any agreement to share authority in this manner. Put tongue-in-cheek, the boss always has the upper hand: "what's mine is mine, and what's yours is negotiable."

Superficially, shared authority resembles delegated authority. Occasionally, the two terms are used interchangeably. However, linguistically, shared and delegated authorities usually refer to a group or to a single individual, respectively; authority is shared with a group and delegated to an individual. Furthermore, by some reckoning, they differ operationally in how the authority is used. As Kimball Wiles puts it, "Persons to whom authority is delegated assume responsibility for its use but not for the decision on how it will be used. They are responsible to their official leader, but not to anyone behind him. . . . On the other hand, persons with whom authority is shared assume responsibility for decisions concerning its use as well as for the execution of decisions. All persons who accept a share in deciding how authority will be used become responsible to each other and to persons outside the group for the utilization of the authority."[2] In other words, by this account, shared authority conveys the responsibility to determine how this authority is used; thus, the recipient has a modicum of control over the limits of the shared authority. In contrast, delegated authority must be used for purposes and within limits imposed by the delegator.

Is this operational distinction between delegated and shared authority just sophistry? Not really, for it poses a challenging conundrum. Formal authority that has been delegated according to policies (for example, bylaws) can be constrained; possible methods include changing policy, making an exception to policy, and disciplining or even firing an individual. Thus, in cases of mismanagement, the governing board assumes institutional accountability but can ease the impact by holding errant individuals accountable for their shortcomings. In contrast, shared authority—shared governance—predicated on a group's well-recognized functional authority cannot easily be constrained or modified. For example, within a university, the governing board possesses the ultimate authority over academic issues but shares this authority with the faculty members, who have generally acknowledged functional authority based on expertise in these matters. If the faculty members make bad decisions, the board cannot realistically discipline them as a group. As Kenneth Mortimer puts it, "the faculty's [shared] authority is without the danger of having to be held responsible for the results."[3] Thus, the governing board must bear the full brunt of accountability. And that's the conundrum: the board shares the authority without any effective control over its use. For the faculty members, that's not a bad position to be in. Fortunately for the board, and unfortunately for the faculty members, shared authority is by nature limited to consultation; it is consultative authority. Indeed, shared and consultative are synonymous in this context.

CONSULTATIVE AUTHORITY

By definition, consultative authority is advisory. That is, management is not necessarily obligated to follow the consultative group's advice, but it is usually expected to offer a good explanation of why it was not followed. Stated differently, consultative authority provides a group the opportunity to influence an administrator's decision, but it does not provide enfranchisement. In that sense, consultative authority is associated with inherently limited power. Realistically, a group's consultative influence depends on its functional authority—its expertise in the object of the decision.

Within many organizations, various employee groups are conferred with consultative authority. As the term implies, these groups are empowered with the authority to represent their constituents' interests in consultation with management. Usually, this empowerment is authorized by formal policy, such as a founding charter or governing board bylaws. Moreover, it is typically limited to just one group that represents a specific constituency, such as a faculty senate. In those cases, the group members are elected or chosen by the constituents because of their special interest or expertise. Reciprocally, management may be required by policy to consult with these designated groups on matters affecting their constituency.

More capaciously, consultative authority may be conferred on the entire population of individuals affected by a decision, not just a smaller representative group. Thus, all stakeholders would be consulted. After they have expressed their viewpoints, the manager in charge makes the final decision, presumably after having given serious consideration to the full range of opinions and recommendations. Importantly, this broad-based consultative authority assigns about the same weight to all stakeholders, regardless of their expertise on the issues. This inclusiveness generates buy-in, which mitigates opposition to a decision, but intrinsically limits the functional authority of any particular individual or alliance of several stakeholders.

In the academic and corporate sectors, consultative authority may exist within the collective-bargaining framework. By way of the collective-bargaining process, the parameters of managerial authority over working conditions are determined through mandatory consultation with union officials, resulting in sharply defined limits of authority and power relationships. Managers then operate within these limits of authority, usually without the requirement of further consultation as long as they remain within these negotiated limits. In the United States, this usually applies only to personnel issues, such as salary, working hours, and workplace conditions. Broader expansion of topics subject to consultation is seldom conferred formally on employees by management. Thus, within a university setting, the collective-bargaining agreement for faculty members as a class sets the parameters for working conditions—salary ranges, fringe benefits, pay raises, working hours, tenure and promotion, and so on. Importantly, the employer, such as a university president, retains authority over these issues for individual employees, but the terms of an individual's employment, such as the teaching load and tenure and promotion criteria, must conform to the general contractual agreement reached through consultation between the university (employer) and the collective employees who are represented by the union.

SHARED GOVERNANCE

Among modern American universities, shared authority has a special name, "shared governance." Parsing the short phrase hints at its hallowed meaning on campus: the governing board, which has authority over all university matters, shares some of this authority with members of the faculty, the student body, or some other employee group. Prima facie, this implies participation of these groups in governing the university. Involvement is usually (but not always) limited to consultation on specific areas where the group has functional authority—that is, expertise or a particularly vested interest. Thus, for faculty members, participation is usually limited to academic matters, such as the curriculum, degree requirements, and so forth. And, for the student body, participation is usually limited to expenditures of certain fees collected for the students' benefit. In general, this shared authority is guarded jealously by the group and acknowledged accordingly by the governing board.

These basic tenets of academic shared governance have been articulated formally in a joint *Statement on Government of Colleges and Universities* issued by the American Association of University Professors (AAUP), the American Council on Education (ACE), and the AGB.

> The faculty has primary responsibility for such fundamental areas as curriculum, subject matter and methods of instruction, research, faculty status, and those aspects of student life which relate to the educational process. On these matters the power of review or final decision lodged in the governing board or delegated by it to the president should be exercised adversely only in exceptional circumstances, and for reasons communicated to the faculty. It is desirable that the faculty should, following such communication, have the opportunity for further consideration and further transmittal of its views to the president or board. Budgets, personnel limitations, the time element, and the policies of other groups, bodies, and agencies having jurisdiction over the institution may set limits to realization of faculty advice.[4]

Notably, this last sentence acknowledges limits to the faculty members' participation in institutional governance. Yes, they have primacy in academic matters, but their authority is strictly consultative. The university president and governing board retain the formal authority, as well as responsibility and accountability, for academic affairs.

Because it was formulated by three highly influential higher-education associations, the *Statement on Government of Colleges and Universities* has been acknowledged as definitive by most universities. *Ipso facto*, faculty members' decisions on academic matters are seldom contested by a governing board. Their decisions are generally final. Indeed, "except in rare instances and for compelling reasons," university governing boards comply with the *Statement on Government* proposition that the faculty has primary responsibility for governance in areas where they have unique academic proficiency. Significantly, as the University of Iowa explains, "primary responsibility also implies that faculty enjoy a certain degree of decision-making autonomy in their areas of expertise—in other words, that the administration maintains a hands-off policy when the faculty are developing recommendations in the areas of curriculum, academic policy, and appointment, reappointment, tenure, and promotion."[5] In this context, it is sometimes said that the faculty possesses "legislative" authority over these matters; it has the license to determine how its shared authority is used in these cases.

In a Supreme Court opinion (*National Labor Relations Board v. Yeshiva University*), Justice William Brennan reiterated this characterization of shared governance.[6] He considered faculty members as part of a "parallel professional network" in a dual-authority system designed to bring their expertise into the decision-making process.

> The primary decisional network is hierarchical in nature: authority is lodged in the administration, and a formal chain of command runs from a lay governing board down through university officers to individual faculty members and students. At the same time, there exists a parallel professional network, in which formal mechanisms have been created to bring the expertise of the faculty into the decision making process . . . whatever influence the faculty wields in university decision making is attributable solely to its collective expertise as professional educators, and not to any managerial or supervisory prerogatives. Although the administration may look to the faculty for advice on matters of professional and academic concern, the faculty offers its recommendations in order to serve its own independent interest in creating the most effective environment for learning, teaching, and scholarship. And while the administration may attempt to defer to the faculty's competence whenever possible, it must and does apply its own distinct perspective to those recommendations, a perspective that is based on fiscal and other managerial policies which the faculty has no part in developing. The University always retains the ultimate decision making authority, and the administration gives what weight

and import to the faculty's collective judgment as it chooses and deems consistent with its own perception of the institution's needs and objectives.

In this dual-authority setting, Justice Brennan recognized the importance of faculty expertise in the decision-making process. But he also recognized the governing board's primacy in determining the institution's future. Thus, in a sense, the two networks—the faculty and the administration—are not truly parallel, as Justice Brennan describes them. Ultimately, they converge into a single network controlled by the administration.

The governing boards of most institutions formalize the faculty members' role in shared governance. For example, according to the University of California Board of Regents, "The Academic Senate, subject to the approval of the Board, shall determine the conditions for admission, for certificates, and for degrees other than honorary degrees" and other academic matters.[7] The State of Wisconsin statutes specify the consultative nature of shared governance at the University of Wisconsin campuses: "Subject to board policy the chancellors of the institutions in consultation with their faculties shall be responsible for designing curricula and setting degree requirements; determining academic standards and establishing grading systems; defining and administering institutional standards for faculty peer evaluation and screening candidates for appointment, promotion and tenure."[8] In short, the chancellors are responsible for academic matters, but they must consult with members of the faculty. But then, in a subsequent paragraph, the law assigns this responsibility to the faculty: "The faculty of each institution, subject to the responsibilities and powers of the board, the president and the chancellor of such institution, shall be vested with responsibility for the immediate governance of such institution and shall actively participate in institutional policy development. As such, the faculty shall have the primary responsibility for academic and educational activities and faculty personnel matters."[9] At first glance, this appears to introduce ambiguity; are the chancellors or the faculty members responsible for academic matters? However, the faculty members' responsibilities (and, therefore, authority) are unambiguously "subject to the responsibilities and powers of . . . the chancellor." Thus, the chancellor's authority supersedes the faculty members' authority.

Traditionally, the venues for faculty participation in shared governance are formally defined in governing board bylaws, university policies, or some other seminal document. In many institutions, the primary venue for shared governance is an assembly (called a council, a senate, or similar name) of all faculty members and higher-level administrators (such as the president, provost, and deans). This large assembly usually elects or appoints a much smaller executive committee (often called the faculty senate) that serves as the official representative of the faculty in communications with the administration; the president or provost may serve ex officio on this legislative body.

The elected faculty senate usually establishes various standing committees that address specific topics, such as promotion and tenure, admissions, academic policy and planning, and budget. Thus, consultative actions communicated to the administration emanate from the formally constituted group (via a report or resolution, for example) and not an individual faculty member (via an email, for example).

Occasionally, a group declares its own shared (consultative) authority, implying that it must be consulted on relevant issues. Unfortunately, self-proclaimed consultative authority has no legitimacy unless it has been endorsed by the governing authority. Otherwise, "just anybody" could claim to represent a particular constituency. And this can cause some confusion about their functional authority to "have the king's ear." For that reason, it is important to ascertain whether the group's shared authority has, in fact, been recognized formally (by the governing board, for example). If it has not, then the group's opinions must be considered in an informal context, and there may be no formal obligation to consult with them. Nonetheless, sometimes these claims of shared authority have a rational provenance. Some aspect of an institution's history or culture may have motivated a group to assert its authority to provide counsel on behalf of what it perceives to be the institution's best interests. In that context, the group's informal advice may be helpful.

The need to establish the legitimacy of a group's claim to shared authority can be illustrated by an anecdotal case involving Provost M. during his first month on the job at Flagship University. Three separate groups declared the right to shared authority, which meant that the provost was obligated to consult with them before major administrative decisions were made. The first group called itself the "council of principal investigators." They explained that they represented the research-active faculty members who were central to the university's status as a top-tier research institution. Unlike the faculty senate, which was elected by all faculty members, this group was self-selected; "We all have active, well-funded research programs, and we understand what it takes to retain the university's research reputation. You can't trust the faculty senate's advice, because many of the elected members haven't done research in years—if ever." The second group was comprised of a group of senior faculty members known as "university professors." Each year, a committee of incumbent university professors recommended several members for inclusion in this group based on scholarly achievements; they were, indeed, eminent in their fields. The governing board, via the provost and the president, routinely endorsed this recommendation and bestowed the honorific title. According to the university professors, "we represent the scholarly interests of the entire university, not just the sciences that have access to federal funding. There's a lot more to maintaining the university's academic reputation than just bringing in money. By the way, the faculty senate members usually have nothing better to do with their time. They're not always attuned to what it takes to achieve quality." The third group was the executive committee of the faculty senate. They were elected by members of the senate, who, in turn, were elected by all tenure-track and tenured university faculty members. "We are the only group authorized to represent the entire faculty; those other two groups represent parochial interests and, frankly, are pretentious elitists."

Confronted by these claims, Provost M. had to decide whether any of these groups warranted formally recognized consultative authority. Although the first two groups raised valid issues, the provost had to agree with the faculty senate that those groups represented only subsets of the university faculty members. Therefore, the legitimacy of their shared authority would most probably be challenged by faculty members not among their constituency. In contrast, most universities recognize the faculty senate as the sole "voice of the faculty." And, sure enough, in its charter, Flagship's faculty senate proclaimed that "the Faculty Senate shall act on behalf of the faculty and shall serve as an advisory body to the President of the University and may consider all matters of university concern" and that "should the President of the University choose not to follow a recommendation of the Faculty Senate, the President shall inform the Senate in writing of the reasons therefore and, upon request of the Senate, the President shall meet with the Senate for discussion of the matter."

This looked to be very convincing, but, since it was documented in the faculty senate's own charter, this was self-proclaimed shared authority. There was no indication in the charter that the president or the governing board endorsed this claim. Nor was there any mention of the faculty senate in the governing board's bylaws. Only after a prolonged search of archived documents, the provost's staff found a note in the minutes of a 1977 governing board meeting saying that it approved the faculty senate's charter. Although there was no explicit mention of shared authority, the board's approval signified its endorsement of the faculty senate's assertion of that right in its charter; the faculty senate had consultative authority on behalf of all faculty members. Since the president had delegated authority over the university's academic matters to the provost, Provost M. was, therefore, obligated to honor the faculty senate's role in shared governance. This was not an unwelcome or surprising outcome, since it conformed to standard university practices of shared governance.

Convinced of their shared authority, Provost M. met regularly once per month with the faculty senate executive committee to "consider matters of university concern." As for the council of principal investigators and the university professors, the provost met with them ad hoc about once or twice per year to discuss issues of mutual interest. Their informal advice was just that: informal advice. But, the provost always listened attentively to their opinions about various topics, which frequently differed from those of the faculty senate.

As illustrated in this anecdote, shared authority is highly prized, because access to decision makers conveys power. This can spawn multiple claims to the rights of consultation. Therefore, as a rule of thumb, administrators must determine early in their tenure what constituencies actually have formally recognized—"legitimate"—shared authority. Also, equally practical, they must remember that shared authority is by nature consultative. They are not formally obligated to follow advice or directives issued by those vested with shared authority.

From a practical point of view, however, university administrators usually pay close attention to advice and recommendations provided through legitimate consultation. For one thing, the advice may be quite helpful; the expertise represented in the faculty can be brought to bear on difficult issues. For another thing, this attention boosts faculty members' engagement in university governance and, along with that, morale. Conversely, failure to pay attention to consultative advice breeds mistrust of the administration and discourages participation in shared governance. Indeed, Rudolph Weingartner posits this as a maxim: "The number and quality of persons who participate in governance activities are directly related to how effectively they influence conditions that matter to them."[10]

LIMITED RIGHTS TO CONSULTATION

Unless it is mandated in law or institutional policy (for example, governing board bylaws), the administration has no legal obligation to confer with faculty members. Stated differently, faculty members do not have constitutional rights to shared governance of their institutions. This was established clearly by the Supreme Court in *Minnesota State Board for Community Colleges v. Knight*, where it declared that "faculty involvement in academic governance has much to recommend it as a matter of academic policy, but it finds no basis in the Constitution."[11]

This case derives from the Minnesota Public Employment Labor Relations Act that mandates collective bargaining over specific terms and conditions of employment in state institutions, including public colleges and universities. The statute also grants professional employees, such as faculty members, the right to "meet and confer" with their employers on matters related to employment that are outside the scope of mandatory bargaining. However, if the bargaining unit designates a specific representative for bargaining mandatory issues, their employer may "meet and confer" on nonmandatory subjects only with that representative.

Within the state's community college system, the Minnesota Community College Faculty Association (MCCFA) is the designated representative. At individual campuses, the MCCFA chapters and the college administrations created local "meet and confer" committees to discuss non-mandatory policy questions applicable only to the campus. By statute, faculty members who did not belong to MCCFA (the designated representative) were not allowed to meet and confer with the administration and vice versa—the administration was not allowed to meet and confer with non-union faculty members.

A group of twenty non-MCCFA faculty members filed a lawsuit challenging the constitutionality of MCCFA's exclusive representation of community college faculty in the meet and confer processes. They claimed that this policy deprived them of their First and Fourteenth Amendment speech and associational rights by denying them an opportunity to participate in their employer's making of policy. The Supreme Court ruled against them, upholding the exclusive policy. In its ruling, the court stated bluntly that the disgruntled faculty members:

> have no constitutional right, either as members of the public, as state employees, or as college instructors, to force officers of the State acting in an official policymaking capacity to listen to [their] views. Nothing in the First Amendment or in this Court's case law interpreting it suggests that the rights to speak, associate, and petition requires government policymakers to listen or respond to communications of members of the public on public issues. Neither appellees' status as public employees nor the fact that an academic setting is involved gives them any special constitutional right to a voice in the making of policy by their employer. Even assuming that First Amendment speech rights take on a special meaning in an academic setting, they do not require government to allow teachers to participate in institutional policymaking.

The Court acknowledged the tradition of shared governance but reiterated that it is not a constitutional right. "To be sure, there is a strong, if not universal or uniform, tradition of faculty participation in school governance, and there are numerous policy arguments to support such participation. . . . But this Court has never recognized a constitutional right of faculty to participate in policymaking in academic institutions."

This strict constitutional judgment does not apply to private institutions. Moreover, in public institutions, its impact depends on internal policies or collective-bargaining agreements concerning faculty consultation.

JURISDICTION OF SHARED GOVERNANCE

In some universities, the faculty's participation in institutional governance may extend beyond traditionally recognized jurisdiction over academic matters. In addition to the AAUP designated responsibility for "curriculum, academic policy, and appointment, reappointment, tenure, and promotion," the faculty may be also responsible for policies covering teaching loads, tuition and enrollment levels, the academic calendar, budget preparation, on-campus parking policies, football tickets, campus architecture, and so forth. Although these less academic responsibilities could be codified as shared governance, they are generally considered as the service component of the faculty members' job expectations, namely "teaching, research, and service." From a practical perspective, these service activities are demarcated from shared governance activities traditionally confined to core academic matters.

However, the courts have broken down this demarcation and expanded the jurisdiction for shared governance to an individual's less-defined service activities. And, ironically, this has not been to the faculty members' benefit.

The first major expansion resulted from a Supreme Court case involving attempts by Yeshiva University faculty members to form a union, *National Labor Relations Board v. Yeshiva University.*[12] In 1974, the Yeshiva University Faculty Association (the union) filed a petition with the National Labor Relations Board (NLRB), seeking certification as the collective bargaining agent for the full-time faculty members in ten (out of thirteen) schools at Yeshiva University. In its hearings, the NLRB heard evidence that university-wide policies are formulated by the central administration but that the faculty members at each autonomous school effectively implement them; they determine the curriculum, grading system, and admission standards, and they provide recommendations on faculty hiring, tenure, sabbaticals, termination, and promotion. As these responsibilities are consistent with traditional shared governance, the NLRB approved the union's petition and directed an election. However, after the union won the election and certification, the university refused to bargain, arguing that its faculty members are managerial employees and, therefore, not eligible for collective-bargaining rights protected under the National Labor Relations Act. The dispute ended up before the Supreme Court, where the university prevailed in its assertion that all of its faculty members are managerial personnel and not eligible for collective bargaining.

In its opinion, the court ruled that the NLRB had ignored the extensive control of Yeshiva's faculty over academic and personnel decisions, as well as its crucial role in determining other central policies of the institution. "The controlling consideration in this case is that the faculty of Yeshiva University exercise authority which in any other context unquestionably would be managerial. Their authority in academic matters is absolute." In a defining statement, the court noted that faculty power at Yeshiva extends beyond strictly academic concerns. "They decide what courses will be offered, when they will be scheduled, and to whom they will be taught. They debate and determine teaching methods, grading policies, and matriculation standards. They effectively decide which students will be admitted, retained, and graduated.

On occasion their views have determined the size of the student body, the tuition to be charged, and the location of a school. When one considers the function of a university, it is difficult to imagine decisions more managerial than these." Accordingly, the court held that the faculty members are endowed with "managerial status" sufficient to remove them from the National Labor Relations Act's coverage.

The decision also addressed faculty loyalty to the university. In their managerial role, as declared by the court, faculty members' decisions are expected to represent the interests of their employer, the university's governing board; they must be loyal to their employer. However, if faculty members were unionized, their loyalty would be divided between the employer and the union. And, the court cannot allow this to occur. In the context of shared governance, the court also noted that faculty members are expected to exercise independent judgment. Although the NLRB argued that a "faculty member exercising independent judgment acts primarily in his own interest and therefore does not represent the interest of his employer," the court held that the interests of the faculty align with those of the university. "The 'business' of a university is education, and its vitality ultimately must depend on academic policies that largely are formulated and generally are implemented by faculty governance decisions. Faculty members enhance their own standing and fulfill their professional mission by ensuring that the university's objectives are met."

The court ruling was limited to "mature" private universities like Yeshiva. The lower courts have been split in subsequent collective-bargaining decisions involving myriad different institutions and circumstances. Given the many possible variations from the circumstances in *Yeshiva*, Kaplin and Lee advise that: "faculty, administrators, and counsel can estimate the case's application to their campus only by comprehensively analyzing the institution's governance structure, the faculty's governance role in this structure, and the resulting decision-making experience."[13]

In a subsequent case, the jurisdiction of faculty governance was expanded to daily professional activities related to university administration, included kibitzing with departmental colleagues. In *Hong v. Grant*, Juan Hong, a professor at the University of California, Irvine (UCI), contended that he was denied a merit pay increase in violation of his First Amendment rights to free speech because he criticized the administration's hiring and promotion of other UCI professors and use of lecturers to teach courses.[14] Mr. Hong had expressed his criticism at faculty meetings and through a series of emails to the department chair, because he believed that he "was under an obligation to do so as a faculty member." The court ruled that Mr. Hong's critical remarks were made in the course of his job duties and were, therefore, not protected by the First Amendment.

In its analysis, the court noted that Mr. Hong was acting within UCI's system of shared governance. "In the University of California system, a faculty member's official duties are not limited to classroom instruction and professional research. While Mr. Hong's professional responsibilities undoubtedly include teaching and research, they also include a wide range of academic, administrative and personnel functions in accordance with UCIs self-governance principle." The court added that "As an active participant in his institution's self-governance, Mr. Hong has a professional responsibility to offer feedback, advice and criticism about his department's administration and operation from his perspective as a tenured, experienced professor. UCI allows for expansive faculty involvement in the interworkings of the University, and it is therefore the professional responsibility of the faculty to exercise that authority." Although he was not part of an official peer review faculty committee, the court ruled that the university had, in fact, "commissioned" Mr. Hong's involvement in the peer-review process and that his participation was part of his official duties under the auspices of shared governance. From this viewpoint, the concept of shared governance includes routine activities outside the formal faculty senate or committee structure. In her comments about this view of faculty governance, Rachel Levinson of the AAUP says that, "he was just speaking in his capacity as a tenured member of the department."[15]

This expansive, nontraditional view of shared governance may appeal to many faculty members. However, beware: it limits a faculty member's freedom of speech and increases the administration's authority to control faculty comments made "pursuant to official duties." In that sense, it does not favor the faculty member. As the court stated ominously, "The University is free to regulate statements made in the course of that process without judicial interference." Therefore, as a best practice, universities should examine their definitions of faculty governance to clarify their legal dimensions.

Parenthetically, some faculty members see shared governance quite differently. They consider themselves as having the ultimate authority for university governance, which they share with the administration. This contrarian viewpoint was expressed by Gary Olson in *The Chronicle of Higher Education*:

A dean chimed in that a faculty leader at her institution actually told her that shared governance means that professors, who are the "heart of the university," delegate the governance of their universities to administrators, whose role is to provide a support network for the faculty. "He said, in all seriousness, that faculty have the primary role of governing the university and that administrators are appointed to spare them from the more distasteful managerial labor," said the dean with incredulity.

That may be a more commonly held notion in academe than it at first appears. I know several faculty senators at one institution who regularly refer

to faculty as "governance," as in "You're administration, and we're governance." That expression reveals a deep misunderstanding of the mechanism of
shared governance—and presupposes an inherently adversarial relationship. [16]

Mr. Olson is right on two counts. First, proponents of this argument mis-
understand the authority vested in the governing board. Second, the relationship between faculty members and the administration may be intrinsically
adversarial. That is an unfortunate corollary to this misunderstanding about
authority within the university. It is also an aspect of most management
versus labor relationships, which crudely depicts the administration versus
faculty relationship in many institutions.

Nonetheless, this alternative perception of shared governance merits further consideration. Historically, medieval universities consisted of a guild of
scholars (the faculty members) who were responsible only to themselves.
They controlled the university in its entirety. Although this model gave way
to externally controlled universities in the United States, this traditional notion of faculty control persists on the basis of one logical argument. Specifically, as a tenet of shared governance, faculty members are responsible for
academic matters. Since all university activities (teaching, research, and service) are ultimately consistent with the academic mission, it follows that the
faculty members are responsible for all university matters. Therefore, they
must have the coupled authority over all university matters. In this scenario,
administrators simply provide support. The fallacy of this logic is that modern governing boards in both public and private universities have a legal
responsibility (a fiduciary duty) to protect the institution's best interests. In
that sense, they cannot be subservient to the faculty; they must retain the final
authority over all university matters.

BREAKDOWN OF SHARED GOVERNANCE: CENSURES AND SANCTIONS

Consequent to misunderstanding of authority and an inherently adversarial
relationship between faculty members and the administration, shared governance sometimes breaks down. And then trouble begins. In a collective-
bargaining environment, the union members may file a grievance or even go
on strike. More commonly, the group sharing governance, such as a faculty
senate, publicly voices its dissatisfaction with the administration, such as the
provost or the president, through a vote of no confidence. This shows "that a
majority does not support the policy of a leader or governing body," and
usually intends to remove an individual from office. [17] The vote of no confidence is addressed to the governing board and anybody else who will pay
attention. Understandably, it must occur rarely and compellingly to have any
effectiveness. And even then, it often goes disregarded.

One route for the faculty to reproach an administration is through the AAUP. This organization, which "has been engaged in developing standards for sound academic practice and in working for the acceptance of these standards by the community of higher education," investigates universities that allegedly violate the principles documented in their so-called *Redbook*.[18] If their investigation reveals serious departures from these principles, they either "censure" or "sanction" the institution. Censures concern violations of academic freedom, while sanctions concern governance. One is not worse than the other; they refer to two different situations. Both reprimands are related, however, because they focus on the administration.

Censure by the AAUP "informs the academic community that the administration of an institution has not adhered to the generally recognized principles of academic freedom and tenure" formulated in their *Statement of Principles on Academic Freedom and Tenure*.[19] Technically, a censure expresses "severe disapproval of (someone or something), especially in a formal statement."[20] In many settings, a vote of censure is often considered to be synonymous with a vote of no confidence. However, in academia, a censure differs from a vote of no confidence. The intent of a censure is not to remove an individual from office but to express that the faculty members have been disrespected by the administration.

The AAUP posts a list of censured institutions "for the purpose of informing Association members, the profession at large, and the public that unsatisfactory conditions of academic freedom and tenure have been found to prevail at these institutions."[21] At any given time, there are about forty-five to fifty institutions on the censure list. Furthermore, they state that "Members of the Association have often considered it to be their duty, in order to indicate their support of the principles violated, to refrain from accepting appointment to an institution so long as it remains on the censure list. Since circumstances differ widely from case to case, the Association does not assert that such an unqualified obligation exists for its members. . . . The Association leaves it to the discretion of the individual, possessed of the facts, to make the proper decision."[22]

Unfortunately, this veiled blacklisting poses little threat to most universities, because it is a highly competitive "buyer's market" for most faculty positions. Indeed, one critic states that "Getting blacklisted by the American Association of University Professors does not usually make college presidents quake in their boots—at least not publicly."[23] Another critic states that "Professors would love it if a censure imposed by the nation's leading faculty group prompted immediate change. But college presidents are more likely to call the association biased and misguided. They complain that the association doesn't really have the right to be investigating and censuring anybody."[24] Nevertheless, that same critic cites one president who said, "I didn't want to be a president of a university on censure." It's a matter of professional pride.

Sanctions are imposed on institutions that do not comply with the AAUP standards for governance, documented in the *Statement on Government of Colleges and Universities*.[25] On their website, the AAUP posts a list of sanctioned universities, with the explanation that "The publication of these sanctions is for the purpose of informing Association members, the profession at large, and the public that unsatisfactory conditions of academic government exist at the institutions in question."[26] Usually, there are five or six institutions on the sanctions list. By publishing these transgressions in their newsletter, the word is out, but its impact is debatable. As one commentator noted, "There is no evidence, either empirical or otherwise, to suggest that institutions that make the AAUP list suffer any negative impact."[27]

What warrants sanctioning by the AAUP? If there are only five or six institutions on the list, whatever actions provoke the sanction must be grim. Idaho State University discovered the answer to that question the hard way. Over a period of several years, friction over one issue or another had developed sore spots in the relationship between President Art Vailas and the faculty members. The soreness increased acutely when the provost announced that he and President Vailas had devised a plan to merge seven colleges into five to save money in response to decreased state support. In deference to shared governance, the provost appointed three task forces comprised of various faculty members (but chaired by associate vice presidents) to vet the proposal and then prepared a revised version based on this feedback. However, members of the faculty complained that their input had been largely ignored and that the revision differed little from the original plan. Consequently, the faculty senate called for a referendum on the proposed reorganization. It came as no surprise when the senate voters flatly rejected the plan. Nonetheless, President Vailas forwarded the reorganization plan to the Idaho State Board of Education, which promptly approved it. But a price was to be paid. About a week afterward, the faculty members voted no confidence in the provost, in apparent retribution for his handling of the proposed reorganization.[28] Regardless, the beleaguered provost remained on the job with President Vailas's tacit support.

Unfortunately, things got worse—much worse. The faculty members' anger at the reorganization plan intensified immeasurably two months later when the State Board of Education instructed President Vailas "to institute a review of the faculty governance structure at Idaho State University and to report back to the Board all findings at the conclusion of the review."[29] As the AAUP reported, the board considered that this review is "a necessary consequence of the board-approved consolidation of the colleges" and that the organizational changes in the University's colleges necessitated "a revision of the faculty governance structure."[30]

In conformity, President Vailas appointed a committee, the Institutional Governance Advisory Committee (IGAC), to review institutional governance. Although two of the committee members were from the academic faculty, general faculty input would be solicited when "a draft report would be presented to the Faculty Senate . . . and also made available to the campus community for comment."[31] The committee finished its assignment in short order. Within six weeks, a draft report was made available for comment, and a final version was submitted a month afterward. It recommended that President Vailas act on his authority "to establish or recognize constituent governance organizations that advise him as part of the decision-making process of the institution and to create advisory groups to make recommendations on particular issues" by creating "four university-wide committees to advise him and his designees on issues critical to the effective operation of the University."[32] These committees would operate independently of the faculty senate, consist of "senior" faculty members and administrators, and report to "the appropriate Vice President." It was generally presumed that the president would appoint the committee members. Thus, the senate's role in faculty governance was effectively marginalized.

All of this landed like a bombshell on the faculty members, who claimed that they had not received any prior notice that the board would consider this action. In haste, the faculty senate passed a resolution calling for an opportunity to vet the proposed governance plan. However, President Vailas promptly submitted the plan as written to the State Board of Education for its endorsement at the next meeting. Predictably, the faculty senate decried the plan because of its preparation during the summer under a cloak of secrecy and, most importantly, its assault on the senate's role in faculty governance: "the concept of faculty-formed governance will have been abandoned and replaced by governance through administrative appointment."[33] Several months later, an overwhelming majority of faculty members voted no confidence in President Vailas, and the faculty senate demanded the president's resignation. But the demand went unheeded.

At its next meeting, one week later, the State Board of Education dropped another bombshell. President Vailas lit the fuse: he asked the board to suspend the current faculty senate structure and bylaws and allow the university to implement an interim governance structure for the next few months. The board complied by passing a motion "To suspend the operation and bylaws of the current Idaho State University Faculty Senate; to authorize President Vailas to implement an interim faculty advisory structure; to direct the President to conclude his review of the faculty governance role as he was previously charged; and to bring a final proposal for a reconstituted Faculty Senate to the Board. . . . Such proposal should include a charge to the reconstituted Faculty Senate to formulate and present to the President for review and approval a proposed Constitution and bylaws in accordance with Board Policy."[34] In many fewer words, the board dissolved the faculty senate and allowed the president to establish his own version of shared governance.

Dissolution of the faculty senate sounded the clarion, and allies jumped into the fray. The AAUP sanctioned Idaho State University in condemnable terms: "what currently passes for shared governance on campus is a conglomeration of administratively appointed and administratively dominated task forces, committees, and ad hoc groups accountable not to the faculty but to the administration."[35] And there were calls for President Vailas's resignation from various sources.[36] Significantly, however, none of these calls was from the Idaho State Board of Education, President Vailas's boss. The board stood firmly behind the president. The war of words may continue, but the war of governance was over. The administration had won.

This epic battle manifested profound differences over what constitutes shared governance. President Vailas adhered to the Idaho State Board of Education policies on institutional governance, which grant him "full power and responsibility . . . for the organization, management, and supervision of the institution," and authorize the faculty to develop procedures for making recommendations to the president "as a part of the decision-making process."[37] Ultimately, the president, not the faculty, "is held accountable by the Board for the successful functioning of the institution."[38] Clearly, the Idaho State University faculty members are not constructionists, for they presume that their recommendations dictate presidential decisions on matters beyond the purely academic realm where they have special expertise, such as the curriculum and student progress. Just as clearly, the AAUP agrees with this point of view. But this presumption oversteps the limits of shared authority as defined in the board's policies. In a *New York Times* editorial, Stanley Fish describes this transgression more bluntly: "It may appear to you, as it does to me, that what is going on at Idaho State is just a petty academic squabble, but to the guardians of faculty prerogatives what is going on at Idaho State is a holy war waged by the forces of good and evil. In fact it is a garden-variety struggle over power between an administration that insists on administrating and a faculty that insists not only on doing its job without being monitored, but on its (God-given?) right to monitor everyone else's job."[39] As Mr. Fish points out, the president is accountable to the governing board, not to the AAUP. For that reason, he must adhere to the board's policies, and the faculty members must respect that necessity.

REFUSAL TO SHARE AUTHORITY

As the Idaho State case demonstrates, faculty members guard their role in shared governance passionately. As an object of passion, this participation in governance can be withheld as a particularly strong protest against an administration's actions. It sends a message: "We disagree strongly with what you're doing, so we are sacrificing something very precious to us in protest."

This is akin to a candidate withdrawing from an election because of a disagreement about the electoral process. It sends another message to the administration: "If you insist on making a decision, you're on your own; we won't have anything to do with it." There is a subliminal message as well: "Since we didn't participate in making the decision, we will oppose it, no matter what it is." This latter unspoken communication poses a potent threat to smooth management.

The tactical refusal to share authority as a means of protesting a decision can be illustrated in the re-telling of a case about disagreements between presidents and provosts first presented by Mortimer and Sathre.[40] In this retold version, a newly appointed provost, Provost M., was excited about the prospects of working for a growing university with world-class resources in various diverse areas. But timing is everything. After decades of growth, the state's economy was on the decline. The university was not immune to this economic misfortune, and its state-funded budget was cut precipitously in Provost M.'s first year on the job. Like most universities, Flagship could not respond rapidly to large budget cuts—at least not in an orderly way. Not with nearly 98 percent of some colleges' operating budgets covering personnel, utilities, and other fixed costs.

Shackled by these constraints, the university faced an enormous challenge. Consistent with the tenets of shared governance, Provost M. consulted weekly with the faculty senate's budget committee in search of an acceptable plan to accommodate the cuts. As a short-term expedient to avert layoffs, the committee recommended the near elimination of repairs and maintenance, library acquisitions, equipment purchases, and state-funded hiring. The latter was tantamount to a hiring freeze. In addition, to arrest this budgetary free-fall, the governing board raised tuition dramatically. This provided some relief, but there were still no resources available to repair the university's fractured infrastructure.

In the absence of any realistic hope for a quick upturn to the economy, the university needed to develop its own long-term solution to this budget predicament. Thus, the governing board instructed the president, and therefore the provost, to develop a plan that "preserves our good programs and eliminates the weak ones." In other words, the board wanted to save money through selective program closures, which meant that some people would lose their jobs. But what programs would go? The provost solicited the faculty senate for advice. In a startling announcement, the senate members openly refused to participate in this or any other process that "pits one faculty member against another." They declared that it was up to the state legislature to find the money needed to maintain a high-quality university. Despite several attempts by the provost to convince the faculty senate members that shared governance means making tough as well as easy decisions, they refused to take part in any decisions that jeopardized a colleague's job. Thus, the provost faced the challenge of identifying which programs would be amputated without the beneficial cooperation of the faculty.

Furthermore, the college and school deans proved to be of little help. They were instructed to identify programs that were superfluous, no longer relevant, or academically inferior for possible closure. Each dean defended his or her programs, arguing that they were all critical to the university's academic mission. Ultimately, despite several aborted attempts, no meaningful closures occurred, for every academic program had a strong, protective constituency.

Provost M. faced a budgetary crisis alone. Neither the faculty members nor the deans provided any meaningful counsel. Meanwhile, the hiring freeze took its toll on departments that were facing ever-larger teaching loads. Several deans implored the provost to "do something about this disaster," but they still refused to make the necessary cuts in their programs. Provost M. decided that the only way to coerce the deans' cooperation in making program cuts was a major reallocation of the operational budget. Careful analysis indicated that 12 percent of the university's operational budget could be held back for reallocation without faculty layoffs. To blunt the impact, the reallocation would be spread over a three-year period—4 percent of each unit's operational budget would be withheld for reallocation per year. Notably, since there was no consensus about which programs should be targeted, the withholding was "across the board." Thus, the deans would be forced into making hard decisions about high and low priority programs. And, presumably, the faculty senate budget committee would participate actively in determining how the withheld funds would be reallocated, consistent with the university's strategic plan.

The university president and the governing board apprehensively approved the concept. The president warned the provost that "you will quickly become a very lonely person. Across the board cuts are offensive to everybody." Truer words are seldom spoken. When the reallocation plan was announced to the deans and the faculty, the immediate reaction was predictable: shock and disbelief. For several months, the plan was debated at many forums. The need for generating resources to heal the infrastructure was generally uncontested. However, the means were hotly debated. Lacking a more persuasive solution to the crisis and with no guidance from the faculty senate or the deans, the provost launched the plan at the beginning of the next fiscal year and issued reduced budget allocations.

In tacit protest, the faculty senate once again waived its consultative authority by choosing not to help determine the recipients of reallocated funds in the first year. In private, it told the provost that "we never agreed to this ill-conceived process in the first place." Therefore, with no input from the faculty, the provost singlehandedly reallocated resources to the neediest programs. Fortunately, as vacant positions were filled, new library books were ordered, and burned-out light bulbs were replaced, the faculty senate's resistance lessened gradually, and it agreed to have its budget committee help oversee the second- and third-year reallocations. Shared governance showed signs of life.

There were predictable consequences. Because of their reduced budgets, all colleges and schools necessarily examined their priorities critically; some low-priority courses were canceled, and many discretionary personnel positions were left unfilled. Some came out ahead and some came out behind in the reallocations. The winners seldom said "thanks," but the losers always said something like "you've inflicted terrible damage to our college." Moreover, there was enhanced pressure to generate extramural resources. It may be coincidental, but the university advanced ten places in the rankings of federal research funding in the next three years. Most importantly in the provost's opinion, the reallocations prompted the colleges and schools to realign academic priorities within the new economic structure.

The reallocations had restored budget stability, despite the faculty's initial recalcitrance and the state's lingering economic malaise. By all reckoning, the reallocation plan's goals had been achieved. But, that success came at a personal cost to the provost. The president, who called the controversial plan "a bad plan whose time had come," had correctly foretold the loss of friends on campus. In one conversation, the president said in a matter-of-fact fashion: "I'm the only ally you have on campus these days." Politically, Provost M. had lost the support of the faculty members and the deans.

Why was the entire experience so contentious? The ideal solution to prolonged budget hardship should be constructive cooperation among the faculty members, the administration, and the governing board in determining selective program reductions or closures. After all, that is the foundation of shared governance. However, as this case illustrates, such an agreement may not occur. Basically, the faculty members were uncomfortable making decisions that potentially cut jobs; indeed, they abrogated the right to shared governance temporarily rather than participate in that destructive process. In that context, university faculty members are far more comfortable with allocations, since they are additive; they are constructive, not destructive. Anything beyond that additive comfort zone lies outside the acceptable limits of their shared authority. And, realistically, as a group they could not be held accountable for this abrogation of shared responsibility and authority.

FAILURE TO ACCEPT RESPONSIBILITY

Fundamentally, shared authority is accompanied by shared responsibility. Failure to accept this responsibility constitutes a serious flaw in shared governance. Refusing to participate in shared governance for ideological reasons is one thing. Agreeing to participate but then refusing to take the responsibility for making decisions is another. Failure to accept responsibility by shifting a difficult decision to someone else is known colloquially as "passing the buck." The phrase is generally pejorative, for it implies a failure to accept the responsibility that accompanies authority. In academia, this can pervert shared governance.

Most observers recognize "passing the buck" when they see it. It occurs in numerous situations on a university campus. Particularly common occurrences arise now and then in a university's tenure and promotion process. Faculty members generally have primary responsibility for decisions about a colleague's tenure or promotion. In fact, this primacy lies at the kernel of shared governance. Positive votes usually come easily, but negative votes often come with surprising difficulty. Sometimes, it is just easier to pass the buck; let somebody else cast the negative vote. As a result, candidates generally acknowledged to have marginal qualifications may receive positive endorsements from various faculty review committees that are simply disinclined to make the tough call.

For experienced administrators, especially provosts, this scenario is not difficult to envision. Anecdotally, it looks like this. At Flagship University, the tenure and promotion process is standard. An applicant's dossier is reviewed and voted upon sequentially by faculty members at the departmental level, the departmental chair, and the dean. It is then voted upon once again by an all-campus committee of faculty members whose purpose is to ensure uniform standards of academic quality across the university. After these steps, the dossier is forwarded to the provost for his or her recommendation before it is sent via the president to the governing board for formal action. Realistically, the provost has the final say in the matter, because the president and the board usually "rubber-stamp" the provost's recommendations. Just as realistically, the provost seldom overturns the all-campus committee's recommendations. However, if there is an apparent disagreement between members of the all-campus committee or apparent inconsistencies in the votes and endorsements along the way, the provost usually meets with the committee to determine why.

These discussions with the all-campus committee often followed a pattern. In a memorable paradigm, Provost M. posed a question: "The department voted seven to five in favor of tenure, the chair voted for, the dean voted against, and your vote was split, four to three in favor of tenure. This isn't a very compelling case." The committee spokesperson replied, "No, it really isn't. None of us thinks that the candidate deserves tenure." In reply, the provost asked the obvious question: "So, why did four of you vote in favor of tenure?" Then came the aggravating answer: "We thought that we'd let you make the tough call." In other words, the committee passed the buck; it failed to accept responsibility. At that point, Provost M. recited conventional university tenure policy: "Because the granting of tenure involves a long-term commitment of the University's resources, the review process is essentially conservative. Unless there is a clear case for tenure, the practice is not to recommend tenure."[41] With those parting words, the provost concluded the meeting, thinking silently, "why don't they do their job?"

The provost had good reasons for asking that last, silent question. By passing the buck, the faculty members weren't doing their job. In its defining statement on shared governance, the AAUP states that the faculty has "primary responsibility for . . . faculty status."[42] Axiomatically, shared authority connotes shared responsibility. Thus, technically, the faculty members have relinquished their shared authority by failing to accept the attendant responsibility to make a difficult decision.

Following the meeting with the all-campus committee, Provost M. wrestled with a dilemma. Despite the closeness of the votes and the all-campus committee's informal negativity, the candidate had received a simple majority of positive endorsements. To deny tenure would expose the provost to charges that he had violated the faculty's primacy over academic matters such as tenure and promotion by vetoing their decision to grant tenure in this situation. After all, members of the department, including the chair, certainly understand the scholarly merits of the case better than the provost, and a majority of them voted in favor of tenure. Likewise, a majority of the all-campus committee members voted positively. It doesn't matter what a committee member said off-the-record; their formal approval was duly recorded.

Under these circumstances, with what authority can the provost second-guess these decisions? The answer to that question is fairly simple. The provost relied on the authority over university academic matters delegated by the governing board via the president. By all accounts, shared governance is consultative, and the provost may overrule the faculty's decisions in "exceptional circumstances, and for reasons communicated to the faculty." [43] In the provost's opinion, this was one of those "rare instances . . . for compelling reasons." Because of the conservative nature of the tenure review process, the provost denied tenure.

As an epilogue to this anecdote, the candidate based an appeal on a purported misapplication of procedural guidelines by members of the all-campus committee (their informal verbal reversal of their endorsement) and prevailed. The disconsolate provost attributed this overruling to the committee's inability to use its authority responsibly.

What can an administrator do when faced with a comparable situation? More to the point: what can an administrator do when lower-level committees shy away from making a difficult decision, thus passing the buck? Unfortunately, the committee cannot be held accountable for this perversion of shared governance. Fortunately, however, an administrator, such as a provost or a dean, retains the authority to make the "tough call." And, he or she should do just that, without doubt or hesitation. The authority is unassailable, as is the responsibility to make the difficult decision. The appeal process may overturn a decision, but, at the very least, the administrator's (and the institution's) integrity has remained intact.

Postscript: purists will contend—and rightly so—that the provost did not deny tenure. He simply did not forward a recommendation to award tenure to the governing board. Likewise, the board never actually denies tenure. Rather, it grants tenure only to those individuals who have been recommended to it. Most boards provide members with a list of who was considered for tenure (or promotion) as an informational item, so they could easily deduce who was not forwarded for their approval. But they never take any formal action tantamount to denial.

SUMMARY

In the academic realm, "shared authority" implies that the authority to govern a university is distributed to not only the governing board but also some other group, such as the faculty members. In theory, this concept of shared authority sounds appealing, because it empowers various constituents in the governance of their affairs. The theoretical conception of shared authority seldom exists in reality. Realistically, the ultimate authority and accountability are not truly shared; they are vested in one individual or group, such as the governing board. Therefore, shared authority is by nature limited to consultation; it is consultative authority, which is advisory. In universities, shared authority has a special name, "shared governance"; the governing board, which has authority over all university matters, shares some of this authority with members of the faculty, the student body, or some other employee group. The governing boards of most institutions formalize the faculty members' role in shared governance, usually by way of a faculty senate. Occasionally, a group declares its own shared authority, implying that it must be consulted on relevant issues. Unfortunately, self-proclaimed shared authority has no legitimacy unless it has been endorsed by the governing authority. Unless it is mandated in law or institutional policy, the administration has no legal obligation to confer with faculty members. Faculty members may be considered managers because of their extensive participation in shared institutional governance, and this can limit their constitutional rights. Shared governance sometimes breaks down; the group sharing governance publicly voices its dissatisfaction with the administration. This can result in a faculty vote of no confidence or an AAUP censure or sanction. Participation in governance can also be withheld as a particularly strong protest against an administration's actions. Agreeing to participate but then refusing to make the tough decisions is another. This implies a failure to accept the responsibility that accompanies authority. In academia, it can pervert shared governance.

NOTES

1. "Merriam Webster Dictionary," Merriam-Webster, Incorporated, http://www.merriam-webster.com/dictionary/. (Accessed January 15, 2014).

2. Kimball Wiles, *Supervision for Better Schools*, 3rd ed. (Englewood Cliffs, NJ: Prentice-Hall, 1967), 181.

3. Kenneth P. Mortimer, personal communication.

4. American Association of University Professors, "Statement on Government of Colleges and Universities," (1966), http://www.aaup.org/AAUP/pubsres/policydocs/contents/governancestatement.htm. (Accessed April 24, 2012).

5. University of Iowa, "What Is Shared Governance Anyway?," (2007), www.uiowa.edu/~aaupweb/principles.html. (Accessed February 22, 2012).

6. *National Labor Relations Board v. Yeshiva University*, 444 U.S. 672 (1980).

7. The Regents of the University of California, "Duties, Powers, and Privileges of the Academic Senate," in *Standing Order 105.2* (2009).

8. State of Wisconsin, "The University of Wisconsin System. The Chancellors" in *Wis. Stats. §36.09 (3)(a)* (2011).

9. "The University of Wisconsin System. The Faculty," in *Wis. Stats. §36.09 (4)* (2011).

10. Rudolph H. Weingartner, *Fitting Form to Function: A Primer on the Organization of Academic Institutions*, 2nd ed. (Lanham, MD: Rowman and Littlefield, 2011), 35.

11. *Minnesota State Board for Community Colleges v. Knight*, 465 U.S. 271 (1984).

12. *National Labor Relations Board v. Yeshiva University*.

13. William A. Kaplin and Barbara A. Lee, *The Law of Higher Education*, 5th ed., 2 vols. (San Francisco: Jossey-Bass, 2013), 570–74.

14. *Hong v. Grant*, 516 F. Supp. 2d 1158 (2007); 403 Fed. Appx. 236 (9th Cir.) (2010).

15. Rachel B. Levinson, "Academic Freedom, Shared Governance, and the First Amendment after Garcetti v. Ceballos," *Stetson University College of Law 31st Annual National Conference on Law and Higher Education* (2011), http://www.aaup.org/NR/rdonlyres/4C126513-1194-4317-8123-459BD9F30A6D/0/Stetson2011AcadFreedomFirstAmdmtoutline.pdf. (Accessed June 27, 2014).

16. Gary A. Olson, "Exactly What Is 'Shared Governance'?," *The Chronicle of Higher Education* (2009), http://chronicle.com/article/Exactly-What-Is-Shared/47065/. (Accessed April 24, 2012).

17. "Oxford Dictionaries Online," Oxford University Press, http://oxforddictionaries.com/?attempted=true. (Accessed April 24, 2012).

18. "Policy Documents and Reports," (Washington, DC: American Association of University Professors, 1995).

19. "Statement of Principles on Academic Freedom and Tenure," (1940), http://www.aaup.org/AAUP/pubsres/policydocs/contents/1940statement.htm. (Accessed April 24, 2012).

20. "Oxford Dictionaries Online."

21. "Censure List," (2011), http://www.aaup.org/AAUP/about/censuredadmins/default.htm. (Accessed April 24, 2012).

22. Jonathan Knight, "The AAUP's Censure List," *Academe Online* (2003), http://www.aaup.org/AAUP/pubsres/academe/2003/JF/Feat/Knig.htm. (Accessed April 24, 2012).

23. Scott Smallwood, "Censure, Be Gone," *Chronicle of Higher Education* (2003), http://chronicle.com.lib-e2.lib.ttu.edu/article/Censure-Be-Gone/8382/. (Accessed April 24, 2012).

24. Ibid.

25. American Association of University Professors, "Sanctioned Institutions," (2011), http://www.aaup.org/AAUP/programs/sharedgovernance/sanctionlist.htm. (Accessed April 24, 2012).

26. Ibid.

27. Audrey Williams June, "AAUP Sanctions 2 Universities and Censures Another," *Chronicle of Higher Education* (2011), http://chronicle.com/article/AAUP-Sanctions-2-Universities/127901/. (Accessed April 24, 2012).

28. Yann Renaivo, "ISU Faculty No-Confidence Vote Goes against Provost Gary Olson," *Idaho State Journal*, 2010, http://idahostatejournal.com/news/local/article_82684212-4487-11df-a98f-001cc4c03286.html. (Accessed April 24, 2012).

29. Idaho State Board of Education, "Idaho State University—Governance Review," *Approved Minutes of the June 16–17, 2010 Meeting* (2010), http://www.boardofed.idaho.gov/meetings/board/archive/2010/06_16_10/index.asp. (Accessed April 24, 2012).

30. American Association of University Professors, "College and University Governance: Idaho State University," (2011), 5, http://www.aaup.org/AAUP/newsroom/prarchives/2011/censuresanction.htm.

31. Idaho State University, "An Advisory Group Has Been Appointed to Review the University's Institutional Governance System," *News and Notes Online* 26, no. 23 (2010), http://www.isu.edu/newsandnotes/100705/facstaff.shtml#governance. (Accessed April 24, 2012).

32. "Report to the ISU President Institutional Governance Advisory Committee," (2010), www.isu.edu/governance/igac-report2010-08sept10.pdf. (Accessed April 24, 2012).

33. Idaho State Journal, "Sep. 21 Faculty Senate Letter," *ISU Voice* (2010), http://isu-voice.com/?p=334493. (Accessed April 24, 2012).

34. Idaho State Board of Education, "Approved Minutes State Board of Education February 16–17, 2011," (2011), http://www.boardofed.idaho.gov/meetings/board/archive/2011/02_16-17_11/index.asp. (Accessed April 24, 2012).

35. American Association of University Professors, "College and University Governance: Idaho State University."

36. Idaho State Journal, "ISU President Should Resign," *Idaho State Journal*, June 26, 2011, http://www.highbeam.com/doc/1P3-2384623691.html. (Accessed April 24, 2012); "New Leader Needed at ISU," (2011), http://www.highbeam.com/doc/1P3-2424966261.html. (Accessed April 24, 2012).

37. Idaho State Board of Education, "Institutional Governance," *Governing Policies and Procedures, §III.C.1–2.* (2002), http://www.boardofed.idaho.gov/policies/iii_policy.asp. (Accessed April 24, 2012).

38. "Institutional Governance," *Governing Policies and Procedures, §III.C.1* (2002), http://www.boardofed.idaho.gov/policies/iii_policy.asp. (Accessed April 24, 2012).

39. Stanley Fish, "Faculty Governance in Idaho," *New York Times* (2011), http://opinionator.blogs.nytimes.com/2011/06/06/faculty-governance-in-idaho/. (Accessed January 26, 2012).

40. Kenneth P. Mortimer and Colleen O'Brien Sathre, *The Art and Politics of Academic Governance* (Westport, CT: Praeger, 2007), 84–86.

41. University of Hawaii at Manoa, "Criteria and Guidelines for Faculty Tenure/Promotion Application," (2011), 6, http://manoa.hawaii.edu/ovcaa/faculty/tenure_promotion_contract_renewal/. (Accessed January 28, 2012).

42. American Association of University Professors, "Statement on Government of Colleges and Universities."

43. Ibid.

Chapter Three

Loyalty

THE NATURE OF LOYALTY

Authority and loyalty are complexly related. On the one hand, authority commands loyalty; leaders expect loyalty from their followers. On the other hand, authority depends on loyalty; leaders rely on loyalty for acceptance of authority. At the extremities, they form two poles on the scale of social interaction between leaders and followers. From the extreme viewpoint, "Two modes of governance emerge that differ in whether the principal opposes or endorses the subordinates' friendship: one based on conflict and authority, the other on trust and loyalty. . . . Authority rests on distance, loyalty on closeness."[1] This dichotomy of interpersonal relations—authority versus loyalty—requires further examination, for it plays a dynamic role in the university environment. To clarify this role, it helps first to define loyalty.

By definition, loyalty is "firm and constant support or allegiance to a person or institution."[2] More generally, in his pioneering treatise on the topic, Josiah Royce speaks about loyalty to a cause: "Loyalty shall mean . . . *The willing and practical and thoroughgoing devotion of a person to a cause.* A man is loyal when first, he has some cause to which he is loyal; when, secondly, he *willingly and thoroughly* devotes himself to this cause; and when, thirdly, he expresses his devotion in some *sustained and practical way*, by acting steadily in the service of his cause."[3] This concept of cause includes not just ideological principles but also individuals, groups of individuals, or institutions.

By its nature, loyalty is self-serving. Individuals must derive some benefit from their loyalty, because otherwise they would not willingly serve some cause. The benefit may be psychological, such as job satisfaction, or material, such as money. Many kinds of personal benefit can be easily imagined.

For example, an employee may be loyal to an employer because the employer has continually provided a fair salary and a steady job during good and bad economic conditions. In another example, a traveler may be loyal to a particular airline because of its generous frequent flier program and other benefits, such as occasional upgrades to first class. Moreover, the strength of these loyalties correlates with their perceived personal value. Pursuant to the airline example, given the choice between two different airlines, a traveler may choose the one with less convenient schedules simply to benefit from the more generous frequent flier rewards, which are based on loyalty.

This self-serving aspect of loyalty can be quite powerful. Indeed, it can readily transcend ethical boundaries. The most egregious cases may involve violations of the law. Financial conflicts of interest fall into this category. For example, a professor may preferentially buy supplies at an inflated price from a company that rewards its best customers with an occasional lavish dinner; the professor benefits from loyalty to the vendor while the university spends more money than necessary. In another example, university employees traveling on business may be required by policy or law to purchase airline tickets at the lowest fare possible. Travelers who circumvent this responsibility by favoring a more expensive airline in order to earn frequent flier miles are disloyal to the university; they place their personal interests above those of the university. And, of course, out of loyalty to their preferred airline, they knowingly violate university policy. Consequently, if caught, they could be chastised.

Loyalty requires discipline, for it may involve submission of natural desires to the will or authority of another person. As Royce puts it, "Loyalty without self-control is impossible. The loyal man serves. That is, he does not merely follow his own impulses. He looks to his cause for guidance. This cause tells him what to do, and he does it."[4] In that sense, loyalty implies an individual's willingness to limit his or her actions to those sanctioned by an authority figure, although those actions may not always comport with his or her moral or ethical convictions. As history sadly demonstrates, a cause is not necessarily good; authority figures with evil and destructive causes, such as "ethnic cleansing," may command many loyal followers, whose actions support the cause.

Despite its dutifulness, loyalty paradoxically connotes free-will. Indeed, Royce incorporates free-will in his definition of loyalty: "the willing . . . devotion of a person to a cause."[5] He continues: "The loyal man's cause is his cause by virtue of the assent of his own will." Importantly, loyalty is not coerced and, theoretically, may be withdrawn or redirected at any time.

The paradox of obligation and free will blurs the distinction between obedience and loyalty. In either case, an individual with authority expects conformance with his or her will. And, in either case, failure to conform can have adverse consequences. In this context, however, there is one noticeable difference. On the one hand, obedience entails following a formal order issued by a superior, whose authority derives from his or her position in an organization. Failure to obey constitutes insubordination, which may result in being fired, fined, or incarcerated. On the other hand, loyalty may not entail following a formal order. Therefore, in some situations, misplaced, divided, or questionable loyalty does not constitute insubordination punishable by formal means. Nonetheless, disloyalty may exact comparable retribution ranging from being transferred out of a desirable job to being beheaded. The hazy difference between obedience and loyalty causes blurring of the limits of authority as well.

LOYALTY OATHS

In the political arena, loyalty is paramount and is often declared by a loyalty oath. Indeed, in his *Apologie for the Oath of Allegiance*, King James I declared that any subject "should make a clear profession of their resolution, faithfully to persist on their obedience to me, according to their natural allegiance."[6] Thus, loyalty to the Crown is a natural obligation derived from an imputed promise "closely sworn, by their birth in their natural allegiance."[7] This precept of loyalty to a sovereign prevails in Western society. In the United States, many states have laws requiring children in public schools to recite the Pledge of Allegiance in the classroom each day. For example, the California education code states that: "In every public secondary [and elementary] school there shall be conducted daily appropriate patriotic exercises. The giving of the Pledge of Allegiance to the Flag of the United States of America shall satisfy such requirement."[8] Likewise, in Florida, "The pledge of allegiance to the flag shall be recited at the beginning of the day in each public elementary, middle, and high school in the state."[9] The Florida statute continues, however, that "Each student shall be informed by posting a notice in a conspicuous place that the student has the right not to participate in reciting the pledge." More generally, in recent years, the courts have ruled that the freedom of speech provisions of the First and Fourteenth Amendments allow a student to refrain from reciting the Pledge of Allegiance or, for that matter, to stand while it is recited by other students.[10]

The body politic itself may require a declaration of loyalty—a loyalty oath—to the state as a condition of public employment. For seventy years now, every new employee of the state of California who is a U.S. citizen, including University of California faculty members, must sign a loyalty oath as a condition of employment. "I do solemnly swear (or affirm) that I will support and defend the Constitution of the United States and the Constitution of the State of California against all enemies, foreign and domestic; that I will bear true faith and allegiance to the Constitution of the United States and the Constitution of the State of California; that I take this obligation freely, without any mental reservation or purpose of evasion; and that I will well and faithfully discharge the duties upon which I am about to enter."[11] The vast majority of new employees sign without hesitation; they want the job. A few individuals have contested the oath and, for the most part, have lost in the contest.

For the record, the exact wording of this oath has varied slightly over the years, but the gist has remained the same. That is, except for a three-year period (1949–1952) when the University of California Board of Regents tacked on an additional clause to this oath. "I do not believe in, and I am not a member of, nor do I support any policy or organization that believes in, advocates, or teaches the overthrow of the United States government, by force or any illegal or unconstitutional methods."[12] At this point, the oath was transformed from a statement of loyalty to the state and the nation into a disclaimer of any kind of involvement with the Communist Party, including belief in its ideology. As David Gardner recounts: "The position of the regents on this was that if you were a member of the Communist Party, you were by definition subject to the discipline of the party, and, therefore, for you the truth was given and could not be freely sought or shared. Such ideological commitments, therefore, were thought to compromise one's impartiality as a scholar and teacher, and rendered one unfit to serve in those roles of responsibility and trust."[13]

With what authority can an individual be required to sign such a disclaimer? Or, more specifically, with what authority can a faculty member be deprived of academic freedom consequent to signing such a disclaimer? This issue arose in an epic confrontation between the University of California's faculty senate and the governing board of regents more than fifty years ago.

Embroiled in the early years of the Cold War that pitted American capitalism against Soviet-inspired communism, the faculty senate took a mildly conciliatory position. They agreed that "proven members of the Communist party were not acceptable as members of the faculty, hoping thereby to persuade the regents to withdraw the disclaimer."[14] As Gardner points out, the response of the faculty was that inflexible adherence to party ideology "may be true in general for communists, but it may not *always* be true. Each case merited its own consideration and such judgments needed to be made case by case."[15] For some faculty members, the disclaimer posed an unacceptable constraint on academic freedom and tenure rights. Therefore, they adamantly refused to sign the oath.

The regents were less inclined to conciliation. Academic freedom aside, for them this became a matter of governance. They asserted their authority to appoint, promote, and dismiss members of the faculty and, accordingly, dismissed faculty members who refused to sign the oath. Stung by this assault on their presumptive authority over these matters, the faculty senate took the quarrel into the courts, where it moved from one jurisdiction to another. In the end, the state supreme court struck down the disclaimer on the grounds that the state already had an oath and that the regents didn't have the authority to impose another one. With that, the court ordered the regents to reappoint faculty members who had been dismissed for not signing the expanded oath. Incidentally, like all state employees, the reinstated faculty members still had to sign the standard loyalty oath.

Significantly, the court remained silent on the fundamental questions about academic freedom, tenure rights, and the authority to hire, fire, and dismiss faculty members. Unchallenged by the court decision, the regents thus remained within the limits of their authority on these points. However, they were judged to have stepped beyond the limits of authority by imposing an oath more expansive than the state's standard loyalty oath. Regardless, the new appointees had to sign the state oath.

After all of this, the pragmatic question is: can prospective California state employees refuse to sign the state's loyalty oath? The answer is yes, of course. However, they cannot expect to be hired under those circumstances.

Loyalty oaths came under scrutiny again in a classic Supreme Court case concerning First Amendment rights in academia, *Keyishian v. Board of Regents*.[16] Under New York's loyalty laws and regulations, faculty members were required to sign a certificate stating that they were not and never had been communists. The intent was to prevent subversives from being employed in the state universities. Four faculty members refused to comply with this requirement to sign the certificate and were subsequently notified that their continued employment would be terminated. They filed a lawsuit claiming that the New York loyalty laws and regulations violated their First Amendment rights to free assembly and were, therefore, unconstitutional.

In its decision, the court struck down the New York teacher loyalty law, declaring it unconstitutional. According to the court, the statute was unconstitutionally vague, not only because it lacked objective measures to evaluate the actions of individuals but also because it unlawfully abridged the faculty members' right to freedom of association. Because of their vague and overbroad nature, the laws threatened a "chilling effect upon the exercise of vital First Amendment rights." Furthermore, the court opined that "Mere knowing membership, without a specific intent to further the unlawful aims of an organization, is not a constitutionally adequate basis for imposing sanctions."

The *Keyishian* decision did not rule out all loyalty oaths, just those that were not sufficiently clear in forbidding individuals from engaging in specific activities. Indeed, a year later, in *Knight v. Board of Regents*, the court upheld an oath requiring employees of New York public universities and tax-exempt private universities to support the federal and state constitutions in performing their duties.[17] Unlike *Keyishian*, where impermissibly vague loyalty oaths were invalidated, the court upheld the oath in *Knight*, ruling that it was not overly vague; nor did it place restrictions on political or philosophical expressions. With that, the court affirmed that state laws, such as those in California, may require faculty members in colleges and universities to sign affirmative loyalty oaths in support of the national and state constitutions as a condition of employment.

DUTY OF LOYALTY

Loyalty is tightly conjoined with another obligation, namely fiduciary duty. Before exploring this relationship, it helps to define the term "fiduciary." In legal jargon, "a fiduciary duty is a legal duty to act solely in another party's interests."[18] Individuals vested with the responsibility to oversee somebody else's interests must always place that person's interests above their own; that is their fiduciary duty. For example, members of a governing board, for example, have a fiduciary duty to act solely in the university's best interests. Individuals with this responsibility are called fiduciaries, and the individuals to whom they owe a duty are called principals or beneficiaries. Thus, as a fundamental principle, fiduciaries may not profit from their relationship with their principals; that is, they have an obligation to avoid any conflicts of interest between themselves and their principals.

Theoretically, all of the situations covered by this fiduciary obligation could be documented in a contract. "When this or that or that, ad infinitum, happens, the fiduciary must serve the beneficiary's interests in this or that or that ad infinitum way." However, all possible situations cannot be foreseen; the perfect contract cannot be written. Therefore, this fiduciary obligation is predicated on loyalty—the fiduciary's loyalty in all situations to the beneficiary's best interests. In this vein, as an adjective fiduciary "involves trust."[19]

In legal parlance, this trust is known as "duty of loyalty." Moreover, "it has been traditional for the duty of loyalty to be articulated capaciously, in a manner that emphasizes not only the obligation of a loyal fiduciary to refrain from advantaging herself at the expense of the corporation but, just as importantly, to act affirmatively to further the corporation's best interests."[20] Failure to abide by this code of behavior constitutes disloyalty, and it can have serious legal consequences, for the courts have imposed duty of loyalty on fiduciaries. Indeed, "A fiduciary duty is the strictest duty of care recognized by the US legal system."[21] There are three reasons for this strict imposition: "(1) the trust relation readily lends itself to secret exploitation, (2) a trustee with a conflict of interest is bound to exploit his trust and (3) the chance of discovering such exploitation is remote."[22]

Thus, the duty of loyalty requires employees to act for the benefit of the organization and not for their own personal benefit. Simply put, the duty of loyalty requires undivided loyalty to the organization. Expanding this simple concept from the perspective of agency law, the duty of loyalty has three key components. From a negative approach, an employee must not:[23]

1. Usurp corporate opportunities for personal gain; that is, an employee cannot misappropriate a business opportunity belonging to the corporation to himself.
2. Engage in so-called interested transactions without governing board approval; that is, without board approval, the employee cannot make a personal profit from a transaction with the corporation, buy or sell assets of the corporation, transact business with another corporation in which he has a financial interest, or transact corporate business with a family member.
3. Divulge the organization's confidential information; that is, an employee may not reveal information about the corporation's business to any third party, unless the information is public knowledge or required by law to be disclosed, or the corporation gives permission to disclose it.

These three components of the duty of loyalty specify that during the period of employment, an employee cannot perform actions that benefit individuals whose interests conflict with those of the employer. That includes other organizations, family members, and the individual himself. Thus, from a lawyer's viewpoint, "in the absence of the employer's consent, 'no man can serve two masters,' at least where the interests of those masters conflict."[24]

The duty of loyalty applies in an academic setting. Universally, it applies to governing board members as trustees. It is "the standard of faithfulness to the school. When making decisions, a trustee must put the school first. This duty is the basis for conflict-of-interest policies that are designed to prevent board members from enriching themselves, their families, and their friends at the expense of the school and from favoring one segment of the school over another."[25] Thus, a member of the governing board must always place the interests of the university above any personal interests; they must put in a good-faith effort to carry out their duties.

Although duty of loyalty applies traditionally to governing board members, it applies technically to other employees, such as institutional officers, who administer an institution's assets. Indeed, fiduciary responsibility at that upper administrative level is generally understood. Moreover, the courts have also extended duty of loyalty to so-called other employees. In Massachusetts, for example: "Employees occupying a position of trust and confidence owe a duty of loyalty to their employer and must protect the interests of the employer. . . . As 'agents' of the corporation, non-management employees have a fiduciary obligation to act in their employers' interests."[26]

By inference, faculty members are agents of the university (the corporation) under this guideline and, therefore, are subject to the duty of loyalty. This may not be documented directly, but it is usually expressed implicitly. For example, Columbia University states that "Each officer of instruction or research is under an obligation to take no action which might affect adversely his or her own independence of judgment or the integrity of the duty of primary loyalty he or she owes the University."[27] In this context, faculty members are fiduciaries and the university is the principal. Similarly, most universities express this relationship in their statements concerning conflicts of interest. In their exemplary statement, Ohio State University says explicitly that "State laws and administrative rules relating to ethics and conflicts of interest grow out of the principle that public employees owe a duty of loyalty to their public employers. In the performance of their university responsibilities, faculty and staff have the obligation to act in the best interests of the university without regard to any personal interests they may have."[28]

Importantly, a faculty member's duty of loyalty is compatible with academic freedom. In its *1940 Statement of Principles on Academic Freedom and Tenure*, the AAUP addresses this linkage: "Institutions of higher education are conducted for the common good and not to further the interest of either the individual teacher or the institution as a whole. The common good depends upon the free search for truth and its free exposition."[29] The statement continues: "As scholars and educational officers, they [faculty members] should remember that the public may judge their profession and their institution by their utterances. Hence they should at all times be accurate, should exercise appropriate restraint, should show respect for the opinions of others, and should make every effort to indicate that they are not speaking for the institution." Thus, while faculty members (teachers) are entitled to full freedom in research and in the classroom when discussing their subject, they are obligated to protect the integrity of the university as a duty of loyalty.

LOYALTY TO THE EMPLOYER

Corollary to the duty of loyalty, employers expect loyalty from their employees. Indeed, an employee is bound to furnish service to the employer according to the terms of any written or oral employment contract. But beyond the agreed employment terms, the employee is also obligated to render loyal, diligent, and faithful service to the employer even in the absence of any specific agreement to that effect. This means, among other things, that an employee owes a duty to act with the utmost good faith in the furtherance and advancement of the employer's interests. It is a duty of loyalty.

Restating this fundamental point, it is an individual's duty—that is, obligation—to be loyal to an employer's cause. Stated conversely, a subordinate's loyalty is to be expected by an individual in a position of authority. Thus, when a boss hires somebody, he or she says implicitly that "I expect loyalty to me personally and to the organization." Stanley Milgram emphasizes this point in his more expansive linkage of loyalty, duty, and discipline with authority: "*Loyalty, duty, discipline*, all are terms heavily saturated with moral meaning and refer to the degree to which a person fulfills his obligations to authority. They refer not to the 'goodness' of the person per se but to the adequacy with which a subordinate fulfills his socially defined role."[30] Thus, in a personal context, a loyal subordinate conforms to the wishes and expectations of an individual possessing authority over a particular domain.

Loyalty to the organization ranks among the most valued assets of any employee. It is manifest when employees become committed to the core objectives set for the institution. In his classic analysis of organizational loyalty, Herbert Simon points out that the values and objectives that guide an employee's decisions are initially "imposed on the individual by the exercise of authority over him; but to a large extent the values gradually become 'internalized' and are incorporated into the psychology and attitudes of the individual participant. He acquires an attachment or loyalty to the organization that automatically—i.e., without the necessity for external stimuli—guarantees that his decisions will be consistent with the organization objectives."[31] In simpler words, the employee develops a commitment to the success of the organization and no longer needs to be reminded what the overall goals are.

Simon restates that point from a different approach: "if that loyalty is lacking, personal motives may interfere with his administrative efficiency."[32] Thus, pragmatically, loyalty is manifest when employees believe that working for this organization is their best option. "Not only do they plan to remain with the organization, but they do not actively search for alternative employment and are not responsive to offers."[33]

The duty of loyalty does not prevent an employee from looking for another job. According to legal counsel, "it is obviously not a violation of the duty of loyalty for an employee to seek employment with a competitor, as long as the job search is conducted outside of company time and not in violation of any written covenant against competition. . . . Nor is it a violation of the duty of loyalty for an employee to use in his new employment the experience, knowledge, memory and skill which he gained in the old."[34] Thus, a university employee can apply for other jobs without violating the duty of loyalty, but, importantly, neither university time nor resources should be used. For example, faculty members or administrators must use vacation time when going on a job interview. Also, they should not use university letterhead or email services when submitting a job application; this use of university resources for personal benefit violates the duty of loyalty (and often, university policies and state laws). In academia, this latter proviso against using letterheads or email services for job applications is often ignored. But technically it is a violation and, in the eyes of a prospective employer, could indicate the applicant's ignorance or disrespect of the law.

Although employees may look for other job opportunities without violating their duty of loyalty, their loyalty to the organization immediately comes into question. And, when the current employer finds out, the consequences are unpredictable. They may range from "good riddance" to "what would it take to keep you here?" At the very least, the employer must assess whether particular work items should be assigned to this individual, since he or she may not be around long enough to complete the assignment. In a sense, that uncertainty erodes the employee's authority. It also causes the employee to question when or whether to inform the employer about the search for another job.

An anecdote illustrates this quandary. After two years on the job, Provost M. received an intriguing email. An executive search consultant (better known as a "headhunter") said that the provost had been nominated for the presidency of a major Western university. Although the provost was reasonably happy in the current job and felt loyal to the institution, this could be a major career advancement. Therefore, Provost M. agreed to become a candidate for the position.

Now the question arose: "Shall I inform my boss about this opportunity?" Provost M. sat on the horns of a dilemma: "What if the president found out about my candidacy in a roundabout way? That would really bring my loyalty into question. But what if I tell the president directly? That might also signal disloyalty. Either way, my effectiveness as provost may suffer."

Unfortunately, Provost M. surmised correctly that loyalty to the president would become an unavoidable issue. In general, the impact on the provost's effectiveness—and the nature of the president's reaction—depends on how long the provost has been on the job. In this case, Provost M. was in the second year, which is not very long. Although there had been no formal agreement about how long the provost would remain in that position, it would be reasonable for the president to insist on at least three years. Indeed, a minimum three-year commitment is an unwritten "rule of thumb." The rationale is that it takes at least that long to make progress on programmatic initiatives. Moreover, there is the underlying desire to realize some return on the costs of recruiting the provost—search, moving, and start-up expenses, for example.

How should Provost M. solve the dilemma? Pundits usually recommend against telling the boss until a new job has been found. For example, a popular internet site advises "don't tell your employer that you're job-searching until you have accepted another offer . . . after all, you may not get this job, and then you could be stuck in an awkward situation for quite some time."[35] In many cases, that is most probably sound advice. However, in some professions, including academe, there is a strong likelihood that "word will get out." This likelihood increases as the size of the professional community decreases. At the level of university president, as in this particular case, this community is fairly small; there aren't that many openings at any given time. Therefore, the best advice is for the provost to inform the president directly before declaring a formal candidacy for the new position. Indeed, few in higher education would argue with the importance of the president learning the news directly from the provost rather than indirectly through a third party. Presumably the president will understand the reasons for pursuing this career opportunity. However, the provost should not be surprised if the president expresses an angry rebuke about disloyalty, with words like: "You owe me three years, and I expect you to honor that commitment." How the provost responds and how this affects future working relationships between the two individuals will depend on the specific circumstances of the situation. The best outcome would be for the president to support the provost's candidacy albeit reluctantly. But, as most people know, there are no guarantees of this level of understanding.

By looking for another job, regardless of the circumstances, Provost M. indirectly ceded a modicum of authority. Loyalty to the president and the institution became compromised. As a corollary, trust in the provost's dedication to the university's well-being also became compromised. The consequences may be subtle. For example, the president may hesitate before sharing confidential information with Provost M., thus marginalizing the provost on certain managerial issues. This is tantamount to a reduction in the provost's authority. On paper, Provost M.'s formal authority remains the same, but in reality, the provost's effective use of the full authority has been eroded.

Could the president fire the provost for this breach of loyalty? The answer is most probably "yes." Of course, the provost's appointment contract may contain some proviso addressing this situation, explicitly restricting or permitting the freedom to explore other job opportunities. However, this would be somewhat unusual. Absent any such proviso, the dismissal would probably stand-up against a legal challenge. Indeed, the courts have recognized "the need to encourage a close and personal relationship between the employee and his superiors, where that relationship calls for loyalty and confidence."[36]

This anecdote featured two high-level administrators, the president and the provost. It could as easily have featured individuals at nearly all levels of an organization, such as a departmental chair and a faculty member. The analysis and the conclusions would be the same.

Incidentally, organizational loyalty can be bought. Despite the cynical aspects of this statement, it reflects common practice. Most organizations, including universities, strive to offer incentives to maintain employee loyalty, ranging from high salaries to free health club memberships. A common strategy is to offer the employee a "golden handcuff." This might be a generous pension if (and only if) the employee stays with the institution for many years; vesting periods usually extend from ten to twenty years, and the benefits increase with time on the job. On a shorter time scale, a rabbi trust may be set up as part of a recruitment package.[37] Typically, on a monthly basis the university deposits some amount of money into an interest-bearing account that it controls. After a certain period in the position, such as five years, the employee gains access to the accumulated funds and may withdraw them for personal use. If the employee leaves voluntarily before five years, he or she forfeits the entire amount—hence the term "golden handcuff." Of course, as the account balance increases, the handcuff becomes tighter. This strategy doesn't always work, but many organizations consider it a wise investment on the presumption that loyalty can be bought. The chronicles of world history bear testimony to the veracity of this presumption.

FAMILIAL LOYALTY

The duty of loyalty to an organization often collides with personal loyalty to family members. Indeed, these collisions caricature family life: "don't wait up for me, I've got to work late tonight." Or, conversely, "I know that the assignment is due tomorrow morning, but I can't work late tonight; we're celebrating our anniversary this evening." In these situations, a personal agenda must yield to the employer's needs. And, as most employees know, a boss's request cannot be turned down very many times without risking a demotion or dismissal. In the worst case scenario, retribution can be swift and unforgiving.

Anecdotes about the conflict between familial and organizational loyalty abound. A prime example occurred at Flagship University not long ago. A wealthy donor had just given stock shares in the family company to the engineering school. At the time of the gift, which was on a Thursday morning, the market value of the shares was roughly $50 million. The university honored this munificent gift by naming the school after the donor. At the naming ceremony, the university president posed with the donor and a six-feet-wide symbolic check for $50 million in front of numerous reporters and news cameras. This was a momentous event.

Late that afternoon, at the conclusion of the day's celebrations, the president instructed the university investment officer to sell all of the donated shares and to deposit the cash into a bank account immediately after trading begins tomorrow—Friday—morning. The investment officer hesitatingly said that it would be done first thing Monday morning; "tomorrow I have a family obligation that I can't cancel." Undeterred, the president replied "I want them sold immediately. Have your assistant do it tomorrow." Again the investment officer hesitated before explaining that the assistant had been given Friday off and was already out of town for the extended weekend. "But don't worry; we'll get it done first thing on Monday morning." Exasperated, the president agreed to the weekend delay.

Bad things happened over the weekend. The overall stock market dropped precipitously in response to discouraging economic forecasts released after the markets had closed on Friday afternoon. The drop was led by the technology sector, including the donor's company, which suffered a serious decline in value. Consequently, when the donated stocks were sold on Monday morning, the original $50 million gift was actually worth only about $40 million to the university. Thus, failure to sell the shares on the preceding Friday had cost the university $10 million.

Predictably, the president was furious. Both the investment officer and the assistant were called into the president's office. After a vituperative scolding about misdirected loyalties, both of them were fired—as of right then. Security personnel, who had been waiting in the nearby hallway, confiscated their office and building keys, handed them a bag containing their personal possessions (coats, photographs, and so forth), and then escorted them off campus. This demeaning departure lasted no more than ten minutes.

Why was the president so harsh on them? Ultimately the president is responsible for university investments and will be held accountable by the governing board. This responsibility was delegated to the investment officer, whom the president entrusted with the authority to manage the university's holdings wisely and prudently. With this delegation of considerable power, the president expected loyalty. Yet in this situation, the investment officer placed familial loyalty ahead of organizational loyalty. If the loss had been only $150,000, would the president have been so irate? Probably not; fluctuations of less than 1 percent hardly warrant attention. But a drop of 20 percent drew everybody's attention. In that sense, the investment officer and the assistant were the victims of bad luck.

This sad parable has several lessons. The first is obvious: don't put off until tomorrow what needs to be done today. Or, more aptly in the context of an inherently volatile stock market, when told to sell on Friday, don't wait until Monday. The second is equally clear: a senior-level office should not be left unattended. The investment officer exhibited blatant bad judgment by allowing the assistant and himself to be absent at the same time, thus leaving nobody to conduct business. Indeed, the investment officer was guilty of mismanagement. The third lesson is a bit more subtle: all decisions have consequences. In this case, choosing the family over the organization resulted in being fired. Of course, vice versa, choosing the organization over the family might have caused similarly unpleasant familial discord. In any event, when forced to choose one loyalty over another, an individual must weigh the potential consequences. And that can be very difficult at times. (Who would have predicted a 20 percent drop in market valuation over a weekend?)

POLITICAL CAMPAIGN CONTRIBUTIONS

Political campaign contributions signify loyalty. Unlike an explicit oath of loyalty, as in the kingdom of James I and the State of California, an expression of loyalty may entail far less explicit demonstrations of allegiance. This is exemplified by a politician's request for contributions to his or her election campaign, which is tantamount to a request for political loyalty. Indeed, in political circles, loyalty is measured by campaign contributions.

In most universities, political activities, like raising campaign contributions on university time, violate the law and institutional policy. The Internal Revenue Service (IRS) explicitly prohibits any institution claiming exemption from federal income taxes, according to section 501(c)(3) of the IRS tax code, from participating or intervening "directly or indirectly, in any political campaign on behalf of or in opposition to any candidate for public office."[38] Nearly all public and private universities fall in that category. Likewise, state laws usually contain similar prohibitions. For example, the State of Wisconsin explicitly states that no public employee shall "solicit or receive subscriptions or contributions for any partisan political party or any political purpose while on state time or engaged in official duties as an employee."[39] That includes soliciting contributions to a politician's campaign fund. Of course, university employees may participate in political activities, but they must occur off campus on their own time and as private citizens; that precludes use of any institutional email accounts, letterhead, or employment title (such as University of Wisconsin professor).

Nonetheless, because of their prominence in the community, university administrators are frequent targets of political fundraising campaigns. And that is where matters can become subtly difficult. An anecdote from Flagship University illustrates the subtle tensions accompanying these requests. It was another one of those lengthy presidential staff meetings. Going around the table, each vice president summarized events of the past week and issues of interest in the forthcoming week. The chief of staff's turn came around: "There is a fundraising event next week to help generate money for Governor K.'s reelection campaign. I'm passing around pledge cards so each of you can make your $500 contribution." Annoyed at the governor's political agenda, Provost M. retorted: "Frankly, I would rather not contribute." With no signs of irritation, the chief of staff said coolly: "That's your choice. However, it would be smart politically to demonstrate support for the governor. It can only be good for the university. Besides, somebody will notice that your name isn't on the list of contributors from the university administration, and that won't help your working relationship with the governor." In contrast to the chief of staff's apparent insouciance, Provost M. grumbled: "I really don't care for Governor K., and I'm not going to make a contribution."

The chief of staff has placed not only Provost M. but also the entire group in an awkward position. Indirectly, they have been asked to declare loyalty to the governor. The money is a minor issue; it merely documents the declaration. There is a deeper principle involved here as well. Governor K., via the chief of staff, is exerting power over the university administration in a feudalistic manner. Reading between the lines, the chief of staff has implied that the governor expects homage and loyalty, manifest as a campaign contribution, in exchange for favorable treatment.

If Provost M. doesn't contribute, will somebody in the governor's office really take notice? It would border on naiveté to assume that nobody would notice this recalcitrance. The governor will know. More importantly, the president and the governing board members will know about Provost M.'s refusal to help the university maintain a good working relationship with the governor. Will there be any adverse consequences? Perhaps, but they may be subtle. Certainly, this could not be used as a reason for seeking Provost M.'s dismissal; there is no legal provision for requiring a political campaign contribution. Any repercussions would probably blend into a broader spectrum of difficulties for the provost. And they may not involve Governor K. directly. The president or members of the governing board (who owe their position to Governor K.) may indirectly extract retribution in the course of their normal interactions with the provost.

Because of the legal restrictions on political activity while on the job, the chief of staff jeopardized the university's tax-exempt status. Loss of the exemption would have serious financial consequences. Yet, nobody raised that issue at the meeting—not the president, not the provost, not the vice president for finance and administration. Surely they knew about the legal prohibitions, so ignorance of the law wasn't an issue. Instead, they tacitly acknowledged the request out of loyalty to their colleagues, the chief of staff and, therefore, the president. It would have been a sign of disrespect and disloyalty to point out that the chief of staff was violating the law. And, there was probably a measure of fear of retribution if they openly snubbed the governor.

Despite the law, the chief of staff's request for campaign contributions was not unusual. Like many other people, members of a university's higher administration receive requests for political contributions both on and off the job. They may be for major elected officials like the governor or a U.S. senator or lesser positions, down to the city council level. Politicians thrive on endorsements from highly visible, important university administrators.

In this case, Provost M. bluntly refused to contribute to the particular candidacy of Governor K. That bluntness was injudiciously provocative. There are better ways to handle this kind of awkward situation. Since the illegality was not to be mentioned, a more tactful answer would be: "As a matter of principle, I prefer not to contribute to any candidates for political office. If I did, I would have to contribute equally to all candidates for that office, and I don't want to go down that pathway." At the very least, this answer evades open opposition to a particular candidate's candidacy. Notably, many corporations adopt a similar approach but follow the other pathway: they contribute to the candidates from both major parties, thus hedging their bets. Although there is no uniformly "best practice" in these situations, the least risky solution to this dilemma would be to contribute equally to both major-party candidates. Loyalty is divided, but at least it is divided evenly.

POLITICAL ENDORSEMENTS

Political endorsements also express loyalty. Like campaign contributions, endorsements from prominent university administrators are highly valued by politicians. Unlike campaign contributions, which usually attract little public attention, endorsements are usually publicized widely to gain maximal exposure for the politician. At the same time, however, this brings broad public exposure for the individual making the endorsement. And that can sometimes prove embarrassing, if not disastrous, especially if the wrong candidate wins the election.

The dangers inherent to political endorsements were demonstrated following political endorsements by two members of the Texas Tech University governing board of regents. Mark Griffin and Wendy Sitton were appointed to the board of regents several years earlier by Texas governor Rick Perry. Then, in a 2010 primary election the incumbent Governor Perry ran unexpectedly for reelection against Senator Kay Bailey Hutchison. Regents Griffin and Sitton publicly endorsed Senator Hutchison. A short time later, regent Griffin unexpectedly resigned his position on the board. Governor Perry denied any involvement in his decision to resign.[40] However, regent Griffin declared openly that he was asked to resign by the governor's office.[41] According to newspaper reports announcing the resignation, Governor Perry's former chief of staff, Brian Newby, had called regent Griffin days after the endorsement with the message that "the governor expects loyalty out of his appointees."[42] Furthermore, according to the university's announcement, "Griffin said he asked Newby if the governor wanted him to resign and Newby said yes." According to regent Griffin, Newby told him, "The governor's not going to ask you himself."[43]

Following her endorsement of Senator Hutchison, regent Sitton was also asked to resign by board of regents chair Scott Dueser. According to the *Lubbock Avalanche-Journal*, "Sitton said Dueser called her to relay a message from the governor's office: 'Cease and desist supporting the senator immediately or resign from the board.'"[44] Despite this pressure to resign, regent Sitton finished the last two months of her term on the board. At the conclusion of the term, she commented that "it's a sad day when politics override and overcome good governance of our public education institutions."[45] Regent Dueser reportedly said that he hopes "politics aren't affecting regents' positions on the board" but explained that "he understands the governor's expectations that go with an appointment to the board."[46] In defense of these pressure tactics on behalf of the governor, regent Dueser added that the governor "appoints those positions and he expects loyalty."

Both Griffin and Sitton claim that they agreed to endorse Senator Hutchison before they knew that Governor Perry would run for reelection. According to Griffin, he agreed to back Senator Hutchison in 2007, before Governor Perry announced his candidacy. But he withheld a public endorsement until after the legislative session ended in June, so his political activity wouldn't harm legislation and funding for Texas Tech.[47] Likewise, Sitton didn't expect Governor Perry to run for an unprecedented third term, so in 2006 she committed to help Senator Hutchison's 2010 campaign. "It's nothing against the governor, it's just more of a support for the senator," she said.[48] Thus, neither regent had expressed displeasure or disagreement with the governor. They simply made premature commitments to his political opponent and then remained loyal to these commitments. Laudable as it may be, that loyalty to their commitments was incompatible with their competing loyalty to the governor who had appointed them to the board in the first place.

Notably, both regents were asked to resign their positions as regents. Must they comply with this gubernatorial request? The answer is no; they may refuse to step down voluntarily, as did Sitton. The governor does not have the authority simply to dismiss the regent from the board. The original appointment required state senate confirmation, so dismissal also requires legislative action. According to Texas statutes, regents can be removed from office through impeachment by the state house of representatives followed by a trial in the state senate.[49] But that would be a drawn-out process guaranteed to bring unfavorable publicity to the university—and to the recalcitrant regent as well. Except in the most unusual cases, a regent (or any other appointed official) would preferably yield to the pressure and resign voluntarily. Pressure, by the way, would come from not only the governor but also the university, which depends on the governor's and the general public's good will for financial support.

This example illustrates the bond between political appointments and expectations of loyalty. As history has shown, political appointments carry political responsibilities, including absolute loyalty to the appointing superior. This unwritten commitment is an expected and generally acknowledged attribute of any organization—governmental, corporate, and academic. For example, in many states, the governor appoints some or all members of the public universities' governing board. Although the board members have an explicit fiduciary duty to the institution, they also have an implicit allegiance to the appointing governor. Failure to honor this responsibility constitutes disloyalty, which is generally unacceptable to the appointer.

Indeed, loyalty is the *raison d'être* for political patronage. The leader, in this case the governor, can thus expect consistency of mission, orders to be followed, and minimal disruptive arguing among the staff members and, in this case, the university regents. These are desirable attributes in any organization. From a more technical perspective, this uniformity consequent to loyalty may reduce diversity of opinion, which could stifle innovation. So there is a pragmatic trade-off between unfettered loyalty and independent approaches to managerial issues. The scales usually tip in favor of loyalty. And that is not necessarily bad from a managerial point of view.

Incidentally, if there is a practical lesson to be learned from this and similar cases of endorsing the wrong candidate, it is this: regents, presidents, and other senior-level administrators of public institutions should demur if at all possible when asked to endorse a candidate for political office. They should simply say no—although in a somewhat more tactful way.

POWER BASE

In all of its manifestations, loyalty constitutes the primary source of an individual's power base. The generic definition of power base is "a source of authority, influence, or support, especially in politics or negotiations."[50] Although this term is used mainly in a political context (e.g., "most of the candidate's power base is in the third precinct"), it is also used in more general situations. Within academia, an administrator's power base can be founded by loyal support from an organized body such as the faculty senate or the governing board, a loosely organized group of individuals such as the deans, or particularly influential single individuals such as the president.

The power base is the group that an administrator can turn to for support during difficult times. For example, if the governing board is unhappy with some aspect of the provost's performance, the faculty senate's strong support—the power base in this case—may be sufficient to mitigate the situation for the provost; the board would rather not act against the provost because that would provoke collateral difficulties with the faculty members. Thus, a strong power base gives critics a reason to pause before taking any adverse action against an individual. Most seasoned administrators are keenly aware of the importance of cultivating a strong power base, consciously or subconsciously.

Although loyalty contributes greatly to a power base, it is not the only contributor. There is also a self-serving factor. Individuals who would normally be at odds may work together if it is politically useful. Depending on the situation, they form a mutual power base. As the proverb puts it, "politics makes strange bedfellows." In fact, sometimes it can be difficult to distinguish between loyalty and political expediency. Regardless, the power base can be a powerful force on campus.

This power was exemplified when a strong power base spearheaded by faculty members at the University of Virginia rallied to support the university president, Teresa Sullivan. As she grappled with shrinking state support, President Sullivan sought buy-in for various solutions from the many campus stakeholders, including the faculty members. This incremental approach was inherently slow and deliberate. Too slow for members of the governing Board of Visitors, who became increasingly concerned that the university was falling behind other benchmark universities such as Harvard and Stanford in innovative developments such as the development and use of online courses. According to board rector Helen Dragas, "the days of incremental decisionmaking in higher education are over, or should be."[51] These concerns motivated the board, headed by Rector Dragas, to ask for President Sullivan's resignation. Consequently, less than three years after she was hired, President Sullivan resigned, citing "philosophical differences" with the board.[52]

The resignation caught the campus by surprise. Responding to the governing board's action, the Faculty Senate Executive Council issued a statement declaring that it was "shocked and dismayed by this news. We were blindsided by this decision." But surprise quickly turned to outrage, as faculty members and students likened the board's action to a coup. As one professor said, "If they can do it to the president, they can do it to anybody."[53] Multiple demonstrations involving faculty members, students, and alumni were held on campus in support of President Sullivan. The AAUP publicly expressed its "deep concern" over the board's action, and the university's faculty senate voted 50-0 for an expression of no confidence in the board's decision.[54] After sixteen days under this pressure, the board voted to reinstate Dr. Sullivan as president of the university.

This example illustrates the influence yielded by a strong power base. The board simply could not stand up to the faculty senate's pressure, which spawned alumnae outrage and threats of donor disengagement. This strength was surprising in some respects, mainly because as a matter of academic culture, faculty members often mistrust university administrators. But in this case, they expressed loyalty to a cause—decision making marked by slow deliberation, extensive faculty consultation, and so forth—that transformed into loyalty to President Sullivan. As George M. Cohen, chair of the faculty senate, commented while praising President Sullivan, she "embodied—and acted upon—a set of principles: honesty, candor, openness, inclusion, consultation, communication, fairness, dignity, and trust."[55] He added that "These are time-honored principles, and they work." The strength of this sentiment fueled the power base needed to defend President Sullivan against her boss, the governing board.

SUMMARY

Authority and loyalty are complexly related. On the one hand, authority commands loyalty; leaders expect loyalty from their followers. On the other hand, authority depends on loyalty; leaders rely on loyalty for acceptance of authority. Individuals must derive some benefit from their loyalty, because otherwise they would not willingly serve some cause. Loyalty requires discipline, for it may involve submission of natural desires to the will or authority of another person. Ultimately, however, loyalty connotes free will. In the political arena, loyalty is paramount and is often declared by a loyalty oath. In fact, a loyalty oath to the state may be a condition of public employment. However, loyalty oaths cannot be overly vague or restrict political or philosophical expression. Loyalty is tightly conjoined with fiduciary duty. Individuals vested with the responsibility to oversee somebody else's interests must always place that person's interests above their own. This obligation to act in the employer's best interests, the fiduciary duty, is predicated on loyalty. Thus, it is known more generally as the duty of loyalty. As agents of the university, faculty members are subject to the duty of loyalty. Corollary to the duty of loyalty, employers expect loyalty from their employees. Loyalty to the organization ranks among the most valued assets of any employee. Thus, when employees look for other job opportunities, their loyalty to the organization comes into question. The duty of loyalty to an organization often collides with personal loyalty to family members. In politics, loyalty plays an important role. Academic administrators are sometimes asked to express loyalty through campaign contributions and endorsements. In this context, perceived disloyalty can have adverse consequences. Loyalty constitutes the primary source of an individual's power base, the group that an administrator can turn to for support during difficult times.

NOTES

1. Samuel Lee and Petra Persson, "Authority Versus Loyalty: Social Incentives and Governance," *New York University Working Paper No. FIN-10-001* (2011), http://www.columbia.edu/~pmp2116/authorityloyalty.pdf. (Accessed January 29, 2013).

2. "Oxford Dictionaries Online," Oxford University Press, http://oxforddictionaries.com/?attempted=true. (Accessed April 24, 2012).

3. Josiah Royce, *The Philosophy of Loyalty* (New York: Macmillan, 1908), 16–17.

4. Ibid., 18.

5. Ibid., 16–17.

6. James I (King of England), *The Political Works of James I* (Cambridge, MA: Harvard University Press, 1918), 71.

7. Ibid., 81–82.; John Dunn, *The Political Thought of John Locke* (Cambridge: Cambridge University Press, 1982), 138.

8. California Education Code § 52720.

9. Florida Statutes § 1003.44.

10. *Frazier v. Alexandre*, 434 F. Supp. 2d 1350, 1352–54 (S.D. Fla) (2006).

11. California Constitution, "Article 20, § 3," (1868).

12. David P. Gardner, *The California Oath Controversy* (Berkeley, CA: University of California Press, 1967), 26.

13. David Gardner, *The California System: Governing and Management Principles and Their Link to Academic Excellence*, Twenty-fifth David Dodds Henry Lecture (Urbana-Champaign, IL: University of Illinois at Urbana-Champaign, 2005), 40.

14. Kenneth P. Mortimer and T. R. McConnell, *Sharing Authority Effectively* (San Francisco: Jossey Bass, 1978), 122.

15. Gardner, *The California System*.

16. *Keyishian v. Board of Regents*, 385 U.S. 589 (1967).

17. *Knight v. Board of Regents of the University of the State of New York*, 269 F. Supp. 339 (S.D.N.Y. 1967), aff'd, 390 U.S. 36 (1968).

18. Legal Information Institute, "Fiduciary Duty," Cornell University Law School, http://www.law.cornell.edu/wex/Fiduciary_Duty?quicktabs_3=1#quicktabs-3. (Accessed February 15, 2013).

19. "Oxford Dictionaries Online."

20. Leo E. Strine et al., "Loyalty's Core Demand: The Defining Role of Good Faith in Corporation Law," *Georgetown Law Journal* 93 (2010), 634.

21. Legal Information Institute, "Fiduciary Duty."

22. Earl R. Hoover, "Basic Principles Underlying Duty of Loyalty," *Cleveland-Marshall Law Review* 7 (1956), 10.

23. Darren B. Moore, "Three Key Components to the Fiduciary Duty of Loyalty," http://moorenonprofitlaw.com/three-key-components-to-the-fiduciary-duty-of-loyalty/. (Accessed May 10, 2014).

24. Wolf Baldwin and Associates, *An Employee's Duty of Loyalty to an Employer in Pennsylvania* (2014), http://www.wolfbaldwin.com/Articles/An-Employees-Duty-of-Loyalty-to-An-Employer.shtml (Accessed July 14, 2014).

25. National Association of Independent Schools, "The Duty of Loyalty," http://www.nais.org/Articles/Pages/The-Duty-of-Loyalty.aspx. (Accessed February 15, 2013).

26. William F. Griffin, "Fiduciary Duties of Officers, Directors, and Business Owners," in *Model Business Corporation Act*, ed. Corporate Laws Committee (Chicago: American Bar Association, 2011). § 8.2.1 (c).

27. Columbia University, "Statement of University Policy on Conflicts of Interest," (1987),http://evpr.columbia.edu/files/evpr/imce_shared/Statement_Conflicts_of_Interest.pdf. (Accessed February 15, 2013).

28. Ohio State University, "The Ohio State University Financial Conflict of Interest Disclosure Process for Colleges and Vice Presidential Units Frequently Asked Questions FY 2011," (2011), http://ehe.osu.edu/downloads/finance/coi-faq.pdf. (Accessed February 15, 2013).

29. American Association of University Professors, "Statement of Principles on Academic Freedom and Tenure," (1940), http://www.aaup.org/AAUP/pubsres/policydocs/contents/1940statement.htm. (Accessed July 30, 2014).

30. Stanley Milgram, *Obedience to Authority* (New York: Harper and Row, 1974), 146.

31. Herbert A. Simon, *Administrative Behavior*, 2nd ed. (New York: Macmillan, 1957), 198.

32. Ibid., 40.

33. Loyalty Research Center, "What Is Employee Loyalty," (2009), http://www. loyaltyresearch.com/media/thought-perspectives/4.3.3%20Employee%20Loyalty%20Part1. pdf. (Accessed March 11, 2011).

34. Wolf Baldwin and Associates.

35. "Should You Tell Your Boss You're Job Hunting?," http://www.askamanager.org/2008/ 09/should-you-tell-your-boss-youre-job.html. (Accessed July 30, 2014).

36. *Clark v. Holmes*, 474 F.2d 928 (7th Cir.) (1972).

37. Dean O. Smith, *Managing the Research University* (New York: Oxford University Press, 2011), 6–7.

38. Internal Revenue Service, "Tax Exempt Status for Your Organization Section 501(c)(3) Political Activity," in *Publication 557* (2013).

39. Wisconsin Statutes *Political Activities; Public Office* § 230.40(1).

40. Enrique Rangel and Adam D. Young, "Tech Regent Mark Griffin Resigns," *Lubbock-Online* (2009), http://lubbockonline.com/stories/090409/loc_489524509.shtml. (Accessed April 24, 2012).

41. Texas Tech University, "Houston Chronicle—Tech Regent Mark Griffin Resigns," Texas Tech University, http://today.ttu.edu/2009/09/tech-regent-mark-griffin-resigns/. (Accessed April 24, 2012).

42. Ibid.

43. Ibid.

44. Adam D. Young, "Sitton Says She Was Pressured to Resign," *LubbockOnline* (2009), http://lubbockonline.com/stories/091209/loc_492306870.shtml. (Accessed March 8, 2011).

45. Ibid.

46. Ibid.

47. April Castro, "Perry Ally Pressured Him to Resign: Tech Regent," (2009), http://www. nbcdfw.com/news/politics/Perry-Ally-Pressured-Him-to-Resign-Tech-Regent-57291597.html. (Accessed April 24, 2012).

48. Young, "Sitton Says She Was Pressured to Resign."

49. Government Code, *Tex. Gov. Code §§ 665.002–028.*

50. "Oxford Dictionaries Online."

51. Sara Hebel, Jack Stripling, and Robin Wilson, "U. of Virginia Board Votes to Reinstate Sullivan," *Chronicle of Higher Education* (2012), https://chronicle.com/article/U-of-Virginia-Board-Votes-to/132603/. (Accessed March 17, 2014).

52. Carol S. Wood, "Full Text of Email Announcing Sullivan's Stepping Down," *UVAToday* (2012), http://news.virginia.edu/node/18788?id=18788. (Accessed March 14, 2014).

53. Andrew Rice, "Anatomy of a Campus Coup," *New York Times* (2012), http://www. nytimes.com/2012/09/16/magazine/teresa-sullivan-uva-ouster.html?pagewanted=6&_r=1&. (Accessed March 14, 2014).

54. American Association of University Professors, "Governing Board's Ouster of University of Virginia President," (2012), http://www.aaup.org/media-release/governing-board%E2%80%99s-ouster-university-virginia-president. (Accessed July 30, 2014); Carol S. Wood, "Faculty Senate Ratifies No-Confidence Vote by Executive Council," *UVAToday* (2012), http://news.virginia.edu/node/18846?id=18846. (Accessed July 30, 2014).

55. Hebel, Stripling, and Wilson, "U. of Virginia Board Votes to Reinstate Sullivan."

Chapter Four

Legal Limits of Authority

LEGAL RIGHTS AND RESPONSIBILITIES

All individuals have fundamental rights protected by law. Logically, these rights come with associated responsibilities. For example, in return for the rights guaranteed by the federal Constitution, an individual is expected to obey the law, remain loyal to the United States, defend the country in case of war, serve as a juror when called, and vote. Numerous statutes, administrative rulings, and internal policies also protect individual rights with correlated responsibilities. In many cases, this protection extends to institutions as well; in return, universities, for example, are expected to teach students and generate new knowledge. The salient sources of rights and responsibilities, their attributes, and primary implementing documents in an academic setting are summarized in table 4.1. A thorough discussion of these rights and responsibilities is the topic of a great many treatises that extend far beyond the scope of this book. However, those that impact academic authority will be discussed here in specific contexts.

THE CONSTITUTION

The federal Constitution, the ultimate source of law in the United States, limits the power of the government by guaranteeing individual rights. In academia, the primary rights are freedom of expression and assembly (First Amendment), freedom from unreasonable searches and seizures (Fourth Amendment), and freedom from unjust deprivation of life, liberty, and property (Fourteenth Amendment). Stated differently, the Constitution prevents the government from infringing on these inherent rights. Each state also has a constitution modeled to a large extent on the federal Constitution but with

Table 4.1. Legal Rights and Responsibilities in Academia

Source	Attributes	Implementing Documents
Constitutional	Limit government powers Protect individual rights	The Constitution First, Fourth, and Fourteenth Amendments
Legislative	Protect civil rights Enact tax laws Approve budget authority	Titles VI, VII, and IX Authorizations Appropriations
Judicial	Interpret statutes for specific cases Base rulings on precedence	Specific rulings Common law
Administrative	Implement laws ("rule making") Issue executive directives	Agency rules and regulations Executive orders
Policies	Establish institutional policies Administer institutional policies Establish de facto academic contracts	Governing board by-laws Operating procedures Student and faculty handbooks

particular attention to statewide concerns. Various statutes and judicial and administrative rulings derive from the federal and state constitutions, applying their principles to specific situations.

Significantly, the Constitution applies to relations between the government and the people. It does not apply to relations between private parties. Consequently, there is an important distinction between public and private institutions: public universities must abide by the Constitution, whereas private universities need not abide by the Constitution. Thus, the extent of the rights and responsibilities varies considerably between institutions, generally with public colleges and universities regulated by federal and state sources more tightly than private colleges and universities. Indeed, this distinction spawned an adage stating that "In the public sector you can't do it until you're told you can. In the private sector, you do it until you're told you can't." So, at a foundational level, private institutions enjoy greater freedom in their actions, such as employment and student disciplinary practices. At a practical level, however, most private universities embrace the constitutional principles voluntarily either in explicit or de facto policies. Moreover, some institutions may have more rigid internal policies and procedures than those embodied in the Constitution. For example, religious institutions may be required to adhere to church dogma as well as conventional rights.

Because of this distinction, it is important to determine whether an institution is public or private. In most cases, that is a simple matter. A college or university established and funded by a state is clearly public, and a college or university established by a nongovernmental charter is private. Ambiguities arise when ostensibly private institutions receive extensive government funding or other formal public involvement. Collectively, these government involvements are known as "state actions." They depend on whether there is a "nexus," a "symbiotic relationship," or a "public function" relationship with the institution.[1] Each of these three terms refers to increasingly intertwined interactions between the state (i.e., the government) and the private institution, to the point where the private entity is performing actions normally undertaken only by the state. Usually, private colleges and universities know whether these relationships exist and whether they must abide by constitutional directives in at least some circumstances. Again, however, this is usually a moot point, since most private institutions adopt constitutional guarantees voluntarily and document this adoption in handbooks, operating procedures, and related material.

DUE PROCESS

Due process is a fundamental constitutional right that limits government power. The term refers to "fair treatment through the normal judicial system, especially as a citizen's entitlement."[2] In a disciplinary action, the phrase "due process" means that an individual is owed the opportunity for a fair hearing of his or her side of the case; process (a fair hearing) is due (owed to) the individual. Thus, due process is a fundamental issue of fairness. As Doug Linder explains:

> The Due Process Clause is essentially a guarantee of basic fairness. Fairness can, in various cases, have many components: notice, an opportunity to be heard at a meaningful time in a meaningful way, a decision supported by substantial evidence, etc. In general, the more important the individual right in question, the more process that must be afforded. No one can be deprived of their life, for example, without the rigorous protections of a criminal trial and special determinations about aggravating factors justifying death. On the other hand, suspension of a driver's license may occur without many of the same protections.[3]

This concept of fairness dates back to the Magna Carta, a collection of individual rights that a group of English barons imposed on King John in the year 1215. Dissatisfied with the king's rule and misuse of his powers, the barons prepared this charter that proclaimed various liberties and constraints on royal authority in the feudal society of the time "for the health of our soul." In particular, Article 39 of the Magna Carta declares that "No free man shall be seized or imprisoned, or stripped of his rights or possessions, or outlawed or exiled, or deprived of his standing in any other way, nor will we proceed with force against him, or send others to do so, except by the lawful judgement of his equals or by the law of the land."[4] In return for the barons' loyalty, King John agreed to honor this agreement that was designed to protect individuals against abuses by the king. Ultimately, the king ignored the agreement because he considered it made under duress.

With this historical foundation, due process imposes limits to authority. As Robert Lane clarifies, these are "limitations that offer protection against arbitrary uses of authority. . . . The philosophical idea that underlies this legal concept is that even legitimate authority cannot be used in just any manner."[5]

Over the ages, the charter survived numerous emendations and became a seminal progenitor of modern American law. Along the way, the words "law of the land" transformed into the synonymous term "due process of law." The insistence on "due process of law"—the Due Process Clause—is repeated twice in the U.S. Constitution, specifically in the Fifth and the Fourteenth Amendments. As declared in the Fifth Amendment, "No person shall . . . be deprived of life, liberty, or property, without due process of law; nor shall private property be taken for public use, without just compensation."[6] The Fourteenth Amendment extends these constitutional rights to the individual states. Most states have similar constitutional protections. For example, like the Magna Carta and the U.S. Constitution, the Texas constitution states that "No citizen of this State shall be deprived of life, liberty, property, privileges or immunities, or in any manner disfranchised, except by the due course of the law of the land."[7] As a result, all citizens of Texas are guaranteed due process by the state.

There are two types of due process that are applicable in an academic setting: procedural and substantive. Procedural due process prohibits the government from arbitrarily depriving individuals of legally protected interests without first giving them notice and the opportunity to be heard. Thus, it requires particular legal procedures to guarantee fundamental fairness and to prevent subjective and impulsive actions by administrators. Procedural due process for minor offenses may be as simple as informing an individual of the offense and offering an opportunity to clarify his or her actions. For more serious offenses, due process may necessitate giving the individual written notice of the offense and the time for a hearing before a review panel. Substantive due process ensures that a valid reason exists if a person is deprived of life, liberty or property; furthermore, the means used to deprive the person must be reasonable. Thus, it addresses the type of the decision made by the institution. For example, "if a student is suspended, a dispute based on substantive due process will contend that the measures taken by the school were arbitrary and capricious. In other words, the decision of the school did not adhere to standards of fundamental fairness."[8] Substantive due process, therefore, concerns the subject matter of the decision. Even though procedural due process was followed—notice of the offense was given, a hearing was held, and an appeal was allowable—the student can argue that the decision was unfair because of the substance of the decision.

In summary, the Due Process Clause provides that no person shall be "deprived of life, liberty, or property without due process of law." When courts face questions concerning procedural due process, the controlling word in this clause is *process*. Courts must determine how much process is due in a particular hearing to satisfy the fairness requirements of the Constitution. When courts face questions concerning substantive due process, the controlling issue is *liberty*. Courts must determine the nature and the scope of the liberty protected by the Constitution before affording litigants a particular freedom.[9]

Although the constitutional and state due process laws apply only to interactions with the federal or state governments, most private educational institutions proactively honor the underlying precept of fairness—that is, due process. Out of respect for commonly held human rights, private universities usually provide the same due process as public universities in cases of student or faculty member discipline or discharge as a matter of policy. This policy may be written explicitly in a handbook or other document or implicitly via adherence to AAUP standards, for example. These documents are interpreted as binding contracts in many states, so due process violations constitute breaches of contract. Moreover, during the past thirty years or so, the courts have upheld "some kind of hearing" requirements for private employers. Consequently, "The private schools feel that state courts may well imply due process principles into their contracts with students or faculty."[10]

DEPRIVATION OF LIFE, LIBERTY AND PROPERTY INTERESTS

To benefit from the constitutional guarantee of fairness, individuals must demonstrate that they have been deprived of a life, liberty, or property interest. If the interest doesn't fall into one of those three categories, no matter how important it is, it doesn't qualify for constitutional protection. Therefore, legal attention often focuses on what exactly constitutes an interest.

A "life" interest is easiest to define. It refers to capital punishment, which obviously lies outside the realm of university administration. Likewise, a most fundamental liberty interest, personal freedom from incarceration, lies outside the realm of university administration.

However, the right to engage freely in society, such as seeking another job of comparable stature, constitutes a liberty interest that may fall within the administrative realm consequent to an employee's demotion or termination. In the employment context, this liberty interest is affected only when an employee is demoted or terminated for reasons that were false, stigmatizing, and made available to the general public. These actions must result in serious damage to the employee's standing in the public's eye. That is, the stigmatization must be sufficiently adverse that it prevents the employee from seeking or obtaining other comparable employment. Furthermore, the standards of evidence are high. To be stigmatizing, for example, the employer's actions must be worse than adverse; they must give rise to a "badge of infamy, public scorn, or the like."[11] Although these kinds of allegations of deprivation of a liberty interest arise occasionally within the university setting, they seldom prevail in the courts. Nonetheless, to avoid deprivation of a liberty interest, an administrator should never divulge publicly the reasons for a disciplinary action; keep them out of the public's eye.

"Property" interests most certainly impact administrators. A faculty member's property interests are involved if he or she has a legitimate claim of entitlement to a given term of employment or to a given benefit. A prime example would be the firing of a tenured faculty member, thus denying the individual of the financial benefits of continued employment. In this context, the financial benefits constitute property. Another example would be the dismissal of a student, thus denying him or her of not only liberty interests such as good reputation, name, honor, and integrity but also property interests. In this context, the right to public education constitutes property. Furthermore, in public institutions, a contract creates a property right. Thus, terminating an employee during the term of the contract requires due process. In fact, in each of these examples, due process must be followed.

Conversely, denying tenure would not infringe on the unsuccessful individual's property interests, since faculty members are not entitled to tenure. They must earn it. Likewise, loss of privileges or special perquisites generally does not involve property or liberty interests; these include situations such as being awarded no merit pay raise, stripped of a specific committee assignment, moved to a smaller office, removed as department chair, or "returned to the faculty" from an administrative position.

Further examples of liberty and property interests are generally nuanced by case specifics. Indeed, the Supreme Court noted in a pivotal case, *Goss v. Lopez*, that "The interpretation and application of the Due Process Clause are intensely practical matters."[12] And, in a separate ruling, that "The very nature of due process negates any concept of inflexible procedures universally applicable to every imaginable situation."[13] This reality places due process and its application squarely in the realm of legal counsel, and consequently it is always wise to consult regularly with counsel prior to any disciplinary actions involving due process. Finally, as Steven Poskanzer points out: "remember that the only legal consequences of having a property or liberty interest implicated is that the affected individual must receive due process before a deprivation of such interests occurs—not that he or she will be able to preserve them."[14]

TITLE IX

Title IX of the Education Amendments of 1972 introduced far-reaching guarantees of fairness in an academic setting.[15] It derives from seminal antidiscrimination legislation contained in the Civil Rights Act of 1964. Title VI of the Civil Rights Act prohibits discrimination on the basis of race, color, or national origin under any program or activity receiving federal financial assistance; Title VII extends this policy to federal employment opportunities by prohibiting discrimination on the basis of race, color, religion, sex, or national origin.[16] Following passage of the Civil Rights Act, and specifically its Title VII, public attention turned to more expansive legislation barring sex discrimination in educational institutions. The result was Title IX, which states that "no person in the United States shall on the basis of sex be excluded from participation in, be denied the benefits of, or be subjected to discrimination under any education program or activity receiving federal financial assistance." It was amended in 1987 to include all the operations of an educational institution, governmental entity, or private employer that receives federal funds. Operationally, Title IX applies primarily to students, thus complementing Title VII, which covers discrimination primarily for employees. Together, the two laws have a far-reaching impact on administrative authority.

Title IX conditions the receipt of federal funding on a commitment by the recipient institution not to discriminate on the basis of gender. In essence, this promise constitutes a contract between the government and the institution. In a university context, federal funding includes not only obvious research grants and contracts but also "scholarships, loans, grants, wages, or other funds extended to any entity for payment to or on behalf of students admitted to that entity, or extended directly to such students for payment to that entity."[17] Notably, financial aid received indirectly via a federal loan to a student counts as federal funding to the institution. In the words of the Supreme Court, there is no "substantial difference" between institutional assistance and aid received by a school through its students.[18]

Because the institution, not a specific student or employee, receives the federal funds, the institution is responsible for compliance with Title IX regulations. For example, if a faculty member is found to have discriminated in violation of Title IX, the university is automatically liable. Furthermore, since the governing board is the official recipient of federal funding, Title IX applies to the entire institution even if only some of its components or programs benefit from federal financial assistance. Consequently, athletic programs and the marching band, for example, are subject to Title IX regulations if the university receives any federal financial assistance, even though there is very little direct federal funding of these particular activities.

According to the law, every institution must have and distribute a policy against sex discrimination and make known its procedures for students to file complaints of discrimination. In addition, every institution must designate one employee who is responsible for coordinating compliance with Title IX; this individual is known as the Title IX coordinator. And, the institution has a responsibility to respond promptly and effectively to any complaints. The regulations require institutions to perform periodic self-evaluations of whether they offer equal opportunities based on sex and to provide written assurances to the Department of Education that they are in compliance for the period that the federal assistance was received.

Because of their close connection, Title VI and especially Title VII legal precedence has provided guidance in the application of Title IX. Indeed, according to the Department of Justice, "In resolving employment actions, the courts have generally held that the substantive standards and policies developed under Title VII to define discriminatory employment conduct apply with equal force to employment actions brought under Title IX."[19] Accordingly, Title VI and Title VII case law can usually be applied to Title IX situations, although there are several exceptions. The most significant exceptions in an academic setting are that educational institutions controlled by a religious organization are exempt if compliance with Title IX would be inconsistent with the religious tenets of the organization. For example, Title IX would not require a religiously controlled organization that trains students for the ministry to offer comparable training to women if the organization's religious tenets hold that all ministers must be men. Title IX also exempts institutions that train individuals for the military or the merchant marine.

In its implementation of Title IX, the Department of Education's Office of Civil Rights regulations prohibit sex discrimination in nearly all routine university activities. They include admissions, financial aid, academic advising, housing, athletics, recreational services, marching band, residential life programs, health services, counseling and psychological services, classroom assignments, grading, and discipline.[20] And, Title IX prohibits sex discrimination in recruitment and employment consideration or selection, whether full time or part time, under any education program or activity operated by an institution receiving or benefiting from federal financial assistance. Furthermore, Title IX regulations protect pregnant and parenting students from discrimination based on pregnant status, marital status, or parenthood. Their condition must be treated as any other medical condition. Students may not be excluded from any activity based on their condition of pregnancy, parenthood, or marital status. If they attend a separate facility, they must elect to do so voluntarily, and the facility must provide comparable programs.

ATHLETICS

Although Title IX regulations encompass nearly all major university activities, none has attracted as much public attention as athletics. According to the regulations, "A recipient which operates or sponsors interscholastic, intercollegiate, club or intramural athletics shall provide equal athletic opportunity for members of both sexes." In determining whether equal opportunities are available, the regulations require consideration of a long list of factors:

(1) Whether the selection of sports and levels of competition effectively accommodate the interests and abilities of members of both sexes;
(2) The provision of equipment and supplies;
(3) Scheduling of games and practice time;
(4) Travel and per diem allowance;
(5) Opportunity to receive coaching and academic tutoring;
(6) Assignment and compensation of coaches and tutors;
(7) Provision of locker rooms, practice and competitive facilities;
(8) Provision of medical and training facilities and services;
(9) Provision of housing and dining facilities and services;
(10) Publicity.

The opportunities for males and females must correlate with their respective numbers in the undergraduate student body. Thus, if females constitute 50 percent of the student body, their opportunities must equal those available to males. Unequal total expenditures for members of each sex or unequal expenditures for male and female teams if the institution operates or sponsors separate teams does not necessarily constitute noncompliance. However, failure to provide necessary funds for teams of one sex may constitute noncompliance if this compromises equality of opportunity for members of each sex. In other words, a university's commitment to the spirit of Title IX is measured by the sufficiency—not the total amount in dollars—of funding and opportunities for both female and male participation. For example, a university may spend a lot of money on a men's football team; that does not mean that an equal amount of money must be spent on a woman's team such as soccer. There must simply be sufficient funding of female teams to equalize the overall opportunities relative to their enrollment numbers.

Implementation of the athletic provisions of Title IX has been costly to many institutions. New teams and facilities have been established to accommodate females—softball stadiums, locker rooms, larger coaching staffs, and so forth. Some universities have dropped predominantly male sports to achieve compliance. For example, Temple University had been out of compliance for years. In 2013, the student body was 51 percent female. But, it had 3 percent more male than female athletes, and 58 percent of its scholarship money went to men. Thus, the opportunities were out of balance. So, Temple dropped seven varsity sports (five male and two female), reallocating funds to its remaining sports to comply with Title IX regulations. According to the university, "With these changes, we will be in compliance with Title IX."[21]

SEXUAL HARASSMENT

Like its counterpart Title VII, Title IX's prohibition of discrimination on the basis of sex also includes sexual harassment or sexual violence, such as rape, sexual assault, sexual battery, and sexual coercion. This aspect of Title IX, which established that sexual harassment of female students could be considered illegal sex discrimination, was first acknowledged by the courts in a classic case, *Alexander v. Yale*.[22] It is significant because for the first time the courts ruled that failing to protect the students from sexual harassment is a form of gender discrimination.

In 1977, nine years after Yale became coeducational, a group of five female students filed a lawsuit against the university, claiming that they had been targets of persistent sexual harassment and that the university had allowed a hostile sexual climate to pervade the campus. One student, Pamela Price, alleged that one of her course instructors, Raymond Duvall, "offered to give her a grade of 'A' in the course in exchange for her compliance with his sexual demands," that she refused, and that she received a grade of C which "was not the result of a fair evaluation of her academic work, but the result of her failure to accede to Professor Duvall's sexual demands." She further alleges that she complained to Yale officials who failed to investigate her complaint and told her that "nothing could be done to remedy her situation." This was a straightforward "sex for grades" allegation. The other four students claimed that the harassment created a hostile environment that negatively affected their educational career. For example, Ronnie Alexander had wanted to pursue a career as a flute player but "'found it impossible to continue playing the flute and abandoned her study of the instrument, thus aborting her desired professional career,' because of the repeated sexual advances, 'including coerced sexual intercourse,' by her flute instructor, Keith Brion." She alleged further that she attempted to complain to Yale officials about her harassment, but "was discouraged and intimidated by unresponsive administrators and complex and ad hoc methods."

The students asserted that the sexual harassment constituted gender discrimination, in violation of Title IX. Their lawsuit was based on the Title IX regulation stipulating that an institution receiving federal funding (like Yale) "shall adopt and publish grievance procedures for prompt and equitable resolution of student and employee complaints alleging any action which would be prohibited by this part." As reported in the *Yale Herald*:

> At that time, there was no recourse for those wishing to bring a complaint against their harasser. The term "sexual harassment" was brand new and seldom used. . . . So instead of asking for financial damages, as is customary today, the plaintiffs requested only that the University set up a means of reporting these crimes—a central grievance procedure so that information about student harassment and assault could be collected in one location, rather than dispersed among the various college deans and masters, who were often ignorant of just how widespread the problem was.[23]

The court ruled in favor of Yale, dismissing four of the allegations as moot because the students had graduated by then and finding that the fifth, Price, had not been sexually propositioned in exchange for better grades as she had alleged. The students' appeal was unsuccessful, partly because they no longer attended Yale and, meanwhile, Yale had implemented a grievance procedure.

Although Yale prevailed, the trial and appellate courts agreed that sexual harassment at an educational institution could constitute sex discrimination and would therefore be illegal under Title IX. Thus, failure to have any grievance procedure for handling sexual harassment claims could make the university liable. Indeed, "the biggest impact of the case is the creation and institutionalization of grievance procedures for complaints of sexual harassment and other forms of discrimination in educational institutions."[24] Within several years of the appellate ruling, most colleges and universities adopted formal policies and procedures about sexual harassment.

Following *Alexander*, the courts and federal agencies now recognize two types of sexual harassment for students and employees: *quid pro quo* and hostile environment. *Quid pro quo* sexual harassment occurs when submission to unwelcome sexual advances becomes a condition of a student's or employee's status or when submission to or rejection of the advances becomes the basis for educational or employment decisions affecting the individual. Examples include: requiring sexual favors in exchange for hiring, a promotion, a raise, or a grade; disciplining, demoting or firing an employee because he or she ends a consensual relationship; refusing to write recommendations for a graduate student because the student refuses sexual advances; and changing work or academic assignments because an employee or student refuses invitations for a date or other private, social meetings. Significantly, the courts have ruled that harassment may have occurred if the plaintiff submits to the sexual advances or threats, even though submission might bring into question whether they were unwelcome. Employers are generally held strictly liable for *quid pro quo* sexual harassment because the harassing employees are deemed to be acting directly on behalf of their employer.

A hostile environment occurs when sexual harassment is sufficiently severe or pervasive to alter the terms or conditions of employment and create an abusive working environment, judged by both an objective and subjective standard. Furthermore, the employer knew or should have known of the harassment. For example, a professor should know that inappropriate hugs, kisses, touches, and sexually oriented suggestive comments to female students constitute sexual harassment.[25] In general, relatively isolated instances of non-severe misconduct will not support a hostile environment claim; sexual harassment must be sufficiently persistent or pervasive that it creates a hostile or abusive educational environment, adversely affecting a student's education. For a one-time incident to rise to the level of harassment, it must be unusually severe.

If an institutional employee knows or reasonably should know about sexual harassment or sexual violence in violation of Title IX, he or she must inform an individual with the authority to intervene—usually the Title IX coordinator. And, the institution must take immediate action to eliminate the sexual harassment or sexual violence, prevent its recurrence, and address its effects. Even when a student or his or her parent does not want to file a complaint or does not request that the institution take any action on the student's behalf, if the institution knows or reasonably should know about possible sexual harassment or sexual violence, it must promptly investigate to determine what occurred and then take appropriate steps to resolve the situation. A criminal investigation into allegations of sexual harassment or sexual violence does not relieve the institution of its duty under Title IX to resolve complaints promptly and equitably.[26]

INSTITUTIONAL POLICIES

Normally, an organization and its employees are expected to follow the organization's policies. This expectation is often stated explicitly in an institutional code of conduct or some other document. For example, the Stanford University employees' code of conduct states that "We all must be cognizant of and comply with the relevant policies, standards, and laws and regulations that guide our work."[27] State governments may also legislate adherence to their policies. For example, North Carolina law states explicitly that "Agencies shall establish requirements for mandatory compliance with the applicable statewide and individual agency . . . standards and policies."[28] In these cases, an individual has little, if any, discretion; the employer requires adherence to policies. Irrespective of formal statements about the need to abide by organizational policies, it is implicit that they must be followed. Indeed, this "follow the rules" doctrine is a well-known best practice.

Often, universities document faculty, staff, and student policies and procedures in faculty, staff, and student handbooks. For all intents and purposes, these handbooks constitute a contract between the university and the faculty members, staff, or students. As a fundamental principle of contract law, the university must follow these documented procedures, although the courts may allow some leeway in how rigidly they adhere to their own policies. As the Foundation for Individual Rights in Education comments, "The consensus of the courts is that the relationship between a student and a university has, as one judge put it, a 'strong, albeit flexible, contractual flavor,' and that the promises made in handbooks have to be 'substantially observed.'"[29] Incidentally, university disclaimers that "a handbook is not a contract" do not allow the university to ignore its own rules.

Legal liability for an action most likely depends on whether institutional policies were followed. Thus, if an employer follows institutional policies when hiring an individual, the employer is reasonably immune to any complaints about the hiring process. In contrast, if an employer flouts policies, then he or she is vulnerable to any complaints, and a legal defense against the complaints is inherently weak because "you didn't follow your own policies." In this context, some organizations document an institutional prerogative to sidestep their own rules; they have an "escape clause," so to speak. For example, as stated in the University of Alabama in Huntsville (UAH) Staff Handbook, "The University also reserves the right to depart from any of the policies or procedures stated herein at any time when in its sole judgment, it is appropriate to do so."[30] Pragmatically, these departures must be rare, for otherwise they become de facto policy, and that can become very confusing and disruptive.

There are two axiomatic limitations on the authority to waive an institutional policy. First, a lower-level administrator does not have the authority to waive a policy set by a higher level administrator. Thus, if the policy is set by the governing board, then no administrator of the university campus has the authority to waive that policy. Second, if the policy is based directly upon a federal or state mandate, then no administrator may waive the policy. For example, if a human resources administrator is going to hire a groundskeeper and the particular groundskeeper under consideration is willing to work for less than the minimum wage, the administrator does not have the authority to waive the requirement that the groundskeeper be paid the minimum wage; that particular policy is set directly by federal statutes. Likewise, if a state statute requires all university employees making $75,000 or more to file an annual statement of economic interest, no university administrator has the authority to waive that requirement.

Not all federal or state mandates are as clear as these examples. For instance, federal law requires the university to have an affirmative action program. However, the federal statute itself is not very specific about what must, or must not, be included in the program. In general, it is actually adopted and approved by the university president. So, under certain circumstances, the president could waive a provision of the affirmative action program if that were in the best interests of the university.

Clearly, careful thought and attention must be given to the circumstances under which an administrator is considering waiving an established policy. The primary considerations should be who set the policy being considered for waiver and what is the administrative level of the person considering making the waiver.

EXHAUSTION OF REMEDIES

Institutional policies generally contain procedures for disputing an administrative action. They provide administrative means for achieving justice—a remedy—in any matter when legal rights are involved. This may involve a hearing before an administrative board, faculty committee, grievance board, or other venue for resolving the issue. As an element of due process, these procedures are designed to resolve disputes within the institution where the underlying issues are understood, in contrast to the courts where expertise in the issues (but not the law) may be limited.

By the doctrine of "exhaustion of remedies," a controversy will not be heard by a state or federal court until all available nonjudicial or administrative remedies have been pursued. That is, all procedures established by statute, contract, or policy "must be initiated and followed before an aggrieved party may seek relief from the courts. After all other available remedies have been exhausted, a lawsuit may be filed."[31] Stated differently, an individual must pursue all opportunities for an appeal available by institutional policy before the courts will consider a lawsuit. The rationale for this doctrine is that it allows the institution with its specialized personnel, experience, and expertise to sort and decide matters that arise under its jurisdiction. The courts become involved as a last resort.

Numerous court cases affirm the need for the exhaustion of remedies in an academic setting. A straightforward example occurred in *Florida Board of Regents v. Armesto*.[32] In this case, a Florida State University law student, Rosa Armesto, allegedly cheated on her final exams. Following an initial investigation to determine whether formal institutional actions should be taken, the law school determined that charges should be filed and investigated according to procedures outlined in the school's student conduct code. These procedures included several steps where Armesto would have an opportunity to challenge the evidence.

However, before matters could proceed according to the conduct code, Armesto filed a lawsuit in circuit court, seeking an injunction against the filing of the charges. She contended that the investigation was conducted improperly for it violated certain student conduct code requirements and that these improprieties created a risk that she would be falsely accused. Furthermore, she argued that the effects of such an accusation could never be remedied; the formal charges would imperil her standing in the legal community, notably the Florida Bar.

The court ruled that by filing her lawsuit before the university's internal procedures had been followed to completion, Armesto had failed to exhaust all remedies. Therefore, the lawsuit was dismissed, in favor of Florida State University. In the words of the court:

> Appellants [Florida State] contended below, and we agree, that appellee [Armesto] was required to exhaust her administrative remedies. . . . These allegations were insufficient to support a conclusion that existing administrative remedies were inadequate. Appellee had the right to move to dismiss the charges under existing university hearing procedures. Additionally, the hearing on those charges provided the accused with the right to defend herself. The possibility that the Florida Board of Bar Examiners might subsequently improperly bar her from practicing law is speculative and does not demonstrate that her administrative remedies were inadequate. The possible consequence of charges is not a basis to bypass the administrative process.

In some situations, exceptions to the doctrine of exhaustion of remedies exist. For example, the exhaustion does not pertain if a federal agency waives the requirement. Also, in some criminal cases, defendants may file suit in a federal court without fully exhausting administrative remedies if state appeals procedures are improper. Additionally, courts grant exemptions in situations where the remedies are inadequate, potentially harmful, or unfairly delayed.

Significantly, in the courts, civil rights actions such as violation of equal employment opportunity (EEO) laws are not subject to the exhaustion of remedies doctrine. In an academic setting, this was established in *Patsy v. Board of Regents*, where the Supreme Court recognized the exception.[33] In that case, Georgia Patsy, alleged that her employer, Florida International University, had denied her employment opportunities solely on the basis of her race and sex. She filed a lawsuit based on a procedural rule, so-called §1983, that allows an individual whose federal statutory or constitutional rights have been violated to bring an action directly to a federal court without needing first to bring suit in a state court.[34] This is based on a court ruling that in these situations: "The federal remedy is supplementary to the state remedy, and the state remedy need not be sought and refused before the federal remedy is invoked."[35] The university asked for dismissal of the case because Patsy had not exhausted all administrative remedies before filing the lawsuit. The court denied the university's request, stating that "When federal claims are premised on §1983—as they are here—we have not required exhaustion of state judicial or administrative remedies, recognizing the paramount role Congress has assigned to the federal courts to protect constitutional rights . . . this Court has stated categorically that exhaustion is not a prerequisite to an action under §1983, and we have not deviated from that position." Thus, the court held that the exhaustion of requirement does not apply in federal civil rights actions concerning freedom of speech, search, and seizure or use of excessive force, cruel and unusual punishment, and claims of due process violation that are encompassed in the First, Fourth, and Fourteenth Amendments as well as Title VI.

SOVEREIGN IMMUNITY

In contrast to due process, which limits the government's authority, the judicial doctrine of sovereign immunity shields the government's authority against lawsuits. Unless the government consents to be sued, that is. But the government makes that decision, not the courts. According to the Supreme Court, "It is an axiom of our jurisprudence. The government is not liable to suit unless it consents thereto, and its liability in suit cannot be extended beyond the plain language of the statute authorizing it." In addition, "The United States cannot be sued in their courts without their consent, and, in granting such consent, congress has an absolute discretion to specify the cases and contingencies in which the liability of the government is submitted to the courts for judicial determination."[36] With these words, the court protects the government and its agencies against most lawsuits. Thus, for most of U.S. history, sovereign immunity almost universally protected federal and state governments and their employees from being sued without their consent. This is a good deal for the government.

Like due process, sovereign immunity goes back a long way. Its roots lie in the precept that the sovereign—that is, the supreme ruler (such as a king, queen, or emperor)—can do no wrong. For example, the sovereign monarch, the king or queen, makes the laws and, therefore, cannot logically break the laws of his or her own making. As the sovereign might say, "If I do something, then that's the law." In other words, the sovereign is immune to prosecution for breaking his or her own laws. This common law principle of sovereign immunity is embedded in the U.S. Constitution.[37] It has been extended to protect not only the federal but also the state governments from being sued by their own citizens.[38] And, the Eleventh Amendment protects a state from being sued in federal courts by another state or the federal government. For example, a citizen of South Carolina cannot sue the state of Georgia.

The modern rationale for sovereign immunity deviates considerably from its historical rationale. Operationally, its modern *raison d'etre* is that the government must be able to pursue its governance and appropriations functions without the hassle of lawsuits that potentially waste the taxpayers' money. Thus, sovereign immunity allows government agencies and officials to avoid being sued for monetary damages in alleged wrongdoing. Claims against the government can be dismissed promptly, regardless of the merits of a case and before any evidence is obtained through pretrial discovery. Notably, only public universities benefit from sovereign immunity.

Parenthetically, "governmental immunity" is technically distinct from sovereign immunity. It applies immunity only to tort liability of local governments, whereas sovereign immunity applies broader immunity to the state and its agencies. Government immunity is based primarily on the premise that governmental agencies should not have to pay monetary damages. Regardless of this technical difference, the courts sometimes consider governmental and sovereign immunity interchangeably.

Despite its historical shield against legal action, sovereign immunity is not a license to exert authority with impunity. Notably, federal sovereign immunity is not a right to be free from trial, but it is a defense against liability in a trial. To be protected, a public official must act with good faith and without malice when fulfilling official duties. Moreover, the official must know and respect the "unquestioned constitutional rights" of the individual to be sanctioned, such as a student, a teacher, or another administrator. In a pivotal case, *Wood v. Strickland*, the Supreme Court ruled that a public official (such as a school teacher or administrator) "is not immune from damages . . . if he knew or reasonably should have known that the action he took within his sphere of official responsibility would violate the constitutional rights of the [person] affected or if he took the action with the malicious intention to cause the deprivation of constitutional rights or other injury to the [person]."[39] In simpler terms, sovereign immunity cannot be claimed if the plaintiff's constitutional rights have been denied.

Until a Supreme Court decision in 1979, it was generally assumed that a state's immunity must be recognized not only in its own courts but also in the courts of other states throughout the country. That case, *Nevada v. Hall*, involved an employee of the University of Nevada who was driving in California on official business and seriously injured a California resident, John Hall, in an automobile accident.[40] The victim sued the university and the state of Nevada for damages in the California courts. In a pretrial motion, Nevada sought to limit the amount that might be awarded, citing a Nevada statute that places a limit of $25,000 on any award in a tort action against the state pursuant to its statutory waiver of sovereign immunity. The California court denied the motion, and the case went to trial, where the jury awarded damages of $1.15 million. On appeal, the Supreme Court held that the common-law doctrine of sovereign immunity had not passed to the states when the United States was created; therefore, it is up to the states to decide whether to recognize and respect the immunity of other states. Thus, the Supreme Court ruled that "a State is not constitutionally immune from suit in the courts of another State" and, therefore, California could properly refuse to respect Nevada's sovereign immunity in the California courts.

Governments can authorize waivers to sovereign immunity. By the reasoning that the "sovereign is exempt from suit [on the] practical ground that there can be no legal right against the authority that makes the law on which the right depends," the sovereign also has the authority to waive this immunity at will.[41] In the United States, the waiver requires an explicit act of Congress. In 1948, for example, Congress passed the Federal Tort Claims Act waiving immunity to lawsuits and liability in federal courts for tort actions committed by persons acting on behalf of the United States.[42] Major waivers authorized by Congress cover: torts when a federal employee causes somebody to suffer loss or harm; claims arising out of contracts to which the federal government is a party; taking of property by the government; and infringement of patent rights. They allow the government to be sued in each of these situations. Importantly, however, Congress retains its right not to pay damages unless it has authorized them according to the Constitution: "No Money shall be drawn from the Treasury, but in Consequence of Appropriations made by Law."[43] Conceivably, the government could lose in court but avoid paying any damages due to sovereign immunity. None of these waivers is iron-clad, for there are numerous statutory exceptions and judicially imposed limitations on them. In general, though, the government is well shielded against most lawsuits.

Sovereign immunity also shields individual states unless it has been waived. Thus, citizens cannot sue their own state unless the state has waived immunity. The extent of sovereign immunity protection against lawsuits varies from state to state. Indeed, many states have enacted statutes defining the limits of immunity for state governmental entities and employees.[44] Typical limitations or waivers include state tort claims. Some states have established a special court of claims, a board, or a commission to determine claims, with the discretion to limit damages or provide for certain exceptions to liability. In a further example, Texas legislation (as determined by the courts) waives immunity from liability when a government entity benefits from an executed contract, voluntarily binding itself like any other party to the terms of an agreement. But Texas law does not waive immunity from a lawsuit claiming damages if the government breaches the contract.[45] Paradoxically, therefore, the state must abide by the terms of a contract like any other party, but it cannot be sued if it chooses not to honor the contract—unless the state legislature passes a joint Senate and House resolution waiving this immunity.

For public universities, sovereign immunity can provide a powerful defense against lawsuits. Indeed, it can thwart even the most compelling legal challenge. The disruptive impact of sovereign immunity was exemplified in a case contesting the firing of Texas Tech football coach Mike Leach, *Leach v. Texas Tech University.*[46]

It all began after a highly successful 2008 season, when Leach's contract was renewed for an additional three years.[47] In addition to salary and endorsement income, the contract also included various incentive bonuses, such as $800,000 if Leach remained as coach through December 31, 2009. Ultimately, this particular bonus would loom large beyond proportions. The contract included a termination section that described the university's right to terminate the agreement "for cause." In this contract, the definition of "cause" included standard events, such as a criminal act or moral turpitude. In addition, "cause" occurred if the coach were to violate or to allow his staff to violate rules set by the National Collegiate Athletic Association (NCAA). And, importantly, the definition of "cause" encompassed failure of the coach to "assure the fair and responsible treatment of student-athletes in relation to their health, welfare, and discipline."[48] If Leach contravened any of these conditions, he would be allowed at least ten days to "cure" the violation. With the contract in place, Leach coached the team through another winning season in 2009, and the team was headed to an appearance in the 2010 Alamo Bowl.

But then the unexpected happened. During a practice session in preparation for the bowl game, a Texas Tech player suffered a concussion. The next day, he was examined and told not to practice that afternoon and to avoid bright lights. Thus, he showed up at practice wearing street clothes and dark glasses. Leach sent the player to a nearby darkened room for the duration of the practice; furthermore, during practice two days later, the player was secluded in another darkened room for three hours. At that point, the concerned parents filed a complaint with the university about their son's treatment after an injury, objecting to the secluded confinement.

In response to all of this, Texas Tech launched an investigation into the incident. Early in the investigation, the university president sent a letter to Leach informing him ominously that "we have been conducting an inquiry into allegations by a student athlete that your treatment of him, subsequent to his being diagnosed with a mild concussion, may have been injurious to his health and served no medical and/or educational purposes. Texas Tech takes these allegations very seriously. In addition to being unacceptable, if proven, these allegations constitute a breach of your employment contract."[49] The news media supplemented the official university press releases. According to the *Lubbock Avalanche-Journal*, Leach "did not dispute the facts, but did not believe he had done anything wrong."[50] Furthermore, it reported that Texas Tech officials gave Leach an ultimatum to apologize to the injured player in writing by December 28, or Leach would be suspended; Leach offered no apology. In court documents, Texas Tech affirms the request for an apology but doesn't couple it to suspension.[51] Another contradictory report claimed that "two sources close to Leach disputed that account, saying the coach was not offered the opportunity to make an apology."[52]

Apparently rebuffed, the university suspended Leach from his coaching position with pay on December 28. The university's press release said simply that a thorough and fair investigation was underway and that "Until the investigation is complete, Texas Tech University is suspending coach Leach from all duties as Head Football Coach effective immediately."[53] Significantly, the suspension would prevent Leach from coaching the team during the Alamo Bowl game on January 2, 2010. Leach promptly filed a motion for a temporary restraining order blocking the suspension, thus allowing him to coach the team during the bowl game. The motion asserted that Leach's contract did not contain any provisions for a suspension; he was suspended "without any process or contractual basis."[54] With this legal filing, the venue for this acrimonious dispute between Leach and the university shifted to the courts. Lawyers were drawn into the scene and would soon upstage the lead players.

But the courts weren't going to have an opportunity to settle this particular issue. On December 30, just minutes before the legal hearing on the injunction motion, the university's chief counsel handed Leach's lawyer a letter announcing formally that Leach was fired "for cause." The Texas Tech press release announcing the firing cut to the point like a dull knife:

> The coach's termination was precipitated by his treatment of a player after the player was diagnosed with a concussion. The player was put at risk for additional injury. After the university was apprised of the treatment, Coach Leach was contacted by the administration of the university in an attempt to resolve the problem. In a defiant act of insubordination, Coach Leach continually refused to cooperate in a meaningful way to help resolve the complaint. He also refused to obey a suspension order and instead sued Texas Tech University. . . . This action, along with his continuous acts of insubordination, resulted in irreconcilable differences that make it impossible for Coach Leach to remain at Texas Tech.[55]

The "for cause" firing had several immediate consequences. First, the motion against the suspension was now irrelevant and was dropped; it didn't matter what the court ruled, because Leach no longer worked for Texas Tech. Second, Leach definitely would not coach Texas Tech during the forthcoming Alamo Bowl game. And third, since Leach was fired on December 30, he would not be employed through December 31, and, as a result, would not receive the $800,000 retention bonus—not to mention any severance pay.

Thus, by firing Leach one day before the year's end, the university saved $800,000.

Not surprisingly, Leach contested his termination. He filed a lawsuit seeking actual, consequential, and punitive damages, attorney's fees, and other legal costs.[56] In the suit, Leach claimed that Texas Tech had breached its contract by "suspending him without any process or contractual basis, failing to give [him] notice as required under the contract and a reasonable opportunity to cure, and allegedly terminating him for cause when no good cause exists." Thus, according to Leach, Texas Tech had violated his rights to due process afforded by the Texas state constitution; the law guarantees Leach a fair hearing of the case brought against him. In addition, his contract explicitly offered Leach an opportunity to "cure" any alleged contract violations—another aspect of due process. According to Leach, he was granted neither his constitutional nor his contractual rights to due process. And he requested a trial by jury to settle the matter.

Jurists debate what constitutes deprivation and due process. More to the immediate point, was Leach deprived of life, liberty, or property? In this case, the answer is presumably yes; he was deprived of the property (money) to be paid according to his contract with Texas Tech, which, by the way, is a state institution and subject to the provisions of the Fourteenth Amendment. Another judicial question is "what kind of process is due?" As far as Leach is concerned, the minimal process would most probably involve the chance for him to hear the specific reasons "for cause" and to rebut them before an impartial party, with his attorney present. Finally, when should this process occur? Can the president summarily fire Leach and then, after the fact, offer the opportunity for a hearing? If Leach had represented an immediate danger to the players, "fire now, listen later" may have been defensible. However, in the absence of any demonstrable urgency, a hearing should precede the termination.

In response, Texas Tech claimed that "Leach is not entitled to permanent relief requested under his breach of contract claim because Tech enjoys sovereign immunity from suit."[57] Ultimately, after some wrangling in the lower courts, the Texas Supreme Court sustained the university's claims to sovereign immunity *in toto*, including immunity to Leach's breach of contract claim.[58] However, the court let stand Leach's right to seek a ruling in trial court that Texas Tech erred in firing him by denying him due process. It granted him the opportunity to pursue his lawsuit seeking due process and, therefore, to plead his side of the story in court. At best, that might clear Leach's reputation. But it was an impecunious victory for Leach, because the ruling did not allow Leach to sue for monetary damages; Texas Tech effectively defended itself against that possibility by invoking sovereign immunity. Leach continued to explore all legal options to clear his reputation until shortly after he was appointed head football coach at Washington State University, starting in the 2012 season. The presiding judge dismissed the case; it was time to move on.

In general, the logical underpinnings of sovereign immunity can be both frustrating and downright maddening in some contexts. To Mike Leach supporters, this is one of those contexts. As Leach's attorney told reporters after an appeals court upheld Texas Tech's claim of sovereign immunity, "In essence, the doctrine permits state institutions such as Texas Tech to deny a man's written contractual rights and steal his hard-earned labor while paying nothing. That is not fair and not what Texas and its citizens stand for."[59] Texas Tech attorneys did little to dispel this notion. In response to the ruling, the university attorney said that: "We're confident he did receive due process. And no matter what, he's not entitled to any monetary claims."[60] Regardless of the viewpoint, this case illustrates how effectively the doctrine of sovereign immunity can protect public universities from potentially damaging lawsuits.

CHARITABLE IMMUNITY

Sovereign immunity applies only to government agents, including public universities. It does not apply to the private sector. Therefore, private institutions cannot invoke sovereign immunity. However, some states offer limited "charitable immunity" to nonprofit institutions, including most private colleges and universities.

By definition, charitable immunity shields a charitable or nonprofit organization (including universities) from civil liability and negligent torts. That is, a charitable organization such as a nonprofit educational institution, church, or hospital is not liable under tort law and is relieved of legal liability for injury due to its negligent acts or decisions. Theoretically, they could pursue their missions without exercising reasonable care, for they are exempt from responsibility for any injuries attributable to their negligence.

The rationale for this doctrine was that imposing liability on a charitable organization could divert its trust funds for purposes other than the charity's benevolent goals and the donor's intent. Furthermore, the normal rules governing vicarious liability should not apply to the injurious behavior of a charity's employees. It was also assumed that imposing liability upon a charity might discourage donors from pledging resources to the organization, thus limiting a charity's ability to perform good works.

Therefore, in some states the doctrine provides private colleges and universities some level of immunity. In Massachusetts, a charitable organization can be required to pay no more than $20,000 in damages even if it is found liable for negligence. Notably, the tort must have been committed in an activity conducted to accomplish the organization's charitable purpose. This concept is illustrated in *Goldberg v. Northeastern University.*[61] On February 13, 1993, Michel Goldberg, a freshman at Northeastern, visited the university's health-care facility, complaining of a dry cough, nausea, dizziness, upper abdominal discomfort, lower back pain, and general malaise. Because it was a Saturday, in accordance with its standard protocol the facility was staffed only by a registered nurse, who was directed to make an initial assessment of all patients and consult an off-site, on-call physician if the nurse determined that it was necessary for a patient to see a doctor. According to court records, without consulting a physician, the registered nurse on duty that day determined that Goldberg had influenza and recommended that she drink fluids, follow a bland diet, rest, and take Tylenol. After declining a bed in the infirmary, she was released to her dormitory room. Subsequently, Goldberg traveled to her parents' home in New Jersey, where she died of acute anemia triggered by leukemia.

The parents filed a lawsuit against Northeastern, claiming that negligence at its health-care facility contributed to Goldberg's death. The jury returned a verdict of $2 million for each parent. However, because Northeastern is a charitable organization, the judge limited the damages award to $20,000. In its ruling, the court clarified the extent of charitable immunity within the university by adding that "a corporate activity is sufficiently connected to the corporation's charitable purposes unless the reasons for conducting that activity are 'primarily commercial,' meaning that the activity is 'entirely disconnected' from the charitable purposes of the corporation." Thus, "Northeastern's entitlement to the protection of the statutory cap extends to the activities of the . . . [health-care facility] because those activities were conducted in pursuit of Northeastern's charitable purposes."

Despite the good intents, many states have now abrogated or limited the extent of charitable immunity. Their repudiation of immunity derives from public embracement of tort law's central tenet: an individual is responsible for harm that he or she negligently causes. And, as Carl Tobias points out, charitable immunity policies "derive from the idea that charities warrant subsidization; however, victims of negligence whose recovery is denied are forced to make a 'coerced donation.'"[62] Thus, in these states private colleges and universities do not enjoy this protection against tort liability.

QUALIFIED IMMUNITY

Government officials such as public university administrators are shielded against liability by so-called qualified immunity. As a form of governmental immunity, qualified immunity protects them from being sued for damages unless they violated clearly established laws that reasonable officials in their position should have known. It only applies to lawsuits against government officials as individuals, not lawsuits against the government for damages caused by the officials' actions. As noted in Kaplin and Lee, "This immunity applies to officials sued in their *personal* (or *individual*) capacities rather than their *official* (or *representational*) capacities."[63] Thus, public officials who are sued individually are not subject to liability unless their actions were malicious, corrupt, or outside the scope of official duties.

From a practical standpoint, in lawsuits where sovereign immunity has been constructively avoided by suing a public official personally instead of the state institution, the defense of qualified immunity can be raised. Qualified immunity may shield the individual from damages or even relieve him or her from defending the suit altogether. In fact, "qualified immunity is not immunity from having to pay money damages, but rather immunity from having to go through the costs of a trial at all. Accordingly, courts resolve qualified immunity issues as early in a case as possible."[64]

The rationale for qualified immunity is to protect public officials from the fear of litigation when performing discretionary functions entrusted to them by law, as long as they act in good faith and with due care. Although qualified immunity is broad, it does not provide absolute immunity against everything public officials might do. Even while acting in the scope of their employment, they can still be sued for intentionally violating a person's constitutional rights. Furthermore, it does not apply to acts performed outside the scope of employment. Thus, in the eyes of the courts, qualified immunity balances the need to shield public officials from harassment, distraction, and liability when they perform their duties reasonably and the need to hold them accountable when they exercise power irresponsibly. In that sense, it is distinct from absolute immunity granted to judges, for example, which extends beyond the immediate scope of official duties; this limitation to the scope of employment "qualifies" absolute immunity—and thus the term qualified immunity.

Technically, qualified immunity applies only to public officials, not to public employees. The courts draw a distinction between these two groups. Generally, public officials have positions created by statute; they take an oath of office and exercise discretion in the performance of their duties. For the most part, this covers public university trustees and administrators such as presidents, provosts, deans, and departmental chairs. School teachers, and by inference, university faculty members, are considered employees and not officials. Therefore, they are not protected by qualified immunity. Consequently, professors are not shielded from personal liability for actions taken in their professional capacity.

The exclusion of teachers is illustrated in a court case, *Daniel v. Morganton*.[65] In 1990, the city of Morganton was building a new softball field. Before it was finished, a local high school varsity softball team began practicing on it, despite the rough playing field. During one of these practices, the team's assistant coach Deborah Gober, a mathematics teacher at the school, was hitting groundballs to players on the field. One of these "grounders" hit either a clump of grass or a rock, took an erratic hop, struck a player (Kristin Daniel) in the face, knocked out one of her teeth, and loosened another. Subsequently, Daniel sued the school board and Gober individually for negligence in using the unfinished playing field.

Gober argued that as a public schoolteacher, she had qualified governmental immunity from liability for acts of negligence. The court denied this argument, commenting that: "defendant Gober is an employee and not an officer and is therefore not entitled to governmental immunity as her duties are purely ministerial and do not, in the instant case, involve the exercise of sovereign power." Citing a precedent, the court commented further: "[A]n employee of a governmental agency . . . is personally liable for his negligence in the performance of his duties proximately causing injury to the property [or person] of another even though his employer is clothed with immunity and not liable." Consequently, as a schoolteacher, the defendant, Gober, is not immune from acts of negligence. She can be held personally liable for negligent acts in the performance of her duties. However, an officer, such as a school principal or provost, is entitled to share in the immunity of the sovereign (e.g., the governing board), and to assert a separate defense of official immunity.

SUMMARY

The federal Constitution limits the power of the government by guaranteeing individual rights. Public but not private universities must abide by the Constitution. However, most private universities embrace the constitutional principles voluntarily. Due process prohibits the government from arbitrarily depriving individuals of legally protected interests without first giving them notice and the opportunity to be heard and ensures that a valid reason exists if a person is deprived of life, liberty or property. Title IX of the Education Amendments of 1972 states that no person shall be discriminated against on the basis of sex under any education program or activity receiving federal financial assistance. In athletics, the opportunities for males and females must correlate with their respective numbers in the undergraduate student body. Title IX's prohibition of discrimination on the basis of sex also includes sexual violence and sexual harassment. If an institution knows about sexual violence or sexual harassment in violation of Title IX, it must take immediate action to correct the situation. Normally, an organization and its employees are expected to follow the organization's policies. Thus, legal liability depends on whether institutional policy was followed. By the doctrine of "exhaustion of remedies," an individual must pursue all opportunities for an appeal available by institutional policy before the courts will consider a lawsuit. The doctrine of sovereign immunity shields the government's authority against lawsuits unless it consents to be sued, thus providing public universities with a powerful defense against lawsuits. Through charitable immunity in some states, a nonprofit private educational institution is relieved of legal liability for injury due to its negligent acts or decisions. Qualified immunity shields public university administrators against liability for acts performed in the scope of their employment. However, faculty members are not shielded from personal liability for actions taken in a professional capacity.

NOTES

1. William A. Kaplin and Barbara A. Lee, *The Law of Higher Education*, 4th ed. (San Francisco: Jossey-Bass, 2006), 45.

2. "Oxford Dictionaries Online," Oxford University Press, http://oxforddictionaries.com/?attempted=true. (Accessed April 25, 2012).

3. Doug Linder, "Procedural Due Process," *Exploring Constitutional Conflicts* (2012), http://law2.umkc.edu/faculty/projects/ftrials/conlaw/proceduraldueprocess.html. (Accessed May 28, 2013).

4. "The Magna Carta," (1215), http://www.bl.uk/treasures/magnacarta/translation/mc_trans.html. (Accessed May 5, 2011).

5. Robert Lane, "Employment at Will vs. Due Process," *Introduction to Ethics* (2010), http://www.westga.edu/~rlane/professional/lecture22_righttowork2.html#_ftnref1. (Accessed July 31, 2014).

6. United States Constitution (1787), http://www.usconstitution.net/const.html. (Accessed April 25, 2012).

7. Texas State Constitution, "Deprivation of Life, Liberty, Etc.; Due Course of Law," Article 1, §19.

8. Dennis Childers, "A Comparison of Procedural and Substantive Due Process," *Yahoo Voices* (2007), http://voices.yahoo.com/a-comparison-procedural-substantive-due-process-189917.html. (Accessed November 12, 2013).

9. "Substantive Due Process," http://legal-dictionary.thefreedictionary.com/Substantive+Due+Process. (Accessed November 12, 2013).

10. Michael Asimow, "The Private Due Process Train Is Leaving the Station," *Administrative and Regulatory Law News* 23, no. 4 (1998), http://apps.americanbar.org/adminlaw/news/vol23no4/statenew.html. (Accessed June 3, 2013).

11. Faculty Rights Coalition, "Faculty Member's Liberty Interest Claim, Phelan v. Texas Tech University," (2008), www.faculty-rights-coalition.com/caselaw/liberty-interest-professional-reputation-of-the-faculty-defamation-slander-libel-claims.html. (Accessed June 15, 2013).

12. *Goss v. Lopez*, 419 U.S. 565, 95 D. Ct. 729, 42 L. Ed. 2d 725 (1975).

13. *Cafeteria Workers v. McElroy*, 367 U.S. 886 (1961).

14. Steven G. Poskanzer, *Higher Education Law: The Faculty* (Baltimore: Johns Hopkins University Press, 2002), 243.

15. *Title IX of the Education Amendments of 1972*, 20 U.S.C. §§1681–1688 (1972).

16. *Title VI of the 1964 Civil Rights Act*, 42 USC §2000d (1964). *Title VII of the Civil Rights Act of 1964*, 42 U.S.C. §2000e (1964).

17. "Nondiscrimination on the Basis of Sex in Education Programs or Activities Receiving Federal Financial Assistance," in *34 C.F.R. §106* (1975).

18. *Grove City College v. Bell*, 465 U.S. 555 (1984).

19. Department of Justice, "Relationship to Title VII, § Iv.B.2," *Title IX Legal Manual*, http://www.justice.gov/. (Accessed December 11, 2013).

20. "Nondiscrimination on the Basis of Sex in Education Programs or Activities Receiving Federal Financial Assistance."

21. Susan Snyder, "Temple to Drop 7 Sports, Incuding Baseball, Rowing," *Philly.com* (2013), http://articles.philly.com/2013-12-08/news/44908784_1_temple-university-the-inquirer-american-athletic-conference. (Accessed December 11, 2013).

22. *Alexander v. Yale University*, 631 F.2d 178 (1980).

23. Alice Buttrick, "A Culture of Silence," *Yale Herald* (2010), http://yaleherald.com/news/cover-stories/a-culture-of-silence/. (Accessed December 13, 2013).

24. Anne E. Simon, "Alexander v. Yale University: An Informal History," in *Directions in Sexual Harassment Law*, ed. Catherine A. McKinnon and Reva B. Siegel (New Haven, CT: Yale University Press, 2012), 56.

25. Robin Wilson, "Harassment Charges at Cornell U.," *Chronicle of Higher Education* (1995), http://chronicle.com/article/Harassment-Charges-at-Cornell/85134/. (Accessed December 11, 2013).

26. Department of Education Office of Civil Rights, "Know Your Rights: Title IX Prohibits Sexual Harassment and Sexual Violence Where You Go to School," http://www2.ed.gov/about/offices/list/ocr/docs/title-ix-rights-201104.pdf. (Accessed December 11, 2013).

27. Stanford University, "University Code of Conduct, §1.B.," *Administrative Guide* (2011), http://adminguide.stanford.edu/1.pdf. (Accessed May 7, 2013).

28. North Carolina, "Complying with Legal and Policy Requirements, §02.120202," *Statewide Information Technology Standards* (2008), https://www.scio.nc.gov/library/pdf/StatewideInformationSecurityManual/Chapter12.pdf. (Accessed May 7, 2013).

29. Harvey Silverglate and Josh Gewolb, "Procedural Fairness at Private Universities," *FIRE's Guide to Due Process and Fair Procedure on Campus* (2013), 37, http://www.thefire.org/pdfs/due-process.pdf.

30. University of Alabama in Huntsville, *Staff Handbook* (Huntsville: University of Alabama in Huntsville, 2003).

31. The Free Dictionary, "Exhausation of Remedies," http://legal-dictionary.thefreedictionary.com/Exhaustion+of+Remedies. (Accessed November 6, 2013).

32. *Florida Board of Regents v. Armesto*, 563 So. 2d 1080 (1990).

33. *Patsy v. Board of Regents of the State of Florida*, 457 U.S. 496 (1982).

34. *Civil Action for Deprivation of Rights*, 42 U.S.C. §1983.

35. *Monroe v. Pape* 365 U.S. 167 (1961).

36. *Price v. United States*, 174 U.S. 373 (1899); *Schillinger v. United States*, 155 U.S. 163 (15 S.Ct. 85, 39 L.Ed. 108) (1894).

37. U.S. Const. art. III §2; U.S. Const. amend. XI.

38. *Hans v. Louisiana*, 1 U.S. 134 (1890).

39. *Wood v. Strickland*, 420 U.S. 308, 95 S. Ct. (1975).

40. *Nevada v. Hall*, 440 U.S. 410 (1979).

41. *Kawananokoa v. Polyblank*, 205 U.S. 349 (1907).

42. *Federal Tort Claims Act*, 28 U.S.C. §1346(b) (1948).

43. U.S. Const. art. I §9 cl. 7.

44. National Conference of State Legislatures, "State Sovereign Immunity and Tort Liability," (2010), http://www.ncsl.org/research/transportation/state-sovereign-immunity-and-tort-liability.aspx. (Accessed January 9, 2014).

45. *Catalina Development, Inc. v. County of El Paso* 121 S.W.3d 704, 705 (Tex.) (2003).

46. *Leach v. Texas Tech University*, 335 S.W. 3d 386 (Tex. App.) (2011).

47. Brandon George, "Texas Tech, Mike Leach Finally Agree to Contract Extension," *SportsDayDFW* (2009), http://collegesportsblog.dallasnews.com/archives/2009/02/texas-tech-mike-leach-finally-agree-to-c.html. (Accessed April 27, 2011).

48. "Employment Contract between Texas Tech University and Mike Leach," http://i.usatoday.net/sports/graphics/2009/coaches-contracts/pdf/leach_texastech.pdf. (Accessed April 22, 2011).

49. Associated Press, "Letter Sent to Leach," *ESPN College Football* (2009), http://sports.espn.go.com/ncf/bowls09/news/story?id=4783361. (Accessed May 4, 2011).

50. Terry Greenberg et al., "Tech Suspends Leach after Complaint," *LubbockOnline* (2009), http://lubbockonline.com/stories/122909/spo_540556326.shtml. (Accessed May 4, 2011).

51. *Mike Leach v. Texas Tech University*, Defendant Texas Tech University's Third Amended Plea to the Jurisdiction Cause No. 2009-550,359 District Court of Lubbock, Texas 99th Judicial District (2010).

52. Joe Schad, "Leach Suspended after Player Complaint," *ESPN College Football* (2009), http://sports.espn.go.com/ncf/bowls09/news/story?id=4776848. (Accessed July 31, 2014).

53. Sally Logue Post, "Statement from Texas Tech on Suspension of Football Coach Mike Leach," *Texas Tech University News* (2009), http://today.ttu.edu/2009/12/statement-from-texas-tech-on-suspension-of-football-coach-mike-leach/. (Accessed May 4, 2011).

54. *Mike Leach vs. Texas Tech University*, Mike Leach's First Amended Petition, Application for Temporary Restraining Order, and Temporary Injunction Cause No. 2009-550,359, 99th District Court, Lubbock County, Texas (2009).

55. "Statement from Texas Tech on Termination of Football Coach Mike Leach," *Texas Tech University News* (2009), http://today.ttu.edu/2009/12/statement-from-texas-tech-on-termination-of-football-coach-mike-leach-2/. (Accessed May 4, 2011).

56. *Mike Leach v. Texas Tech University,*, Plaintiff Mike Leach's Second Amended Petition Cause No. 2009-550,359 District Court of Lubbock, Texas 99th Judicial District (2010).

57. *Leach v. Texas Tech University*, Cause No. 2009-550,359, 99th District Court, Defendant's response (and alternative plea to the jurisdiction) in opposition to plaintiff's application for temporary restraining order (2009).

58. Tommy Magelssen, "Texas Supreme Court Denies Mike Leach, Texas Tech Appeals; Leach to Seek Declaratory Judgment," *Lubbock Avalanche-Journal* (2012), http://m.lubbockonline.com/crime-and-courts/2012-02-17/texas-supreme-court-denies-mike-leach-texas-tech-appeals-leach-seek. (Accessed February 21, 2012).

59. Betsy Blaney, "Appeals Court Rues against Ex-Tech Coach Mike Leach," *Houston Chronicle* (2011), http://www.chron.com/disp/story.mpl/sports/fb/fbc/7391500.html. (Accessed May 23, 2011).

60. Ibid.

61. *Goldberg v. Northeastern University*, 60 Mass. App. Ct. 707 (2004).

62. Carl Tobias, "Reassessing Charitable Immunity in Virginia," *University of Richmond Law Review* 41, no. 1 (2006), http://lawreview.richmond.edu/v/. (Accessed January 9, 2014).

63. Kaplin and Lee, *The Law of Higher Education*, 346.

64. Legal Information Institute, "Qualified Immunity," Cornell University Law School, http://www.law.cornell.edu/wex/qualified_immunity. (Accessed July 23, 2014).

65. *Daniel v. Morganton*, 125 N.C. App 47 (1997).

Chapter Five

Academic Authority

ACADEMIC FREEDOM

Academic freedom is the keystone of academic authority. It is a hallowed principle of higher education. In common academic lore, the term refers to the freedom to inquire, to teach, and to learn without unreasonable interference or restriction from law, institutional regulations, or public pressure. In encyclopedic lore, its basic elements include "the freedom of teachers to inquire into any subject that evokes their intellectual concern; to present their findings to their students, colleagues, and others; to publish their data and conclusions without control or censorship; and to teach in the manner they consider professionally appropriate."[1] Thus, academic freedom gives both faculty and students the right to express their views in speech, writing, and through electronic communication, both on and off campus, without fear of sanction. This freedom, incidentally, extends to part-time and adjunct faculty members as well.

The *Statement of Principles on Academic Freedom and Tenure* developed by the AAUP in 1940 has become the definitive document on academic freedom.[2] It has been endorsed by more than two hundred educational and professional institutions. Many institutions, including accrediting organizations, incorporate these principles by reference into their policies, thus establishing a contractual commitment to honor them. With this broad legal and professional basis, academic freedom has become the conceptual lifeblood of academia. It applies to all constituents of the academic enterprise: faculty members, students, even the institution itself.

The courts endorse academic freedom as well. In a paean praising academic freedom, the Supreme Court voiced its support in *Keyishian*.[3] In the Court's words:

> Our nation is deeply committed to safeguarding academic freedom, which is of
> transcendent value to all of us and not merely to the teachers concerned. That
> freedom is therefore a special concern of the First Amendment, which does not
> tolerate laws that cast a pall of orthodoxy over the classroom. . . . The class-
> room is peculiarly the "marketplace of ideas." The nation's future depends
> upon leaders trained through wide exposure to that robust exchange of ideas
> which discovers truth "out of a multitude of tongues, [rather] than through any
> kind of authoritative selection."

In a now classic opinion arguing for the exclusion of governmental intervention in the intellectual life of a university, *Sweezy v. New Hampshire*, Supreme Court Justice Felix Frankfurter parsed academic freedom into four
essential freedoms: "It is the business of a university to provide that atmosphere which is most conducive to speculation, experiment and creation. It is
an atmosphere in which there prevail 'the four essential freedoms' of a university—to determine for itself on academic grounds who may teach, what
may be taught, how it shall be taught, and who may be admitted to study."[4]
These four freedoms derive primarily from the constitutional right to free
expression guaranteed to all U.S. citizens in the First Amendment. But they
also originate in part from contract law and professional standards.

Consistent with these ringing endorsements, the courts honor academic
freedom through the doctrine of "judicial deference." By this principle, the
courts usually hesitate to consider academic matters, deferring to the highly
specialized judgment of university administrators and faculty members. Indeed, courts and juries are usually reluctant to question or overturn the specialized knowledge of faculty members about scholarly issues unless it is
such an arbitrary and capricious departure from academic standards that it
indicates "bad faith" rather than actual professional assessment. This respect
for academic expertise is an aspect of judicial deference, sometimes aptly
called "academic deference."

STUDENTS' ACADEMIC FREEDOM

In general, students enjoy the same academic freedom as faculty members.
For the most part, the basic tenets of academic freedom simply transpose into
the student's context. Thus, the fundamental freedom is to learn—to study
subjects that concern them, to form conclusions for themselves, and to express their opinions. This includes the freedom to explore controversial ideas
and engage in creative work.

Like faculty members, students have both rights and responsibilities. A
student has, for example, the right to disagree with a professor in class. With
the right to disagree comes the responsibility to maintain appropriate behavior in class. The student may not steer the conversation off to an unrelated

topic or monopolize the discussion to the point that others cannot participate. Importantly, regardless of their personal views, students remain responsible for learning the course material. That is, students' academic freedom does not deny faculty members the right to require the students to master course material and the fundamentals of the disciplines that faculty teach. Institutions usually explain these rights and responsibilities in their handbooks and policies.

FUNDAMENTAL LIMITATIONS

Despite its centrality, academic freedom has fundamental limitations. Academic freedom does not pertain if the manner of expression substantially impairs the rights of others. Consequently, faculty members cannot harass, threaten, intimidate, ridicule, or impose their views on students. Nor does academic freedom pertain to faculty members if their views demonstrate professional ignorance, incompetence, or dishonesty with regard to their discipline or fields of expertise. And, of course, it does not protect a faculty member who repeatedly skips class or refuses to teach the classes or subject matter assigned.

Significantly, academic freedom does not apply to university administrators such as members of the governing board, the president, the provost, and the deans when they are acting in their official administrative capacity. That limitation arises because governing board members have a fiduciary responsibility to the university—a duty of loyalty—that requires them to act in the institution's best interest. This limits their expression and, therefore, their academic freedom. Similarly, the president represents the institution and is accountable to the governing board. This also limits free expression. The same concept applies to other academic administrators. Caveat: although they do not have academic freedom in their administrative roles, these individuals would have academic freedom if they also engaged in teaching or research.

FREEDOM OF EXPRESSION

Because of protection afforded by the First Amendment, freedom of expression is a primary element of academic freedom. All citizens, whether in public or private universities, are protected by the First Amendment from government infringement on the freedoms of speech, press, and association. In public institutions, this constitutional protection extends to infringement by internal administrators, since they are government employees. In private institutions, the First Amendment does not apply to restraint by internal administrators. However, most private institutions adhere by contract law to this constitutional level of protection as well. This commitment is usually documented in general policy statements. For example, in its Rights and Responsibilities statement for the general college community, Colorado College (which is private) asserts that "all members of the college community have such basic rights as freedom of speech, freedom of press, freedom of peaceful assembly and association, freedom of personal beliefs, and freedom from personal force and violence, threats of violence and personal abuse."[5] Notably, one state, California, extends First Amendment and state constitutional freedom of expression rights to private colleges and universities via the so-called "Leonard law."[6]

Importantly, however, there are limits to free expression. Most university policies contain a clause insisting on the maintenance of decorum and civility. For example, the Colorado College assertion of rights is followed in the next sentence by a caveat: "The exercise of such rights is subject to the college's obligation to maintain an atmosphere consistent with the purposes of academic freedom, social responsibility, and civil order." The college states this more bluntly in its policy on dissent: "Reasoned dissent is welcome at Colorado College. Disruption of college activities is not, and such behavior will not be tolerated."[7] This blunt limitation on freedom of expression is quite representative of most academic institutions; courteous dissent is okay, but disruptive dissent is not.

A prime example of this limitation on freedom of expression occurred at Stanford University in 1972. At that time, the United States was in the throes of the Vietnam War, which triggered antiwar protests on many campuses nationwide. In that context, a tenured associate professor at Stanford, H. Bruce Franklin, delivered three speeches critical of the U.S. war effort on campus that, according to the university, "led or contributed to anti-war demonstrations on campus, including one night of fighting and near-riots."[8] Furthermore, he led an illegal occupation of the campus computing center that resulted in confrontation with the police. In response, the university president, Richard Lyman, indicated his intention to fire Professor Franklin because his actions "constituted a substantial and manifest neglect of duty and a substantial impairment of his performance of his appropriate functions within this University community all in violation of . . . the University's Statement of Policy on Appointment and Tenure."[9] Because this case involved freedom of speech, Stanford (in the words of Donald Kennedy) "had to decide whether it would adopt the applicable Constitutional interpretations, as though Stanford were a state institution, or claim private status. We decided on the former."[10] So, as a matter of due process, a faculty advisory board reviewed the charges and concluded that "Professor Franklin intentionally urged and incited his audience to engage in conduct which would disrupt activities of the University community and threaten injury to individuals and property."[11] Therefore, the Advisory Board sustained the charges, and Professor Franklin was fired. (Incidentally, H. Bruce Franklin is now a professor at Rutgers University–Newark.)

In another limitation, free expression in the classroom applies only to the content of the course being taught. According to the AAUP principles, "Teachers are entitled to freedom in the classroom in discussing their subject, but they should be careful not to introduce into their teaching controversial matter which has no relation to their subject."[12] Most universities document this limitation in faculty, staff, or student handbooks, or similar publications. For example, the University of Wisconsin–Madison confines this aspect of academic freedom to the course material: "Adherence to the right of freedom of speech and to the principle of academic freedom requires that all thoughts presented as ideas or the advocacy of ideas in instructional settings, if they are germane to the subject matter of the course being taught, must be protected."[13] Thus, a faculty member's comments on a particular religious or political issue in a class on organic chemistry may not be protected under the principle of academic freedom. Likewise, derogatory comments are not protected. At the University of Wisconsin–Madison: "The use, in addressing a specific student, university employee, or recipient of university services, of an epithet or a comment concerning that student, employee or recipient of services that clearly derogates and debases him or her on the basis of his or her gender, gender identity and expression, race, religion, ethnicity, sexual orientation, or disability is not appropriate and therefore is not protected." The basic constraint is that the form of expression must not disrupt operation of the educational process.

A landmark case, *Pickering v. Board of Education*, established legal criteria for First Amendment protection of freedom of expression for all public employees inside and outside the classroom.[14] In this case, a public high school teacher, Marvin Pickering, was fired for writing a letter to the local newspaper criticizing the board of education's financial plans for the high schools. The board justified the dismissal because the letter purportedly damaged the reputations of the board members and school administrators, disrupted faculty discipline, and fomented "controversy, conflict and dissension among teachers, administrators, the Board of Education, and the residents of the district." In short, the letter was "detrimental to the efficient operation and administration of the schools of the district." In his lawsuit, Pickering asserted that this dismissal violated his First Amendment rights to freedom of speech. The Supreme Court ruled in favor of Pickering. Thus, his employment was reinstated.

The significance of this ruling lies in its legal reasoning. The court raised five defining questions to determine whether Pickering's letter was protected by the First Amendment. This line of reasoning, which balances the employee's right to free speech against the harm likely to result from the state's interest in promoting efficient performance of its employees, is now known as the "Pickering line" or the "Pickering rule." It is embodied in these questions and the Court's answers ("findings"), which are summarized in table 5.1. All five of the findings, by the way, argued in favor of First Amendment protection.

The first two elements in the Pickering line, numbers one and two in table 5.1, are critical and are highlighted accordingly in italics. The first critical element is the importance of the topic. If it is of major public concern, the balance shifts to the employee's First Amendment rights. In contrast, if the topic is of negligible public concern—an internal office matter, for example—the balance shifts to the employer (i.e., no First Amendment protection). The second critical element of this line of reasoning is the hierarchical proximity of the employee to the object of criticism. At one pole, if the relationship is impersonal, the criticism would probably not interfere with their working relationship and, by inference, not seriously disrupt management of the organization. This minimal impact would favor the employee. At the opposite pole, however, if the relationship is personal and intimate, the criticism would most probably undermine the working relationship between them. In that situation, the balance would shift away from First Amendment protection of the employee to the employer, and the employee could be dismissed. Items three and four elaborate on this second critical element. Operationally, they address the employer's need to maintain effective organizational management; expression that seriously disrupts this managerial necessity cedes constitutional protection. The last element (number five) stresses that if the expression, such as a pamphlet or essay, is written and distributed in the performance of the employee's official duties, it is not protected under the First Amendment.

Table 5.1.   The Pickering Line of Reasoning

The Court's Defining Questions	The Court's Findings
1 *Is the substance of the letter a matter of legitimate public concern?*	*The letter dealt with a matter of public concern.*
2 *Was there a close working relationship between Pickering and those he criticized, namely the board?*	*Pickering had no working relationship with the board.*
3 Was Pickering's performance of his daily duties impaired?	His performance as a teacher was not hindered by the letter.
4 Did the letter have a detrimental impact on the administration of the educational system?	The letter was greeted with public apathy and therefore had no detrimental effect on the schools.
5 Was Pickering writing in his professional capacity or as a private citizen?	He wrote as a citizen and not as a teacher.

Thus, digesting the Pickering line to its two critical elements, the court ruled that First Amendment protection of freedom of expression requires that the expression (1) must be of public importance and (2) must not cause a disruptive impact between the employee and a proximate supervisor. Based on its findings along this line of reasoning, the court concluded that the board's interest in limiting Pickering's commentary is no greater than its interest in limiting anybody else's similar commentary.[15] Therefore, Pickering was entitled to protection under the First Amendment.

Subsequently, two Supreme Court cases clarified the applicability of the Pickering line of reasoning. In the first case, *Givhan v. Western Line Consolidated School District*, the Supreme Court ruled that it does not matter whether individuals express their views in public or in private; First Amendment protection, subject to the Pickering rule, applies in both situations. "The First Amendment forbids abridgment of the 'freedom of speech.' Neither the Amendment itself nor our decisions indicate that this freedom is lost to the public employee who arranges to communicate privately with his employer rather than to spread his views before the public."[16] In the second case, *Connick v. Myers*, the court ruled that the Pickering line of reasoning did not protect public employees who communicate views to office staff about internal office matters; the topics must be of demonstrable concern to a broader public than just office colleagues. There is a very practical rationale for this criterion, as stated by Justice Byron White: "To presume that all matters which transpire within a government office are of public concern would mean that virtually every remark—and certainly every criticism directed at a public official—would plant the seed of a constitutional case."[17] Thus, there is a common-sense realization that government offices could not function if every employment decision became a constitutional matter. As a corollary, the court also posited: "Whether an employee's speech addresses a matter of public concern must be determined by the content, form, and context of a given statement, as revealed by the whole record."[18] "Context" is the key word here, for it delimits the scope of protection. Furthermore, in this decision, the Court emphasized the subtlety of the balancing process, writing that "the State's burden in justifying a particular [discipline] varies depending upon the nature of the employee's expression. Although such particularized balancing is difficult, the courts must reach the most appropriate possible balance of the competing interests." Appreciating the significance of this ruling, it is sometimes appended to the Pickering line of reasoning: the "Pickering/Connick line."

In summary, two inquiries guide interpretations of the constitutional protections accorded to public employee's speech. The first inquiry is whether the employee spoke as a citizen on a matter of public concern. If the answer is no, the employee has no First Amendment cause of action based on the employer's reaction to the speech. If the answer is yes, a constitutional claim may arise. The second inquiry then becomes whether the government entity (the employer) had adequate justification for treating the employee differently from any other member of the general public. This inquiry requires a judge to balance the interests of employees in commenting upon matters of public concern against the interest of government employers in promoting the efficiency of public service.

Numerous legal cases involving teacher expression in a classroom setting have been settled using the Pickering/Connick line of reasoning, usually in the faculty members' favor.[19] However, some concern the use of words that are religious, sexual, or vulgar in nature. The courts generally favor the institution in these situations, ruling, for example, that "such language was not germane to the subject matter in [the] class and had no educational function."[20]

FACULTY CRITICISM OF THE ADMINISTRATION

Faculty members must be somewhat circumspect in their expressions about institutional governance. They may criticize the administration, but the criticism must not disrupt the efficient management of the university. Two examples illustrate the courts' application of the Pickering line of reasoning in this setting. In both cases, faculty members spoke out critically on governance matters within their departments. The first, *Roseman v. Indiana University*, involves an associate professor, Eleanor Roseman, who was fired for criticizing the acting chair of her department at a faculty meeting.[21] Specifically, she alleged to her teaching colleagues and the College dean that "the Acting Chairman of the Foreign Languages Department . . . may have suppressed the application of one [candidate] for chairmanship of the Department." After a faculty meeting where the disgruntled professor presented the allegations, the other faculty members voted their confidence in the acting chair. Subsequently, the departmental committee on merit and tenure recommended nonrenewal of Professor Roseman's contract, which the university administration ratified. Professor Roseman filed a lawsuit, seeking reinstatement. In applying the Pickering line of reasoning, the court ruled that the professor's statements did not rise to the level of public importance. Furthermore, they had a disruptive impact; indeed, it is easy to imagine that a harsh verbal attack on the chair in a faculty meeting would have a serious effect, interfering with the harmonious relationship between the employee, coworkers, and the supervisor. Consequently, the professor's statements did not meet the Pickering-rule criteria necessary for protection under the First Amendment. Thus, the statements could be (and were) used as a basis for dismissal.

The second example, *Maples v. Martin*, involved five faculty members in the mechanical engineering department at Auburn University who had disagreed with the personnel and administrative decisions of successive departmental chairs over a period of about ten years.[22] Their disagreement was visible in numerous hostile memoranda and personal confrontations, including a written review of the department administration that was highly critical of the chair. Besides distributing the critical review to faculty members, students, some alumni administrators, they also sent a copy to the American Board of Engineering and Technology (ABET) just prior to ABET's accreditation appraisal of the college. After an on-site visit, ABET concluded that the schism in the department was seriously disrupting the educational process there and affecting faculty members in other engineering programs. According to court records, "The visiting team characterized the review as 'academic terrorism' which was aimed at discrediting the chair and cited the frequent turnover of department heads as evidence that the situation required drastic action."[23] Recognizing that the departmental in-fighting was injuring the entire college, the dean (with the support of the president) reassigned the five disgruntled faculty members to other departments in the university. None of them suffered any loss of income, rank, or tenure as a result of the transfer.

The professors filed a lawsuit against the university, arguing that reassignment for having published and distributed the review was a violation of their rights to freedom of speech. The courts disagreed. Applying the Pickering/Connick line of reasoning, the court found initially that the review contained some information that was of public interest, because it alerted the public to "substantive issues that could influence the public's perception of the quality of education provided by the department." With this finding, the court took the next step, which was to weigh the professors' free speech interests in publishing the review against the review's disruptive impact on the workplace (the balancing test). It came down firmly on the administration's side as it noted that:

> by subjecting internal administrative policies to public scrutiny, [the review] distracted both students and faculty from the primary academic tasks of education and research. Further, the review was produced in an atmosphere of tension created by the authors' longstanding grievance that they were not being sufficiently involved in departmental decision making. . . . The publication of the review contributed to a lack of harmony among the faculty and interfered substantially with the regular operation of the [Mechanical Engineering] Department. It severely hampered communication between members of the faculty and the Department Head.

In conclusion, the court found that the review addresses a matter of public concern—the quality of education provided by a state-sponsored institution—but that the interest of the university in the orderly administration of the mechanical engineering department outweighs the professors' interest in speaking on this issue. The faculty members' reassignment was affirmed.

In both of these cases, the courts initially questioned whether the faculty members' expression was a matter of public concern. Thus, from a practical point of view, when criticizing the administration an irate faculty member should elevate the criticism above a strictly personal level by focusing on a "bigger issue" to attain constitutional protection. And, he or she should stop short of provoking disruptive actions that might justify discipline, for that pushes the Pickering balance in favor of the administration.

An all-too-common strategy among some disgruntled faculty members has been to bring an issue to public attention by alerting the news media about alleged administrative problems, via letters to the editor, op-ed columns, and so forth. This does not guarantee First Amendment protection. Just because they are published does not automatically mean that their content is now a matter of public concern. Ruling to this effect in a case involving a physics professor who had published letters to the editor criticizing his departmental colleagues, a judge noted that publishing letters in the newspaper was simply "publicly complaining about private disputes that were unique to him and not a matter of public concern."[24] Clearly, the courts must address nuances of each case about what warrants First Amendment protection, and this is the subject of considerable legal scholarship.[25]

More recently, a public university faculty member's freedom to criticize the administration was sharply curtailed. In a landmark case, *Garcetti v. Ceballos*, the Supreme Court ruled that the First Amendment does not protect public employees whose statements are made as part of their official employment responsibilities.[26] In this case, the defense attorney in a pending criminal case contacted a deputy district attorney in the Los Angeles District Attorney's office, Richard Ceballos, informing him about inaccuracies in a search-warrant affidavit. Ceballos conducted his own investigation and concluded that a sheriff had, indeed, misrepresented facts in the affidavit. After questioning the sheriff about the inaccuracies and receiving an unconvincing explanation, as part of his official job responsibility to advise his supervisor how best to proceed with a pending case, Ceballos presented the prosecuting attorneys a memorandum documenting the inaccuracies and recommending dismissal of the case. Although they all agreed that the affidavit was questionable, the District Attorney's office refused to dismiss the case. Later, Ceballos told the defense attorney that, in his opinion, the affidavit contained false statements. Not surprisingly, the defense counsel subpoenaed Ceballos to testify at a trial-court hearing, where he recounted his reservations about the affidavit. Following that, Ceballos was reassigned to a different position, transferred to another courthouse, and denied a promotion. He initiated an employment grievance claiming retaliation for cooperating with the defense, but the grievance was denied based on a finding that he had not suffered any retaliation. Unsatisfied, Ceballos filed a lawsuit alleging that his employer (the District Attorney's office) had violated the First and Fourteenth Amendments by retaliating against him based on his memorandum about the affidavit's inaccuracies.

In a 5-to-4 decision, the Supreme Court held that Ceballos was speaking "pursuant to his official duties" and not as a private citizen. Therefore, his speech was not protected by the First Amendment. In other words, speech by a public official is only protected if the official is speaking on a matter of public concern as a private citizen; it is not protected if the official is speaking as part of his public duties. As a result, Ceballos's employers were justified in taking action against him based on his testimony and cooperation with the defense because it happened as part of his official duties. It did not matter that Ceballos was "just doing his job" when he wrote the memorandum. According to the court, "The fact that his duties sometimes required him to speak or write does not mean his supervisors were prohibited from evaluating his performance."

The court elaborated on the employer's right to control an employee's speech. "Employers have heightened interests in controlling speech made by an employee in his or her professional capacity. Official communications have official consequences, creating a need for substantive consistency and clarity. Supervisors must ensure that their employees' official communications are accurate, demonstrate sound judgment, and promote the employer's mission." Thus, the court emphasized the importance of the relationship between the person speaking and his employment. Because public employees often occupy trusted positions in society, their expression of views that contravene governmental policies may impair the proper performance of governmental operations. Therefore, without some control over employees' words and actions, a government entity may not provide services efficiently or effectively.

Importantly, employees speaking as citizens about matters of public concern face only those restrictions on First Amendment rights necessary for their employers to operate efficiently or effectively. Restricting speech that owes its existence to a public employee's professional responsibilities does not infringe on any liberties the employee might have enjoyed as a private citizen. It simply reflects the exercise of employer control over what the employer itself has commissioned or created.

The *Garcetti* decision sent a chilling message to public employees. Basically, it said that if an employee discovers misconduct and reports it to a supervisor who doesn't want to hear about it, the supervisor may retaliate against the employee for presenting the bad news. For many employees, that message raised the fear of retaliation if their speech displeased their employer. The court attempted to assuage this fear somewhat by noting that a government employee who speaks out against an employer's dishonesty or unethical behavior can be protected from any retaliation by a vindictive employer under whistleblower laws even if he is unsuccessful in asserting a First Amendment violation. In other words, *Garcetti* had no impact on existing state and federal whistleblower laws. But that limited assurance is of little comfort for everyday decisions and actions.

Does this restriction on an employee's freedom of speech, known as the "*Garcetti* reservation" and the "official duty rule," apply to public university faculty members engaged in scholarship or teaching as part of their job? In a dissenting opinion, Justice Souter raised this concern: "I have to hope that today's majority does not mean to imperil First Amendment protection of academic freedom in public colleges and universities, whose teachers necessarily speak and write 'pursuant to . . . official duties.'" The majority opinion declined to address this vital topic: "There is some argument that expression related to academic scholarship or classroom instruction implicates additional constitutional interests that are not fully accounted for by this Court's customary employee-speech jurisprudence. We need not, and for that reason do not, decide whether the analysis we conduct today would apply in the same manner to a case involving speech related to scholarship or teaching." Thus, the door was left open for subsequent court intrusions into freedom of speech issues while on the job. In this context, it should be remembered that private university faculty members are not necessarily any better off than their public university counterparts; regardless of *Garcetti*, they have no constitutional protections against dismissal for speech that their employers dislike.

In the immediate aftermath, citing *Garcetti*, three court decisions quickly confirmed a public university faculty member's worst fears. In *Hong v. Grant*, Juan Hong, a professor at the University of California, Irvine, contended that he was denied a merit pay increase in violation of his First Amendment rights to free speech because he criticized the administration's hiring and promotion of other university professors and the use of lecturers to teach courses.[27] The court ruled that Hong's critical remarks were made in the course of his job duties as a participant in shared governance and were, therefore, not protected. It added that the University of California "is entitled to unfettered discretion when it restricts statements an employee makes on the job and according to his professional responsibilities." In two other cases, *Renken v. Gregory* and *Gorum v. Sessoms*, the courts adopted similarly restrictive interpretations of faculty free speech rights.[28]

Nonetheless, two more recent decisions have concluded that *Garcetti* does not apply to a faculty member's classroom speech, even if it is "pursuant to official duties."[29] In a dispute over a faculty member's particularly conservative viewpoints on social issues, *Adams v. Trustees of the University of North Carolina-Wilmington*, the court ruled explicitly that "We are . . . persuaded that *Garcetti* would not apply in the academic context of a public university as represented by the facts of this case."[30] However, the court qualified this statement: "There may be instances in which a public university faculty member's assigned duties include a specific role in declaring or administering university policy, as opposed to scholarship or teaching. In that circumstance, *Garcetti* may apply to the specific instances of the faculty member's speech carrying out those duties. However, that is clearly not the circumstance in the case at bar." Thus, it left some ambiguity in the breadth of its ruling.

The more notable example is *Demers v. Austin.*[31] In this case, a tenured associate professor at Washington State University (WSU), David Demers, served on a "structure committee" that was debating the administrative structure of the university's Murrow School of Communication. While serving on the committee, Demers wrote a pamphlet describing a plan to restructure the school's faculty, which he distributed to the provost, "members of the print and broadcast media in Washington state, administrators at WSU, to some of my colleagues, to the Murrow Professional Advisory Board, and others." He also circulated a draft book manuscript (*The Ivory Tower of Babel*) that was critical of the university administration. Subsequently, Demers argued in a lawsuit against several university administrators that he had been subjected to unfairly bad performance reviews, changes in his class assignments, an unwarranted investigation for improper behavior, and other negative management actions in response to his pamphlet and book manuscript, in violation of his First Amendment rights. According to Demers, these retaliatory actions adversely affected his compensation and his reputation as an academic.

The university's lawyers countered that the actions taken against him were justified and unrelated to his speech, contending, among other things, that he had reoriented his priorities away from academia after receiving tenure; he failed to publish in refereed journals, attended faculty committee meetings sporadically, gave online quizzes instead of appearing in person to teach his Friday classes despite repeated requests to comply with university policies that required him to appear in person, and failed to perform his appropriate share of university service. Furthermore, they contended that the pamphlet was written and circulated pursuant to Demers's official duties and according to *Garcetti* was, therefore, not protected.

The court ruled in Demers's favor, noting that the First Amendment protects his calls for change at the university. Importantly, the court concluded that "*Garcetti* does not—indeed, consistent with the First Amendment, cannot—apply to teaching and academic writing that are performed 'pursuant to the official duties' of a teacher and professor. We hold that academic employee speech not covered by *Garcetti* is protected under the First Amendment, using the analysis established in *Pickering*." With that, the court remanded the case to the district court, where it will balance Demers's First

Amendment rights with the university's interest in controlling his speech and determine whether the pamphlet was the impetus for adverse actions against him. Apropos *Pickering*, the court noted that "protected academic writing is not confined to scholarship" and that Demers's pamphlet addressed matters of public concern because it "made broad proposals to change the direction and focus of the School." Thus, although Demers has not yet prevailed in court on the merits of the case, this decision was a major victory for advocates of the idea that college faculty members have speech rights beyond those afforded other public employees.

Despite this victory, the federal courts are split currently on the matter of faculty members' free speech "pursuant to official duty." Thus, faculty members must still tread apprehensively in this arena until the Supreme Court ultimately clarifies the issue. The AAUP recommends the inclusion of a statement explicitly protecting faculty members' speech regarding institutional matters in university policies, providing specific examples online.[32] As a conservative best practice, public university faculty members should not assume that their speech—especially if it is critical of the administration—will be protected under the First Amendment. And, of course, private university faculty members should not assume that they have any protections in this regard, unless the institution has specific policies providing protection.

EXPRESSION IN PRIVATE LIFE

A faculty member may speak out on any topic as a private citizen with reasonable expectations of protection by the First Amendment. Therefore, as shown in the Pickering line of reasoning, it is important to distinguish between expression as an employee and as a private citizen. However, this distinction between the two venues—professional and private—is not always easily demarcated. Whether speaking within or outside the university community, faculty members are generally identified by title (e.g., Professor) and academic affiliation (e.g., Flagship University). Thus, they represent the university directly or indirectly regardless of intention. The AAUP recognizes this in the *1940 Statement*:

> College and university teachers are citizens, members of a learned profession, and officers of an educational institution. When they speak or write as citizens, they should be free from institutional censorship or discipline, but their special position in the community imposes special obligations. As scholars and educational officers, they should remember that the public may judge their profession and their institution by their utterances. Hence they should at all times be accurate, should exercise appropriate restraint, should show respect for the opinions of others, and should make every effort to indicate that they are not speaking for the institution.

In a separate document, the AAUP notes further that "The controlling principle is that a faculty member's expression of opinion as a citizen cannot constitute grounds for dismissal unless it clearly demonstrates the faculty member's unfitness for his or her position. Extramural utterances rarely bear upon the faculty member's fitness for the position. Moreover, a final decision should take into account the faculty member's entire record as a teacher and scholar."[33]

The courts have a more focused viewpoint. When a faculty member at a public institution is penalized for expression as a private citizen, the dispute generally involves the First Amendment along the Pickering line of reasoning.[34] *Starsky v. Williams* provides a fairly straightforward example.[35] A professor at Arizona State University, Morris Starsky, irritated the Arizona Board of Regents with his dissemination of information about socialism. The irritation was compounded when Professor Starsky canceled a class to attend a rally at the University of Arizona, where he was one of several speakers protesting the arrest of certain University of Arizona students. The entire incident attracted a considerable amount of public attention that caused the regents to initiate disciplinary proceedings against Professor Starsky for his participation in this and seven other incidents involving allegedly unprofessional conduct. The animosity was further inflamed when Professor Starsky criticized the board in a television appearance and in a press release. Ultimately, the board fired him for "intemperate and unrestrained behavior, inaccurate and misleading statements." Professor Starsky filed a lawsuit, claiming violation of his First Amendment rights.

The court ruled that the dismissal violated Professor Starsky's constitutional right to free speech. In the court's opinion:

> we are dealing with speech away from the campus on which plaintiff is employed. The television speech, the press release and the speech at the University of Arizona raise our most serious questions of violation of constitutional rights, the Board's own avowed standards of academic freedom, and of federal due process. In each of these communications, plaintiff spoke or wrote as a private citizen on a public issue, and in a place and context apart from his role as faculty member. In none of these public utterances did he appear as a spokesman for the University, or claim any kind of expertise related to his profession. He spoke as any citizen might speak and the Board was, therefore, subject to its own avowed standard that when a faculty member "speaks or writes as a citizen, he should be free from institutional censorship or discipline."[36]

In arriving at this decision, the court applied the Pickering line of reasoning. Did Professor Starsky's constitutional right to freedom of speech outweigh the university's right to forbid conduct which would materially and substantially interfere with the requirements of appropriate discipline in the operation of the school? The court ruled that it did, in Professor Starsky's favor.

Thus, when speaking on any topic as a private citizen, a faculty member has reasonable expectations of protection by the First Amendment. Pragmatically, however, as *Starsky* illustrates, common sense and legal caution would recommend that he or she speak off-campus and carefully avoid any overt references to personal faculty status or institutional affiliation.

This case highlights the difference between First Amendment constitutional rights and academic freedom. In general, the First Amendment provides broader protection than academic freedom. A simple anecdote by former AAUP counsel Ann Franke illustrates this point.

> A citizen could lawfully proclaim in the town square that the moon is made of green cheese. The government could not punish the person for making that statement. What if an astronomy professor from a public university, in all seriousness, made the same statement in the town square? Her peers and her university could decide that the statement cast serious doubt on her competence to teach astronomy. The university could discipline the professor for making the statement, provided the university met its obligations to provide academic due process. [37]

Thus, expression protected by the First Amendment may not be protected by academic freedom.

CURRICULUM

As expounded by Justice Frankfurter in his four essential freedoms, the university has the academic freedom to determine what may be taught and how it shall be taught. [38] There is a noteworthy caveat to this principle of the university's academic freedom to determine what may be taught. In some states, the curricular offerings of their public colleges and universities are coordinated by a central higher education coordinating board (or some variation on that name). In Alabama, for example, all academic degree programs must be approved by the state's coordinating board, the Alabama Commission on Higher Education (ACHE). [39] Therefore, when the faculty members via the administration at the University of Alabama in Huntsville chose to offer a PhD in chemistry, they would have to petition ACHE for approval. But, informally, ACHE indicated that it would disapprove the request, citing the competing programs at other universities in the state. Therefore, the petition was never filed. And, as in most other states, only a few of the public universities may offer the MD degree. Thus, both the faculty's and the administration's authority to determine what may be taught (one of Justice Frankfurter's four fundamental freedoms) is constrained within limits imposed by the state. In this context, their recognized primacy in the academic domain must comport with overall statewide planning and coordination of higher education.

As a matter of institutional academic freedom, the university administration has the ultimate authority over course content. When disputes between a faculty member and the administration over course content end up in court, the university's authority in these matters almost always prevails. Stated in different terms, institutional academic freedom takes precedence over individual academic freedom. One judge noted bluntly that when the university (through a dean or provost, for example) and a faculty member disagree about course content, "the University must have the final say in such a dispute."[40] This emphatic dictum derives in part from the administration's need to coordinate the prerequisite requirements in the progression of courses toward a degree. An individual faculty member may not necessarily see this bigger picture. It is also manifest in the need to maintain uniform standards in various sections of the same course. Therefore, a faculty member does not necessarily have the freedom to deviate significantly from an established syllabus or pedagogical approach. Indeed, even a well-intentioned deviation may evoke institutional resistance.

The university's prevailing interest in these curricular matters has been affirmed by the courts. For example, in *Scallet v. Rosenblum*, a nontenured instructor at the University of Virginia's Darden Graduate School of Business, Robert Scallet, alleged that the university violated his First Amendment by refusing to renew his teaching contract in retaliation for his outspokenness on issues of "diversity."[41] At Darden, all first-year students must take an Analysis and Communications (A&C) course. To accommodate all of the students, the course was offered at three different times. Scallet was the instructor in one of the three sections. A strong advocate of diversity, Scallet expounded on issues of diversity and business ethics, adding two new cases on those topics. Several other faculty members objected to this divergence from the uniform approach of the other two sections. They claimed that failure to teach the same material taught in the other two sections disrupted the ability of the students to interact outside the classroom. Furthermore, the defendants alleged that Scallet's classroom material "trenched upon material taught by other teachers throughout Darden, some of whom expressed concerns about Scallet's course content." They maintained "that it is the school's prerogative to decide whether business ethics and diversity issues are taught in the first-year Business Ethics class by a professor with an M.B.A., or by an instructor in the first-year writing and speech class who has no business background. In short, defendants maintain that they needed to take control of the A&C curriculum and that the First Amendment does not prohibit them from doing so." Ultimately, this disagreement led to non-renewal of Scallet's contract, with the university claiming that "the material he taught and through the ways in which he abrasively interacted with his colleagues, created an untenable situation that warranted, indeed necessitated, the action taken."

In applying the Pickering balancing test, the court ruled first that Scallet's classroom speech concerning diversity clearly relates to a core issue of public concern. Thus, it then considered whether Scallet's exercise of free speech is outweighed by the "countervailing interest of the state in providing the public service the teacher was hired to provide." The court found that Scallet's "in-class speech, that is, his use of certain materials for classroom discussion" disrupted Darden's pedagogical mission, which required uniformity across class sections. Moreover, his "in-class pedagogy adversely affected the functioning of Darden as a whole." Thus, the court concluded that the interests of the university outweighed Scallet's First Amendment right to free expression, and the case was decided in favor of the university.

Pragmatically, *Scallet* demonstrates that when several professors teach the same course their rights may be somewhat narrower than if they were teaching entirely different courses. Faculty members teaching multiple sections of a course often collaborate on designing the course, and as a group they may decide on the general topics to be covered in each class session. Furthermore, they may all agree to use the same textbook. These reasonable requirements for teaching multisection courses, especially requirements designed by the faculty for the faculty, do not violate academic freedom. However, colleges and universities have a legitimate interest in the content of their courses and course sections, and, as a matter of institutional academic freedom, they may enforce these requirements if necessary.

This outcome was reinforced in a particularly far-reaching case (*Edwards v. California University of Pennsylvania*) involving a tenured professor, Dilawar Edwards, who was assigned to teach an Introduction to Educational Media course using a syllabus provided by the departmental chair and other faculty members.[42] This traditional syllabus focused on how teachers can effectively use various classroom tools, such as projection equipment, chalkboards, photographs, and films. In his syllabus, however, Professor Edwards included a new emphasis on issues of bias, censorship, religion, and humanism. Following student complaints that Professor Edwards was using the class to advance religious ideas, the department chair determined that he was teaching from an unapproved syllabus, and the faculty members voted to reinstate the original syllabus. In response, Professor Edwards sued the university, alleging First Amendment free speech violations.

The court ruled in favor of the university, with the stern commentary that "the First Amendment does not place restrictions on a public university's ability to control its curriculum" and "a public university professor does not have a First Amendment right to decide what will be taught in the classroom." Moreover, it found that the university acts as a "speaker" that engages faculty members to convey its message or course content to the students. And, as the speaker, the university is "entitled to make content-based choices in restricting Edwards's syllabus." In agency-law terms, the university (the speaker) is the principal, and the faculty member is an agent. This last point—the faculty member is an agent of the university—has become the basis for several subsequent opinions favoring the administration.

Expressing religious viewpoints can trigger administrative constraints on academic freedom in the classroom. This has been established in the courts in cases such as *Bishop v. Aronov.*[43] An exercise physiology assistant professor at the University of Alabama, Phillip Bishop, sued the university after it instructed him not to lecture on "evidences of God in human physiology" in class or to teach intelligent design theory in an extracurricular class. In essence, the university sought to prevent Professor Bishop from presenting his religious viewpoint during instructional time, even to the extent that it represented his professional opinion about the matter. The court ruled that during instructional time the classroom was not an open forum and that the university had a right to set the curriculum. "In short, Dr. Bishop and the University disagree about a matter of content in the courses he teaches. The University must have the final say in such a dispute. Though Dr. Bishop's sincerity cannot be doubted, his educational judgment can be questioned and redirected by the University when he is acting under its auspices as a course instructor, but not when he acts as an independent educator or researcher. The University's conclusions about course content must be allowed to hold sway over an individual professor's judgments." Thus, the court concluded that the university as an employer and educator can direct a faculty member to refrain from expression of religious viewpoints in the classroom and similar settings.

As these cases illustrate, the main legal basis for regulating a faculty member's conduct in the classroom is that the conduct violated institutional teaching interests. All of that boils down to this: within reason, the institution prevails over individual faculty members on issues of course content.

Otherwise, faculty members have relatively free reign in the classroom. Summarizing the faculty member's authority in the classroom, Steven Poskanzer comments that: "As long as faculty do not act abusively towards students, ignore established course content (though they can probably put their own slant even on this), use the classroom for blatant proselytizing (especially in circumstances where it looks like compulsion) or repeated discussion of extraneous matter, or aim their teaching at a different audience from their students (including pegging the course at a wildly inappropriate intellectual level), the classroom largely remains their domain."[44]

These cases demonstrating institutional primacy in the determination of course content involved First Amendment considerations in public universities. The principle extends to private universities as well. In fact, the limitations to an individual faculty member's discretion in the classroom may be more profound in a private setting, where individual constitutional protections are not an issue.

RELIGIOUS INSTITUTIONS

Some private institutions have religious goals and define academic freedom in the context of their doctrinal responsibilities. These responsibilities can limit freedom of expression, for faculty members may be prohibited from contradicting religious doctrine. As a matter of good practice, these religiously affiliated colleges generally give faculty members advance notice of restrictions they may place on customary understandings of academic freedom, as directed by the AAUP in its *1940 Statement*: "Limitations of academic freedom because of religious or other aims of the institution should be clearly stated in writing at the time of the appointment."[45] This is the so-called limitations clause. Incidentally, in a footnote, the AAUP comments that "Most church-related institutions no longer need or desire the departure from the principle of academic freedom implied in the *1940 Statement*, and we do not now endorse such a departure." Nonetheless, disputes arise occasionally, and they generally favor the institution.

When a religious institution invokes the limitations clause, thus imposing limits on academic freedom, contract issues may arise concerning the interpretation and the extent of these limits. And this may involve both the courts and the AAUP, as shown in *McEnroy v. Saint Meinrad School of Theology.*[46] This case involved the dismissal of a tenured faculty member from the Saint Meinrad School of Theology, Carmel McEnroy, who signed an open letter to Pope John Paul II asking that continued discussion be permitted concerning the question of ordaining women to the priesthood. Professor McEnroy signed the open letter as a private citizen, without any indication of her academic or religious affiliations, consistent with the AAUP *Statement* that had been adopted without the limitations clause by the school. Nonetheless, Professor McEnroy was fired for "public dissent." According to the school, "she had publicly dissented from the teaching of the Church and was therefore disqualified [by the Church's canon law] from continuing in her faculty position."[47] Insisting that she was exercising her right as a private citizen, Professor McEnroy sued the institution for breach of contract. The AAUP filed an amicus brief arguing that the professor's dismissal violated the institution's own policies emphasizing the importance of academic freedom and the due process rights of faculty members at religiously affiliated institutions. In its defense, the school maintained that it had fired Professor McEnroy on ecclesiastical and not academic grounds and that the AAUP *Statement* did not apply in this nonacademic situation. Regardless, the AAUP censured Saint Meinrad on due process and academic freedom grounds.

The court dismissed the case, thus ruling against Professor McEnroy. It noted the Supreme Court's contention that the First Amendment requires civil courts to refrain from interfering in matters of church discipline, faith, practice, and religious law. This precludes the courts from resolving disputes involving church-affiliated institutions if resolution of the disputes cannot be made "without extensive inquiry . . . into religious law and polity." Accordingly, personnel decisions are protected from court interference that would require the court to interpret and apply religious doctrine or ecclesiastical law. Furthermore, the court ruled that Professor McEnroy's contract contained a clause acknowledging the church's jurisdiction over the school. Thus, the court lacked jurisdiction over the case because that would "excessively entangle the court in religious matters in violation of the First Amendment."

As this sample case demonstrates, the courts are very reluctant to become involved in employment matters within religious organizations. To the AAUP's dissatisfaction, this reluctance reinforces the institution's authority in this realm at the expense of individual academic freedom.

Although the legal system imposes few restraints in this regard, eligibility for receipt of federal funds requires a religiously affiliated institution to respect academic freedom. To receive federal funds, including student financial aid, an institution must be accredited by an association approved by the Department of Education.[48] Furthermore, if an institution is not recognized by an accrediting association, students cannot use federal financial aid there. Thus, the accrediting associations serve as de facto "gatekeepers" because they determine which institutions are eligible for federal funding. And therein lies the linkage. Academic freedom is a *sine qua non* for accreditation. For example, WASC has as one of its primary criteria for review that "The institution publicly states its commitment to academic freedom for faculty, staff, and students, and acts accordingly." Many religiously affiliated colleges and universities are accredited by regional associations such as WASC. Importantly, accrediting organizations specifically for religious institutions also include this criterion. For example, the Christian Association for Biblical Higher Education requires "A published statement of academic freedom and adherence to its principles within the context of the institutional mission."[49] Eligibility for federal funding, of course, is a powerful motivation, so most religious colleges and universities honor this commitment to academic freedom.

However, some schools have turned down this eligibility on strong religious grounds. A noteworthy example is Grove City College, a private, nondenominational Christian college in Pennsylvania. Historically, it has sought to preserve its institutional autonomy by consistently refusing state and federal financial assistance. The college did, however, enroll a large number of students who received Basic Educational Opportunity Grants (now known as Pell grants) through a program administered by the Department of Education. As a recipient of federal assistance, the college was subject to the nondiscrimination requirements of Title IX of the Education Amendments of 1972. When the college refused to comply with the requirements, arguing that the indirect aid received by its students did not constitute federal financial assistance to the college, the Department of Education attempted to terminate funding of the student financial aid program. The college challenged this action in a lawsuit, *Grove City College v. Bell*, that reached the Supreme Court.[50]

The Court held that there was no "substantive difference" between federal financial assistance received directly by the institution and federal financial aid received by the institution through its students. Furthermore, the Court concluded that prohibiting discrimination as a condition for federal assistance did not infringe upon the institutional First Amendment rights of the college. Therefore, if the college did not file an assurance that it would comply with Title IX, the Department of Education could terminate the student financial aid, which it did.

RESEARCH

Academic freedom extends first and foremost to research and scholarly activities, including publication, by faculty members. Indeed, it tops the list of academic freedoms in the AAUP's *1940 Statement of Principles on Academic Freedom and Tenure*: "Teachers are entitled to full freedom in research and in the publication of the results, subject to the adequate performance of their other academic duties."[51] In *Bishop*, the court limited the professor's speech on intelligent design in the classroom, but it emphasized his freedom to conduct research and to publish on the topic. "The University has not suggested that Dr. Bishop cannot hold his particular views; express them, on his own time, far and wide and to whomever will listen; or write and publish, no doubt authoritatively, on them; nor could it so prohibit him."[52] The encyclopedic "freedom of teachers to inquire into any subject that evokes their intellectual concern" practically defines academia. Most faculty members interpret this freedom to mean that "I can study and publish whatever I want to." And that is generally true, although there are some limitations that must be observed.

The federal government imposes numerous regulatory limitations on research using human subjects, animals, radioactive isotopes, hazardous agents, and recombinant DNA. Although research using these resources is not prohibited, there are specific guidelines concerning their use. These guidelines are designed to protect human and animal subjects against unethical treatment and experimenters and the general public against hazardous biological agents and chemicals. They are discussed in depth in *Managing the Research University.* [53]

Universities also impose limitations on permissible research voluntarily. For example, most institutions have strict policies limiting classified research. "Classified research" (also called "research of a classified nature") covers any research that entails access to classified information, whether top secret, secret, or confidential. Extending these definitions, classified information is information that the sponsor (usually the federal government) has declared in need of protection against unauthorized disclosure for the sake of national security. This restriction on publication violates the basic principles of academic freedom that entitle faculty members to full freedom in research and the publication of the results. That violation of academic freedom is why most universities have policies limiting or prohibiting classified research on campus.

Despite assertions against classified research, many universities conduct substantial amounts of classified research, ostensibly because it is in the national interest. (It can also be quite lucrative.) Most universities reconcile this contradiction of policies that explicitly disapprove of classified research by moving it off campus, thus eliminating the need to have classified facilities on campus and greatly reducing any participation of students in the research projects. Johns Hopkins University, for example, administers a huge classified research portfolio at its off-campus Applied Research Laboratory. Its policy states that "Classified research will not be carried out on any academic campus of Johns Hopkins University. . . . Any member of the research community at Johns Hopkins who is planning to participate in a project conducted under the auspices of the University that may involve classified research . . . must include a plan for a non-academic site where the expected research will be conducted." [54]

Universities that do conduct classified research, either on or off campus, generally refuse to consider any student thesis or faculty member's tenure or promotion dossier based on classified research, mainly because of the restrictions on publication. As an example, at Johns Hopkins "Research programs using classified materials cannot be used to satisfy the criteria for completion of academic degree requirements, faculty or scholarly appointments, or promotions." [55] Similar constraints apply to any proprietary results arising from research sponsored by a corporation or foundation. In this vein, "most universities have a clause that recognizes the possibility that a project may unexpectedly generate results that must become classified. In those cases, when classification was not known a priori, the project is generally moved off-campus as quickly as practical, and at least the non-classified results may be admissible in a thesis (subject to necessary security regulations)." [56]

These restrictions on conducting classified research may appear to limit academic freedom. But, they are self-imposed by the institution's faculty members. Paradoxically, the faculty members are exercising their authority to determine what can be studied. Thus, the academic freedom of an individual who desires to conduct classified research may be violated, but the academic freedom of the institution to limit this research is preserved.

GRADES

Axiomatically, the assessment of student academic performance, including the assignment of particular grades, is a primary faculty responsibility. This authority to evaluate the academic performance of students enrolled in a course derives from the generally accepted freedom in the classroom conferred on the instructor. Stated from a different point of view, "the faculty member offering the course should be responsible for the evaluation of student course work and, under normal circumstances, is the sole judge of the grades received by the students in that course."[57] According to the AAUP's *Statement on Professional Ethics*, "professors make every reasonable effort . . . to ensure that their evaluations of students reflect each student's true merit."[58] The academic community proceeds under the strong presumption that the instructor's evaluations are authoritative. But sometimes, circumstances deviate from normal, limiting the faculty member's authority over this domain.

The most common deviation occurs when a student disputes a grade. The basis of an appeal to change a grade can range from a benign arithmetic error to more sinister civil rights discrimination. And, as most faculty members recognize, the appeal may be more personal. Examples include: "If I don't get a B in this course, I'll lose my scholarship"; "if I don't pass this course, I won't graduate this spring"; "I had the flu the day of the final exam"; and so forth. In fact, these disputes occur with such regularity that most faculty members quickly develop personal strategies for resolving them informally. However, occasionally, a dissatisfied student will persist in a "higher-level" resolution of the dispute. When a student alleges that a grade he or she has received is wrong and the faculty member is unwilling to change it, the AAUP *Joint Statement on Rights and Freedoms of Students* asserts that "students should have protection through orderly procedures against prejudiced or capricious academic evaluation."[59] Accordingly, the AAUP further claims that: "A suitable mechanism for appeal, one which respects both the prerogatives of instructors and the rights of students in this regard, should thus be available for reviewing allegations that inappropriate criteria were used in determining the grade or that the instructor did not adhere to stated procedures or grading standards."[60]

Consequently, some—but not all—institutions have written policies for accommodating these appeals. At Texas Tech University, for example, the operating policy states that "A [final] grade can be formally appealed only when there is demonstrable evidence that prejudice or arbitrary or capricious action on the part of the instructor has influenced the grade."[61] The policy calls for due process, with the burden of proof that an unfair influence has affected a grade resting with the student who appeals the grade. The appeal is reviewed by a committee comprised of faculty members and students, who submit their conclusion and recommendation to the college dean for any action. In contrast, Harvard College does not provide a formal appeals process beyond the level of the department chair. "A student may request that the instructor review a grade that has been received and may also ask to consult with the chair of the department or committee of instruction offering the course. However, final authority for the assignment of grades rests with the instructor in charge of the course. Once a grade has been reported to the Registrar, it can be changed only upon the written request of the instructor to the Registrar."[62] Significantly, "The Registrar must be satisfied that all students in the course will have been treated equitably before authorizing any grade change." In other words, a faculty member may be required to review every other student's grade as well, which could be a very daunting prospect. Even less permissive, the University of Alabama tersely states: "If you believe that your grade is incorrect or was assigned in error, please consult with the course instructor."[63] And some institutions (such as the University of Wisconsin–Madison) simply remain silent on the matter.

The lack of a formal institutional policy for appealing a grade does not imply the absence of an appeals process. It may be embedded in a more general grievance policy, including one designed to cover discrimination based on gender or disability. In fact, all institutions receiving federal funds are required by law to provide procedures for students to challenge grades that they believe may have been biased by gender or disability discrimination. This derives from the more general requirement that "A recipient shall adopt and publish grievance procedures providing for prompt and equitable resolution of student and employee complaints alleging any action which would be prohibited by this part."[64] The Department of Education's Office for Civil Rights and the AAUP provide information on the necessary components of these procedures.[65]

Although the faculty member has the responsibility to assign a grade, the university administration has the authority to change the grade without the faculty member's consent. At first glance, responsibility and authority appear to be disconnected in this regard. Furthermore, this contradicts the AAUP's assertion that "no grade may be assigned or changed without faculty authorization" and that "administrators should not substitute their judgment for that of the faculty concerning the assignment of a grade."[66] On what basis, then, can it be stated that the university administration has this authority?

Several court rulings help resolve these contradictions. The first case, *Parate v. Isibor*, established both the faculty member's First Amendment rights in assigning the grade and the administration's authority to change it.[67] Specifically, a dean, Edward Isibor, ordered a nontenured professor, Natthu Parate, to raise the grade of a student in his class from a B to an A. Professor Parate objected repeatedly but ultimately complied with the order. His recalcitrance escalated into a stormy relationship with Dean Isibor, eventually resulting in Professor Parate's dismissal. Seeking redress, Professor Parate filed a lawsuit claiming that the dean had violated his First Amendment rights when asking him to change the grade. The court agreed that under the free speech clause, "because the assignment of a letter grade is symbolic communication intended to send a specific message to the student, the individual professor's communicative act is entitled to some measure of First Amendment protection." This was a transitory victory, however, because the court also held that the university administrators could have changed the student's grade themselves: "If they deemed Parate's grade assignments improper, however, the defendants could have achieved their goals by administratively changing [the student's] grade." The unconstitutional act was compelling the professor to change the grade. So, if an administrator, such as a chair or a dean, wants a student's grade changed, the advice is: "just do it." Don't involve the instructor who assigned it in the first place.

The second case, *Brown v. Armenti*, affirms the administration's authority to change grades, arguing that the professor is acting as an agent of the university.[68] Specifically, at the conclusion of a semester, a tenured professor, Robert Brown, assigned an "F," or "failing," grade to one of his students in a practicum course because the student had attended only three of fifteen class sessions. The university president, Angelo Armenti, ordered that the grade be changed to "Incomplete," but Professor Brown refused. The professor was suspended from teaching the course and eventually terminated. Subsequently, Professor Brown filed a complaint claiming that the defendant, President Armenti, had retaliated against him for refusing to change the student's grade, thus violating his First Amendment rights to free speech. Citing the *Edwards* proposition that "in the classroom, the university was the speaker and the professor was the agent of the university for First Amendment purposes," the court held that the professor had no First Amendment right to expression regarding grade assignment. Elaborating on this point, the court further commented that "Because grading is pedagogic, the assignment of the grade is subsumed under the university's freedom to determine how a course is to be taught." This latter comment is significant, because it shifts the concept of academic freedom from the individual faculty member to the institution.

A third case, *Stronach v. Virginia State University*, reinforced the primacy of institutional academic freedom in grading matters.[69] A tenured professor of physics at Virginia State University (VSU), Carey E. Stronach, assigned a student a final grade of D after he had failed three classroom quizzes. The student claimed to have received A's on two of the quizzes. He submitted faxed copies of his score sheets to Professor Stronach, who concluded that the student had doctored his scores. The student appealed to the chairman of the physics department, who sided with the student and changed his final course grade to an A. Consequently, Professor Stronach sued the department chairman and other university officials on the grounds that they had violated his constitutionally protected right to academic freedom by changing the grade that he, as the course instructor, had assigned. The judge dismissed the suit, stating that "the Court finds that no constitutional right to academic freedom exists that would prohibit senior VSU officials from changing a grade given by Stronach to one of his physics students against his will." Furthermore, the judge declared that academic freedom "is the university's right and not the professor's right."

In summary, these three cases establish that academic freedom in public universities arguably protects a professor's right to assign a grade. But, more compellingly, they also protect the prerogative of the university through its academic administrators (chairs, deans, provost, et cetera) to change the grade over the professor's objection. Since First Amendment rights do not apply to private universities, legal constraints on the freedom to teach (and to change grades) in these institutions are usually based on contract law. Therefore, institutional policies will generally serve as the starting point for resolving any disputes over freedom of expression. In particular, if the institution incorporates the AAUP terms on teaching and grading into its policies, faculty members are given sole responsibility for grading, with the highly significant caveat "under normal circumstances." Thus, in any dispute, the courts may be called upon to determine what constitutes "normal circumstances."

An institution may also require a faculty member to alter the overall difficulty of a course or grading standards. This was ascertained in a fourth case, *Lovelace v. Southeastern Massachusetts University*.[70] Matthew Lovelace was a nontenured instructor in computer courses, whose students complained to the dean that his homework assignments were too time-consuming and his courses were too hard. The dean first threatened not to renew Lovelace's contract unless he appeased the students by inflating his grades or lowering his expectations and teaching standards. When Lovelace refused to lower his standards, his contract was not renewed. In the lawsuit, Lovelace claimed that the university's actions had interfered with his academic freedom, which is protected by the First Amendment. The court rejected the claim because the university has the freedom to set its own grading standards. Specifically,

Whether a school sets itself up to attract and serve only the best and the brightest students or whether it instead gears its standard to a broader, more average population is a policy decision which, we think, universities must be allowed to set. And matters such as course content, homework load, and grading policy are core university concerns, integral to implementation of this policy decision. To accept plaintiff's contention that an untenured teacher's grading policy is constitutionally protected and insulates him from discharge when his standards conflict with those of the university would be to constrict the university in defining and performing its educational mission. The First Amendment does not require that each non-tenured professor be made a sovereign unto himself.

Significantly, in its comments, the court referred to the third of Justice Frankfurter's four essential freedoms of a university: "to determine on academic grounds . . . how it shall be taught." In no uncertain terms, it assigned priority to institutional academic freedom over individual faculty members' academic freedom. Thus, a departmental chair or dean may legally require an individual faculty member to adjust the difficulty of his or her course content.

Although the courts have generally favored the administration's authority to change grades unilaterally, many observers would question the usefulness of that legal right. An administrator such as a chair, dean, or provost might prevail when changing a single grade now and then. But, if the changes were sufficiently frequent or extensive to attract the attention of the faculty senate, they could register their dissatisfaction in several ways, ranging from a public rebuke to a censure or vote of no confidence. The potential negative publicity and damaged working relationship with the faculty from any of these actions would certainly compel an administrator to pause before making a grade change. When told about the court's rulings in this matter, a seasoned provost commented: "It doesn't matter what the law says. I could never get away with it."

CONFERRING DEGREES

When a student satisfactorily completes a prescribed course of study, universities routinely confer a degree. In definitional terms, the degree is "an academic rank conferred by a college or university after examination or after completion of a course of study, or conferred as an honor on a distinguished person."[71] The latter refers to honorary degrees. A diploma certifies conferral of the degree. In definitional terms, the diploma is "a certificate awarded by an educational establishment to show that someone has successfully completed a course of study." Typically, the diploma documents the university's authority to confer the degree. For example, the Arizona State University diploma reads: "The Arizona Board of Regents by virtue of the authority vested in it by law and on recommendation of the University Faculty does hereby confer on John D. Sample who has satisfactorily completed the Studies prescribed therefore the Degree of Bachelor of Arts English in the College of Liberal Arts and Sciences with all the Rights, Privileges and Honors thereunto appertaining this eighteenth day of December, two thousand and eight." It is signed by various dignitaries, including the chair of the governing board, the university president, and, in this example, the state governor. [72]

In most institutions, the faculty determines who qualifies for the degree, but the governing board has the sole authority to confer the degree. This general truth, documented on the sample Arizona State diploma, is stated explicitly in the AAUP's *Statement on Government in Universities and Colleges*: "The faculty sets the requirements for the degrees offered in course, determines when the requirements have been met, and authorizes the president and board to grant the degrees thus achieved." [73] It may be an overstatement to claim that the faculty authorizes the governing board, since the board has the ultimate authority over all university matters and could overrule faculty recommendations. Nonetheless, the faculty members possess considerable power over this cardinal academic domain.

From a legal perspective, a student's enrollment at a university establishes a contractual relationship. If the student complies with the institution's graduation requirements, it agrees to award the degree. In the words of Bernard Reams, "The university cannot take the student's money, allow him to remain and spend his time, and then arbitrarily expel him or refuse to confer on him that which it promised, the degree." [74] That would be a breach of contract. As part of this contractual arrangement, the requirements for a degree are listed in campus publications, such as course catalogues, student handbooks, and departmental websites. It is generally accepted that the terms and conditions for graduation with the degree are those offered by university publications at the time of enrollment.

The authority to confer a degree is broad, providing school administrators and faculty members with a large amount of discretion. In fact, they have almost unlimited discretion to determine whether a student has satisfied the academic requirements for a degree, diploma, certificate, or other recognition that an academic program has been successfully completed. This includes the discretion not to confer a degree if, in their judgment, the requirements have not been satisfied. According to the courts, "the University is under a discretionary and not a mandatory duty to issue degrees to persons participating in its curricula . . . [However] the University may not act maliciously or in bad faith by arbitrarily and capriciously refusing to award a degree to a student who fulfills its degree requirements." [75] The courts have interpreted "arbitrary and capricious" to impose an onerous burden on the student. The few cases where students have prevailed on claims challenging academic performance involve "unusual fact patterns." [76] In other words, this broad authority to confer degrees "requires the exercise of quasi-judicial functions, in which capacity the university's decisions are conclusive. The only apparent limitation on the conferral power is that a degree may not be refused arbitrarily."[77]

REVOKING DEGREES

Just as the university has the authority to confer a degree, it has the authority to revoke a degree if it has been awarded improperly. The revocation must be for good cause and not arbitrary and capricious. In the courts, causes include "instances where the institution learned that a student failed to complete degree requirements, fabricated data in a thesis, or violated the honor code because the student was convicted after graduation for embezzlement of university property."[78] Other causes for revocation include plagiarism and altered grades.

Whether a university has the authority to revoke a degree has been challenged in the courts on several occasions. The earliest case occurred in 1334. In *The King v. University of Cambridge*, the plaintiff sought the restoration of his doctoral degree, which the University had rescinded without a judicial hearing.[79] Although the court granted the plaintiff's petition compelling the University to restore the degree because it had been taken from him without a hearing, the court clearly recognized the right of the University to "revoke a degree for a reasonable cause."[80] More recently, in a seminal case, *Waliga v. Board of Trustees of Kent State University*, the Ohio Supreme Court ruled that Kent State University had the authority to rescind a degree because the student had not completed the appropriate number of courses for graduation.[81] In a widely cited opinion, the court noted that "Academic degrees are a university's certification to the world at large of the recipient's educational achievement and the fulfillment of the institution's standards. To hold that a university may never withdraw a degree effectively requires the university to continue making a false certification to the public at large of the accomplishments of persons who in fact lack the very qualifications that are certified." In fewer words, the authority to revoke a degree derives from the institution's right to preserve its reputation and credibility. Furthermore, "since a university can confer or refuse to confer a diploma for noncompliance with graduation requirements, it follows that the institution should also be able to rescind a degree for the same shortcomings."[82]

The right to rescind a degree is also a matter of contract law. This point of view arose in 1975, when a Virginia university wanted to rescind the degree of a student when it learned that he had altered his grades while working at the university's computing center. When asked for an opinion on the situation, the Virginia attorney general commented that: "if a party is fraudulently induced to perform a contract, the law allows the defrauded party to rescind the agreement and obtain restoration of the benefit of property conferred by him."[83] In this context, the university was fraudulently induced to award the degree based on fraudulent grades. Therefore, as a principle of contract law, the university was entitled to take back the degree.

The revocation process requires adherence to Fourteenth Amendment and contract-law rights. Presumably, students have a property interest in their degree. Therefore, in public universities they have a constitutional right to due process in any revocation proceedings. In general, that involves a fair hearing with the benefit of legal counsel and the opportunity to present witnesses. In private universities, they do not necessarily have this right. However, in a California case of a contested degree revocation, the court ruled that, according to the California common law of fair procedures required of non-profit groups, the student was entitled to "the minimum requisites of procedural fairness. These minimum requisites included notice of the charges, and the probable consequences of a finding that the charges would be upheld, a fair opportunity to present his position and a fair hearing."[84] In most institutions, similar rights are generally incorporated into their operating policies and procedures.

According to the fundamental principle of reversing an authoritative action, revocation of a degree must reverse the process of conferring the degree. Accordingly, "Although institutions of higher education appear to have the authority to revoke degrees, the revocation must be an act of the same entity that has the authority to award the degree."[85] Thus, if the governing board formally confers a degree, it must formally revoke the degree.

This principle can be illustrated by a counter-example, where the courts over-ruled revocation of a degree by the New Mexico State University administration because the governing Board of Regents was not involved.[86] The case, *Hand v. Matchett*, began with allegations of plagiarism in a student's dissertation; these allegations were confirmed by two faculty members from other universities. In response, the university executive vice president directed the graduate dean to develop a policy to investigate academic misconduct allegations such as this. A policy was developed and approved by the board. Shortly after board approval, the graduate dean established an ad hoc committee of graduate school faculty members to investigate the allegations, which confirmed the plagiarism. Singlehandedly, the graduate dean decided that the appropriate response was revocation of the student's degree and instructed the registrar to make this change on the student's transcript.

The student filed a lawsuit in district court, claiming that the revocation violated state law. The court agreed. Specifically, according to New Mexico statutes, the New Mexico State University Board of Regents is vested with exclusive authority to confer degrees and diplomas—"the regents shall have the power to . . . confer such degrees and grant such diplomas."[87] Therefore, according to the court, "Implicit in that power must be the authority to revoke degrees." [88] If the board does not delegate the ultimate authority to confer degrees, it cannot "delegate its authority to revoke a degree to a subordinate individual or body."[89] And, since the board was not involved in the revocation, the university had violated state law. This decision was affirmed by the appeals court. So, the student prevailed.

In general, whenever the administration decides to revoke a degree, it must clearly identify the conferring authority. This is usually the governing board; delegation of this authority seldom extends beyond the president. Thus, for example at a commencement, a dean announces: "Madame President, I recommend the following candidates for the degree." And the president responds: "By the authority vested in me by the Board of Regents, I bestow on you the degree with all the rights and privileges appertaining thereto." The official revocation must emanate from the conferring authority. In this example, that is the president whose authority in the matter has been "vested in me by the Board." As a best practice, the governing board should always be well informed in these situations, especially if there are ambiguities in its ability to delegate—to vest—the authority to confer degrees.

SUMMARY

Academic freedom gives both faculty and students the right to express their views in speech, writing, and through electronic communication, both on and off campus without fear of sanction. It does not pertain if the manner of expression substantially impairs the rights of others. Nor does it pertain to faculty members if their views demonstrate professional ignorance, incompetence, or dishonesty with regard to their discipline or fields of expertise. And it does not protect a faculty member who repeatedly skips class or refuses to teach the classes or subject matter assigned. Significantly, academic freedom does not apply to university administrators. Because of protection afforded by the First Amendment, freedom of expression is a primary element of academic freedom. Most private institutions adhere by policy to First Amendment levels of protection as well. There are limits to free expression. First Amendment protection requires that the expression must be of public importance and must not disrupt the working relationship between the employee and a proximate supervisor. Faculty members may criticize the administration, but the criticism must not disrupt the efficient management of the university. Moreover, the First Amendment does not protect public university employees whose statements are made as part of their official job duties. A faculty member may speak out on any topic as a private citizen with reasonable expectations of protection by the First Amendment. The university has the academic freedom to determine what may be taught and how it shall be taught. In disputes between a faculty member and the administration over course content, the administration's authority in these matters almost always prevails. Although the faculty member has the responsibility to assign a grade, the university administration has the authority to change the grade without the faculty member's consent. An institution may require a faculty member to alter the overall difficulty of a course or grading standards. In most institutions, the faculty determines who qualifies for the degree, but the governing board usually has the sole authority to confer the degree and to revoke a degree. Revocation of a degree must reverse the process of conferring the degree.

NOTES

1. Encyclopedia Britannica, "Academic Freedom," (2013), http://www.britannica.com/EBchecked/topic/2591/academic-freedom. (Accessed September 19, 2013).

2. American Association of University Professors, "Statement of Principles on Academic Freedom and Tenure," (1940), http://www.aaup.org/AAUP/pubsres/policydocs/contents/1940statement.htm. (Accessed September 5, 2013).

3. *Keyishian v. Board of Regents*, 385 U.S. 589 (1967).

4. *Sweezy v. New Hampshire*, 354 U.S. 234 (1957).

5. Colorado College, "Rights and Responsibilities: The General College Community," *The Pathfinder*, http://www.coloradocollege.edu/other/studentguide/pathfinder/. (Accessed September 6, 2013).

6. *Freedom of Speech; Students' Remedies; Hate Violence*, California Education Code Section 94367.

7. "Protest and Dissent: Procedure—Guidelines for Dissent and Protest," *The Pathfinder*, http://www.coloradocollege.edu/other/studentguide/pathfinder/college-policies/protest-and-dissent.dot. (Accessed September 6, 2013).

8. Don Kazak, "Stanford: Faculty Firing Questioned 26 Years Later," *Palo Alto Weekly* (1998), http://www.paloaltoonline.com/weekly/morgue/news/1998_Jun_17.FRANKLIN.html. (Accessed September 6, 2013).

9. Richard W. Lyman, "Statement of Charges," *In the Matter of Associate Professor Howard Bruce Franklin* (1972), http://a3m2009.org/archive/1971-1972/71-72_franklin_advisory/files_71-72_advisory/71-72FranklinBoard_Charges.pdf. (Accessed September 6, 2013).

10. Donald Kennedy, *Academic Duty* (Cambridge, MA: Harvard University Press, 1997), 133.

11. Donald Kennedy et al., "Summary of Advisory Board Report," *Decision Advisory Board In the Matter of Associate Professor Howard Bruce Franklin* (1972), http://a3m2009.org/archive/1971-1972/71-72_franklin_advisory/files_71-72_advisory/71-72FranklinBoard_Summary_of_Report.pdf. (Accessed September 6, 2013).

12. American Association of University Professors, "Statement of Principles on Academic Freedom and Tenure."

13. University of Wisconsin–Madison, "Expression in Instructional Settings," *Faculty Legislation* (2007), http://www.secfac.wisc.edu/governance/legislation/pages300-399.htm. (Accessed July 25, 2014).

14. *Pickering v. Board of Education*, 391 U.S. 563 (1968).

15. William A. Kaplin and Barbara A. Lee, *The Law of Higher Education*, 4th ed. (San Francisco: Jossey-Bass, 2006), 606.

16. *Givhan v. Western Line Consolidated School District*, 439 U.S. 410 (1979).

17. *Connick v. Myers*, 461 U.S. 138 (1983).

18. Ibid.

19. Kaplin and Lee, *Law of Higher Education*, 628–44.

20. *Martin v. Parrish*, 805 F.2d 583 (5th Cir.) (1986).

21. *Roseman v. Indiana University*, 520 F. 2d 1364 (3rd Cir.) (1975).

22. *Maples v. Martin*, 858 F.2d 1546 (1988).

23. Ibid.

24. *De Llano v. Berglund*, 282 F.3d. 1031 (8th Cir.) (2002).

25. Kaplin and Lee, *Law of Higher Education*, 605–722.

26. *Garcetti v. Ceballos*, 547 U.S. 410 (2006).

27. *Hong v. Grant*, 516 F. Supp. 2d 1158 (2007); 403 Fed. Appx. 236 (9th Cir.) (2010).

28. *Renken v. Gregory*, 541 F.3d 769 (C.A. 7) (2008). *Gorum v. Sessoms*, 561 F.3d 179 (3rd Cir.) (2009).

29. Peter Schmidt, "Appeals Court Shields Professor's Criticism of Washington State U. Administration," *Chronicle of Higher Education* (2012), http://chronicle.com/article/Appeals-Court-Shields/141455/. (Accessed June 19, 2014).

30. *Adams v. Trustees of the University of North Carolina-Wilmington*, 640 F.3d 550 (2011).

31. *Demers v. Austin*, 729 F. 3d 1011 (2013); No. 11-35558, WL 306321 (9th Cir.) (2014).

32. American Association of University Professor, "Protecting an Independent Faculty Voice: Academic Freedom after Garcetti v. Ceballos," (2009), http://www.aaup.org/file/Protecting-Independent-Voice.pdf. (Accessed June 22, 2014).

33. American Association of University Professors, "Committee A Statement on Extramural Utterances," (1964), http://www.aaup.org/report/committee-statement-extramural-utterances. (Accessed October 21, 2013).

34. Kaplin and Lee, *Law of Higher Education*, 688–92.

35. *Starsky v. Williams*, 512 F.2d 109 (1975).

36. *Starsky v. Williams*, 353 F.Supp. 900 (1972).

37. Ann Franke, "Academic Freedom Primer," *Difficult Dialogues Program* (2006), http://agb.org/sites/agb.org/files/u1525/Academic%20Freedom%20Primer.pdf. (Accessed October 29, 2013).

38. *Sweezy v. New Hampshire*.

39. Alabama Commission on Higher Education, "Responsibilities," http://www.ache.alabama.gov/Content/About%20Us/Responsibilities.aspx. (Accessed July 25, 2014).

40. *Bishop v. Aronov*, 926 F.2d 1066 (11th Cir.) (1991).

41. *Scallet v. Rosenblum*, 911 F. Supp. 999 (W.D. Va) (1996).

42. *Edwards v. California University of Pennsylvania*, 156 F.3d 488 (3rd Cir.) (1998).

43. *Bishop v. Aronov*.

44. Steven G. Poskanzer, *Higher Education Law: The Faculty* (Baltimore: Johns Hopkins University Press, 2002), 102.

45. American Association of University Professors, "Statement of Principles on Academic Freedom and Tenure."

46. *McEnroy v. St. Meinrad School of Theology*, 713 N.E.2d 334 (1999).

47. Bertram H. Davis, Marie Gabriel Hungerman, and Robert M. O'Neil, "Academic Freedom and Tenure: Saint Meinrad School of Theology (Indiana)," *Academe* 82, no. 4 (1996): 55.

48. Department of Education, "Approved Accrediting Organizations," http://www.chea.org/pdf/CHEA_USDE_AllAccred.pdf. (Accessed October 23, 2013).

49. Association for Biblical Higher Education, "Faculty Qualifications, Development, and Welfare, Standard 9a , Essential Element 10," *ABHE Commission on Accreditation Manual* (2013), http://www.abhe-resources.com/pdfResources/COA/2013_COA_Manual.pdf. (Accessed October 23, 2013).

50. *Grove City College v. Bell*, 465 U.S. 555 (1984).

51. American Association of University Professors, "Statement of Principles on Academic Freedom and Tenure."

52. *Bishop v. Aronov*.

53. Dean O. Smith, *Managing the Research University* (New York: Oxford University Press, 2011), 145–238.

54. Johns Hopkins University, "Policy on Classified and Otherwise Restricted Research," http://jhuresearch.jhu.edu/JHU_Classified_Research%20Policy.pdf. (Accessed October 29, 2013).

55. Ibid., 3.

56. Smith, *Managing the Research University*, 193.

57. American Association of University Professors, "The Right of an Instructor to Assign Grades," *The Assignment of Course Grades and Student Appeals* (1998), http://www.aaup.org/report/assignment-course-grades-and-student-appeals. (Accessed September 13, 2013).

58. "Statement on Professional Ethics," (2009), http://www.aaup.org/report/statement-professional-ethics. (Accessed September 16, 2013).

59. "Protection against Improper Academic Evaluation," *Joint Statement on Rights and Freedoms of Students* (1992), http://www.aaup.org/AAUP/pubsres/policydocs/contents/studrights.htm#4. (Accessed September 16, 2013).

60. "The Right of an Instructor to Assign Grades."

61. Texas Tech University, "Grade Appeals Policy," *OP 34.03: Student Grade Appeal* (2007), http://www.depts.ttu.edu/opmanual/OP34.03.pdf. (Accessed September 16, 2013).

62. Harvard University, "The Grading System," *Harvard College Student Handbook* (2013), http://handbook.fas.harvard.edu/icb/icb.do?keyword=k95151&tabgroupid=icb.tabgroup162919. (Accessed September 16, 2013).

63. University of Alabama, "What Should I Do If a Grade Is Incorrect?," *University Registrar* (2011), http://ua.intelliresponse.com/student_services/index.jsp. (Accessed September 16, 2013).

64. Department of Education, "Nondiscrimination on the Basis of Sex in Education Programs or Activities Receiving Federal Financial Assistance," *34 C.F.R. §106.8* (1975). Also, 28 C.F.R. §35.107.

65. "Prompt and Equitable Grievance," *Revised Sexual Harassment Guidance: Harassment of Students By School Employees, Other Students, or Third Parties* (2001), 19–21, http://www2.ed.gov/about/offices/list/ocr/docs/shguide.pdf. (Accessed September 16, 2013); American Association of University Professors, "The Right of an Instructor to Assign Grades."

66. Donna R. Euben, "Who Grades Students? Some Legal Cases, Some Best Practices," *American Association of University Professors* (2001), http://www.aaup.org/issues/grading/who-grades-students. (Accessed April 25, 2012).

67. *Parate v. Isibor*, 868 F.2d 821 (6th Cir.) (1989).

68. *Brown v. Armenti*, 247 F. 3d 69 (3rd Cir.) (2001).

69. *Stronach v. Virginia State University*, 631 F.Supp. 2d 743 (2008).

70. *Lovelace v. Southeastern Massachusetts University*, 793 F. 2d 419 (1986).

71. "Oxford Dictionaries Online," Oxford University Press, http://oxforddictionaries.com/?attempted=true. (Accessed July 31, 2014).

72. Arizona State University, "Diploma," (2008), http://grad.arizona.edu/gccouncil/system/files/PrintCollege.pdf. (Accessed August 28, 2013).

73. American Association of University Professors, "Statement on Government of Colleges and Universities," (1966), http://www.aaup.org/AAUP/pubsres/policydocs/contents/governancestatement.htm. (Accessed August 28, 2013).

74. Bernard D. Reams Jr., "Revocation of Academic Degrees by Colleges and Universities," *Journal of College and University Law* 14, no. 2 (1987).

75. *Tanner v. Board of Trustees, University of Illinois*, 48 Ill.App.3d 680, 363 N.E.2d 208 (1977).

76. Michael Prairie and Timothy Garfield, *College and School Law: Analysis, Prevention, and Forms* (Chicago: American Bar Association, 2010), 184.

77. Reams, "Revocation of Academic Degrees by Colleges and Universities."

78. Prairie and Garfield, *College and School Law: Analysis, Prevention, and Forms*, 184.

79. *The King v. University of Cambridge (Bentley's Case) (K.B. 1723)*, 8 Modern Rep. (Select Cases) 148, 92 E.R. 818, 2 Ld. Raym. 1334 (1334).

80. Mary Ann Connell and Mayo Mallette, "The Right of Educational Institutions to Withhold or Revoke Academic Degrees," http://www.stetson.edu/law/conferences/highered/archive/2005/RevokeDegrees.pdf. (Accessed August 21, 2013).

81. *Waliga v. Board of Trustees of Kent State University*, 488 N.E. 2d (Ohio) (1986).

82. Reams, "Revocation of Academic Degrees by Colleges and Universities."

83. Patricia A. Hollander, *Legal Handbook for Educators* (Boulder, CO: Westview Press, 1978), 93.

84. Kaplin and Lee, *Law of Higher Education*, 940–41.
85. Ibid., 941.
86. *Hand v. Matchett*, 957 F.2d 791 (10th Cir.) (1992).
87. *N.M.Stat.Ann. § 21-8-7.*
88. *Hand v. Matchett.*
89. Kaplin and Lee, *Law of Higher Education*, 941.

Chapter Six

Admissions

AUTHORITY TO ADMIT

The authority to determine "who may be admitted to study" constitutes one of the university's four essential freedoms.[1] Like all other matters concerning the university, the admissions authority is granted to the governing board. It is then delegated down into the academic hierarchy, usually to the level of a dean or director who bears administrative responsibility for vetting the applications and selecting those who will be offered admission to his or her particular realm within the university. The AAUP promotes the faculty's participation in this aspect of institutional governance: "With regard to student admissions, the faculty should have a meaningful role in establishing institutional policies, including the setting of standards for admission, and should be afforded opportunity for oversight of the entire admissions process."[2] And, in fact, faculty members generally participate in setting institutional policies, including standards.

The process of reviewing the applications and recommending those to be admitted varies between academic units (e.g., colleges and schools). The faculty is usually represented, but staff members may play the predominant role. In most institutions, the actual composition of the admissions committee is confidential to protect against attempted interference from external sources. Technically, their decisions can be overruled by higher authorities such as the provost, the president, and the governing board. Indeed, Texas Tech University's admissions policy states specifically that "The president or her/his designee may waive the admission requirements for a limited number of applicants under unusual or special circumstances."[3] In contrast, Harvard College asserts that "No one may overrule admissions decisions made by the

Committee on Admissions and Financial Aid."[4] Despite this dogmatic policy assertion, the final authority resides in the governing board.

FUNDAMENTAL CONSTRAINTS

Universities are generally protected from legal intrusions into the admissions process by the doctrine of judicial deference. Accordingly, the courts are quite reluctant to second-guess the expertise of academic administrators and faculty members in this realm. Nonetheless, universities must be mindful of fundamental legal constraints.[5]

Primarily, the selection process must not be arbitrary or capricious. An institution may select almost any admissions criteria it wishes, but they must be made known to all applicants and applied equally to all of them. Under the arbitrariness standard, the court will overturn an institution's decision if there is no reasonable explanation for the institution's actions. However, this rarely happens, as the courts almost always defer to the institution's judgment.

The courts' deference is exemplified in *Grove v. Ohio State University*.[6] At Ohio State, the Veterinary School's admissions procedure required submission of an applicant's overall grade-point average, the average grade in selected preprofessional courses, and the results of an interview with two members of the six-member admissions committee. The interview counted heavily in the admissions process, with an assigned weight of forty-five out of a total one hundred points. An Ohio State undergraduate student, Jack Grove, had applied and been denied for admission to Veterinary School three times. He filed a lawsuit, claiming among other things, that the committee's use of a personal interview score, especially with such heavy weighting, introduced subjective factors that were arbitrary and capricious. Thus, he claimed that the school's rejection denied his constitutional liberty interests without due process.

Although the court agreed that Grove had a liberty interest in pursuing veterinary medicine, it disagreed that he had been denied due process. Yes, the interviews were subjective. But they were only one component of the overall admissions process, along with grades, test scores, and so forth. Thus, the court concluded that despite the interviews' subjective nature, Grove had the benefit of sufficient due process. Significantly, in that context, the court deferred to the university's academic judgment of how much weight should be attached to the interviews. "This Court does not consider the determination of the proper weight to be accorded an interview score in a university's admissions evaluation to be properly within its purview unless it is clearly erroneous. . . . While this Court recognizes that there is a certain degree of subjectivity present in all personal interviews, . . . this particular procedure is not so arbitrary as to make it irrelevant to the determination of an applicant's prospective performance in the veterinary college program and therefore a denial of due process of law." As in this case, barring any substantive departure from its published criteria, a university can reasonably expect the courts to steer clear of any involvement in the admissions process.

Rare cases of judicial intervention occur when a university ostensibly reneges on an admissions commitment. In *State ex. rel. Bartlett v. Pantzer*, the University of Montana Law School told an applicant, James Bartlett, that he would be accepted if he took a course in financial accounting.[7] He took the course, receiving a grade of D. The school refused to admit him, asserting that a D was an "acceptable" but not a "satisfactory" grade. Bartlett filed a lawsuit, claiming that it was unreasonable for the school to stipulate the need for a "satisfactory" grade after he had taken the course. In its judgment, the court agreed; to add the distinction between acceptable and satisfactory *post hoc* was an abuse of institutional discretion, and the university was ordered to admit Bartlett.

In a related situation, *Levine v. George Washington University*, a medical student had done poorly in his first year but was allowed to repeat the year with the proviso that he would be expelled if he turned in a "repeated performance of marginal quality."[8] On his second attempt, he passed but ranked low in each of his courses. Thus, the school expelled him, and he filed a lawsuit. Citing contract theory, the court ruled that subjective interpretation of "marginal quality" without prior notice to the student violated the agreement between the student and the medical school. Thus, the expulsion was overruled. Both of these cases illustrate the need for an institution to have explicit policies on provisional admission and readmission. And, importantly, they must abide by these policies.

Of course, under the principles of contract theory, the institution is expected to adhere to its published admissions standards and to honor its admissions decisions. *The Law of Higher Education* advises that "if the individuals and groups who make admissions decisions adhere carefully to their published (or unwritten) criteria, give consideration to every applicant, and provide reasonable explanations for the criteria used in making decisions, judicial review will be deferential."[9] It provides further advice: because an institution must honor its published policies in deciding whom to admit and to reject, "the institution may wish to omit standards and criteria from its policies in order to avoid being pinned down under the contract theory." By following these pieces of advice, the university can exercise its authority over the admissions process with negligible concerns about legal repercussions.

Parenthetically, it should be mentioned that the recruitment and admissions procedure for prospective student athletes must abide by stringent guidelines set by an independent organization, the NCAA. Representing over one thousand colleges and universities, the NCAA establishes and enforces academic and "amateurism" rules designed to ensure that student athletes at these institutions all compete on equal footing. [10] Although these sometimes complex rules (which go well beyond the scope of this book) do not carry the force of law, compliance with them generally involves oversight by not only an athletic department but also legal counsel.

DISCRIMINATION

Another fundamental constraint, namely discrimination, warrants special attention because of its societal impact. As a primary limitation on institutional authority, a university may not have admissions policies that unjustifiably discriminate on the basis of characteristics such as race, sex, disability, age, national origin, or citizenship. Like EEO laws, these limitations derive from the Fourteenth Amendment equal protection clause and the various civil rights acts prohibiting discrimination. Numerous court cases affirm these protections in an educational setting, and equally numerous books and articles elaborate on the details.

Historically, legal protection against discrimination has evolved with the social attitudes of the time. This evolution is most evident in the approach to race. For the first half of the twentieth century, discrimination based on race relied on the "separate but equal" doctrine emanating from a particularly influential Supreme Court decision in 1896, *Plessy v. Ferguson*. [11] In 1892, Homer Plessy, who was seven-eighths Caucasian but was considered black by Louisiana law, took a seat in a "whites only" car of a Louisiana train, in violation of a state law that required separate railway cars for blacks and whites. He refused to move to the car reserved for blacks and was arrested. Plessy filed a lawsuit, claiming that the Louisiana law requiring segregated trains violated the Fourteenth Amendment. The judge ruled against Plessy; Louisiana did, indeed, have the right to regulate railways, as long as they operated within the state.

The decision was appealed to the U.S. Supreme Court and was upheld. In its opinion, the Court stated that:

> The object of the [Fourteenth] amendment was undoubtedly to enforce the absolute equality of the two races before the law, but, in the nature of things, it could not have been intended to abolish distinctions based upon color, or to enforce social, as distinguished from political, equality, or a commingling of the two races upon terms unsatisfactory to either. Laws permitting, and even requiring, their separation in places where they are liable to be brought into contact do not necessarily imply the inferiority of either race to the other, and have been generally, if not universally, recognized as within the competency of the state legislatures in the exercise of their police power. The most common instance of this is connected with the establishment of separate schools for white and colored children, which has been held to be a valid exercise of

the legislative power even by courts of States where the political rights of the colored race have been longest and most earnestly enforced.

This opinion had far-reaching consequences, for it condoned segregation. The "separate but equal" doctrine meant that segregated educational institutions were constitutional if tangible facilities at the schools and colleges were equal. That is, "if buildings, books, teachers, and other tangible features of both black and white schools and colleges were substantially equal, the courts found no constitutional violation of equal protection by the laws."[12] Despite the presumption of equal tangible facilities, the funding for black and white institutions began to diverge.

The "separate but equal" doctrine characterized American society for sixty years, until it was overturned by a landmark 1954 Supreme Court decision, *Brown v. Board of Education*.[13] At the time, Topeka, Kansas, had a segregated school system. Challenging segregation, thirteen black parents attempted to enroll their children in the closest neighborhood school. They were each refused enrollment and directed to the segregated schools. Thus, they filed a class action lawsuit claiming that they were deprived of their equal protection laws under the Fourteenth Amendment; they contended that "segregated public schools are not 'equal' and cannot be made 'equal,' and that hence they are deprived of the equal protection of the laws."[14] The Supreme Court took up the case and ruled unanimously in favor of the plaintiffs, thus reversing the longstanding *Plessy* ruling that condoned segregation.

In its decision, the court ruled that "separate educational facilities are inherently unequal." The argument was based in part on psychological factors.

> Does segregation of children in public schools solely on the basis of race, even though the physical facilities and other "tangible" factors may be equal, deprive the children of the minority group of equal educational opportunities? We believe that it does. . . . To separate them from others of similar age and qualifications solely because of their race generates a feeling of inferiority as to their status in the community that may affect their hearts and minds in a way unlikely ever to be undone. . . . A sense of inferiority affects the motivation of a child to learn. Segregation with the sanction of law, therefore, has a tendency to [retard] the educational and mental development of negro children and to deprive them of some of the benefits they would receive in a racial[ly] integrated school system. We conclude that, in the field of public education, the doctrine of "separate but equal" has no place.

Although this decision focuses on elementary and secondary schools, a subsequent case, *Board of Trustees v. Frasier*, ruled that it applies to higher education as well.[15] Furthermore, desegregation must occur quickly; institutions were to desegregate at "all deliberate speed."

The federal government amplified desegregation requirements to include most private institutions. Title VI of the Civil Rights Act of 1964, in particular, imposes basically the same constitutional protections as the equal protections clause of the Fourteenth Amendment on any institution receiving federal funds.[16] The law states that "No person in the United States shall, on the ground of race, color, or national origin, be excluded from participation in, be denied the benefits of, or be subjected to discrimination under any program or activity receiving Federal financial assistance." Since most public and private universities receive some form of federal financial assistance, this is far-reaching legislation. In addition, the Internal Revenue Service issued a ruling that extends nondiscrimination policies to private institutions claiming tax-exempt status under section 501(c)(3) of the federal tax code; a "private school that does not have a racially nondiscriminatory policy as to students does not qualify for exemption."[17]

Furthermore, the Supreme Court also ruled that private institutions may not discriminate on the basis of race in *Runyon v. McCrary*.[18] Michael McCrary and Colin Gonzales were black children who were denied admission to Bobbe's School, a private school. Gonzales was also denied admission to Fairfax-Brewster School, another private school. Their parents filed a class action lawsuit against the schools, suspecting the denials were due to their children's race. They cited an 1871 federal law, the so-called Ku Klux Klan Act, that provided "All persons within the jurisdiction of the United States shall have the same right in every State . . . to make and enforce contracts . . . as is enjoyed by white citizens"[19] In its ruling, the court asked the fundamental question about this federal law, codified at the time as 42 U.S.C. 1981: does it "prohibit private schools from excluding qualified children solely because they are Negroes"? Significantly, the court limited its question strictly to discrimination based on race and not on other factors such as gender or religion.

> It is worth noting at the outset some of the questions that these cases do not present. They do not present any question of the right of a private social organization to limit its membership on racial or any other grounds. They do not present any question of the right of a private school to limit its student body to boys, to girls, or to adherents of a particular religious faith, since 42 U.S.C. 1981 is in no way addressed to such categories of selectivity. They do not even present the application of 1981 to private sectarian schools that practice racial exclusion on religious grounds. Rather, these cases present only two basic questions: whether 1981 prohibits private, commercially operated, nonsectarian schools from denying admission to prospective students because they are Negroes, and, if so, whether that federal law is constitutional as so applied.

The court ruled in the affirmative; private schools' admissions policies may not discriminate on the basis of race. Thus, the combination of constitutional, statutory, tax, and judicial provisos effectively bars discrimination in the admissions process in both public and private institutions.

Despite these protections, pockets of racial segregation still exist in the academic setting. By 2004, eleven of the nineteen states that once operated segregated public colleges had yet to receive official declarations from the federal government that they are desegregated.[20] And, in 2013, a U.S. District Court ruled that Maryland had still failed to fully desegregate its public higher-education system.[21] Four other states, Florida, Oklahoma, Pennsylvania, and Texas, allegedly may also be impacted by that ruling.[22] Furthermore, in 2013, a black student at the University of Alabama was allegedly excluded from a sorority because of her race. According to the *New York Times* account, "The student, Melanie Gotz, said the sorority had bowed to alumnae influence and considered race when it evaluated potential new members earlier this year. Other sorority members shared similar stories."[23] In a historic admission, the university's president, Judy Bonner, acknowledged that the university's "Greek system remains segregated" and ordered the sororities and fraternities to extend their admissions process to re-consider minority candidates. Subsequently, the sororities admitted six minority members. Governor Robert Bentley hailed the news as a "positive first step" but said that it may be too early to tell if the changes would be lasting.[24] These examples illustrate the lingering vestige of racial segregation in American academic institutions.

AFFIRMATIVE ACTION ADMISSIONS PROGRAMS

When an institution has discriminated in the present or past, Title VI regulations require it to put into practice an affirmative action program designed to remedy the effects of that discrimination. According to the regulations: "In administering a program regarding which the recipient has previously discriminated against persons on the ground of race, color, or national origin, the recipient must take affirmative action to overcome the effects of prior discrimination."[25] The regulations continue: "Even in the absence of such prior discrimination, a recipient in administering a program may take affirmative action to overcome the effects of conditions which resulted in limiting participation by persons of a particular race, color, or national origin." Thus, a university may adopt either a mandatory or voluntary affirmative action admissions policy to correct any past discrimination. Notably, the regulations contain a proviso that the affirmative action policies are designed to remedy prior discrimination by only the institution and not society as a whole.

As a result, many universities implemented affirmative action into their admissions policies. Ideally, the goal was for the composition of the student body to match the diversity of the community they came from. The community for comparison would range from a city or county in the case of a community college to the entire United States for an elite Ivy League school. Operationally, more underrepresented applicants were admitted to each class using methods that ranged from adding "bonus points" to setting aside a specific number of slots—a quota—for racially under-represented applicants. Over time, these methods should allow the goal to be achieved. However, corollary to the admission of more underrepresented applicants was the admission of fewer overrepresented individuals. And that led to complaints of "reverse discrimination," which would also be a violation of the Fourteenth Amendment and Title VI. Thus, a legal conundrum arose; affirmative action to correct past or present discrimination generated further discrimination, only in reverse.

A landmark case involving reverse discrimination, *Regents of the University of California v. Bakke*, addressed this conundrum.[26] As part of its affirmative action program to redress longstanding, unfair minority exclusions from the medical profession, the University of California, Davis Medical School reserved sixteen places in each entering class of one hundred for "qualified" minorities, whose applications were considered separately from the other applicants. Operationally, this constituted a quota of sixteen places for underrepresented minority applicants in each entering class. Allan Bakke, a thirty-five-year-old white man, had twice applied for admission to the school and had been rejected both times. In both years that his applications were rejected, Bakke's qualifications (college grade-point average and test scores) exceeded those of all the minority students admitted under the quota system. Thus, after the second rejection, he filed a lawsuit alleging that the Medical School's special admissions program excluded him from the school on the basis of his race, in violation of his rights under the equal protection clauses of the Fourteenth Amendment and the California Constitution and of Title VI of the Civil Rights Act of 1964. That is, he contended that he was excluded from admission solely on the basis of race.

Ultimately, the case went before the Supreme Court. Notably, because the special admissions program involved a racial classification, the court held itself bound to apply a "strict scrutiny" standard of judicial review. Under this level of scrutiny, a race-conscious affirmative action plan must be "narrowly tailored" to further a "compelling government interest" to be constitutional.

In a highly divided ruling marked by six separate opinions, the court contended that race could be used as one criterion in the admissions decisions of institutions of higher education. Citing Justice Frankfurter's four essential freedoms that constitute academic freedom, the court found that the university's consideration of race to attain a diverse student body "clearly is a constitutionally permissible goal for an institution of higher education."

Moreover, "the State has a substantial interest that legitimately may be served by a properly devised admissions program involving the competitive consideration of race and ethnic origin."

However, the court ruled that the university's use of strict racial quotas was an unconstitutional violation of Fourteenth Amendment rights and ordered the medical school to admit Bakke. Likewise, separate systems for reviewing minority applications with procedures and criteria different from those used for nonminority applications are impermissible. According to the court, an affirmative action program must serve a "compelling state interest," and the diversity that furthers this interest must encompass "a far broader array of qualifications and characteristics, of which racial or ethnic origin is but a single, though important, element." In other words, ethnic diversity is only one element in a range of factors a university may consider in attaining the goal of a heterogeneous student body. A university's authority must have wide discretion in making the sensitive judgments as to who should be admitted, but constitutional limitations protecting individual rights may not be disregarded. Accordingly, many public and private universities refined their affirmative action admissions processes to conform to the guidance provided in this ruling.

The divisiveness of the court in the *Bakke* case left lingering doubts about the legality of affirmative action programs. These doubts were diminished in a 2003 case, *Grutter v. Bollinger*, when the Supreme Court reaffirmed higher education affirmative action programs.[27] The case tested the University of Michigan Law School's use of race as a factor in making admissions decisions. Importantly, the Law School considered not only race but numerous other factors in its admission process; it did not use a quota system. In 1997, Barbara Grutter, a white resident of Michigan, applied for admission to the University of Michigan Law School but was turned down. She filed a lawsuit, claiming that the law school had discriminated against her on the basis of race, violating the Fourteenth Amendment and Title VI. According to her argument, the law school's use of race as a "predominant" factor gave applicants belonging to certain minority groups a significantly greater chance of admission than students with similar credentials from disfavored racial groups. Moreover, the school had no compelling interest to justify that use of race. In its defense, the law school claimed that its consideration of race was strictly to obtain "the educational benefits that flow from a diverse student body."

With references to *Bakke* (in quotation marks in the following quote), the court articulated the compelling interest that justifies race-conscious policies.

Attaining a diverse student body is at the heart of the Law School's proper institutional mission, and its "good faith" is "presumed" absent "a showing to the contrary." Enrolling a "critical mass" of minority students simply to assure

some specified percentage of a particular group merely because of its race or
ethnic origin would be patently unconstitutional. But the Law School defines
its critical mass concept by reference to the substantial, important, and laudable educational benefits that diversity is designed to produce, including cross-
racial understanding and the breaking down of racial stereotypes. The Law
School's claim is further bolstered by numerous expert studies and reports
showing that such diversity promotes learning outcomes and better prepares
students for an increasingly diverse work force, for society, and for the legal
profession.

Applying a strict-scrutiny standard of review, the court concluded that the
law school's consideration of race was sufficiently narrow, because race was
only one element of its affirmative action program to achieve its compelling
interest, namely diversity. It dismissed Grutter's assertion that the law
school's plan was not narrowly tailored because race-neutral means existed
to obtain the educational benefits of student body diversity that the law
school seeks: "Narrow tailoring does not require exhaustion of every con-
ceivable race-neutral alternative. Nor does it require a university to choose
between maintaining a reputation for excellence or fulfilling a commitment
to provide educational opportunities to members of all racial groups." The
court held that universities may consider race or ethnicity as a "plus" factor
in the context of individualized review of each applicant and that admissions
programs must be "flexible enough to consider all pertinent elements of
diversity in light of the particular qualifications of each applicant." The law
school policy met these requirements—it was "a highly individualized, holis-
tic review of each applicant's file, giving serious consideration to all the
ways an applicant might contribute to a diverse educational environment."

Consistent with *Bakke*, the court ruled further that institutions may not
"establish quotas for members of certain racial groups or put members of
those groups on separate admissions tracks." The court defined a quota as a
"program in which a certain number or proportion of opportunities are reserved exclusively for certain minority groups," and held that "[t]he Law
School's goal of attaining a critical mass of underrepresented minority students does not transform its program into a quota." Citing *Bakke*, the court
stated that "some attention to numbers, without more, does not transform a
flexible admissions system into a rigid quota." Thus, in its decision, the court
upheld the law school's use of race in its affirmative action program, noting
that "the Equal Protection Clause does not prohibit the Law School's narrowly tailored use of race in admissions decisions to further a compelling interest
in obtaining the educational benefits that flow from a diverse student body."

This landmark ruling removed most doubts about the legality of considering race in the admissions process. Furthermore, it reaffirmed judicial deference to the university's primary authority in determining who may be admitted to study. "The Court defers to the Law School's educational judgment

that diversity is essential to its educational mission. The Court's scrutiny of that interest is no less strict for taking into account complex educational judgments in an area that lies primarily within the university's expertise."

In a companion case, *Gratz v. Bollinger*, the race-conscious admissions policy of the University of Michigan's largest undergraduate college, the College of Literature, Science, and the Arts, was also challenged, with a different outcome.[28] Like the law school, the college considered a variety of factors including, among others, whether the student was socioeconomically disadvantaged or came from an educational environment that was socioeconomically disadvantaged, and whether the student was a member of an underrepresented racial or ethnic community or came from a school that served those communities. A point system was used to evaluate each applicant. Most of the points (110 out of 150) were based on academic criteria, with the remainder based on personal characteristics and accomplishments that could contribute to the diversity of the class as a whole. Importantly, unlike the law school, the college automatically awarded twenty points to all applicants from underrepresented minority groups, without further consideration of their other individual attributes.

Two unsuccessful white applicants, Jennifer Gratz and Patrick Hamacher, sued the university, claiming that it violated the Fourteenth Amendment and Title VI because it gave too much weight to race. In its ruling, the court reaffirmed the use of race in the admissions process but claimed that the automatic awarding of twenty points based on race was unconstitutional. As noted, predetermined point allocations that award twenty points to underrepresented minorities "ensures that the diversity contributions of applicants cannot be individually assessed" and "has the effect of making the factor of race . . . decisive for virtually every minimally qualified underrepresented minority applicant." Similar to an outright quota, this automatic bonus to a minority applicant is impermissible.

Predictably, the use of race-conscious affirmative action in college admissions is not universally popular. Indeed, according to a 2013 Gallup poll, a clear majority of Americans, 67 percent, are opposed to considering race and ethnicity in college admissions decisions, instead saying that students should be admitted solely based on merit.[29] Consequently, there are continuous legal challenges against race-conscious admissions policies.

Several states have prohibited the use of race as an admissions criterion. For example, California's public universities have been barred from using race as a factor in admissions since voters approved Proposition 209 in 1996.[30] The proposition forbids universities from using race, sex, ethnicity, or national origin in admissions: "The State shall not discriminate against, or grant preferential treatment to, any individual or group on the basis of race, sex, color, ethnicity, or national origin in the operation of public employment, public education, or public contracting." Likewise, in 2006, Michigan voters approved Proposal 2, which amended the state's constitution to make affirmative action illegal in public education unless it is mandated by federal law or is necessary for an institution to receive federal funding. Recently, in *Schuette v. BAMN*, the Supreme Court upheld the rights of voters to ban the use of affirmative action when making college admission decisions, ruling that a ban on affirmative action through a state constitutional amendment is permissible under the U.S. Constitution.[31]

Many universities have implemented various less provocative, race-neutral strategies to increase minority enrollment. The University of Texas at Austin, for example, guarantees admission to any applicants who are in the top 10 percent of their high school class. Although this enables admission of relatively high numbers of black and Hispanic students without explicitly considering race, the university has argued that such an alternative to race-conscious admissions policies does not provide it with sufficient levels of diversity, especially considering the state's large black and Hispanic populations. Therefore, Texas adopted a supplemental race-conscious admissions policy that allows applicants who fail to graduate in the top 10 percent of their class a further opportunity to gain admission to the university by scoring highly in a process that evaluates their talents, leadership qualities, family circumstances, and race.

This supplemental consideration of race spawned another, more recent lawsuit challenging affirmative action: *Fisher v. University of Texas*.[32] The case was brought by Abigail Fisher, a white woman who applied to the university in 2008 and was denied admission. She claimed that her constitutional rights and federal civil rights laws were violated. In its decision, the court allowed affirmative action to survive in college admissions but imposed a tough legal standard, warning that schools must prove there are "no workable race-neutral alternatives" to achieve diversity on campus before adopting a race-conscious policy. The standard of strict scrutiny "does not permit a court to accept a school's assertion that its admissions process uses race in a permissible way without closely examining how the process works in practice." Instead, the burden of proof is on a university to show that "each applicant is evaluated as an individual and not in a way that makes an applicant's race or ethnicity the defining feature of his or her application." In these words, the Supreme Court further limited the authority of the university to determine who will be admitted. Nonetheless, even with these constraints, affirmative action was allowed to continue as a vital element of the admissions process. The university's authority over admissions remained intact, albeit with tightened limits to this authority.

LEGACY PREFERENCES

Some institutions preferentially admit individuals with so-called legacy ties to the institution. These are applicants whose parents or other close family members attended the same university, sometimes for multiple generations, thus establishing the legacy.

Prima facie, the rationale is simple: money. Families with strong legacy ties to the university are expected to donate more generously, although there are no publicly available data quantifying this expectation.[33] The University of Virginia's admissions dean John Blackburn clearly states the reason for the preference. "In light of very deep budget cuts from the state, our private support particularly from alumni is crucial to maintaining the quality of the institution," he says. "The legacy preference helps ensure that support by recognizing their financial contributions and their service on university committees and task forces."[34] While this mercenary rationale is intuitively true, according to Jerome Karabel, legacy preferences arose for a less acceptable reason: the exclusion of Jews and immigrants.[35] That history may taint the practice, but the mercenary reasoning is generally acceptable to public opinion, and many admissions committees continue legacy preferences on the premise that donations will follow.

The consideration of legacy is widespread among selective institutions. Indeed, according to Richard Kahlenberg, "Legacy preferences, which provide a leg up in college admissions to applicants who are the offspring of alumni, are employed at almost three-quarters of selective research universities and virtually all elite liberal-arts colleges."[36] The Ivy League schools readily acknowledge preferential consideration of legacy applicants. At Harvard, for example, the Dean of Admissions and Financial Aid, William Fitzsimmons, reported in a 2011 interview that the acceptance rate for legacy applicants has hovered around 30 percent—more than four times the regular admissions rate—in recent admissions cycles and that the undergraduate population is comprised of approximately 12 to 13 percent legacies, a group he defined as children of Harvard College alumni and Radcliffe College alumnae.[37] Princeton and Yale report similar numbers.[38] Notably, neither MIT nor Caltech consider legacy in their admissions process.

As the Harvard data imply, legacy status can confer a considerable advantage to an applicant. In a study of thirty highly selective colleges, Michael Hurwitz found that applicants with at least one parent who attended the college as an undergraduate got an average 45-percentage-point increase in their probability of admission.[39] In other words, the odds of admission are multiplied by a factor 7.6 due to primary legacy status. Ostensibly, the legacy factor serves mainly as a "tie-breaker"; if all other factors are equal, preference will be given to the legacy applicant. "Other factors," such as test scores, grade-point average, and so forth, are nearly equal for many, if not most, applicants to elite colleges. Therefore, because of the subjective nature of the admissions process, the legacy preference can become a decisive factor.

Legacy-conscious admissions policies constitute a variation on affirmative action. One class of individuals—the children of alumni—is given an advantage because of ancestry. And that advantage is a disadvantage to all other applicants, which constitutes discrimination. But, in *Grutter*, Justice Thomas commented that legacy preferences were constitutional and upheld the university's authority in this matter. "The Equal Protection Clause does not, however, prohibit the use of unseemly legacy preferences or many other kinds of arbitrary admissions procedures. . . . So while legacy preferences can stand under the Constitution, racial discrimination cannot. I will not twist the Constitution to invalidate legacy preferences or otherwise impose my vision of higher education admissions on the Nation."

Nonetheless, legal challenges to legacy preferences might be expected to arise. However, there have been remarkably few. In 1976, they were challenged indirectly in a breach of contract lawsuit, *Steinberg v. University of Health Sciences, Chicago Medical School.*[40] The plaintiff, Robert Steinberg, applied to a private medical school, submitting a written application and $15 application fee. His application was rejected. Consequently, Steinberg filed a class action lawsuit, claiming that the medical school's acceptance of his application fee created a contract to evaluate his application on the basis of criteria documented in the school's bulletin. Allegedly, the school failed to honor that contract because its decisions to accept or reject applicants were based on unpublished criteria, such as "familial relationships to the school's faculty and board of trustees and the ability of the applicant or his family to pledge or make payment of large sums of money to the school." These preferred candidates allegedly did not have to meet the criteria published in the bulletin. By considering these unpublished criteria, Steinberg claimed that the school had breached its contract to judge his application by published criteria. The court agreed that a contract existed and that the school had not honored it, thus ruling in favor of Steinberg. Although this case did not address legacy preferences directly, it raised the shadow of a doubt over their legality. However, the shadow was not sufficiently dark to stop the practice.

There has only been one other significant test in federal courts, namely *Rosenstock v. The Board of Governors of the University of North Carolina.*[41] According to governing board policy, the University of North Carolina freshman undergraduate class consists of 15 percent and 85 percent of nonresident and resident students, respectively. Because of the smaller number of available slots, out-of-state applicants face stiffer competition for admission than in-state applicants. That is, using the quota (15 percent versus 85 percent) results in different treatment of residents and nonresidents with respect to the level of academic achievement necessary for admission.

However, there is an exception to this policy based on legacy. Children of out-of-state alumni of the university must meet the same requirements necessary for admission as in-state residents, thus improving their chances of admission. The university's reason for this exception is that the alumni, through their monetary support of the university, contribute substantially to its well-being. In return for their support, the university admits their children under the less stringent requirements for resident student admission. (Likewise, underrepresented minority students and athletes are given preference.)

A New York resident, Jane Rosenstock, applied to the university but was denied admission because her credentials were not competitive in the out-of-state application pool. She sued the university, claiming that the more stringent standards applicable to out-of-state residents seeking admission to the university and the alleged preferential treatment given to applicants who are children of alumni deny her equal protection of the law and due process and violate her constitutional rights.

The court ruled against Rosenstock. It asserted "that the alumni provide monetary support for the University and that out-of-state alumni contribute close to one-half of the total given. To grant children of this latter group a preference then is a reasonable basis and is not constitutionally defective. Plaintiff's attack on this policy is, therefore, rejected." This decision affirmed the practice of giving legacy applicants preference, predicated on financial benefit to the university.

Despite this ruling, there is continued opposition to legacy-conscious admissions on theoretical grounds. For example, Carlton Larson argues that legacy preferences in public university admissions violate the Constitution's prohibition on the granting of titles of nobility.[42] He claims that the nobility clauses were not limited to the prohibition of certain distinctive titles, such as "duke" or "earl," but had a substantive content that included a prohibition on all hereditary privileges with respect to state institutions. Thus, he concludes that legacy preferences are blatantly inconsistent with the Constitution's prohibition on hereditary privilege. In another example, Steve Shadowen, Sozi Tulante, and Shara Alpern argue that legacy preferences are a violation of the Fourteenth Amendment's equal-protection clause.[43] Although the amendment was aimed primarily at stamping out discrimination against black Americans, they claim that it also extends more broadly to all preferences based on lineage. Since racial discrimination is unlawful in large part because it is a type of discrimination based on ancestry or lineage, they deduce that legacy preferences are also a violation of the Civil Rights Act of 1866, which prohibits discrimination on the basis of race.[44] Accordingly, they conclude that in both public and private institutions, individuals should be judged on their own merits, not by their lineage. And that would rule out legacy preferences.

Despite their eloquence, neither of these theoretical arguments has been validated in the courts. Consequently, in the absence of any legal constraint, under the premise of academic freedom universities retain the authority to use legacy status as a criterion when determining "who may be admitted to study."

BRIBERY

Bribery—or attempted bribery—can play a role in admissions, corrupting the university's authority. Indeed, if they are associated with a donation to the university, legacy preferences involve a subtle form of bribery. Fundamentally, they satisfy the definition of bribery, which involves offering money or a favor "in order to influence the judgment or conduct of a person in a position of trust."[45] Legal pedants may modify this definition for judicial reasons, such as distinguishing between bribery and influence peddling or limiting it to public officials. Or they may point out that technically bribery benefits an individual—or as the dictionary puts it, "a person in a position of trust."[46] The money goes into that person's pocket. In contrast, a donation benefits the university as a whole; furthermore, the money must be spent transparently in accordance with well-established accounting rules. Likewise, academic purists may bristle at the use of the term bribery in the context of academic freedom. In more subtle situations, the college may not agree explicitly to admit the student, but the donor buys access and a sympathetic hearing. But the simple concept remains the same: there is a *quid pro quo*. "If you admit my child, I will donate money to the university." Despite pedantic definitional distinctions, when there appears to be a relationship between a donation and admission to the university, many observers consider this bribery.

Although there are certainly few published policies to this effect, it is believed in many circles that a significant contribution would greatly increase an applicant's chances of admission—legacy preferences aside. In fact, anecdotes abound about the influence of contribution money on the admissions process at many different universities ranging from the elite to the less elite. A well-known stereotype was portrayed in the movie *Back to School*, when an academically unqualified Thornton Melon, played by actor Rodney Dangerfield, bought (bribed) his way into the fictitious Grand Lakes University by donating the money to build a new business school.[47] In a *Newsweek* posting on the Internet titled *The Year to Bribe Your Way In*, the relationship is clearly stated in the first paragraph: "The recession is dramatically changing the college admissions game, as cash-strapped schools court students with ties to big donors. Why it's easier than ever to buy your way in."[48] The article continues with a sequence of testimonials about "buying your way in." The linkage between donations and admissions commonly refers to bribery.

The University of Virginia provides a far more real example. In 1999, a headline in *The Chronicle of Higher Education* stated that, "U. of Virginia Considers Possibility of Future Donations in Admissions Decisions."[49] According to the dean of admissions, if an applicant who would otherwise have been rejected shows the potential for "a significant gift to the university . . . there are a few cases where I will actually change the decision [to admit the student]."[50] Furthermore, the university's chief development officer reportedly stated that "it's not wrong to consider an individual's past involvement in philanthropy" when making a handful of admissions decisions. He continued: "If an institution says it does not pay attention to the applications from its most-important benefactors, legislators, and friends, it either does not have a very competent development program, or it is being disingenuous. . . . Every important, highly selective institution has to pay attention to this."[51]

Is it wrong to grant admission in return for a financial contribution to the university development office? Technically, the answer is no. Unless the institution has policies explicitly prohibiting this practice, it is permissible. Realistically, however, including financial contributions as a criterion for acceptance detracts from the meritocratic admissions process. In that sense, it ironically "cheapens" the institution. Thus, despite their preferential treatment of legacy applicants, most elite universities claim that admissions are independent of donations to the institution; their answer to the question would be "yes, it is wrong to grant admission in return for a financial contribution." Unfortunately, these claims are often met by cynical smiles.

For some individuals, there is a presumption that admission can be bought—that an admissions officer can be bribed. After all, the practice of bribery is as old as the hills and is certainly not limited to legacy preferences. A straightforward attempt at bribery can be very direct. Consider an anecdote based on a real-life case when Provost M. was offered bribes. Each fall, the local public school district sponsors an informational college fair. The objective is to provide high school students and their parents the opportunity to visit with representatives from about fifty different universities. Routinely, a representative of Flagship University attended, answering questions about its admissions process and handing out informational brochures. On this occasion, Provost M. represented the university for the first time.

Midway through the evening, a father, mother, and their teenage son approached the booth. After a few minutes of pleasantries, the father posed the question: "What will it take to get our son admitted into Flagship?" Mother continued: "We're prepared to pay whatever you usually charge." Meanwhile, the son looked away in apparent embarrassment. The directness of the question surprised the provost. Resisting the temptation to propose a ludicrous sum of money as a joke, Provost M. answered that "Flagship doesn't work that way. Admissibility depends on various criteria, including high-school grades, standardized test scores, and other personal qualifications." The father replied: "Then how much do you charge to help prepare our son's application to ensure that he will get admitted? Surely we can reach an agreement." At that point, the provost was interrupted by another potential applicant and was able to disengage successfully from the uncomfortable conversation.

Most observers would agree that this was an attempt at outright bribery. Its crudeness caught Provost M. off guard, who, fortunately, was extricated from the awkward situation with minimal embarrassment for either the parents or the university. As if that one experience weren't enough, about an hour later, another individual—this time a grandfather—offered the provost a bribe in an attempt to help his grandchild get admitted to Flagship. Provost M. thought: "Twice in one evening! What are the odds of this happening? Is bribery that common in college admissions?"

If it is of any solace, Provost M.'s experience is hardly unique. Most seasoned admissions officers have had similar moments. According to Mary Anne Schwalbe, former associate dean for admissions at Harvard, "Everyone in my position was offered bribes."[52] Parents would come in for their child's interview and then ask to speak to her privately. They would say "Not only will I give Harvard $1 million, but I'll give you and your husband a house or a cruise." Many admissions officers have similar stories of parents, independent admissions counselors, even corporate attorneys offering a monetary incentive to facilitate a student's admission. For example, in an interview, the dean of admissions at Hamilton College claims to have been offered bribes four or five times at three different colleges.[53] "I have had people show up with a check in hand asking how much it will cost," she says. And every time she explains to them that that is not the way business is done. "We let the family know that the conversation is no longer appropriate, nor is it helping their son or daughter."[54]

Unfortunately, not everybody turns down the bribe. For example, in 2007, a California State University, Fullerton employee was arrested and charged with accepting up to $2,500 per student in return for preferential admission.[55] The motive was not stated explicitly, but presumably it involved money. At the arraignment, the employee claimed to have "considered the money a gift."[56] Ultimately, the employee was found guilty, convicted on four felony counts of taking a bribe in exchange for admission to the university, and sentenced to jail.[57] Moreover, the four students involved in the bribery scheme were expelled from the university.

Most probably, the vast majority of admissions officers or other university administrators would never accept a bribe in return for granting admission to the university. However, true or not, the university as a whole is perceived to favor applicants who donate generously. This duality blurs the limits of propriety. If a contribution to the university is an acceptable way to improve the chances for admission, why wouldn't a contribution to an officer of the university also be acceptable? Ethicists can argue intellectually all they want about this topic, but parents eager to help their children may be deaf to their erudition. In their eyes, money buys acceptance into the university.

Is it wrong for a university employee to grant admission in return for a bribe? The knee-jerk answer is "yes, of course it is wrong." And the legal answer agrees; it is wrong—at least in public institutions. State and federal penal codes explicitly prohibit bribery involving public-sector employees.[58] For example, the California state penal code says that: "Every executive or ministerial officer, employee, or appointee of the State of California, a county or city therein, or a political subdivision thereof, who asks, receives, or agrees to receive, any bribe, upon any agreement or understanding that his or her vote, opinion, or action upon any matter then pending, or that may be brought before him or her in his or her official capacity, shall be influenced thereby, is punishable by imprisonment" and other punitive measures.[59] Texas amplifies this prohibition by stating that it is "no defense to prosecution . . . that a person whom the actor sought to influence was not qualified to act in the desired way whether because he had not yet assumed office or he lacked jurisdiction or for any other reason."[60] Furthermore, "It is no defense to prosecution . . . that the benefit is not offered or conferred or that the benefit is not solicited or accepted until after: (1) the decision, opinion, recommendation, vote, or other exercise of discretion has occurred; or (2) the public servant ceases to be a public servant."[61] In other words, it doesn't matter if the person receiving the bribe has no authority to deliver on the favor or if the bribe is offered or received after the favor has already been granted.

Notably, these state anti-bribery laws apply specifically to public employees. That includes all state university personnel. How about the private sector? Is bribery legal in private institutions? The obverse answer is that bribery per se may not be illegal in private universities. Although some penal codes outlaw bribery in designated classes of private endeavors, such as bribery of labor-union officials, they do not address most areas in the private sector. That is, unless any aspect of interstate commerce, including email, or, importantly, federal money (such as scholarships or loans) was involved in the bribe. Then various federal criminal statutes come into play. However, just because it isn't illegal most certainly does not imply that bribery is acceptable in private universities. Most institutions—private and public— have codes of conduct that mandate adherence to commonly accepted ethical and moral standards. Stanford's code of conduct provides a good example: "Frequently, Stanford's business activities and the other conduct of its community members are not governed by specific laws or regulations. In these instances, rules of fairness, honesty, and respect for the rights of others will govern our conduct at all times."[62] Bribery in the admissions process would definitely run afoul of these rules of conduct.

Why would seemingly decent people resort to measures such as bribery? In most cases that isn't so difficult to imagine; they were simply caring for their children. More disturbing was why they would assume that university officials would respond to the offer. Do the officials broadcast some signal—overtly or subliminally—suggesting that a bribe would be accepted? Self-assuredly, most admissions officers would deny the suggestion. But perhaps some other university practice breeds confusion in this ethical milieu.

In one publicly acceptable variation on the *quid pro quo* scenario, the athletic departments at many universities have ticket policies that are openly influenced by financial contributions. To get good seats, season ticketholders must donate a defined amount to the athletic program in addition to the regular season ticket price. At the University for Wisconsin–Madison, for example, regular season football tickets cost $294 in 2011. This will buy seats in less desirable sections, usually near the goal line. According to the university, "Requests for changing seating locations within seating sections are reviewed first based on annual giving level."[63] An annual contribution of at least $400 to the athletic department is the minimum required to get a seat in sections straddling the fifty-yard line in the football stadium. But even that is usually not enough. The official policy states: "Please note many donors looking to obtain seats closer in proximity to midfield, contribute more than the recommended minimum amount, prior to the specified deadline, on an annual basis."[64] To retain preferred seating, the contribution must be made every season; failure to pay will result in a "demotion" to a less desirable location.

Very few individuals would equate this ticket practice with an illegal activity. Indeed, most university administrators would vehemently deny that these seating policies constitute bribery. After all, "everybody does it." That justification—everybody else is doing the same thing—points out the importance of context. What constitutes bribery in one setting metamorphoses into an acceptable way of doing business in another setting. As former Indonesian president Suharto once told former president of the World Bank James Wolfensohn "You know, what you regard as corruption in your part of the world, we regard as family values."[65] But it reinforces the perception that donating money is the key to favorable treatment from the university.

Incidentally, from a technical point of view, this ticket-pricing practice amounts more to extortion than to bribery. Extortion differs from bribery. Bribery involves the giving of money in return for a favor. Extortion is "the practice of obtaining something, especially money, through force or threats."[66] The threat is loss of premium seats. In simple words: "pay the extra money or you'll lose your good seats."

PERSONAL FAVORS

Occasionally, challenges to the administration's authority over the admission process come from within the institution's constituency, beyond the normal reach of the law. They often entail a request for the university to admit a friend or relative. A governing board member, staunch alumnus or alumna, generous donor, or other influential individual may cloak this request as a personal favor. The request may be straightforward and direct or less innocuous, with a subtly implicit *quid pro quo* characteristic of bribery or extortion. Either way, it is unpleasant to deal with. There is seldom any legal protection or universal guideline about how to respond.

However, when an influential member of the university's broad community requests preferential admission as a personal favor, the president generally becomes involved. Indeed, as a rule of thumb, if the provost, graduate dean, or other administrator receives such a request, he or she should always inform the president. An experienced president usually develops an instinctive sense of what requests can and cannot be rejected. With the formal authority of the office, the president is in the position to educate the person who made the request about the admissions process and university governance. This educational discussion may also touch upon the pragmatic constraints imposed by negative public opinion and threatened accreditation. It may be directly with the person who made the request or, depending on who made the request, indirectly via the chair of the governing board or alumni association, for example.

A hypothetical example illustrates the inherent uneasiness in responding to these requests. Flagship University was renowned for its clinical psychology program. Every year, it ranked among the top ten clinical programs based on how well their graduates performed on the licensing exam, the Examination for Professional Practice in Psychology.[67] Furthermore, the university guaranteed four years of financial support for all doctoral students in the program, thus increasing its attractiveness even more. Consequently, admission into the doctoral program was extremely competitive. Only about 3 percent of the applicants are admitted each year.

In 2007, Ms. S. applied for admission to the university's clinical psychology program. On paper, she was a strong candidate. Going into her senior year at Flagship, she had a 3.5 grade-point average, graduate record exam scores in the upper six hundreds, and very supportive letters of recommendation. Importantly, she also had strong legacy ties to the university; she, her parents, and siblings all graduated from Flagship. Plus, her father was a member of the governing board of regents.

Despite these impressive credentials, Ms. S. was not admitted to the program. Unlike the undergraduate admissions office, the graduate programs did not consider legacy, so that was not an advantage. Of the 175 applicants, only three were admitted that year. And they all accepted the admission promptly, so there was no waiting list. Understandably, Ms. S. was deeply disappointed. Neither she nor her family could understand why she failed to make the cut. Her father, Regent S., was particularly stunned. After all he had done for the university, financially and professionally, this just didn't seem right.

So, Regent S. made an appointment to discuss the matter with Provost M. The conversation was brief and to the point, with the regent making a request: "My daughter applied to the clinical psychology program but didn't get in. Surely something can be done about this. I'd like for you to talk with the program chair." Provost M. replied that as a matter of academic policy, the provost is not involved with the graduate admissions process. That authority has been delegated to the graduate school dean and further to the departmental level. Undeterred, Regent S. continued that "good policy always allows for exceptions. My daughter is very highly qualified, and there's no reason why you shouldn't speak with the program chair about admitting her on a one-time exceptional basis as a personal favor to me." Provost M. did not yield: "I'm sorry, but I cannot interfere with the admissions process. That would exceed my authority."

The meeting did not end well for either Regent S. or Provost M. The regent left somewhat confused and angry. Didn't his authority as a member of the governing board confer the power to control the provost in a situation like this? He thought: "How dare the provost refuse to honor my request? As a regent, I work very hard in support of this university, and I donate generously to their fund-raising efforts. At the very least, the provost could make this one exception." Likewise, Provost M. departed the meeting unsettled. True, Ms. S. was a very strong candidate. Furthermore, it was highly unlikely that the admissions process could accurately distinguish between the top 10 percent of the candidates. If financial aid were an issue, the provost certainly had the resources to provide the necessary funding. But, pondering further, "I simply cannot disrespect the admissions process. That would constitute a serious violation of academic governance." With that conclusion, Provost M. told the university president about the incident. The president winced but promptly defended the provost's refusal to intervene in a discussion with the board chair, who agreed to explain the impropriety of the request to Regent S.

Could the regent have ordered the clinical psychology program chair to accept his daughter into the program, thus bypassing the provost? At Flagship and most other universities, the answer is no. According to the Board of Regents' bylaws, all actions by the board must emanate from the board as a whole; a single regent does not have the authority to act independently of the rest of the board. Technically, the board as a whole could vote to admit Ms. S. into the program. That would fall within their formal authority over all matters of the university. Similarly, Provost M. has the authority to overrule the department and the graduate dean and admit Ms. S, for they report to him; thus, the provost misspoke when he claimed that this would exceed his authority. But realistically, an action like this would draw such negative attention to the board or the provost and the university that there is little chance that it would ever happen. Negative public attention is a very practical limitation to the board's and the administration's authority.

There is another, far more compelling reason why a governing board (or the provost) would not impose its authority over the admissions procedures: this would seriously jeopardize the institution's accreditation. Each of the five major accrediting associations expects the institution to operate "with integrity in all matters."[68] Moreover, "Failure of an institution to adhere to the integrity principle may result in a loss of accreditation."[69] Granting such a special favor to one regent would surely breach the limits of integrity. Also, the accrediting associations expect the institution to establish clearly defined organizational responsibilities and delegated authority, including the admissions process. For example, in their accreditation criteria, the North Central Association of Colleges and Schools' accreditation states that the organization must consistently implement "clear and fair policies regarding the rights and responsibilities of each of its internal constituencies."[70] The Southern Association of Colleges and Schools states this criterion even more crisply: "There is a clear and appropriate distinction, in writing and practice, between the policy-making functions of the governing board and the responsibility of the administration and faculty to administer and implement policy."[71] A single transgression, such as Regent S.'s insistence on admitting his daughter into the clinical psychology program, might not doom the institution's accreditation, but the risk would certainly deter honoring the request.

SUMMARY

Admissions authority is granted to the governing board. It is then delegated down into the academic hierarchy, usually to the level of a dean or director who bears administrative responsibility. Faculty members usually play a major role in the admissions process. The courts are quite reluctant to second-guess the expertise of academic administrators and faculty members in this realm. The selection process must not be arbitrary or capricious. An institution may select almost any admissions criteria it wishes, but they must be made known to all applicants and applied equally to all of them. Under contract theory, the institution is expected to adhere to its published admissions standards and to honor its admissions decisions. As a primary limitation on institutional authority, a university may not have admissions policies that unjustifiably discriminate on the basis of characteristics such as race, sex, disability, age, national origin, or citizenship. When an institution has discriminated in the present or past, it must put into practice an affirmative action program designed to remedy the effects of that discrimination. In several landmark cases, the Supreme Court declared affirmative action constitutional but invalidated the use of racial quotas. Some institutions preferentially admit individuals with legacy ties; their parents or other close family members attended the same university. Admission in return for a financial contribution to the university is permissible unless the institution has policies explicitly prohibiting the practice. However, bribery per se is generally illegal in public universities and is contrary to commonly accepted ethical and moral standards in private universities. Occasionally, a governing board member, staunch alumnae member, generous donor, or other influential individual requests the university to admit a friend or relative as a personal favor. An experienced president usually develops an instinctive sense of what requests can and cannot be rejected.

NOTES

1. *Sweezy v. New Hampshire*, 354 U.S. 234 (1957).

2. American Association of University Professors, "Statement on Government of Colleges and Universities," (1966), http://www.aaup.org/AAUP/pubsres/policydocs/contents/governancestatement.htm. (Accessed July 15, 2014).

3. Texas Tech University, "Op 34.01: Undergraduate Admissions," *Operating Policy and Procedure* (2010), http://www.depts.ttu.edu/opmanual/OP34.01.pdf. (Accessed September 25, 2013).

4. Harvard College Standing Committee on Admissions and Financial Aid, personal communication, Admissions Officer, (2013).

5. William A. Kaplin and Barbara A. Lee, *The Law of Higher Education*, 4th ed. (San Francisco: Jossey-Bass, 2006), 317.

6. *Grove v. Ohio State University*, 424 F. Supp. 377 (S.D. Ohio) (1976).

7. *State Ex. Rel. Bartlett v. Pantzer*, 489 P.2d 375 (Mont.) (1971). Cited in Kaplan and Lee, *The Law of Higher Education*, 755.

8. *Levine v. George Washington University*, C.A. (Civil Action) 8230-76 (D.C. Super. Ct.) (1976). Cited in *The Law of Higher Education*, 803–4.

9. Kaplan and Lee, *The Law of Higher Education*, 755.

10. "National Collegiate Athletic Association," http://www.ncaa.org/wps/wcm/connect/public/ncaa/eligibility/index.html. (Accessed October 19, 2013).

11. *Plessy v. Ferguson*, 163 U.S. 537 (1986).

12. Patricia A. Hollander, *Legal Handbook for Educators* (Boulder, CO: Westview Press, 1978), 59.

13. *Brown v. Board of Education*, 347 U.S. 483 (1954).

14. Ibid.

15. *Board of Trustees v. Frasier*, 350 U.S. 979 (1956).

16. *Title VI of the 1964 Civil Rights Act*, 42 USC § 2000d (1964).

17. Internal Revenue Service, "Revenue Ruling 71-447, 1971-2 C.B. 230," (1971).

18. *Runyon v. McCrary*, 427 U.S. 160 (1976).

19. *Enforcement Act of 1871*, 42 U.S.C. §1981 (1871).

20. Sara Hebel, "Segregation's Legacy Still Troubles Campuses," *Chronicle of Higher Education* (2004), http://chronicle.com/article/Segregations-Legacy-Still/9675/. (Accessed October 8, 2013).

21. *The Coalition for Equity and Excellence in Maryland Higher Education v. Maryland Higher Education Commission Et Al.*, United States District Court for the District of Maryland Civil No. CCB-06-2773 (2013).

22. Eric Kelderman, "Four Other States Could Be Affected by Desegregation Ruling in Maryland," *Chronicle of Higher Education* (2013), http://chronicle.com/article/4-Other-States-Could-Be/142217/?cid=at&utm_source=at&utm_medium=en. (Accessed October 11, 2013).

23. Alan Blinder, "At Alabama, a Renewed Stand for Integration," *New York Times* (2013), http://www.nytimes.com/2013/09/19/us/at-alabama-a-renewed-stand-for-integration.html?_r= 0. (Accessed October 8, 2013).

24. Charles Huckabee, "U. Of Alabama Sororities Admit 6 Minority Members in a Widely Watched 'First Step,'" *Chronicle of Higher Education* (2013), http://chronicle.com/blogs/ticker/jp/u-of-alabama-sororities-admit-6-minority-members-in-a-widely-watched-first-step. (Accessed October 8, 2013).

25. Department of Education, "Discrimination Prohibited," *34 C.F.R. §100.3 (b)(6)(i)* (1975).

26. *Regents of the University of California v. Bakke*, 438 U.S. 265 (1978).

27. *Grutter v. Bollinger*, 539 U.S. 306 (2003).

28. *Gratz v. Bollinger*, 539 U.S. 244 (2003).

29. Jeffrey M. Jones, "In U.S., Most Reject Considering Race in College Admissions," *Gallup Politics* (2013), http://www.gallup.com/poll/163655/reject-considering-race-college-admissions.aspx?utm_source=alert&utm_medium=email&utm_campaign=syndication&utm_content=morelink&utm_term=All%20Gallup%20Headlines. (Accessed October 4, 2013).

30. *Declaration of Rights*, Article 1 §31 (a) (1996).

31. *Schuette, Attorney General of Michigan v. Coalition to Defend Affirmative Action, Integration and Immigration Rights and Fight for Equality by Any Means Necessary (BAMN) Et Al.*, 572 U.S. ___ (2014).

32. *Fisher v. University of Texas at Austin*, 570 U.S. ___ (2013).

33. Chad Coffman, Tara O'Neill, and Brian Starr, "An Emprical Analaysis of the Impact of Legacy Preferences on Alumni Giving at Top Universities," in *Affirmative Action for the Rich: Legacy Preferences in College Admissions*, ed. Richard D. Kahlenberg (New York: Century Foundation, 2010).

34. Daniel Golden, "Admissions Preferences Given to Alumni Draws Fire," *Wall Street Journal* (2003), http://online.wsj.com/public/resources/documents/golden3.htm. (Accessed October 18, 2013).

35. Jerome Karabel, *The Chosen: The Hidden History of Admission and Exclusion at Harvard, Yale, and Princeton* (New York: Houghton Mifflin Harcourt, 2005), 2; Peter Jacobs, "Legacy Admissions Policies Were Originally Created to Keep Jewish Students Out of Elite Colleges," *Business Insider* (2013), http://www.businessinsider.com/legacy-admissions-originally-created-keep-jewish-students-out-elite-colleges-2013-10. (Accessed October 29, 2013).

36. Richard D. Kahlenberg, "Ten Myths About Legacy Preferences in College Admissions," *Chronicle of Higher Education* (2011), http://chronicle.com/article/10-Myths-About-Legacy/ 124561/. (Accessed October 16, 2013).

37. Justin C. Worland, "Legacy Admit Rate at 30 Percent," *Harvard Crimson* (2011), http:// www.thecrimson.com/article/2011/5/11/admissions-fitzsimmons-legacy-legacies/. (Accessed October 16, 2013).

38. Pamela Paul, "Being a Legacy Has Its Burden," *New York Times* (2011), http://www. nytimes.com/2011/11/06/education/edlife/being-a-legacy-has-its-burden.html?_r=2&ref= edlife&. (Accessed October 16, 2013).

39. Michael Hurwitz, "The Impact of Legacy Status on Undergraduate Admissions at Elite Colleges and Universities," *Economics of Education Review* 30, no. 3 (2011).

40. *Steinberg v. University of Health Sciences, Chicago Medical School*, 354 N.E. 2d 586 (1976).

41. *Rosenstock v. The Board of Governors of the University of North Carolina*, 423 F. Supp. 1321 (1976).

42. Carlton F. W. Larson, "Titles of Nobility, Hereditary Privilege, and the Unconstitutionality of Legacy Preferences in Public School Admissions," *Washington University Law Review* 84, no. 6 (2006).

43. Steve D. Shadowen, Sozi P. Tulante, and Shara L. Alpern, "No Distinctions except Those Which Merit Originates: The Unlawfulness of Legacy Preferences in Public and Private Universities," *Santa Clara Law Review* 49, no. 1/2 (2009).

44. *Civil Rights Act of 1866*, 14 Stat. 27-30 (1866). Codified as *Enforcement Act of 1871*.

45. "Merriam-Webster Dictionary," http://www.merriam-webster.com/dictionary/bribe. (Accessed April 11, 2011).

46. Ibid.

47. Alan Mettler, "Back to School," (USA: Orion Pictures, 1986).

48. Kathleen Kingsbury, "The Year to Bribe Your Way In," *Daily Beast* (2009), http://www.thedailybeast.com/blogs-and-stories/2009-02-27/the-year-to-bribe-your-way-in/#. (Accessed April 13, 2011).

49. John L. Pulley, "U. Of Virginia Considers Possibility of Future Donations in Admissions Decisions," *Chronicle of Higher Education*, November 12, 1999, http://chronicle.com/article/U-of-Virginia-Considers/6408/. (Accessed April 25, 2012).

50. Ibid.

51. Ibid.

52. Daniel Golden, *The Price of Admission: How America's Ruling Class Buys Its Way into Elite Colleges—and Who Gets Left Outside the Gates* (New York: Three Rivers Press, 2006), 60.

53. Alvin P. Sanoff, "Bribery Attempts, the Unbearable Pushiness of Parents, and Other Admissions Tales," *Chronicle of Higher Education* (2006), http://chronicle.com/article/Bribery-Attempts-the/21230. (Accessed July 31, 2014).

54. Ibid.

55. Seema Mehta, "Campus Staffer Is Accused of Taking Bribes," *Los Angeles Times*, August 8, 2007, http://articles.latimes.com/2007/aug/08/local/me-admissions8. (Accessed April 25, 2012).

56. Christine Hanley, "Ex-Campus Staffer Pleads Not Guilty to Bribery," *Los Angeles Times*, September 8, 2007, http://articles.latimes.com/2007/sep/08/local/me-bribes8. (Accessed April 25, 2012).

57. Orange County District Attorney, "CSUF Employee Convicted of Accepting Bribes in Exchange for Admitting Foreign Students to the University" in *Press Release, Case # 07CF2984* (Santa Ana, CA 2008).

58. 18 U.S.C. §201 Bribery of public officials and witnesses.

59. California Penal Code §68 (a), http://codes.lp.findlaw.com/cacode/PEN/3/1/5/s68. (Accessed April 25, 2011).

60. Texas Penal Code, "Bribery," *§36.02 (4)(b)*, http://www.statutes.legis.state.tx.us/docs/pe/htm/pe.36.htm. (Accessed April 25, 2012).

61. Ibid., *§36.02 (4)(c)*

62. Stanford University, "Standards of Integrity and Quality," *University Code of Conduct, Administrative Guide Memo 1* (2007).

63. University of Wisconsin–Madison, "Football, Men's Basketball and Men's Hockey Seating," http://www.uwbadgers.com/development/seating-info.html. (Accessed March 15, 2011).

64. Ibid.

65. Sebastian Mallaby, *The World's Banker: A Story of Failed States, Financial Crises, and the Wealth and Poverty of Nations* (New York: Penguin Books, 2006), 179.

66. "Oxford Dictionaries Online," Oxford University Press, http://oxforddictionaries.com/?attempted=true. (Accessed April 15, 2011).

67. "Examination for Professional Practice of Psychology (EPPP)," (2011), http://www.asppb.net/i4a/pages/index.cfm?pageid=3279. (Accessed March 14, 2011).

68. Southern Association of Colleges and Schools Commission on Colleges, *The Principles of Accreditation: Foundations for Quality Enhancement* (Decatur, GA 2010), 11.

69. Ibid.

70. North Central Association of Colleges and Schools, *Handbook of Accreditation*, Third ed. (Chicago, IL: Higher Learning Commission, 2003). Chapter 3.1, Core Component 1e.

71. Southern Association of Colleges and Schools Commission on Colleges, *The Principles of Accreditation: Foundations for Quality Enhancement*, 24.

Chapter Seven

Student Affairs

RELATIONSHIP WITH THE INSTITUTION

Students are the university's *raison d'être*. Indeed, they are the common element of all institutions of higher education, regardless of their mission. The commonality extends from purely undergraduate colleges to highly complex research universities. Whether the institution concentrates on imparting existing knowledge or generating new knowledge, students play a primary role. Thus, there is an inherently tight-knit relationship between the institution and the students.

This relationship has evolved over the years. For several hundred years, it was based on the doctrine of *in loco parentis* ("in the place of the parent"), with the university sharing the responsibility for the students' well-being with the parents. In 1765, Sir William Blackstone articulated this doctrine of shared responsibility by asserting that part of parental authority is delegated to schoolmasters, including the powers of "restraint and correction" that may be necessary to educate the children.[1] This authority was reinforced by the courts in a 1913 case, *Gott v. Berea College*.[2] At that time, Berea College (located in Berea, Kentucky) had a rule that "eating houses and places of amusement in Berea, not controlled by the College, must not be entered by students on pain of immediate dismission [dismissal]. The institution provides for the recreation of its students, and ample accommodation for meals and refreshments, and cannot permit outside parties to solicit student patronage for gain." A nearby tavern owner, J. S. Gott, brought a lawsuit against the college, charging that its policy "unlawfully and maliciously" injured his business. The court ruled in favor of Berea College, noting specifically that "College authorities stand *in loco parentis* concerning the physical and moral welfare and mental training of the pupils, and we are unable to see why, to

165

that end, they may not make any rule or regulation for the government or betterment of their pupils that a parent could for the same purpose . . . unless the rules and aims are unlawful or against public policy."

The *Gott* case made it explicitly clear that a university had broad authority to do as it pleased with its students. As stated by Kaplin and Lee, "By placing the educational institution in the parents' shoes, the doctrine permitted the institution to exert almost untrammeled authority over students' lives."[3] This meant that universities could regulate the students' personal lives, including speech, association, and movement, and take disciplinary action against students without concern for their right to due process.

A corollary of *in loco parentis* is the institution's duty to protect the students, just like the natural parents. Universities owe the same degree of care and supervision to their students that reasonable and prudent parents would employ in the same circumstances for their children. In the words of Theodore Stamatakos, "The exercise of legal authority is inextricably bound with the obligations of legal duty, and *Gott* suggests that the *in loco parentis* doctrine imposes a duty to protect the physical welfare of students. So, as college administrators governed students with parental authority, courts began to recognize a correlative legal duty to protect the students over which such authority was exercised."[4]

Moreover, under tort principles of negligence, universities owe students a duty to anticipate foreseeable dangers and to take reasonable steps to protect those students from that danger. Thus, under the two aspects of *in loco parentis*, universities had the right to act as parents when controlling students. At the same time, they had the duty to act like the parent when protecting students from foreseeable harm. Public institutions have the additional responsibility to protect the constitutional rights of students, which parents do not have.

The relationship between the university and its students changed noticeably following World War II, turning away from the traditional *in loco parentis*. Several factors drove this change. Bolstered by the G.I. Bill, the number of older students increased on campus. Also, the Twenty-sixth Amendment lowered the legal voting age to eighteen, and most states lowered the legal age of majority to eighteen years. Consequently, after age eighteen, students were no longer a parent's legal responsibility; college students were perceived as adults who were entitled to their own rights. The advent of online courses and other nontraditional teaching methods added to the changing student-body demography. Since most college students reached the age of majority while still enrolled, universities could not easily justify temporary parental status over these young adults. Conceptually, the doctrine of *in loco parentis* lost much of its earlier meaning.

This evolutionary change away from *in loco parentis* was highlighted by a landmark court case, *Dixon v. Alabama State Board of Education*, which established for the first time minimal due process for students as legal adults with constitutional rights.[5] A public higher education institution, Alabama State College, attempted to expel students without offering any type of due process prior to their suspensions, such as notification of the reasons for expulsion or an opportunity for a disciplinary hearing. Specifically, twenty-nine African American students of Alabama State College participated in a sit-in demonstration that sought to desegregate a variety of public services, including segregated seating areas at the lunch grill in the basement of the Montgomery County Courthouse. Provoked by several other civil rights demonstrations, the president presented the names of the sit-in students to the State Board of Education, citing fears of campus disruption. The board expelled nine students and placed twenty of them on probation. Notably, no formal charges were filed against the students, and no hearing was granted to them prior to the expulsion; they were not told what specific misconduct they were charged with or for what reason they were expelled. Six of them filed for a permanent injunction to restrain the board from obstructing their right to attend college, claiming that due process guaranteed by the Fourteenth Amendment in the Constitution was violated.

An appeals court ruled that students at public universities were entitled to at least fundamental due process. This decision overruled a preceding *in loco parentis* opinion of the district court, which commented that "the courts have consistently upheld the validity of regulations that have the effect of reserving to the college the right to dismiss students at any time for any reason without divulging its reason other than its being for the general benefit of the institution." In its reversal of that opinion, the appeals court stated that formal notice of the charges justifying the expulsion and an opportunity for a judicial hearing constitute minimal due process prior to permanent expulsion. The court reasoned further that education is so basic and vital in modern society that public, tax-supported universities must meet minimum constitutional due process requirements when dealing with students. In short, a university could not just discipline a student with "untrammeled authority." With this reasoning, the court effectively ended the traditional *in loco parentis* relationship.

The *Dixon* court limited its holding to public institutions by observing "that the relations between a student and a private university are a matter of contract." Students at private institutions are not necessarily guaranteed rights comparable to constitutional rights of due process. Nonetheless, many private institutions incorporate the right to due process contractually in student handbooks, for example, thus blunting the severity of *in loco parentis* policies. Furthermore, most private universities have been affected by the same post–World War II demographic and attitudinal changes that have transformed the relationships between students and public universities; most of their students are legally adults. These changes have compelled many private universities to adopt policies commensurate with those of public institutions.

After the demise of traditional *in loco parentis*, the relationship between students and universities continued to evolve. The immediate reaction to *Dixon* was several cases suggesting that universities should have little or no affirmative involvement or duty over their students' lives outside of academic pursuits. They should no longer have the role of protective parents. For example, in *Bradshaw v. Rawlings*, the court refused to impose liability on Delaware Valley College for serious injuries suffered by a student, Donald Bradshaw, in an automobile accident following an off-campus class picnic where alcohol was served to underage students.[6] The driver of the car, Bruce Rawlings, was another student who became intoxicated at the picnic; on the drive back to campus, he lost control of his car and struck a parked vehicle. As a result of the collision, Bradshaw suffered a cervical fracture which caused quadriplegic paralysis. He filed a lawsuit alleging, among other things, that the college was negligent in its supervision of the sophomore class picnic. In its defense, the college argued that the student failed to establish that the college owed him a legal duty of care under the law of negligence.

The court ruled in favor of the college, commenting specifically on the demise of *in loco parentis*: "College administrators no longer control the broad arena of general morals. At one time, exercising their rights and duties *in loco parentis*, colleges were able to impose strict regulations. But today, students vigorously claim the right to define and regulate their own lives. Especially they have demanded and received satisfaction of their interest in self-assertion in both physical and mental activities, and have vindicated what may be called the interest in freedom of the individual will." The court commented further on the underlying societal changes: "Thus, for purposes of examining fundamental relationships that underlie tort liability, the competing interests of the student and of the institution of higher learning are much different today than they were in the past. At the risk of oversimplification, the change has occurred because society considers the modern college student an adult, not a child of tender years." This case illustrates what has been called a "bystander" model of university-student relations, where universities have little or no involvement or duty over their students' lives outside of academic pursuits.[7]

More recently, this bystander approach has been moderated significantly. Despite the downplaying of *in loco parentis* relationships, the courts have been finding that colleges indeed have a duty to take reasonable measures to ensure their students' safety. This is illustrated in *Mullins v. Pine Manor College*.[8] A female college student, Lisa Mullins, was raped on the Pine Manor College campus by an unidentified assailant who was able to get onto campus and into the victim's room unescorted. With a pillowcase covering her head, he walked Mullins out of her building and across campus unde-tected to an unlocked building where he raped her. Mullins filed a personal injury lawsuit against the college for not taking reasonable steps to protect her from the attack. Specifically, she asserted that the college was negligent due to an inadequate security system characterized by unsecured locks and gates, too few guards patrolling the grounds, and an insufficient key system.

The court ruled in favor of Mullins. It reasoned that "Of course, changes in college life, reflected in the general decline of the theory that a college stands *in loco parentis* to its students, arguably cut against this view. The fact that a college need not police the morals of its resident students, however, does not entitle it to abandon any effort to ensure their physical safety. Parents, students, and the general community still have a reasonable expecta-tion, fostered in part by colleges themselves, that reasonable care will be exercised to protect resident students from foreseeable harm."

This more moderate approach follows the fundamental principle of law that "one who voluntarily takes custody of another is under a duty to protect that person."[9] In their analysis of student-university relationships, Robert Bickel and Peter Lake characterize this as the "duty era," characterized by "an implicit search for a balance between university authority and student freedom and for shared responsibility for student safety/risk."[10] In the court's words (*Furek v. The University of Delaware*):

> The university-student relationship is certainly unique. While its primary func-tion is to foster intellectual development through an academic curriculum, the institution is involved in all aspects of student life. By providing food, hous-ing, security, and a range of extracurricular activities the modern university provides a setting in which every aspect of student life is, to some degree, university guided. This attempt at control, however, is directed toward a group whose members are adults in the contemplation of law and thus free agents in many aspects of their lives and life styles.[11]

Despite the clarity of the courts' pronouncements about the end of *in loco parentis*, the universities' relationship with their students is sufficiently close and direct to impose a duty to regulate and supervise foreseeable dangerous activities occurring on university property. In that sense, the courts are im-posing the same standards of duty—of responsibility—on universities that are imposed on businesses, landlords, and other nonacademic entities. As a fundamental principle, the universities must have the authority to meet this responsibility. Thus, in the eyes of today's courts, universities no longer stand *in loco parentis* to their students as they had in the past. But, the universities still retain the necessary authority over student activities and behavior needed to protect their safety and well-being.

AUTHORITY OVER STUDENT LIFE

As custodians of their well-being, universities still have broad authority over student activities and behavior. In that regard, they expect students to comply with society's basic ethical standards: be honest, maintain integrity, treat people with fairness and respect, accept personal accountability, obey the law, and so forth. Often, universities emphasize these axiomatic expectations in student handbooks or other official documents. In its *Handbook for Students*, Harvard College, for example, declares that: "It is the expectation of the College that all students, whether or not they are on campus or are currently enrolled as degree candidates, will behave in a mature and responsible manner." This understatement is then amplified by a long list of general regulations eschewing physical violence, sexual assault, possession of firecrackers, theft, bookmaking, hazing, possession of stolen goods, et cetera. [12] Despite the length of this list, the college adds further that "Because students are expected to show good judgment and use common sense at all times, not all kinds of misconduct or behavioral standards are codified here." Most other institutions have similar—if not more abbreviated—statements of behavioral expectations. And, as a rule of thumb, student conduct is subject to these guidelines from the time of application through the actual awarding of a degree, even before classes begin or after a semester is complete.

The university's custodial authority extends to student behavior both on and off campus. This was articulated in a defining judicial memorandum issued by a U.S. District Court following a flood of campus disciplinary cases during the civil rights and Vietnam War era: "In the field of discipline, scholastic and behavioral, an institution may establish any standard reasonably relevant to the lawful mission, processes, and functions of the institution. . . . Standards so established may apply to student behavior on and off the campus when relevant to any lawful mission process, or function of the university." [13] Although this pronouncement emanated in the context of public universities, it applies equally to public and private universities. Actually, private university students generally receive fewer procedural safeguards against the long arm of university custodial authority than public university students. Indeed, the courts hold that "attendance at a private school is not a right but a privilege which may be discontinued at the option of the university." [14] By inference, private universities have broad authority to regulate all aspects of student life both on and off campus.

Although the rationale for on-campus authority is readily apparent because it falls within the university's immediate purview, the rationale for off-campus authority is less apparent. Nonetheless, this authority has been upheld in the courts. For example, in *Ray v. Wilmington College*, a student, Jerry Ray, was suspended indefinitely for allegedly violating campus policy by sexually assaulting a female student at his off-campus apartment. [15] Ray contended that the college could not discipline him for an incident that occurred off campus. However, in the court's opinion, "this argument is meritless." It added that "An educational institution's authority to discipline its students does not necessarily stop at the physical boundaries of the institution's premises." Numerous other cases sustain the basic premise that universities, indeed, have authority over student activities that occur off campus. [16]

However, this authority over off-campus activities and behavior has its limits. In general, it is limited to student behavior that is incompatible with vital university interests. Some university student-conduct codes document this limitation explicitly. For example, Florida State University defines it within a broader scope of authority: "Florida State University jurisdiction regarding student conduct is generally limited to conduct of any student that occurs on Florida State University premises. In addition, the University reserves the right to impose discipline based on any student conduct, regardless of location, when that conduct may adversely affect the University community or its international programs. The University further reserves the right to restrict contact with specified people when facts and circumstances dictate such action." [17]

The courts have generally insisted on the coupling between off-campus authority and university interests. In various legal opinions, they have stated that there must be some nexus between the off-campus offense and a vital interest of the university. "Any statute or university rule authorizing an institution to sanction [student] conduct must limit disciplinary actions to misconduct that is detrimental to the institutions' interests." [18] In that context, off-campus conduct such as sexual assaults, stalking, rape, and murder clearly create a nexus that negatively impacts the institution; they relate to the safety of the university community. The nexus is less clear in cases of off-campus drug possession and burglary of non-university victims. The courts vary in their treatment of cases like these. For example, a Texas court found that drug possession did not implicate a university interest, despite the university's argument that drug users pose a threat to other students who might be convinced to use illegal drugs themselves. [19] In contrast, a Virginia court ruled that a university could assume that off-campus illegal drug possession had a negative impact on campus, noting that students "may be required to possess and exhibit superior moral standards, which may be set by the institution." [20] In these and similar cases, the courts must weigh and balance the nature of the university, its relationship with the larger community, and the extent of overlap of the criminal justice system and the university judicial processes. [21]

HONOR CODES

Many institutions share their authority over student conduct with the students via an honor code. These codes set guidelines for academic and, in some cases, social conduct. Primarily, they affirm a student's integrity during examinations and preparation of class materials. Moreover, they usually require a student to report any evidence of academic misconduct. These expectations are summarized succinctly in Texas A&M University's honor pledge: "An Aggie does not lie, cheat or steal, or tolerate those who do."[22] These abbreviated codes are usually backed up by extensive lists of intolerable academic behavior, including cheating on an exam, plagiarism, fabrication of data, falsification of research materials, and so forth. Some honor codes also set guidelines for nonacademic social behavior, such as drinking, smoking, drug use, and premarital sex. And, they have well-documented procedures for enforcing the honor code. Students, faculty members, and administrators (mainly from the office of student affairs) participate in any adjudication procedures.

Faculty members and administrators are usually expected to respect the honor code by refraining from proctoring examinations or taking unusual and unreasonable precautions to prevent dishonesty. The point is not to convey mistrust of the students' honor. And administrators are expected to avoid creating situations conducive to cheating. For example, they should provide examination rooms large enough to allow ample space between students, thus reducing the temptation to look at other students' answer sheets. As Stanford puts it: "While the faculty alone has the right and obligation to set academic requirements, the students and faculty will work together to establish optimal conditions for honorable academic work."[23]

Inevitably, the question arises: "do honor codes work?" The quick answer is "yes." In a classic study, Donald McCabe, Linda Treviño, and Kenneth Butterfield report that about 75 and 50 percent of students at universities without and with honor codes, respectively, admit to having cheated one way or another—that is, copied on an exam, used unauthorized crib notes, plagiarized, et cetera.[24] Concluding from these data, the prevalence of cheating was about one-third less in universities with honor codes. Other studies report varying percentages of cheaters, but their conclusions are roughly the same. Although honor codes reduce the prevalence of cheating, they certainly do not eliminate it. About half of the students still admit to cheating. Thus, the quick answer to the question should be modified: "Yes, honor codes work but not perfectly." Reflecting this modified answer and muted expectations, under its newly devised honor code (the first in its 377-year history), Harvard College will continue to proctor exams.[25]

According to McCabe and his colleagues, the honor code's effectiveness can be attributed to a fundamental attribute of shared authority, the students' sense of participation in the university community—its governance. "Most code students see themselves as part of a moral community that offers significant trust and freedom and has corresponding rules and expectations that must be honored to preserve that trust and freedom."[26] As pointed out by David Callahan, it derives from a fundamental premise of social contracts: "People are more likely to obey rules when they feel like they are stakeholders in a community and when they believe they have a say in how the rules are made and enforced."[27]

The importance of the community, a student's peers, is restated in game-theory terms in an alternative explanation of an honor code's effectiveness. "When a student perceives that there is a high probability his peers will report him for cheating, he will tend to cheat less in an effort not to get caught. Once this individual cheats less, the lower cheating level is observed by others and contributes to a lower aggregate level of cheating, which further encourages the original student to cheat even less. These effects feedback off of each other until a steady low-cheating equilibrium is reached, which we observe at schools that have strong honor codes."[28] This explanation reinforces the premise that the success of an honor code depends on student expectations.

DISCIPLINARY ACTIONS

Violations of university regulations regarding academic and personal student behavior can lead to disciplinary action. This authority to discipline students is stated expressly in a District Court memorandum clarifying the judicial standards for student discipline in tax-supported institutions:

> The voluntary attendance of a student . . . is a voluntary entrance into the academic community. By such voluntary entrance, the student voluntarily assumes obligations of performance and behavior reasonably imposed by the institution of choice relevant to its lawful missions, processes, and functions. These obligations are generally much higher than those imposed on all citizens by the civil and criminal law. So long as there is no invidious discrimination, no deprival of due process, no abridgement of a right protected in the circumstances, and no capricious, clearly unreasonable or unlawful action employed, the institution may discipline students to secure compliance with these higher obligations as a teaching method or to sever the student from the academic community.[29]

According to these widely cited guidelines, public university disciplinary actions must adhere to constitutional rights of due process and legislative guarantees of civil rights. And, importantly, they must not be arbitrary or capricious. That is, the disciplinary process must be applied uniformly to all individuals and not be malicious, dishonest, or utterly outrageous.

Private institutions have more latitude in their disciplinary authority. They are not obligated to honor rights of due process, for example. The courts have upheld their right to "dismiss a student at any time on whatever grounds the university judges advisable."[30] Although private universities are not bound to constitutional guarantees in student disciplinary cases, they may be sued for breach of contract, discrimination, or arbitrary and capricious actions. This last point is important and bears repeating; like public universities, private universities must not mete out discipline in an arbitrary or capricious manner. Although universities seldom lose cases based on this claim, "the mere presence of a legal doctrine placing some limit on an institution's power, where that limit is not clearly drawn, often has the effect of restraining the arrogance of power."[31] Furthermore, the standards of conduct must be deemed reasonable, and the student should have been aware of them. Pragmatically, as a "best practice," private universities are advised to follow fundamental rules of due process in student disciplinary proceedings to ensure a thoughtful and fair outcome. Indeed, Kaplin and Lee advise private institutions "to adhere to much the same guidelines for promulgating rules as are suggested for public institutions, despite the fact that private institutions are not required by law to do so."[32]

For the most part, universities describe their disciplinary processes from an educational perspective. For example, the Rutgers University Code of Student Conduct states that: "The primary purpose of the student conduct process should be to foster the personal, educational, and social development of students. The process should also serve as deterrence to misconduct to enhance the safety and security of the community. Students are expected to take responsibility for their conduct. Disciplinary consequences therefore serve both educational and deterrence objectives."[33] The University of Wisconsin–Madison expands on this basic premise: "The nonacademic misconduct process is designed to provide and help maintain an educational atmosphere with emphasis on developing individual understanding and acceptance of personal and social responsibilities; creating a sense of belonging within a welcoming environment; and challenging and supporting students to reflect, integrate, and act upon their Wisconsin Experience."[34] Accordingly, the university adds that "The Dean of Students Office seeks to employ a compassionate, educational, and supportive approach to the student misconduct process—a philosophy that seeks to guide behavior for the common good while respecting the rights and responsibilities of all members of the University community." From that perspective, discipline is considered part of the student's overall university learning experience. In a sense, the universities are invoking the old "tough-love" adage that "you'll thank me for this someday." Of course, at the time, the students might disagree with that assertion.

Furthermore, to maintain an educational tone, universities strive to ensure that the process is as nonadversarial as possible, while safeguarding the rights of students. According to the University of Chicago, "the relation of collegiality and trust that binds all members of the University community entails an obligation of truthfulness and candor on the part of everyone who participates in a disciplinary proceeding."[35] In principle, an accused student is expected to participate in a disciplinary action in a manner that helps the university reach a complete and fair understanding of the facts of the incident at issue.

Because of their educational focus, university disciplinary systems differ fundamentally from the judicial systems of society in general. Although the disciplinary process adjudicates misconduct, it is not a legal system; it is not subject to the judicial processes of courts of law. The disciplinary process does not use the same procedures, burdens of proof, or rules of evidence as the legal systems. This fundamental difference between universities and courts of law is manifest in their jargon. "The University's regulations are applied to incidents that are not 'cases,' the bodies that hear and dispose of incidents are not 'courts,' individuals who may accompany a student in the course of a disciplinary proceeding are not 'counsel' advocating on behalf of the student and scrutinizing procedures for compliance with 'rules of evidence,' and requests for review of disciplinary decisions are not 'appeals.'"[36] Importantly, students involved in university discipline do not automatically abdicate any of the rights—constitutional and statutory—that are guaranteed to them by the civil society. At all times they remain free to claim and assert those rights through the courts.

Student misconduct may be subject simultaneously to a university's disciplinary system and external legal or administrative proceedings, particularly in conjunction with criminal charges. Under those circumstances, the university's disciplinary system normally proceeds independently. Furthermore, university disciplinary committees are not bound by external findings, adjudications, or processes. Ideally, their judgments on a matter are made independent of any external legal proceedings.

Most disciplinary cases are settled "in house," observing fundamental aspects of due process: notification of the charges, a hearing, the opportunity to call witnesses, and the right to a review of a decision. These minimal due process requirements were set by the Supreme Court in *Goss v. Lopez*.[37] In this case, nine Columbus, Ohio, high school students were suspended for destroying school property and disrupting the educational environment. In a lawsuit, they alleged that they had been suspended for up to ten days without a hearing, in violation of the procedural due process clause of the Fourteenth Amendment. Noting that the due process clause forbids arbitrary deprivations of liberty, the court held that a student facing suspension of ten days or less "must be given oral or written notice of the charges against him, an explanation of the evidence against him and, if he denies them, an explanation of the evidence the authorities have and an opportunity to present his side of the story. The [due process] Clause requires at least these rudimentary precautions against unfair or mistaken findings of misconduct and arbitrary exclusion from school." Longer suspensions or expulsions might require more formal procedures. The court noted further that "Generally, notice and hearing should precede the student's removal from school, since the hearing may almost immediately follow the misconduct, but if prior notice and hearing are not feasible, as where the student's presence endangers persons or property or threatens disruption of the academic process, thus justifying immediate removal from school, the necessary notice and hearing should follow as soon as practicable."

In *Goss*, the court made an important distinction between nonacademic and academic judicial matters. In student behavioral disciplinary actions involving temporary suspensions, the court upheld the need for due process, requiring that a student be given oral or written notice of the charges against him, an explanation of the evidence, and an opportunity for a hearing to present his side of the story. However, in student academic disciplinary actions, the *Goss* opinion stopped short of requiring a formal hearing. Rather, it required nothing more than an "informal give and take" between the student and the administrative body that would give the student the opportunity to characterize his conduct and put it in what he deems the proper context.

This lenience in academic due process was made clearer by the Supreme Court in *Board of Curators of the University of Missouri v. Horowitz*, where it stated that it "would grant greater deference to institutions in academic, as opposed to disciplinary, dismissals and, indeed, would require more stringent procedural requirements in dismissals based purely on disciplinary matters."[38] Thus, the court again raised the distinction that academic disciplinary cases do not necessarily require a formal hearing, whereas the hearing is a key element of due process in nonacademic cases. This case involved a medical student at the University of Missouri, Kansas City who contested her dismissal from the medical school.[39] At the end of Horowitz's first year, an academic review team, known as the Council on Evaluation, recommended her continuation on a probationary basis. During the second year, council faculty members expressed additional concerns about her capacity to perform the required clinical skills and indicated that unless Horowitz displayed dramatic improvement in her poor clinical performance, she should be dismissed from the school. Affording Horowitz another opportunity to demonstrate her academic competencies, officials at the medical school allowed her to participate in a set of oral and clinical examinations. As part of the examinations, seven well-regarded practicing physicians evaluated Horowitz's performance. The evaluations drew mixed results: two recommended passing her, two suggested immediate dismissal, and three called for deferring a decision until other evaluations of her clinical experiences were received. Later that academic year, the council reconvened after receiving additional poor ratings of Horowitz's clinical requirements and recommended her dismissal from the school. A committee of the faculty known as the Coordinating Board affirmed that recommendation to the dean, who agreed with the decision and notified Horowitz of her dismissal. Horowitz appealed to the university provost for health sciences. On review, the provost upheld the medical school's decision.

Subsequently, Horowitz unsuccessfully filed a lawsuit based on constitutional claims, alleging that the school had deprived her of a liberty or property interest without the benefit of procedural due process rights protected by the Fourteenth Amendment. The trial court was convinced that Horowitz received due process, ruling in favor of the university. On appeal, the Eighth Circuit reversed in favor of Horowitz, concluding that dismissal would make it very difficult for Horowitz to obtain employment in the medical field. Because the stigma of dismissal would deprive Horowitz of "liberty," the court ruled that the university could not dismiss her without a due process hearing where she would have the opportunity to rebut the evidence against her. The University of Missouri appealed. On final appeal, the Supreme Court reversed back in favor of the university, concluding that Horowitz had been afforded full due process by the university.

But, relying on the distinction between academic and disciplinary cases, the court ruled significantly that she had no right to a hearing. "Academic evaluations of a student, in contrast to disciplinary determinations, bear little resemblance to the judicial and administrative fact finding proceedings to which we have traditionally attached a full hearing requirement." These judgments are, by their nature, more subjective than the typical factual questions raised in the normal disciplinary decision. In the words of the court, "Like the decision of an individual professor as to the proper grade for a student in his course, the determination whether to dismiss a student for academic reasons requires an expert evaluation of cumulative information, and is not readily adapted to the procedural tools of judicial or administrative decision making." This ruling opened the door for university administrators to forego the formal hearing in academic disciplinary cases.

Because of this less stringent standard for due process, the courts must decide if a disciplinary case is academic or nonacademic. Given the complexity of educational missions, this can be a challenging decision. A particularly vexing situation arose in *University of Texas Medical School in Houston v. Than.*[40] During an exam, two proctors observed a third-year medical student, Allan Than, looking repeatedly at the answer sheet of another student. The school instituted disciplinary proceedings that included a formal hearing with witnesses and cross-examination. Afterward, the hearing officer viewed the testing room; notably, Than's request to accompany her was denied. Inside the room, the hearing officer "sat in the chair occupied by Mr. Than during the examination and could clearly see the paper from the examination chair occupied by [the other student]." Relying, at least in part, on this evidence, the school expelled Than for academic dishonesty.

Than filed a lawsuit requesting an injunction against the expulsion, claiming that he had been denied due process when he was not allowed to visit the testing room with the hearing officer. The school argued that Than's dismissal was not solely for disciplinary reasons, but was for academic reasons as well, thus requiring less stringent procedural due process than is required under *Goss* for disciplinary actions. However, the court held that "This argument is specious. Academic dismissals arise from a failure to attain a standard of excellence in studies whereas disciplinary dismissals arise from acts of misconduct. Than's dismissal for academic dishonesty unquestionably is a disciplinary action for misconduct." In other words, cheating on an exam is disciplinary and not academic misconduct. For that reason, in these cases, administrators must adhere to the more stringent standards of due process. The court ordered the university to reinstate Than as a student in good standing and to grant a new hearing on the charge of academic dishonesty.

This case stresses the diligent attention to due process necessary in disciplinary cases. Than prevailed because the university did not allow him to be present when the hearing officer visited the examination room. The case turned on what might have appeared a priori to be a minor issue.

In the eyes of some faculty members, this necessary diligence accorded to due process equates to unnecessary hassle. Thus, they may resort to "frontier justice," circumventing the disciplinary procedures dictated in university policy. Rather than formally confronting a student with allegations of academic misconduct and, therefore, going through formal due process, they mete out punishment by assigning a low (if not failing) grade. As former Stanford president Donald Kennedy commented, "if [disciplinary] prosecutions encounter regular difficulty, either because the standard of proof is too exacting or because the hearing body is overcome with mercy, then faculty members are more likely to take matters into their own hands." [41] In fact, Kennedy commented that "the most serious challenge to Stanford's honor code that I encountered came when faculty members take matters into their own hands and administer frontier justice through the grading system when they were convinced cheating had occurred." And, as most faculty members realize, disputes about grades are far less likely to end up in court. As a best practice, therefore, universities should routinely evaluate faculty satisfaction with their disciplinary procedures to maximize compliance.

HOUSING

The universities' authority is manifest further in their control over student living arrangements. For example, they may require some students to live on campus in university-affiliated housing, under their watchful eye. This requirement was upheld by the court in *Postrollo v. University of South Dakota*.[42] The university policy required all single freshman and sophomore students to live in university residence halls, with few exceptions (e.g., they have dependent children or live with their parents). According to the university, there are two main justifications for this requirement. First, "it was intended to provide a standard level of occupancy to ensure repayment of the government bonds which provided capital for the dormitory construction." In other words, the university needs the money. Second, "it was meant to ensure that younger students who must of necessity live away from home while attending the University would avail themselves of the learning experience in self-government, group discipline, and community living that dorm life provides, as well as the increased opportunity for enriching relationships with the staff and other students."[43] In other words, university officials believe that dormitory living provides an educational atmosphere that assists younger students, namely underclassmen, in adjusting to college life.

Challenging that notion, two incoming students at the University of South Dakota, Gail Prostrollo and Lynn Severson, filed a lawsuit claiming that this requirement encroached on their constitutional right of privacy and denied them equal protection of the laws under the Fourteenth Amendment. The court ruled against the students and upheld university policy. Noting that the need for revenue to defray construction costs was not illegal, the court chose not to focus on that mercenary aspect of the rationale. Instead, it based its opinion on the requirement's second rationale, the university's belief that "dormitory living provides an educational atmosphere which assists younger students, as underclassmen, in adjusting to college life." Because living in dormitories contributed to their adjustment to college, the court held that requiring freshmen and sophomores to live in dormitories was not a denial of equal protection; there was a justifiable reason for this housing requirement. Basically, the court deferred to the university's judgment on these matters. Furthermore, it held that the housing requirement did not violate fundamental rights of privacy and freedom of association, noting wryly that "The interest in living precisely where one chooses is not fundamental within our constitutional scheme."

Bolstered by this ruling, the University of South Dakota and many other universities—large and small—continue to require freshmen and, in some cases, sophomores to live in university-affiliated housing. Because of their university affiliation, fraternities and sororities generally satisfy this requirement. Subsequent cases established specific guidelines defining the universities' authority in this context. Examples include: a regulation allowing male but not female students to live off campus was found to be unconstitutional; a student may keep a guinea pig in her residence hall room as a "service animal"; universities may prohibit visits by members of the opposite sex in dormitory bedrooms; and numerous other cases summarized in Kaplin and Lee.[44]

ROOM SEARCHES AND SEIZURES

Once ensconced in their rooms, whether on or off campus, students expect privacy. Just like any other citizen, they are protected from unwarranted intrusions by the Fourth Amendment, which states that: "The right of the people to be secure in their persons, houses, papers, and effects, against unreasonable searches and seizures, shall not be violated, and no warrants shall issue, but upon probable cause, supported by oath or affirmation, and particularly describing the place to be searched, and the persons or things to be seized." This constitutional right protects against unwarranted state actions, such as a raid by the police.

Therefore, as agents of the government, local, state, and federal police officers may search properties where there is a legitimate expectation of privacy only if they have probable cause to believe that they can find evidence of criminal activity. In most circumstances, a judge must first issue a warrant authorizing the search. Thus, if police officers wish to enter a dormitory room for evidence of wrongdoing, they must first obtain a search warrant. In exceptional circumstances, a warrantless search may be conducted. Searches with probable cause but no warrant may be conducted with the individual's consent, incidental to a lawful arrest, or under exigent circumstances when the police have probable cause but no time to obtain a warrant. Furthermore, according to the "plain sight" doctrine, police do not need a search warrant to seize evidence that is in plain view by the police when they are in a place where are they legally authorized to be. (Incidentally, the same Fourth Amendment protections also apply to searches of faculty or staff offices).

Local, state, and federal law enforcement officers are generally commissioned; they carry a badge and a weapon, have arrest powers, and must abide by the Fourth Amendment. Whether campus police are commissioned depends on state and local laws as well as agreements between the university and the local police force. Campus police at most (e.g., Texas) but not all (e.g., Hawaii) public universities are commissioned with the same authority as other police officers, such as state troopers.[45] Either way, at public universities, they are state employees and must abide by the Fourth Amendment.

At private universities, however, campus security officers are not state employees. So, in principle, if they are not commissioned by a governmental agency, they are exempt from the Fourth Amendment protections. Notably, as Elizabeth Jones points out, since the "Fourth Amendment only limits governmental activity, evidence obtained by a warrantless or nonconsensual search performed by a private person, 'perhaps by illegal means,' is not obligatorily excluded from evidence in a criminal trial."[46] In that respect, warrantless searches performed in private college or university dormitories by noncommissioned individuals (such as security personnel or other institutional officials) are most likely valid. However, this exemption is not iron-clad. If local, state, or federal police officers participate in a search by campus security officers, their involvement may be sufficient to invoke Fourth Amendment guarantees, thus requiring a warrant before conducting the search. In addition, a student whose room is searched contrary to the institution's housing agreement or housing policies may have a claim for breach of contract. And, students whose rooms are searched in an arbitrary and capricious manner, or otherwise without a legitimate basis, also may have claims for invasion of privacy based on traditional landlord-tenant jurisprudence.

In some situations, the right to privacy pertains to not only the residence hall room but also the hallways. This was established in *State v. Houvener*.[47] At 5:45 a.m., a WSU police officer responded to the reported burglary of a student's computer and guitar in a campus dormitory. While walking the halls searching for the burglar, the officer heard voices and loud music coming from one of the rooms, which he considered suspicious that early in the morning. He listened at the threshold of the door and heard one voice say "I'm just paranoid we are going to get caught" and a second voice say "I don't think he would call the cops." The officer then put his finger over the peephole to prevent the occupants from seeing him and knocked on the door while stating, "Let me in, this is Matt." After the students ignored the knock, the officer identified himself as a policeman and ordered the occupants to open the door. After opening the door, one of the students, Jacob Houvener, was asked to step into the hallway, where he admitted the theft; subsequently, the second suspect was asked into the hallway and also admitted to the theft. Houvener was then placed under arrest and told to retrieve the stolen items from his room.

At the trial, the court noted that Houvener had a reasonable expectation of privacy in the hallway. Unlike an apartment, "each dormitory floor is treated by the university as an independent residential area and students are members of a living group-with shared bathroom, study facilities, lobbies, and hallways for which the residents are responsible and may govern." Furthermore, "Because of the intimate nature of the activities in the hallway—most remarkably, towel-clad residents navigating the hallways to and from the shared shower facilities—it is reasonable to hold that this area is protected [by the Fourth Amendment]." For these reasons, private citizens could not enter the hallway uninvited; they are restricted to the lobby.

Thus, the court dismissed the burglary charges against Houvener, citing several reasons predicated on Houvener's reasonable expectation of privacy in the hallway. Without a warrant, the police had no greater right to the hallway than a private citizen. Thus, they were not lawfully present in the hallways. Moreover, the officer's eavesdropping at the door's threshold constituted a warrantless search, and without a warrant, the officer had no legal authority to order Houvener to open his door. Expanding on this last point, the court asserted that the order to open the door "constituted a warrantless, unconsensual search/seizure contrary to . . . the Washington State Constitution and the Fourth Amendment of the United States Constitution. All evidence obtained thereafter should be considered fruit of the poisonous tree. Had the Defendant not been ordered to open his door, he would not have agreed to exit his room, be interviewed by the police, give incriminating statements and thereafter, turn over to the police the stolen guitar and computer." With the evidence excluded by the court, Houvener evaded criminal prosecution for burglary.

Conducting a search in violation of a student's Fourth Amendment rights can render public university employees, and potentially the university itself, liable for damages. In addition, as *Houvener* illustrates, any evidence of criminal activity obtained in the search likely may be tainted as "fruit of the poisonous tree" and, therefore, suppressed in ensuing criminal proceedings. It should also be noted that public institutions also may be subject to a state constitution's analogous "search and seizure" provisions. These state constitutional provisions sometimes provide even greater protections against warrantless searches and seizures than the Fourth Amendment.[48]

If an individual voluntarily consents to a search, a warrant is not required. Thus, the police may enter a student's apartment without a warrant if the student agrees to the search beforehand. The police are not required to mention that the consent is voluntary. Furthermore, the Supreme Court ruled that a third party with common authority over the premises can give consent for a search without violating a suspect's Fourth Amendment rights.[49] That is, unless the suspect is present and denies the consent given by the third party. Then, the consent of one individual with common authority cannot override the refusal of the other who is present.[50]

These rulings raise questions about who actually has common authority. A roommate has common authority and could consent to the search of a suspect's dormitory room, unless the suspect is present and objects. If a student shares an apartment with a roommate, the roommate has the power to give police permission to search common areas in the apartment, such as the living room or kitchen, but not the suspect's personal bedroom.

However, in the sometimes casual living arrangements among students, how do the police know who is a roommate with common authority and who isn't? Fortunately for the police, the court ruled in *Illinois v. Rodriguez* that a warrantless search is still considered valid if they accept in good faith the consent given by an apparent authority, even if it is determined later that the third party did not have authority over the property in question.[51] That case began when Gail Fischer phoned police claiming that Edward Rodriguez had beaten her. She escorted the police to Rodriguez's apartment, maintaining that it was "our apartment" and that she had belongings there. Moreover, she opened the apartment door with a key. Believing that Fischer had common authority over the apartment, police entered without a search warrant and found several items of drugs and related material. They proceeded to the bedroom, where they found Rodriguez asleep and discovered additional containers of white powder in two open attaché cases. The officers arrested Rodriguez and seized the drugs and related paraphernalia. He was charged with possession of a controlled substance with intent to deliver. At the trial, Rodriguez moved to suppress all evidence seized at his residence, claiming that Fischer had vacated the apartment several weeks earlier and had no authority to consent to the entry—that is, she did not possess common authority over the apartment.

The Supreme Court ruled in favor of the police. It held that searches are valid if, at the time of the search, the authorities "reasonably believe" the third party possesses common authority over the premises. In reaching its decision, the court noted that "reasonableness," not consent, is the touchstone of Fourth Amendment jurisprudence; the Constitution only prohibits "unreasonable" searches and seizures. Therefore, the constitutional validity of a police determination of consent to enter is not judged by whether the police were correct in their assessment, but by whether, based on the facts available at the moment, it was reasonable to conclude that the consenting party had authority over the premises. In the words of the court, "Because many situations which confront officers in the course of executing their duties are more or less ambiguous, room must be allowed for some mistakes on their part. But the mistakes must be those of reasonable men, acting on facts leading sensibly to their conclusions of probability."

In most university housing contracts, students must agree to a consent clause that allows college and university officials the right to enter and search a room for specific, institutionally vital purposes, such as protecting university property and maintaining a sound educational environment. These are "administrative" or "health and safety" searches. The courts almost uniformly uphold the university's right to conduct these searches, provided the underlying purposes are reasonable. Examples include searches for violations of campus drug, alcohol, or weapons policies. Importantly, by signing this waiver of privacy, students are not waiving their Fourth Amendment rights; the courts have not upheld provisions in housing agreements that require students to waive constitutional rights as a condition of campus housing.[52] Thus, if an administrative search turns up illegal drugs and police are called in, Fourth Amendment rights pertain.

Commonwealth v. Neilson is an amusing, frequently cited case that illustrates the general validity of housing agreements that allow administrative searches but also illustrates the legal limits of these searches.[53] A student at Fitchburg State College, Eric Neilson, signed a residence hall contract that stated "residence life staff members will enter student rooms to inspect for hazards to health or personal safety." One morning, a maintenance worker believed that he heard a cat inside a four-bedroom dormitory suite where Neilson lived. He reported the information to college officials, who visited the suite and informed one of the residents (not Neilson) that "any cat must be removed pursuant to the college's health and safety regulations." That afternoon, a college official posted notices on all four bedroom doors of the suite, informing the students of the possible violation of college policy and alerting them that a "door to door check" would be conducted that night to ensure that the cat had been removed. Neilson was not present when the officials returned that evening. While searching his bedroom, they noticed a light shining in the closet. Concerned that the light might pose a fire hazard, they opened the closet door and discovered two four-foot tall marijuana plants, along with growth lights, fertilizer, and numerous other materials for marijuana cultivation and use.

At this point, the officials stopped their investigation and requested the assistance of the Fitchburg State College campus police, who have commissioned powers of arrest. They arrived at the suite, entered the bedroom, took photographs of the marijuana plants and other paraphernalia, and, with the help of the college officials, removed the evidence from the room. At no time did the police seek, obtain, or possess a warrant for the search. Subsequently, Neilson was charged with illegal possession, cultivation, and distribution of marijuana.

The court ruled that the warrantless search of the dormitory room by the campus police violated Neilson's constitutional rights and that all evidence obtained as a result of the search should be suppressed. Significantly, however, the court also noted that the initial search to locate the "elusive feline" and the decision to open the closet door were permissible, for they were based on reasonable concerns for the students' health and safety. In the words of the court, "the initial search was reasonable because it was intended to enforce a legitimate health and safety rule that related to the college's function as an educational institution." The constitutional violation occurred when the police searched the room and seized the evidence without a warrant. Although Neilson had consented entry to his room by residence life staff, he had not consented entry to the police. Furthermore, the plain view doctrine does not apply to the police seizure of the evidence, because the officers were not lawfully present in the dormitory room when they made their plain view observations. Therefore, the court concluded that "when the campus police entered the defendant's dormitory room without a warrant, they violated the defendant's Fourth Amendment rights. All evidence obtained as a result of that illegal search was properly suppressed." Lack of a warrant was the crux of the matter.

In their summary of this case, Kaplin and Lee offer sage advice.[54] Before entering a student's room under the auspices of a housing agreement or an administrative search, it is advisable to obtain the occupant's consent beforehand if that is feasible. "Such a policy not only evidences courtesy and respect for privacy but would also augment the validity of the entry under circumstances in which there might be some doubt about the scope of the administrator's authority under the housing agreement or the judicial precedents on administrative searches."

FAMILY EDUCATIONAL RIGHTS AND PRIVACY ACT

The university's authority to control student educational records is limited by the Family Educational Rights and Privacy Act (FERPA), which governs the privacy of student educational records.[55] Sometimes called the Buckley amendment (after its proponent Senator James Buckley), FERPA is administered by the Family Policy Compliance Office in the U.S. Department of Education. It applies to all educational agencies and institutions that receive funding under any program administered by the department, which includes funds received directly (e.g., research grants) or indirectly from students who pay them to the institutions (e.g., a Direct Loan). Nearly all universities fall into this category.

What constitutes an educational record? "Education records" include nearly all records maintained by an educational institution in any format that are directly related to its past or present students. A record is directly related to a student if the student's identity is stated expressly or if the student's identity could be deduced from the demographic, descriptive, or other information contained in the record, either alone or in combination with other publicly available information. The material contained in these education records, as summarized by the National Association of College and University Attorneys (NACUA), include "not only registrar's office records, transcripts, papers, exams and the like, but also non-academic student information database systems, class schedules, financial aid records, financial account records, disability accommodation records, disciplinary records, and even 'unofficial' files, photographs, e-mail messages, hand-scrawled Post-it notes, and records that are publicly available elsewhere or that the student herself has publicly disclosed."[56]

FERPA gives students enrolled at a postsecondary institution three fundamental rights concerning their educational records—that is, any records maintained by the institution that contain information directly related to a student. The eligible students have the right to:

1. gain access to their education records
2. seek to have the records amended if information was recorded inaccurately
3. have control over the disclosure of personally identifiable information from the records

The first right is straightforward. The institution must provide students the opportunity to inspect their education records and a copy of the records. However, the institution is not required to provide or create information that is not normally maintained in these records. Also, it is not required to provide more general information not related to a specific student, such as course syllabi, academic calendars, general notices, announcements, and so forth.

The second right is equally straightforward. The institution must consider a student's request to amend information. This may entail providing the student a hearing on the matter. However, the institution is not required to amend the information—just provide the hearing. This right is limited; it may not be invoked to contest a grade, an opinion, or a substantive decision made by the institution about the student.

The third right is more complicated. An institution may not disclose personally identifiable information from a student's education records to a third party without the student's written consent. There are numerous exceptions, however. Institutions are permitted, but not required, to disclose education records without consent to institutional officials (such as professors, administrators, health staff, counselors, and attorneys) if they have a "legitimate educational interest" in the information. That is, if they need the information to fulfill their professional responsibilities. Also, an institution may disclose relevant information to: another institution where the student seeks to enroll; financial aid offices if it is needed to determine eligibility, amounts, and so forth; appropriate parties in connection with health or safety emergencies; and directories. However, students may edit or block directory information. Significantly, except in cases of health and safety emergencies, institutions may not release educational records to a student's parents without consent unless at least one of the parents claims the student as a dependent on a federal income tax return. In no case may the institution release the student's social security number without consent.

The institution must notify students annually about these rights. This notification may be in a student handbook, a schedule of classes, or some other general announcement. In addition, students have the right to file a complaint with the Department of Education if an institution violates any of these fundamental rights.

FERPA does not establish recordkeeping requirements. Under FERPA, an institution is not generally required to maintain particular education records or education records that contain specific information. Rather, it is required to provide certain privacy protections for those education records that it does maintain. Also, unless there is an outstanding request by an eligible student to inspect and review education records, FERPA permits the institution to destroy the records without notice to the student.

In general, therefore, FERPA prohibits the improper disclosure of personally identifiable information derived strictly from education records. However, information that an official has obtained through personal knowledge or observation or has heard secondhand from others is not protected under FERPA. In other words, if a university employee develops a concern about a student based on personal observations or interactions with the student, the employee may disclose that concern to anyone without violating FERPA regulations. This apparent "loophole" applies if even if education records containing that information exist, unless, of course, the employee had an official role in establishing that protected education record.

The FERPA guidelines contain an element of permissiveness based in semantics. The fundamental provisions are written using the legally absolute "shall." For example, "No funds shall be made available under any applicable program to any educational agency or institution which has a policy or practice of permitting the release of educational records." However, most of the exemptions are written using the legally permissive word "may." For example, "An educational agency or institution may disclose personally identifiable information from an education record of a student without the consent required . . . if the disclosure meets one or more of the following conditions."[57] The semantics are important. Based on use of the word "may" instead of "shall," releasing the education records is an option but not a requirement. Institutional policies would dictate whether the records were released in specific circumstances.

An anecdotal case illustrates this permissiveness. A seventeen-year-old freshman at Flagstaff University was placed on academic probation because of low grades at the end of the first semester. Embarrassed, he refused to discuss the poor performance with his parents. The alarmed parents called the dean of students asking to see the specific grades. The dean denied the request, citing FERPA restrictions on disclosure of educational records. "But he is only seventeen years old. He is still a minor, and we are his legal parents," they objected. In response, the dean reminded them that age didn't matter, since the student was enrolled at the university. After studying the FERPA regulations, the parents returned a week later. "According to the law, we are entitled to see our son's educational records because we claim him as a dependent on our federal income taxes." Patiently, the dean replied: "Yes, according to the law, the university may disclose the educational records to you under these circumstances. However, we are not required to do so. And, it is university policy to maintain the privacy of these records unless the student consents to their release, which he has not done." That ended the discussion; the university would not release the student's educational records to the parents.

In this case, the university chose not to release information. Other universities may have different policies in this regard. As a "best practice," all faculty members and senior-level administrators should be familiar with institutional policies on the release of educational records. Incidentally, after discussing the permissiveness embedded in FERPA from a faculty member's perspective, Ethan Watrall offers sound advice: "Because the implementation will be different for different institutions, it behooves you, dear readers, to go find the information out for yourself. Because, in all honestly, you can't afford not to."[58]

Incidentally, campus law enforcement records are not "educational records" according to FERPA and may be disclosed freely to anybody deemed appropriate by the institution. Thus, for example, campus police, whether commissioned or not, may share an incident report documenting their response to a student's threatening statements or behavior with an external law enforcement agency without concern for FERPA. However, as NACUA notes, "any copies of that report that are shared with other campus offices would become subject to FERPA, though the original in the law enforcement unit would continue not to be."[59] That is, if the police provided a copy of an incident report to a dean, the dean must treat this copy according to FERPA guidelines. Furthermore, any student education records provided to campus police (as school officials with a legitimate educational interest) by other campus offices remain subject to FERPA.

SUMMARY

Historically, under the doctrine of *in loco parentis*, universities shared the responsibility for the students' well-being with the parents. However, as the legal age of majority was lowered to eighteen years, most university students were perceived as adults who were entitled to their own rights, leading to a demise of *in loco parentis*. Nonetheless, as custodians of their well-being, universities still have broad authority over student activities and behavior. The university's custodial authority extends to student behavior both on and off campus. This authority over off-campus activities is limited to student behavior that is incompatible with vital university interests. Some universities share authority over student conduct with the students and faculty members through honor codes. Student misconduct may be subject simultaneously to a university's disciplinary system and external legal or administrative proceedings. Academic disciplinary actions must follow due process but do not require a hearing. Universities may require some students to live on campus in university-affiliated housing, where they are protected by the provisions of the Fourth Amendment. Therefore, police officers may search properties where there is a legitimate expectation of privacy only if they have a warrant. Warrantless searches may be conducted with the individual's consent. A third party such as a roommate with common authority over the premises can give consent for a search. In most university housing contracts, students must agree to a consent clause that allows university officials the right to enter and search a room for specific, institutionally vital purposes. The university's authority to control student educational records is limited by the FERPA, which governs the privacy of student educational records, giving students the right to gain access to their education records, seek to have the records amended if information was recorded inaccurately, and have control over the disclosure of personally identifiable information from the records.

NOTES

1. Todd A. DeMitchell, "In Loco Parentis," *Education Law* (2012), http://educational-law.org/345-in-loco-parentis.html. (Accessed April 23, 2014).

2. *Gott v. Berea College*, 156 Ky. 376; 161 S.W. 204 (1913).

3. William A. Kaplin and Barbara A. Lee, *The Law of Higher Education*, 5th ed. (San Francisco: Jossey-Bass, 2013),10.

4. Theodore C. Stamatakos, "The Doctrine of in Loco Parentis, Tort Liability and the Student-College Relationship," *Indiana Law Journal* 65, no. 2 (1990), http://www.repository.law.indiana.edu/cgi/viewcontent.cgi?article=1293andcontext=ilj. (Accessed April 29, 2014).

5. *Dixon v. Alabama State Board of Education*, 294 F.2D 150 (5th Cir.) (1961).

6. *Bradshaw v. Rawlings*, 612 F.2d 135 (1979).

7. Philip Lee, "The Curious Life of *in Loco Parentis* in American Universities," *Higher Education in Review* 8 (2011).

8. *Mullins v. Pine Manor College*, 389 Mass. 47 (1983).

9. William A. Kaplin and Barbara A. Lee, *The Law of Higher Education*, 4th ed. (San Francisco: Jossey-Bass, 2006), 196.

10. Robert D. Bickel and Peter F. Lake, *The Rights and Responsibilities of the Modern University: Who Assumes the Risks of College Life?* (Durham, NC: Carolina Academic Press, 1999), 157.

11. *Furek v. The University of Delaware*, 594 A.2d 506 (1991).

12. Harvard College, "General Regulations," *Handbook for Students* (2013), http://handbook.fas.harvard.edu/icb/icb.do?keyword=k95151andpageid=icb.page584330. (Accessed June 6, 2014).

13. *General Order on Judicial Standards of Procedure and Substance in Review of Student Discipline in Tax Supported Institutions of Higher Education*, 45 F.R.D. 133 (W.D. Mo.) (en banc). (1968).

14. "An Overview: The Private University and Due Process," *Duke Law Journal* 1970, no. 4 (1970): 795.

15. *Ray v. Wilmington College*, 106 Ohio App. 3d 707 (1995).

16. Lucien Capone, III, "Jurisdiction over Off-Campus Offenses: How Long Is the University's Arm?," *National Association of College and University Attorneys* Annual Conference (2003), http://www.nacua.org/LRSSearch/Advanced. (Accessed June 22, 2014).

17. Florida State University, "Student Conduct Code 6c2r-3.004," http://srr.fsu.edu/content/download/89267/929484/file/conduct.pdf. (Accessed June 8, 2014).

18. *74 Md. Op. Atty. Gen. 147, 1986*, Cited in Capone III, *op cit.* (2003).

19. *Paine v. Board of Regents of the University of Texas System*, 355 F. Supp. 199 (W.D. Tex.) (1973).

20. *Krasnow v. Virginia Polytech Institute and State University*, 474 F.Supp. 55 (W.D. Va.) (1976).

21. J. Wes Kiplinger, "Defining Off-Campus Misconduct That Impacts the Mission: A New Approach," *University of St. Thomas Law Journal* 4, no. 1 (2006).

22. Texas A&M University, "Honor System Rules," http://aggiehonor.tamu.edu/RulesAnd-Procedures/. (Accessed June 13, 2014).

23. Stanford University, "Honor Code," http://studentaffairs.stanford.edu/communitystan-dards/policy/honor-code. (Accessed June 13, 2014).

24. Donald L. McCabe, Linda Treviño, and Kenneth Butterfield, "Cheating in Academic Institutions: A Decade of Research," *Ethics and Behavior* 11, no. 3 (2001).

25. Dev A. Patel and Steven R. Watros, "Faculty Approves College's First Honor Code, Likely Effective Fall 2015," *Harvard Crimson* (2014), http://www.thecrimson.com/article/2014/5/6/faculty-passes-honor-code/?page=1. (Accessed July 2, 2014).

26. McCabe, Treviño, and Butterfield, "Cheating in Academic Institutions: A Decade of Research."

27. David Callahan, "Why Honor Codes Reduce Student Cheating," *Huffingtonpost College* (2010), http://www.huffingtonpost.com/david-callahan/why-honor-codes-reduce-st_b_795898.html. (Accessed July 2, 2014).

28. Alexander C. Cartwright and Jennifer Dirmeyer, "The Honor Code Works at H-SC, but It Won't Save Harvard," *Hampton Sydney* (2012), http://www.hsctiger.com/2012/09/the-hon-or-code-works-at-h-sc-but-it-wont-save-harvard/. (Accessed July 2, 2014).

29. *General Order on Judicial Standards of Procedure and Substance in Review of Student Discipline in Tax Supported Institutions of Higher Education.*

30. *Carr v. St. Johns University*, 231 N.Y.S. 2d 410 (1962).

31. Harvey Silverglate and Josh Gewolb, "Procedural Fairness at Private Universities," *FIRE's Guide to Due Process and Fair Procedure on Campus* (2013), 44, http://www.thefire.org/pdfs/due-process.pdf. (Accessed June 9, 2014).

32. Kaplin and Lee, *The Law of Higher Education*, 5th ed., 1174.

33. Rutgers University, "Code of Student Conduct, Section 10.2.11," *Rutgers Policy* (2013), http://studentconduct.rutgers.edu/files/documents/UCSC_2013.pdf.(Accessed June 9, 2014).

34. University of Wisconsin–Madison, "Non-Academic Misconduct, Standards Statement," http://students.wisc.edu/doso/nonacadmisconduct-statement.html. (Accessed June 9, 2014).

35. University of Chicago, "University Disciplinary Systems," https://studentmanual.uchicago.edu/disciplinary. (Accessed June 10, 2014).

36. Ibid.

37. *Goss v. Lopez*, 419 U.S. 565, 95 D. Ct. 729, 42 L. Ed. 2d 725 (1975).

38. Lisa Tenerowicz, "Student Misconduct at Private Colleges and Universities: A Road-map for "Fundamental Fairness" in Disciplinary Proceedings," *Boston College Law Review* 42, no. 3 (2001), http://lawdigitalcommons.bc.edu/bclr/vol42/iss3/4/. (Accessed June 9, 2014).

39. *Board of Curators, University of Missouri v. Horowitz*, 435 U.S. 78 (1978).

40. *University of Texas Medical School at Houston v. Than*, 901 S.W.d 926 (1995).

41. Donald Kennedy, *Academic Duty* (Cambridge, MA: Harvard University Press, 1997), 88.

42. *Postrollo v. University of South Dakota*, 507 F.2d 775 (1974).

43. Ibid.

44. Kaplin and Lee, *The Law of Higher Education*, 5th ed., 987–97.

45. *Texas Education Code, Title 3. Higher Education. § 51.203. Campus Peace Officers*; University of Hawaii at Manoa, "2013 Annual Security and Fire Safety Report, Enforcement," (2013), http://www.hawaii.edu/security/resources/PDFs/annual_report13.pdf. (Accessed May 3, 2014).

46. Elizabeth O. Jones, "The Fourth Amendment and Dormitory Searches," *Journal of College and University Law* 33, no. 3 (2007): 606.

47. *State of Washington v. Houvener*, 186 P 3d 370 (2008).

48. Kevin O'Leary, Daryl J. Lapp, and Thomas V. Wintner, "Whose Room Is It Anyway? Lawful Entry and Search of Student Dormitory Rooms," *NACUA Notes* 3 (2009): 2.

49. *United States v. Matlock*, 415 U.S. 164 (1974).

50. *Georgia v. Randolph*, 547 U.S. 103 (2006).

51. *Illinois v. Rodriguez*, 497 U.S. 177 (1990).

52. *Piazzola v. Watkins*, 442 F.2d 284 (1971).

53. *Commonwealth v. Neilson*, 666 N.E. 2d 984 (Mass.) (1996).

54. Kaplin and Lee, *The Law of Higher Education*, 5th ed., 1000.

55. "Family Educational Right to Privacy Act (Buckley Amendment)," in *20 U.S.C. §1232g; 34 C.F.R. §99.1* (1974).

56. Nancy E. Tribbensee and Steven J. McDonald, "FERPA and Campus Safety," *NACUA Notes* 5, no. 4 (2007), http://www.nacua.org/documents/ferpa1.pdf. (Accessed May 9, 2014).

57. *Family Educational Rights and Privacy, under What Conditions Is Prior Consent Not Required to Disclose Information?*, 34 C.F.R. §99.31 (2014).

58. Ethan Watrall, "Understanding FERPA and Educational Records Disclosure," *Chronicle of Higher Education* (2010), http://chronicle.com/blogs/profhacker/understanding-ferpa-educational-records-disclosure/25002. (Accessed May 9, 2014).

59. Tribbensee and McDonald, "FERPA and Campus Safety."

Chapter Eight

Hiring

THE GENERIC HIRING PROCESS

A primary role of management is to hire individuals to accomplish institutional goals.[1] This begins at the top—the governing board—and extends on down the organizational hierarchy. As former Chairman of the Federal Reserve Paul Volcker states, "The board's inescapable and prime responsibility is hiring and firing the CEO."[2] In a university setting, the governing board hires the president, who hires a provost, who hires the deans, who appoint the departmental chairs, and so forth. And authority is delegated *pari passu* throughout the institution. The governing board has the authority to appoint the president, who has the authority to appoint the provost, and so on.

Because of the hierarchical nature of the organization, the qualities of a manager with line authority hired at one level may impact the qualities of managers hired at all lower levels. Rudolph Weingartner states this as a blunt maxim, "'A' people hire 'A' people, while 'B' people hire 'C' people."[3] At each level, therefore, the manager must strive to hire competent individuals to optimize the chances that they, in turn, will hire competent individuals at the next lower level. The importance of this maxim cannot be overestimated. Since this linear chain of competence starts at the top, "Hiring a manager may be the most important decision a . . . governing board makes."[4] And that pertains to not just the governing board but also every line manager.

Parenthetically, Rudolph Weingartner states another maxim concerning the hiring process. "The best is the enemy of the good."[5] According to this cryptic maxim, an individual may be the best candidate available for a job but not necessarily a good candidate. Thus, in an academic context, an administrator should hire only individuals well qualified to do the assigned job; that job may include hiring competent administrators further down in the organization. At any level, hiring just the best available from a pool of mediocre candidates introduces risk into future appointments by this candidate. Ideally, therefore, it is preferable to prolong a search until a satisfactory applicant pool has been obtained. Of course, timing issues in any particular situation can complicate the hiring process, leaving an administrator with few options.

Because of its importance, the hiring process has become far more sophisticated as institutions, including universities, strive to recruit highly skilled, competent managerial personnel. Filling a vacant managerial position requires far more than simply hanging the iconic sign "Help wanted. Apply within" on the office door and waiting for the right person to walk in. Most institutions now have detailed hiring guidelines developed by professional human resources personnel. Furthermore, an entire industry has flourished: the executive search firms, which offer expertise in identifying, recruiting, and vetting qualified candidates for an open position. In a sense, the hiring process has become a science mastered by skilled experts.

Among academic institutions, recruitment and selection procedures usually involve a search process that follows a fairly common pathway mapped out clearly in institutional policy. The steps are sequential: a well-publicized national search, a search and screen committee to vet the applications, on-site interviews of several finalists, selection of the candidate by the immediate superior, and approval by authorities at least one level higher in the organizational hierarchy. Thus, in a university setting, the provost's appointment of a dean must be approved by the president (the provost's immediate superior). Of course, some institutions' processes may vary slightly from this general procedure. For example, approval may extend two levels higher in the organization; in that case, the provost's appointment of a dean would require approval by both the president (the provost's immediate superior) and the governing board (the president's immediate supervisor). Nonetheless, despite minor variations, by and large this is a fairly standard hiring protocol.

Restating the point from a different approach, appointment authority usually projects indirectly at least one level down the organizational hierarchy. So, the governing board must approve appointments made by the president (such as the provost and other vice presidents), the president must approve appointments made by the vice presidents (such as deans), and on down the line. In some institutions, this approval process may even project two steps downstream. The rationale for this overlapping approval process is the need for checks and balances and, perhaps more important, consistency of mission. The higher-level approving authority has the opportunity to ensure that the line subordinates share their values and goals for the organization. It also reduces the chances of an incompetent appointment at lower organizational levels. In practice, of course, the higher approving authority (such as the governing board, the president, and so forth) should be consulted before a job offer is made to confirm their ultimate concurrence with the chosen individual.

FEDERAL EQUAL EMPLOYMENT OPPORTUNITY LAWS

This generic hiring process must abide by several major federal laws, known collectively as equal employment opportunity (EEO) laws, to ensure nondiscriminatory policies. These pieces of legislation have become the centerpiece of modern hiring practices. They originated in the Civil Rights Act of 1964.[6] In that statute, Title VI prohibits discrimination on the basis of race, color, or national origin under any program or activity receiving federal financial assistance.[7] This applies to employment discrimination if the primary objective of the federal financial assistance is to provide employment or if discriminatory employment practices cause further discrimination when providing services under any activity receiving federal funding. Title VII addresses employment more explicitly. It prohibits discrimination in employment on the basis of race, religion, color, sex, or national origin.[8] This historic legislation, which launched the age of nondiscrimination, was amplified by the Civil Rights Act of 1991 that provides for possible compensatory and punitive damages in cases of intentional discrimination in violation of the 1964 act.[9] Moreover, the burden of proof was shifted to the employer.

Discriminatory hiring on the basis of age was also drawn under the civil rights mantel in the Age Discrimination in Employment Act of 1967.[10] It banned not only age discrimination in hiring, promotion, wages, or layoffs but also any statements indicating preferences based on age.[11] Except for certain occupations, such as firefighters and some higher-level executives, the act also banned mandatory retirement based on age. Thus, in a university setting, faculty members cannot be forced to retire because of their advanced age. The rationale is that age has no impact on professors' abilities to teach or conduct research. In contrast, advanced age (usually fifty-five years or older) presumably diminishes firefighters' abilities to perform their jobs. Interestingly, the act does not prohibit favoring the old over the young. An employer might say "you're too young for this job" but cannot say "you're too old for this job."

Two related federal laws barring discriminatory hiring practices extend coverage to individuals with physical or mental disabilities. Although the Rehabilitation Act of 1973 introduced legislation promoting the hiring of handicapped individuals,[12] it was the Americans with Disabilities Act of 1990 (ADA) that set the current standards.[13] According to the ADA's general rule, "No covered entity shall discriminate against a qualified individual with a disability because of the disability of such individual in regard to job application procedures, the hiring, advancement, or discharge of employees, employee compensation, job training, and other terms, conditions, and privileges of employment."[14] In this context, a "covered entity" simply means an employer.

Responding to the potentially intrusive assault on personal privacy revealed by emergent techniques for rapid DNA analysis, the most recent federal hiring legislation bars employment discrimination on the basis of genetic information.[15] This law put a spotlight on several dark shadows in modern American history. In a rather chilling preamble to the legislation, Congress noted that "The early science of genetics became the basis of State laws that provided for the sterilization of persons having presumed genetic 'defects' such as mental retardation, mental disease, epilepsy, blindness, and hearing loss, among other conditions. The first sterilization law was enacted in the State of Indiana in 1907. By 1981, a majority of States adopted sterilization laws to 'correct' apparent genetic traits or tendencies."[16] Moreover, Congress cites state legislation "mandating genetic screening of all African Americans for sickle cell anemia, leading to discrimination and unnecessary fear" beginning in the 1970s.[17] With the passage of this "Genetic Information Nondiscrimination Act of 2008," the federal government fully opened its umbrella to protect against discrimination in the employment process, ranging from recruitment to termination.

In a notable exception to the EEO laws, a university may hire individuals of a specific religion if it is "owned, supported, controlled, or managed by a particular religion or by a particular religious corporation, association, or society, or if the curriculum of such school, college, university, or other educational institution or institution of learning is directed toward the propagation of a particular religion."[18] Thus, the exception applies only to those institutions whose purpose and character are primarily religious, allowing them to employ preferentially individuals who share their religion. So, for example, a Jesuit university can limit its hiring to Roman Catholics and stay within the law. However, this exception does not allow religious organizations to discriminate further on the basis of race, color, national origin, sex, age, or disability. Thus, a religious organization is not permitted to engage in racially discriminatory hiring by asserting that a tenet of its religious beliefs is not to associate with people of other races.[19]

These EEO laws are enforced by the Equal Employment Opportunity Commission (EEOC). The EEOC is a bipartisan commission comprised of five presidentially appointed members, plus a general counsel to support litigation programs. The commission monitors employer compliance with EEO laws and, when appropriate, issues charges of discrimination and authorizes the filing of lawsuits in cases of noncompliance.

Subsequently, the federal government went one step beyond the EEO laws to protect against discrimination in the hiring process. In 1965, President Lyndon Johnson issued Executive Order 11246.[20] This order prohibits employment discrimination based on race, color, religion, sex, and national origin by organizations receiving federal contracts and subcontracts. And in 1972, nondiscrimination on the basis of sex was enacted in Title IX of the Educational Amendments Act of 1972.[21] Specifically, Title IX prohibits sex discrimination in recruitment and employment consideration or selection, whether full time or part time, under any education program or activity operated by an institution receiving or benefiting from federal financial assistance. These nondiscrimination requirements basically overlap the rights protected by the EEO laws. Importantly, however, they extend these protections to any university—public or private—that receives federal funding, including financial aid. Thus, nearly all colleges and universities in the country are subject to this prohibition against employment discrimination based on race or gender.

AFFIRMATIVE ACTION

Executive Order 11246 added another requirement, namely affirmative action. "The contractor will take affirmative action to ensure that applicants are employed, and that employees are treated during employment, without regard to their race, color, religion, sex or national origin. Such action shall include, but not be limited to the following: employment, upgrading, demotion, or transfer; recruitment or recruitment advertising; layoff or termination; rates of pay or other forms of compensation; and selection for training, including apprenticeship."[22] In other words, Executive Order 11246 requires federal contractors to promote actively the full realization of equal opportunity for women and minorities; they must proactively comply with the EEO laws. In addition, the contractor must "post in conspicuous places, available to employees and applicants for employment, notices to be provided by the contracting officer setting forth the provisions of this nondiscrimination clause." These postings have become a familiar part of the academic workplace.

The scope of affirmative action has been expanded beyond women and minorities to include certain armed forces veterans and individuals with disabilities. Specifically, under the Vietnam Era Veterans' Readjustment Assistance Act of 1974, as amended, employers must extend affirmative action to several categories of "covered veterans," such as disabled veterans, armed forces service medal veterans, recently separated veterans, and veterans who "participated in a United States military operation for which an Armed Forces service medal was awarded."[23] Furthermore, the Rehabilitation Act of 1973 mandates affirmative action measures to benefit individuals with disabilities.[24]

The central premise of affirmative action is that ideally, in the absence of discrimination, a contractor's workforce should reflect the gender, racial, and ethnic profile of the labor pools from which the contractor recruits and selects. Therefore, any imbalances between the demographic labor pool and the workforce must result from biases—discrimination—in the hiring and retention process. So, at its roots, affirmative action is based on a moral and social obligation to amend historical wrongs and eliminate the present effects of past discrimination. The ultimate goal is to achieve the ideal balance between the labor pool and the workforce.

Under the Department of Labor, the Office of Federal Contract Compliance Programs (OFCCP) monitors these affirmative action requirements and has developed regulations for all federal contractors. For contractors employing more than fifty people and having federal contracts totaling more than $50,000, which includes nearly all universities, compliance with these regulations includes: disseminating and enforcing a nondiscrimination policy; establishing a written affirmative action program and placement goals for women and minorities; and implementing programs for accomplishing these goals. In addition, an official of the organization must be assigned responsibility for implementation of equal employment opportunity and the affirmative action program.

The affirmative action program, also called an affirmative action plan, is a key element of these requirements for federal contractors. It is basically a management tool designed to ensure EEO, for it defines an employer's procedures and standards for proactively recruiting, hiring, and promoting women, minorities, disabled individuals, and veterans. In addition, many states also have affirmative action program requirements for state government contractors. Notably, the EEO laws themselves usually do not require formal affirmative action programs, so only universities with federal contracts must comply with this requirement. Nonetheless, most educational institutions develop affirmative action programs based on core moral values.

Affirmative action programs can be quite complex to create. For starters, they include a diagnostic institutional analysis of employment data to determine quantitatively any imbalances between the labor pool and the actual workforce. If imbalances exist, the program must describe the employer's good faith efforts to correct any deficiencies. Effective affirmative action programs also include internal auditing and reporting systems as a means of measuring the employer's progress toward achieving the workforce that would be expected in the absence of discrimination. To help an employer in these efforts, the Department of Labor provides an online sample affirmative action program.[25]

The affirmative action program reporting requirements are quite extensive. Employers with federal government contracts ($50,000 or more and fifty or more employees) and employers who do not have a federal government contract but have one hundred or more employees must file an "Employer Information Report" (the EEO-1 report, named after the form number) annually to both the EEOC and the OFCCP. On the one hand, the EEOC uses the data to support civil rights enforcement and to analyze employment patterns, such as the representation of female and minority workers within companies, industries, or regions. On the other hand, the OFCCP uses EEO-1 data to determine which employer facilities to select for compliance evaluations. Accordingly, "OFCCP's system uses statistical assessment of EEO-1 data to select facilities where the likelihood of systematic discrimination is the greatest."[26]

Prima facie, the report is not daunting; it consists of two pages that can be filed online. However, the backup information, which must be retained by the employer for one or two years, depending on the number of employees, is voluminous. In a single, massive 252-word sentence, the OFCCP summarizes the required information:

> Such records include, but are not necessarily limited to, records pertaining to hiring, assignment, promotion, demotion, transfer, lay off or termination, rates of pay or other terms of compensation, and selection for training or apprenticeship, and other records having to do with requests for reasonable accommodation, the results of any physical examination, job advertisements and postings, applications, resumes, and any and all expressions of interest through the Internet or related electronic data technologies as to which the contractor considered the individual for a particular position, such as on-line resumes or internal resume databases, records identifying job seekers contacted regarding their interest in a particular position (for purposes of recordkeeping with respect to internal resume databases, the contractor must maintain a record of each resume added to the database, a record of the date each resume was added to the database, the position for which each search of the database was made, and corresponding to each search, the substantive search criteria used and the date of the search; for purposes of recordkeeping with respect to external resume databases, the contractor must maintain a record of the position for which each search of the database was made, and corresponding to each search, the substantive search criteria used, the date of the search, and the resumes of job seekers who met the basic qualifications for the particular position who are considered by the contractor), regardless of whether the individual qualifies as an Internet Applicant under 41 CFR 60-1.3, tests and test results, and interview notes.[27]

In addition, the law requires up-to-date maintenance of the affirmative action program. An employer must "develop and maintain a written affirmative action program (AAP), must maintain its current AAP and documentation of good faith effort, and must preserve its AAP and documentation of good faith effort for the immediately preceding AAP year." These records must be made available to federal officials when requested. There is little margin for error in this recordkeeping, and OFCCP conducts periodic "desk" and on-site audits to monitor compliance. These usually require the employer (e.g., the university) to submit to OFCCP its affirmative action program, and numerous other documents, such as faculty and staff handbooks, job vacancy advertisements, compensation policies, maternity leave policies, and so forth. Furthermore, explanations must be provided regarding applicants not hired for particular jobs, salary differentials between individuals with similar positions, certain terminations, disability accommodation requests, and myriad other matters.

All in all, affirmative action programs are a substantial administrative load. However, for employers, including universities, they are a necessary condition of doing business with the federal government.

INSTITUTIONAL RECRUITMENT AND EMPLOYMENT POLICIES

As long as they comply with federal EEO laws, individual institutions may devise their own recruitment and employment policies. Stated differently, federal antidiscrimination laws set statutory limits to the institution's hiring authority, but beyond that, it's up to the employer to set the rules. These hiring rules are normally codified in organizational policy. As such, they may be part of governing board bylaws, institutional policies and procedures manuals, a faculty handbook, a union contract, or other comparable document.

Typically, university policies require hiring senior administrators through a generic search process because of the high level of responsibilities associated with these positions and the desire to engage broad participation in the hiring decisions. Likewise, they require hiring tenure-track and tenured faculty members as well as continuous staff positions through the search process because of the long-term institutional commitment involved with these types of appointments.

Nonetheless, many institutions have policies that allow for specific exceptions to the generic search process for certain individuals, such as a candidate with extraordinary skills unique to the position. They may also allow exceptions for qualified "in-house" candidates and other individuals if they contribute uniquely to institutional affirmative action goals. For example, Stanford University's Faculty Handbook explicitly allows waivers: "On occasion, the Provost may approve a search waiver for a professorial position when an exceptionally talented person (usually an eminent scholar who is clearly a leader in his or her field) is unexpectedly available."[28] Stanford's Administrative Guide for staff hiring implicitly acknowledges the possibility of waivers: "All regular staff vacancies not posted for the minimum posting period must have an approved waiver of posting before an employment offer can be made. The local Human Resources Office may approve waiver requests."[29] The approval by a human resources office or an affirmative action officer is required to ensure compliance with EEO laws. The University of Minnesota policy states this explicitly: "To hire without a search, units must obtain written approval from both the vice president for the Office of Human Resources and the director of the Office of Equal Opportunity/Affirmative Action prior to offering a position to ensure the candidate's qualifications are demonstrated, unit diversity and affirmative action goals are furthered, and hiring without a search is otherwise justified."[30] By requiring this approval, the university monitors adherence to EEO laws and its affirmative action program.

Deviations from standard hiring practices occur occasionally. Sometimes, search processes are circumvented by reassigning an employee from one position to another. This kind of deviation is generally permissible, because technically a new employee is not being hired *de novo*. However, as a general rule, it is always advisable to consult with the human resources department before making an "in-house" reassignment, regardless of whether it is required by policy. In unusual cases, reassignments may be subject to EEO legislation.

If deviations are not permissible by institutional policy, they are technically unallowable. Nonetheless, in some situations they may be acceptable to the public and can occur with sometimes disconcerting impunity. The circumstances dividing public disapproval and acceptance of deviations from standard hiring practices and the impact on individual hiring authority will be examined in the context of several generic situations.

IMPOSED HIRING: PATRONAGE

Many common deviations from standard hiring practices involve the imposition of an employee on an administrator without regard to institutional policies. This vexing assault on an administrator's hiring authority constitutes patronage. By definition, patronage involves "the power to control appointments to office or the right to privileges."[31] Its insidiousness is reflected in the dictionary's usage counterexample: "The recruits are selected on merit, not through political patronage." Another dictionary defines the word in a political context: "the power to make appointments to government jobs especially for political advantage."[32] In that setting, patronage may be an accepted cultural norm. Regardless of the context, the patronage concept applies in any situation when job appointments are based on a superior's power and influence.

Through a managerial lens, patronage occurs when some higher authority, such as the chief executive officer, the governing board, a legislator, the state's governor, or a generous donor, imposes the hiring of an individual on an organization. For example, an influential legislator recommends a former loyal aide or relative for a university administrative position, regardless of whether there is a need or desire for an additional staff member. Rather than provoking the legislator, the university hires the individual under the presumption that the new person simply must be accommodated somehow. There are many variations on this theme, and all of them are equally undesirable. Patronage like this often shows disrespect for the recipient's office and, by extrapolation, raises questions about the overall commitment to the office as a whole.

Imposed hiring does not always originate from outside an institution. A superior, such as a president, dean, or other boss, can impose the hiring of an in-house individual on a subordinate's office. This may involve, for example, a promotion, a lateral transfer, or a fallback position after stepping down from another post. Since these are reassignments of individuals who have already been hired, institutional search and affirmative action policies may not apply to these in-house appointments. Union or civil service guidelines may limit reassignment options at some organizational levels, but usually they don't apply to administrative positions. Regardless, if somebody higher in the organization exercises power to control the appointment, these imposed assignments constitute patronage.

An anecdotal scenario illustrates several dimensions of patronage. It had been an already stressful morning for Provost M. when the university president interrupted a meeting and walked into Provost M.'s office accompanied by a distinguished looking older gentleman. The president made the introduction: "I would like you to meet Mr. B. He served for six years as governor K.'s chief of staff and is now preparing to retire from public service. To help make this transition, the governor has suggested that Mr. B. would fit well in your office. And I agree." After a courteous handshake, Provost M. replied that there really weren't any openings in the provost's office right now; they were fully staffed. The president continued more sternly: "Mr. B. brings a wealth of experience with him. I'm sure that he'll prove to be valuable colleague." Trying to retain composure, Provost M. replied unconvincingly: "There may be other opportunities in the university more closely aligned with Mr. B.'s experience. Let me think about this." The president quickly ended the conversation: "There's no need to. Besides, my executive assistant has already begun the formal appointment paperwork."

What formal paperwork? In a situation like this, working with the human resources department, the experienced executive assistant most probably would create a new position in the provost's office with a title such as "special assistant," or something similar, with desirable qualifications matching those of Mr. B.'s. Conforming to institutional search policy, the position could be posted on the university's job-opening website for a minimum time (e.g., three days). After a perfunctory review of all applicants (if there were any others), Mr. B. would be selected. All university hiring policies would be followed, and the appointment would be final in a matter of several days. Governor K., via the university president, would have usurped the provost's delegated authority to manage his office. This is raw patronage.

Is there any recourse to this kind of patronage? At first glance, it appears as if Provost M. can do nothing about this case of usurped authority; Mr. B.'s appointment looks like "a done deal." Of course, Provost M. may just say "No. I won't accept this individual's appointment to my staff," creating a situation akin to "it's him or me." Unfortunately, this simplistic answer, which requires considerable thought beforehand, carries an acute risk of retribution—one way or another—and is, therefore, not advisable.

Will looking more carefully at the situation detect any way to resist this imposed appointment? Probably not; the governor and the president may simply fall back on their higher authority to enforce an appointment. Nonetheless, it's worth a peek. To put patronage in perspective, the first look should examine standard hiring procedures and any legal constraints. Did Governor K. and the president flout some institutional employment policy or break some EEO law, thus giving Provost M. a possible escape route from this unpleasant situation? Not really, since there was a properly advertised job opening in the provost's office and none of the federal antidiscrimination laws were technically broken. In fact, if there were no other candidates, discrimination is not an issue. Did Governor K. discriminate against some other individual when choosing Mr. B. for this patronage appointment? That would be a very difficult case to prove, since the university did the actual hiring. Furthermore, the job had been advertised, thus ostensibly giving other individuals an opportunity to apply. Are there any further legal limitations to management's hiring authority that might help Provost M. deter this imposed appointment? No; most of them fall into the category of "there ought to be a law." If this were a highly visible appointment, the only possible relief might come from public outrage—the court of public opinion.

In this anecdote, Provost M. is viewing fairly ordinary-looking patronage. However, patronage has many different faces. While interesting, this variability complicates efforts to render broad generalizations about managing specific cases. Thus, against this generic procedural and legal backdrop, several other aspects of patronage will be examined in the hope that a composite image of managing with authority in these situations will emerge.

POLITICAL PATRONAGE

Patronage is a standard feature of the political landscape. Throughout history, newly anointed leaders have had an informally recognized right to appoint a certain number of individuals to jobs in their government. As they say, "To the victor go the spoils." Within the U.S. federal government, the patronage system is usually confined to presidential appointments of cabinet members, department heads, and foreign ambassadorships. It may project sporadically farther down into the bureaucracy, but this, too, is generally considered acceptable if it occurs in conjunction with a new administration.

At the state level, the political patronage system operates in about the same way. An incoming governor has the acknowledged authority to hand-pick cabinet members and major department heads. This authority seldom extends directly to the public universities, even if the university's chief executive officer (president or chancellor) serves ex officio on the governor's cabinet. The University of Puerto Rico is an exception, for a change in the governorship is usually accompanied by a change in university administrators from the president down to the deans' level. Gubernatorial patronage may extend indirectly in states where the governor has the authority to appoint members of the public universities' governing boards (usually subject to the legislature's confirmation), which opens the door for political patronage at that level. Clearly, this empowers the governor to influence appointment of the university's chief executive officer, who is appointed technically by the board.

Importantly, public acceptance quickly evaporates when political patronage occurs at lower levels of government, especially when it is not synchronized with the election of a new administration. Then, it becomes much less acceptable to a wary public. In that context, state universities are particularly susceptible to patronage. They are large, bureaucratic organizations that, in many people's eyes, receive overly generous public funding. In simpler terms, they have "deep pockets." Indeed, political patronage scandals in academe appear once every several months in the news media. Curiously, some cases receive little attention beyond the initial headlines and others trigger an explosion of public outrage. Large pay raises predictably catch the public's eye, but this alone is usually insufficient to attract a forceful response. However, sizeable pay raises conjoined with personal conflicts of interest generally draw an aggressive public reaction.

The muted public response to a large pay raise alone is exemplified by an alleged case of patronage in Wisconsin. A 2010 newspaper headline declared that "Lawmaker accuses UW's Reilly of patronage in job filling."[33] The article goes on to elaborate: "A state lawmaker accused University of Wisconsin System President Kevin Reilly of engaging in political patronage for giving a high-paying state job to Gov. Jim Doyle's top lieutenant without considering other candidates." The governor's explicit role in this appointment was left unsaid in the news coverage, although the headlines implied as much. The job offer as the University of Wisconsin system's senior vice president for administration and fiscal affairs provided the new appointee with a 79 percent boost in pay, which understandably added fuel to the fire surrounding the appointment. Furthermore, in an apparent departure from normal, the job opening was not advertised, there was no national search, and no other candidates were considered for the job.[34]

An aide to president Reilly said that the hiring was "appropriate and the UW System was simply trying to avoid a protracted and costly search to fill the job at a time when the system is in the midst of major projects."[35] Significantly, the university added that the normal search-and-screen process was not needed because the appointment was considered to be interim—that is, for up to three years.

Echoing the headline, this appointment appears to constitute political patronage. But only one of the two signposts that attract attention was clearly visible to the public: a large pay raise. The other signpost, namely a conflict of interest, was not evident. The candidate was unrelated to the governor or the university president, and there were no noticeable *quid pro quo* arrangements. As in many cases of patronage—political and otherwise—the appointee was eminently qualified, and the rationale for the appointment was credible. Thus, regardless of the large publically funded pay raise, this case of political patronage went relatively uncontested.

Can anything be done about cases like this? Not likely. The UW System president has the authority to make a vice presidential appointment. Furthermore, as a matter of policy, interim appointments do not require the normal national search.[36] Thus, unless the need for a generic search-and-screen process for interim appointments is codified in board policy or state law, no legal issues have been raised in situations like this. The only meaningful defense against this kind of appointment would be politically threatening public indignation. In this particular case, that did not transpire. Public interest in the appointment was short lived.

In contrast, the inflammatory effect of a large pay raise coupled to a conflict of interest is illustrated in a 2009 political patronage incident at North Carolina State University that went much less smoothly. Indeed, it proved to be disastrous. Looking forward to the endpoint: "North Carolina State University Chancellor James Oblinger submitted his resignation Monday, becoming the third top university official to step down in recent weeks."[37] The chancellor, the chair of the board of trustees, and the provost all lost their jobs. So did the governor's wife. How did this happen? It's a matter of patronage gone awry.

It all started when Michael Easley was elected governor of North Carolina. Shortly after assuming office in 2001, Governor Easley appointed a good friend, McQueen Campbell, to the North Carolina State University board of trustees. This constituted political patronage, but it fell within the acceptable range of gubernatorial authority. However, a series of personnel appointments in 2005 heralded impending changes in fortune. Governor Easley reappointed Campbell for a second term on the board. At about the same time, the board of trustees promoted Dr. James Oblinger from his position as the university's provost to chancellor. Subsequently, Dr. Larry Nielsen was appointed interim provost with the public understanding that he would not be a candidate for the permanent position.[38]

The turning point came several months later when an aide to Governor Easley began enquiring about a job for the governor's wife, Mary Easley. In late April, Campbell informed Chancellor Oblinger that Ms. Easley, an accomplished lawyer, was interested in a university position. Within about two weeks, Ms. Easley entered contract negotiations with interim provost Nielsen, which culminated in a three-year appointment starting in August at $80,000 per year.[39] Notably, provost Nielsen created Ms. Easley's new position *de novo* and waived all of the usual search requirements.[40] Shortly after these contract negotiations, Chancellor Oblinger announced that interim provost Nielsen "should have the opportunity to be a candidate" for the permanent position.[41] And in July 2005, Dr. Nielsen was appointed permanent provost without participating in the search process that had already identified four finalists. A month later, Ms. Easley's appointment was announced publicly.[42] Two years later, in 2007, Campbell was named board chair.

Despite some procedural anomalies, the appointments of Ms. Easley, provost Nielsen, and Campbell to board chair were uncontested in the court of public opinion. Although they came perilously close to violating the North Carolina ethics act and university hiring policies, the appointment procedures were not questioned formally.[43] *Quid pro quo* political patronage lurked in the shadows, but its shadowed visage failed to generate meaningful public reaction.

The entire situation took a sharp turn for the worse in September 2008. Like most universities, North Carolina State was facing serious budget duress at that time. To control spending, the governor had recommended a meager 1.5 percent pay raise for state employees. In that economic climate, Ms. Easley's appointment was renewed for another five years with a salary of $170,000 per year. That represented an 88 percent pay hike, which caught an uneasy public's attention. Chancellor Oblinger defended the higher salary, citing the depth of Ms. Easley's experience and her expanded duties.[44] Nonetheless, the huge pay raise—88 percent—for the governor's wife evoked outrage from the public already stressed by economic worries. Patronage stepped out of the shadows into full view. And it wasn't pretty.

The news media launched a barrage of reports documenting the sequence of appointments and the conflicts of interest inherent to them that had lain dormant for the past three years. They raised penetrating questions.[45] Did Campbell relay a request from Governor Easley for his wife's position to Chancellor Oblinger? Did Chancellor Oblinger ask interim provost Nielsen to create a position for Ms. Easley and then offer the permanent provost's position to Nielsen as a reward for arranging the university job for Ms. Easley? Did Governor Easley facilitate Campbell's appointment as chair of the board of trustees as a reward for helping get the university job for his wife? Answers to these questions were not readily forthcoming. However, initial denials and memory lapses slowly gave way to affirmations—some implied and some explicit.

The case came to a quick conclusion in late spring 2009. Within less than a month, provost Nielsen, board of trustees chair Campbell, and chancellor Oblinger resigned in response to public pressure.[46] Furthermore, the board of trustees fired Ms. Easley.[47] In a letter announcing his resignation, provost Nielsen denied that he had hired Ms. Easley in return for being appointed to the permanent provost position; he states that "I have chosen to resign because of the intense public attention and criticism from my hiring of Mrs. Mary Easley and now because of questions surrounding the way I was hired as provost."[48] Chancellor Oblinger's resignation statement was less explicit: "I am (resigning) because that is what leaders do when the institutions they lead come under distracting and undue public scrutiny. This is particularly true for leaders of public institutions like N.C. State."[49]

As if that weren't enough, federal prosecutors launched a grand jury inquiry of the case as part of a broader investigation into other charges against Governor Easley. No charges were filed against either Oblinger or Nielsen, and both denied any wrongdoing.[50] However, emailed communications released by the university and turned over to the grand jury "showed Campbell communicated several times with the former governor about a potential N.C. State job for his wife and then communicated with Oblinger and Nielsen to make it happen."[51] These emails irrefutably established the "worst-case" linkage between the governor, the board of trustees, chancellor Oblinger, and provost Nielsen. Incidentally, Governor Easley was ultimately found guilty of a felony for failure to report a $1,600 helicopter ride in violation of campaign financing laws.[52] This conviction terminated the grand jury investigation.

Why did this case of political patronage go so terribly wrong when other cases slip fleetingly across the public's radar screen? The limits of authority were transgressed early on—in 2005. Financial conflicts of interest were evident. Yet the public let them pass without major turmoil. The huge pay raise triggered the outcry. As usual, the adage "follow the money" rang true. Speculatively, the question arises: if Ms. Easley had settled for a more modest pay raise—such as 5 percent—would the court of public opinion ruled differently? The answer is probably yes. Laws were not proved to be broken in a court of law, but public trust in leadership was shattered by what was perceived to be egregious greed. The court of public opinion handed down its decision: guilty by perception.

The next question is whether Ms. Easley could have been reappointed without incident. With the acuity of hindsight, the best strategy would have been for Nielsen not to have ruled out his candidacy for the permanent position when he accepted the interim provost's job. Conversely, if he didn't plan on being a candidate, then he should not have waivered in this commitment. In addition, when he was approached about a job for Ms. Easley, interim provost Nielsen should have created the position that he wanted Ms. Easley to fill, which is within his authority, and then gone through a normal search and selection process. With her incumbent advantage and admirable credentials, Ms. Easley would have been a strong, plausible candidate. Furthermore, most experienced administrators know how to manage a search process within the limits of authority to generate the desired result. Unfortunately, as most experienced administrators also know, hindsight is just that—hindsight.

INVISIBLE PATRONAGE

Patronage is not always visible. It may occur invisibly. In the simplest case, a person possessing power does not make an appointment but influences those who do. Control of the appointment is exerted by an invisible hand. For example, a governor's ability to influence high-level executive appointments extends beyond straightforward political patronage. Because the governor controls state spending, agency directors and governing boards must always heed any signs of gubernatorial support or displeasure of a particular job candidate. These signs can be communicated quite subtly, but their meaning is usually crystal clear: "the governor can work with candidate Smith but not with Jones." If the employer gets the message, then Smith gets the job. The patronage is indirect but unmistakable.

Notably, in this context, the governor's comment also constitutes what might be called "inverse patronage" because it lessens Jones's appointment chances. Because it can eliminate candidates, inverse patronage can be just as effective as indirect and even direct patronage.

In a clandestine environment, there may be few written records documenting this kind of political pressure. The higher-level authority may simply comment verbally about a job candidate to an aide, thus leaving a protective gap in any subsequent paper trail. The aide then communicates these instructions to the employer—again verbally. Of course, this cloak of invisibility can hide unscrupulous activities. Indeed, any rent in the cloak usually attracts suspicious onlookers, as the previous North Carolina State case illustrated. Thus, corollary to its invisibility, this kind of patronage arouses suspicions whenever it is glimpsed.

Invisible patronage and inverse patronage may occur informally at many different levels in an organization—not just at the highest levels. If appointments must be approved one or two levels up the organizational hierarchy, it would not be unusual for a higher-level authority to comment positively or negatively on a particular job candidate before an offer is made, thus influencing the ultimate decision. And that is not necessarily bad; indeed, it informally complements the more formal approval process. Managerial disruption occurs, however, if this form of invisible patronage dominates the lower-level appointment process, thus obfuscating the limits of authority.

PATRONAGE SANCTIONED BY POLICY

University employment policies usually leave sufficient "wiggle room" to allow for patronage. Unlike the federal EEO guidelines that are generally inflexible, institutional hiring policies may be much more elastic. For example, the rationale for allowing exceptions to the generic search process is to allow institutional flexibility when compelling opportunities arise unexpectedly. That is a reasonable guiding principle, as long as the exceptions are rare. However, with this elasticity comes the opportunity for patronage. Indeed, allowing exceptions to standard hiring policy may inadvertently sanction patronage. And, of course, the president generally has the ultimate authority to hire an individual without following institutional search procedures, although EEO laws must be followed.

The boundary between opportunistic hiring and patronage can be barely distinguishable in some situations. An interesting example of this blurred distinction occurred in 2009, when Alberto Gonzales, the attorney general under former President George W. Bush, was appointed to a faculty position as a visiting assistant professor in the political science department at Texas Tech University. The appointment did not arise through the usual departmental search and selection process, which includes a national search initiated by the departmental chair for qualified candidates to fill an open faculty position and extensive vetting by members of the faculty. Instead, it was initiated and orchestrated by a higher authority, namely the university system's chancellor, with minimal faculty involvement. According to newspaper accounts, Texas Tech chancellor Kent Hance "began recruiting the former attorney general to Tech after watching him deliver a talk."[53] The appointment was supported by the interim dean of the college of arts and sciences, who claimed that "Judge Gonzales brings a unique experience to our classroom. His career in law, government and public service will provide our political science students a rich perspective of the executive branch and issues and challenges facing our nation."[54] Nonetheless, in a newspaper reporter's understatement, "the chancellor acknowledged some people may be critical of Gonzales' appointment." [55]

Indeed, an outcry of opposition began immediately. "Should Texas Tech Employ Alberto Gonzales?" blared the *New York Times* headline.[56] The article continued: "Hiring Gonzales was cronyism, undertaken at the behest of Tech's chancellor . . . [who is] a 'good friend' of Gonzales's." And a Texas Tech faculty petition opposing the appointment declared that "Hiring faculty is paradigmatically the responsibility of academic departments. . . . It is not appropriate for the chancellor to be calling the deans of the various colleges asking them to hire particular individuals."[57]

The uproar about hiring Alberto Gonzales wasn't entirely about process. There were political and legal considerations as well. Prima facie this should have been a coveted recruitment. After all, Gonzales had been the U.S. attorney general for two and a half years. However, in its report of his resignation in 2007, the *New York Times* noted that "Mr. Gonzales faced increasing scrutiny for his leadership of the Justice Department over issues including his role in the dismissals of nine United States attorneys late last year and whether he testified truthfully about the National Security Agency's surveillance programs."[58] Deserved or not, reports like this cast a shadow over Gonzales.

According to these published comments, the appointment certainly conformed to the definition of patronage. The chancellor imposed the appointment on the university. But did the chancellor overstep the limits of his authority? No, he did not. The Texas Tech governing board policies authorize the chancellor "to exercise the powers and authorities of the board in the governance of the TTU system. The chancellor will act through the appropriate officers of the TTU system regarding the matters delegated to them. . . . The chancellor, however, shall not be precluded from direct participation and communication with any TTU system officers, staff, faculty members, or groups."[59] This last caveat explicitly allows the chancellor to influence the appointment through "direct participation." Furthermore, the university's currently posted operating procedures allow for exceptions to the normal search process: "On limited occasions, with the authorization of the [provost] and dean of the college involved, an opportunity may arise to hire an extraordinarily talented faculty member (typically one who is a nationally recognized scholar in his or her field), therefore presenting a need to truncate the search process."[60] Thus, with this policy in place, the hiring clearly fell within the limits of the chancellor's and the dean's authority. The truncated process was sanctioned by board and campus policies.

Was the hiring "cronyism" as the *New York Times* asserted? Before answering that question, it helps to review the exact definition of the word. According to the *Oxford Dictionary*, cronyism is "the appointment of friends and associates to positions of authority, without proper regard to their qualifications."[61] Ignoring political biases, Gonzales was not put in a position of noteworthy authority, nor were his qualifications egregiously ignored. Indeed, he was highly qualified for the position. Furthermore, cynics might argue that cronyism occurs technically when any "in-house" candidates are hired, which is permissible according to nearly all university operating procedures. Thus, from a pedantic point of view, there may have been an element of cronyism in the recruitment of Gonzales, but it hardly warrants serious consideration.

Arguing the technicalities of patronage and cronyism detracts from a more pragmatic issue. Could the political sciences department have resisted the appointment? According to hearsay, that's what the law school did when they were asked earlier to accept the appointment; the faculty members just said no, they would not accept this.[62] University policy allows the chancellor to participate directly in departmental affairs, so he could have imposed the appointment on the law school regardless of faculty protests. But, he received a more welcoming response from the political sciences department. Of course, from its perspective, the department faced a realistic dilemma when considering the possible consequences of resistance. Would they somehow be punished if they defied the chancellor? Understandably, that fear always lurks in the background. According to the author of a faculty petition opposing the Gonzales hiring, "Strictly speaking, no rules were broken. I don't have any sense that the [arts and sciences] dean was pressured into it. But there is a built-in conflict: if you say no to the chancellor, you don't know what goodies you're giving up. The chancellor should not be suggesting appointments for his friends."[63]

The only remaining procedural question is whether the appointment passed the test of public opinion. The answer is "not quite"; this appointment did not "seem right" to some members of the university community and the general public. Otherwise there would not have been such criticism in the news media and faculty petitions protesting the hiring. The limits of authority were not trespassed. But respect for the institution suffered in some, but not all, quarters, and that carries an incalculable cost.

FALLBACK APPOINTMENTS

There are two additional forms of imposed appointments that constitute sanctioned in-house patronage: fallback appointments and spousal hires. Fallback appointments usually occur when faculty members are guaranteed the right to return to their academic department as a condition of becoming a member of the university's administration. Thus, when professors take on administrative jobs, they typically retain a tenured position on the faculty. Furthermore, a tenured fallback position is almost always an integral component of any administrative job offer to academic appointees, ranging from a dean to a president, when they come from another university—that is, if they had a tenured position at the previous institution. Because of these fallback positions, stepping down from an administrative post is called "returning to the faculty" in academic parlance.

Fallback positions pose a novel type of patronage. When returning to the faculty, the administrator has the right to join an academic department whether he or she is welcome or not. In a sense, the appointment is imposed on the department, which is a defining element of patronage. If the individual had been a member of the department prior to joining the administration, at least there is a historical link with the department. That doesn't necessarily guarantee a welcome reception, however; unpopular administrative decisions, conflicting claims on office space, inability or unwillingness to teach specific courses, and other easily imagined reasons could dampen any enthusiasm for the returnee. Nonetheless, the department has no choice in the matter. The return rights prevail.

Administrators recruited from outside the institution face a more complicated reentry into a faculty role. Stepping back to the beginning, in the recruitment process, applicants for an administrative position are asked to identify which department would be most appropriate as a locus of tenure. Typically, the applicant will meet the chair and perhaps members of the faculty of the chosen department during a recruitment visit to campus. If the candidate accepts an offered administrative position, the chosen department is then informed by its dean to prepare the tenure application dossier according to normal procedures. Incidentally, salary money is not an issue; the provost routinely promises that the necessary funding will be added to the departmental budget when and if the candidate returns to the faculty. Likewise, the provost usually promises that the fallback position will not be subtracted from the department's position count. In other words, the position is free.

Technically, the departmental faculty members could vote against granting tenure to the candidate; that is tantamount to saying "No. We don't want you." That happens rarely for two reasons. First, higher-level administrators, including the dean, the provost, the president, and the governing board, have the authority to overrule a negative departmental vote. So, the faculty members would accomplish little more than expressing their a priori disapproval of the candidate as a colleague. Second, the departmental faculty members generally recognize the potential for recrimination if they defy the higher-level authorities. For example, an angry provost might not allow them to fill their next vacancy. This realistic angst motivates cooperation.

More optimistically, fallback appointments imposed on a department can be a windfall. The candidate may have credentials that merit an enthusiastic welcome from the fallback department. The affiliation enhances the department's reputation and prestige. Furthermore, if the credentials are at least acceptable, there is always the hope that some favors will accrue to the department from the loyal candidate. Of course, this may or may not happen. Since there is usually little that a department can do about an imposed fall-back appointment, the best strategy is to accommodate the newcomer with courtesy. In the end, he or she may never take advantage of the position.

SPOUSAL HIRES

In-house imposed hiring takes another guise: spousal hires. The visage is familiar. The institution wants to hire a candidate, but the individual will not accept the position unless his or her spouse is also offered a job. So, the institution arranges an appointment for the spouse as well—the spousal hire. This additional position may be external to the university, but commonly it is within the institution. And in those cases, the spousal hire is frequently imposed on a department or other unit within the organization. This imposition constitutes patronage.

Like fallback appointments, a spouse who is hired under these conditions—often called the "trailing spouse"—may or may not receive a warm welcome from the department. The degree of warmth will depend, of course, on the candidate and the circumstances. Compounding the anxiety inherent to the imposed appointment, the trailing spouse may also harbor a sense of uneasiness due to the imposition. And the new colleagues may be oblivious to these concerns.

The psychological complexities of a spousal hire can be quite subtle but daunting. An anecdote illustrates this point. During a lengthy career, Provost M. changed institutions three times, and each time the provost's spouse received a faculty appointment as a spousal hire. Although the details of each occasion varied slightly, the general experience remained the same: uneasy. During the recruitment process at Flagship University, for example, Provost M. insisted that a spousal appointment in the chemistry department was a deal-breaking requirement. Because the spouse had tenure at their previous institution, a Flagship peer, tenure was also a requirement. On one of the recruitment visits, the provost's spouse met with the chemistry department chair and several faculty members. The visit was pleasant, as they discussed mutual research interests and possible teaching assignments. A short time later, the chair prepared the necessary tenure dossier, and the appointment was finalized.

On the first day of the new job, the spouse was assigned an office. It was small, with an old wooden desk, a well-worn swivel chair, a filing cabinet, a telephone, and a computer that appeared to be about five years old. The dusty window looked out onto the brick wall of an adjoining building. Noticing the spouse's disappointment, the chair said that this was "only temporary until something better becomes available." During the first several days, colleagues dropped in occasionally to introduce themselves. They seemed to be quite sincere, although one individual boorishly said "so you're the new provost's spouse" and walked away.

During the next several months, the spouse wrestled with a sense of uneasiness. What caused this? The chair had found a newer, more attractive office, and the teaching assignment was acceptable. Most of the new colleagues were congenial, but the spouse perceived a subtle resentment in some of them. When the provost asked for specific examples, the spouse had difficulty providing detailed instances. But the feeling prevailed. It occurred to the spouse that maybe there was an element of guilt for getting the job without going through the normal hiring process; the appointment had not been on the spouse's merits but on the provost's merits. The spouse countered *sotto voce*: "perhaps, but I'm a good chemist, and they know it. I'll be an asset to this department, just like I was in my previous university." Provost M. was attentive when the spouse raised these issues but was incapable of providing soothing consolation. After all, the provost, who was preoccupied with other professional matters, had never been a trailing spouse and, therefore, lacked empathy. The spouse was alone on this one. And that realization compounded the overall uneasiness.

Fortunately, "time heals all wounds." In the due course of time, the spouse had, indeed, proved to be an asset to the department. Self-confidence had triumphed over the uneasiness inherent to the atypical appointment process. Not all stories about spousal hires end this way, however. Stresses, such as guilt, resentment, and other insecurities exert pressure that can easily amplify other personal difficulties, resulting in broken relationships and other unhappy outcomes.

Compassionate administrators strive to minimize these stresses, but the foibles of human nature complicate the effort. As always, when confronted with a patronage appointment, the best strategy from a managerial perspective is to accommodate the newcomer with courtesy. Thus, initial concerns about the imposed appointment should be discussed with the superior in private, not in the presence of the appointee, who may be very uneasy about the situation. In addition, any temptations to marginalize the new appointee must be resisted; the trailing spouse should be given a fair chance to succeed. If performance is unsatisfactory, then routine disciplinary processes should be followed.

Clearly, patronage is an undesirable practice in many settings, but it is also an accepted managerial practice in others. Fallback positions are the norm for upper-level academic administrators. Moreover, spousal hires are an important component of any university employment policy. In all settings, these kinds of patronage fall within the limits of authority. Whether they fall within the limits of propriety, however, depends on the integrity of the individuals imposing the appointment.

SUMMARY

Among academic institutions, hiring usually involves a search process that follows a fairly common pathway mapped out clearly in institutional policy. The generic hiring process must abide by federal equal employment opportunity laws that prohibit discrimination in employment on the basis of race, religion, color sex, national origin, age, disability, or genetic information. These laws apply to any institution that receives federal funding, which includes nearly all public and private universities. Furthermore, employers must have an affirmative action program to comply with antidiscrimination laws. If the labor pool and the actual workforce are unbalanced, the program must describe the employer's good faith efforts to correct any deficiencies. Beyond the coverage provided by the federal government's antidiscrimination laws, individual institutions may devise their own recruitment and employment policies. Typically, university policies require hiring senior administrators and faculty members through a search process because of the high level of responsibilities associated with these positions, the desire to engage broad participation in the hiring decisions, and the long-term institutional commitment involved with these types of appointments. Nonetheless, many institutions have policies that allow for specific exceptions to this generic search process for certain individuals with extraordinary qualifications. Patronage involves the imposition of an individual on a position without regard to standard institutional search and selection policies. It is not always visible; a person possessing power does not make an appointment but influences those who do. Fallback appointments resemble patronage when an administrator new to the university is guaranteed an appointment in an academic department as a condition of hiring. Likewise, spousal hires resemble patronage when the spouse of a newly recruited employee is imposed on a department. Thus, patronage is an undesirable practice in many settings, but it is also an accepted managerial practice in others.

NOTES

1. Kenneth P. Mortimer and Colleen O'Brien Sathre, *The Art and Politics of Academic Governance* (Westport, CT: Praeger, 2007), 51.

2. Paul Volcker, quoted in William G. Bowen, *The Board Book: An Insider's Guide for Directors and Trustees* (New York: W. W. Norton, 2008), 46–47.

3. Rudolph H. Weingartner, *Fitting Form to Function: A Primer on the Organization of Academic Institutions*, 2nd ed. (Lanham, MD: Rowman and Littlefield, 2011), 102.

4. Vaughn Mamlin Upshaw, John A. Rible IV, and Carl W. Stenberg, *Getting the Right Fit: The Governing Board's Role in Hiring a Manager* (Chapel Hill: School of Government,

University of North Carolina, 2011), 1, http://sogpubs.unc.edu//electronicversions/pdfs/gettin-grightfittoc.pdf? (Accessed April 16, 2013).

5. Weingartner, *Fitting Form to Function*, 118.

6. *Civil Rights Act of 1964*, Pub.L. 88–352, 78 Stat. 241, (1964).

7. *Title VI of the 1964 Civil Rights Act*, 42 USC §2000d (1964).

8. *Title VII of the Civil Rights Act of 1964*, 42 U.S.C. §2000e (1964).

9. Civil Rights Act of 1991, *Equal Rights under the Law*, 42 U.S.C. §1981 (1991).

10. Age Discrimination in Employment Act of 1967, 29 U.S.C. §§621–634 (1967).

11. Ibid., §623(e).

12. Rehabilitation Act of 1973, *Employment of Individuals with Disabilities*, 29 U.S.C. §791 (1973).

13. Americans with Disabilities Act of 1990, *Title I Employment*, 42 U.S.C. §§12111–12117 (1990).

14. Ibid., §12112(a).

15. Genetic Information Nondiscrimination Act of 2008, Public Law No. 110-233, §§ 201–213,122 Stat. 881, 110th Cong., 2nd Sess. (May 21, 2008).

16. Ibid., §2(2).

17. Ibid., §2(3).

18. Civil Rights Act of 1964, 42 U.S.C. 21 §2000e–2.e.

19. U.S. Equal Employment Opportunity Commission, "Questions and Answers: Religious Discrimination in the Workplace," (2011), http://www.eeoc.gov/policy/docs/qanda_religion. html. (Accessed July 26, 2014).

20. Lyndon B. Johnson, "Executive Order 11246," (1965), http://portal.hud.gov/hudportal/ HUD?src=/program_offices/fair_housing_equal_opp/FHLaws/EXO11246. (Accessed April 25, 2013).

21. *Nondiscrimination on the Basis of Sex in Education Programs or Activities Receiving Federal Financial Assistance*, 34 C.F.R. §106 (1975).

22. "Executive Order 11246." §202 (1).

23. "Affirmative Action and Nondiscrimination Obligations of Contractors and Subcontractors Regarding Special Disabled Veterans, Veterans of the Vietnam Era, Recently Separated Veterans, and Other Protected Veterans," *41 C.F.R. §60-250* (2013), http://www.ecfr.gov/cgi-bin/text-idx?c=ecfr&tpl=/ecfrbrowse/Title41/41cfr60-250_main_02.tpl. (Accessed May 6, 2013); Department of Labor, "The Vietnam Era Veterans' Readjustment Assistance Act (VEV-RAA)," http://www.dol.gov/compliance/laws/comp-vevraa.htm. (Accessed May 6, 2013).

24. "Section 503 of the Rehabilitation Act of 1973, as Amended," *29 USC §793* (1993), http://www.dol.gov/ofccp/regs/compliance/sec503.htm. (Accessed May 6, 2013); United States Department of Labor, "The Rehabilitation Act of 1973, Section 503," http://www.dol.gov/ compliance/laws/comp-rehab.htm. (Accessed May 6, 2013).

25. Department of Labor, "Sample Affirmative Action Program (AAP)," http://www.dol. gov/ofccp/regs/compliance/pdf/sampleaap.pdf. (Accessed May 2, 2013).

26. Equal Employment Opportunity Commission, "Questions and Answers: Revisions to the EEO-1 Report," (2006), http://www.eeoc.gov/employers/eeo1/qanda.cfm. (Accessed April 29, 2013).

27. *Obligations of Contractors and Subcontractors Record Retention 41 C.F.R. §60-1.12 (a)*.

28. Stanford University, "Search Waivers, § 2.7.C(5)," *Faculty Handbook* (2010), http:// facultyhandbook.stanford.edu/ch2.html. (Accessed May 15, 2013).

29. "Waiver of Posting, § 3.D," *Administrative Guide Memo 22.1, Recruiting and Hiring of Regular Staff* (2012), http://adminguide.stanford.edu/22_1.pdf. (Accessed May 15, 2013).

30. University of Minnesota, "Recruitment and Selection of Faculty and Academic Professional and Administrative Employees," (2013), http://policy.umn.edu/Policies/hr/Hiring/RE-CRUITFACPA.html. (Accessed May 6, 2013).

31. "Oxford Dictionaries Online," Oxford University Press, http://oxforddictionaries.com/ ?attempted=true. (Accessed April 25, 2012).

32. "Merriam Webster Dictionary," Merriam-Webster, Incorporated, http://www.merriam-webster.com/dictionary/. (Accessed April 25, 2012).

33. Patrick Marley, "Lawmaker Accuses UW's Reilly of Patronage in Filling Job," *Journal Sentinel* (2010), http://www.jsonline.com/news/statepolitics/96574199.html. (Accessed March 3, 2011).

34. Ibid.

35. Ibid.

36. University of Wisconsin System, "Section 6-4 Search and Screen Procedures for Chancellors, Senior Vice Presidents or Vice Presidents, Interim Appointments," *Regent Policy Documents* (2010).

37. Bruce Mildwurf, "N.C. State Chancellor Resigns," *WRAL.com*, June 8, 2009 (2010), http://www.wral.com/news/local/story/5303995/. (Accessed March 3, 2011).

38. J. Andrew Curliss, "Easley Family, Friend Forge Rewarding Bond," *newsobserver.com* October 19 (2009), http://www.newsobserver.com/2009/05/10/90575/easley-family-friend-forge-rewarding.html#storylink=misearch. (Accessed March 4, 2011).

39. "E-Mail: Easley Involved in Wife's Hiring," *WRAL.com* (2009), http://www.wral.com/news/local/politics/story/5305943/. (Accessed March 4, 2011).

40. "Easley Family, Friend Forge Rewarding Bond."

41. Ibid.

42. "Mary Easley to Start Teaching Appointment at N.C. State," *WRAL.com*, August 15 2005, http://www.wral.com/news/local/story/119212/. (Accessed March 4, 2011).

43. "Use of Public Position for Private Gain," in *North Carolina State Government Ethics Act §138A-31.* (2006).

44. Erin Hartness, "UNC Board of Governors Approves Pay Raise for First Lady," *WRAL.com*, September 12, 2008, http://www.wral.com/news/state/story/3533482/. (Accessed July 26, 2014).

45. Paul Fain, "Scandal at N.C. State Exposes Dark Side of Politically Connected Trustees," *Chronicle of Higher Education* (2009), http://chronicle.com/article/Scandal-at-NC-State-Exposes/47277/. (Accessed July 16, 2014).

46. Mildwurf, "N.C. State Chancellor Resigns."

47. Martha Waggoner, "N.C. State Terminates Mary Easley's Job," *news-record.com*, June 9, 2009, http://www.news-record.com/content/2009/06/08/article/mary_easley_fired_from_nc_state_job. (Accessed March 6, 2011).

48. "Nielsen Quits as NCSU Provost over Easley Flap," *Triangle Business Journal*, May 14, 2009, http://www.bizjournals.com/triangle/stories/2009/05/11/daily54.html. (Accessed April 25, 2012).

49. Mildwurf, "N.C. State Chancellor Resigns."

50. Fain, "Scandal at N.C. State Exposes Dark Side of Politically Connected Trustees."

51. Cullen Browder, "E-Mail: Easley Involved in Wife's Hiring," *WRAL.com*, June 8, 2009, http://www.wral.com/news/local/politics/story/5305943/. (Accessed March 6, 2011).

52. J. Andrew Curliss and Anne Blythe, "Easley Enters Plea to Felony Campaign Finance Charge," *Newsobserver.com*, November 23, 2010, http://www.newsobserver.com/search_results?&sf_pubsys_story_keywords=privilege%20mike. (Accessed March 6, 2011).

53. Sarah Nightingale and Shelly Gonzales, "First Hispanic AG to Teach at Tech," *Lubbock Avalanche-Journal*, July 7, 2009, http://lubbockonline.com/stories/070709/loc_460926283.shtml. (Accessed March 6, 2011).

54. Sally Logue Post, "Alberto Gonzales Brings Expertise, Experience to Texas Tech," *Texas Tech University News*, July 7, 2009, http://today.ttu.edu/2009/07/alberto-gonzales-brings-expertise-experience-to-texas-tech/. (Accessed March 7, 2011).

55. Nightingale and Gonzales, "First Hispanic AG to Teach at Tech."

56. Randy Cohen, "Should Texas Tech Employ Alberto Gonzales?," *New York Times* (2009), http://ethicist.blogs.nytimes.com/2009/08/31/should-texas-tech-employ-alberto-gonzales/. (Accessed March 6, 2011).

57. Texas Tech Faculty, "Faculty Petition Regarding the Hiring of Alberto Gonzales," (2009), http://webpages.acs.ttu.edu. (Accessed March 7, 2011).

58. Steven Lee Myers and Philip Shenon, "Embattled Attorney General Resigns," *New York Times* (2007), http://www.nytimes.com/2007/08/27/washington/27cnd-gonzales.html?_r=1. (Accessed April 25, 2012).

59. Texas Tech University Board of Regents, "Chapter 2—Administration Section 02.01 Chancellor," in *The Rules and Regulations of the Board of Regents of the Texas Tech University System* (Lubbock, TX: Texas Tech University, 2010).

60. Texas Tech University, "Exception to the Search Process for Strategic Hires, Op 32.16 Faculty Recruitment Procedure," in *Operating Policy and Procedure* (Lubbock, TX: Texas Tech University, 2010).

61. "Oxford Dictionaries Online."

62. Cohen, "Should Texas Tech Employ Alberto Gonzales?"

63. Ibid.

Chapter Nine

Exceeding Authority

EXCEEDING THE LIMITS

Axiomatically, formal authority cannot be exceeded. Therefore, an institution cannot exceed the authority granted to it in its originating document, such as a charter or statute. Likewise, individuals cannot act or make decisions unless the requisite authority has been delegated to them. This axiom pertains to authority in its broadest legal manifestations: express, implied, and inherent authority. Accordingly, formal authority is granted and delegated with the expectation that the recipient recognizes the limits to this authority and will not exceed them.

It is generally understood that authority is limited to the parameters created by the oral or written hiring agreement between the employer and the employee. For example, a provost's job description conveys authority to administer academic matters. It does not mention operations such as campus parking policies or football ticket prices. Since these operations are not inherent to the provost's job, the provost has no authority over them. Of course, like any other employee, the provost is expected to know these inherent boundaries. Any incursions by the provost into nonacademic realms of authority might be rebuffed with "mind your own business."

Is there ever an excuse for exceeding the limits of authority? As a fundamental principle, the answer is no. In that sense, exceeding the limits of authority may be likened to exceeding the speed limit. Hoping to avoid the inevitable ticket, a driver may offer excuses to the police officer: "The truck in front of me was driving erratically. I had to get around it for my own safety." Without compassion, however, the officer will most probably hand over the citation with a stern rebuke: "there is never an excuse for exceeding the speed limit." Equally impassionate, there is never an excuse for exceeding the limits of authority.

Nonetheless, some individuals by nature of their personality find it challenging to operate consistently within their specific realms of authority. Sometimes they stray beyond their boundaries. This may be unintentional or, in worse cases, deliberate. Regardless, these transgressions are inexcusable in principle. How an institution or the courts react to them depends on the specific details of the situation, of course.

LACK OF AUTHORITY

If an individual acts without authority, the limits of authority have clearly been exceeded. For example, if university regulations prohibit the use of its operating funds for food but a dean does it anyway, he has acted without authority. The requisite authority is lacking. By extension, the same applies when an individual has been granted authority of limited scope and acts beyond the limits of that authority. Expanding the example, if university operating funds can be spent on food but not alcoholic beverages, but a dean includes wine in a meal paid with these funds, he has acted without authority. Again, that specific authority is lacking.

This fundamental tenet can be expressed in agency law terms. If an agent acts without authority, the principal and the third party are not bound to each other. Thus, in the previous example, if the dean (the agent) exceeds his authority by including wine in a restaurant (third party) bill paid with university (the principal) funds, the university is not obligated to pay for the wine. However, the dean is considered to be a "false agent" and will be held liable; he must pay the restaurant for the wine. In more general terms, an agent acting without authority or exceeding its authority is liable for damages to the third party. Stated differently, by entering into a contract without authority, the agent has violated his or her fiduciary duty to the principal and is financially responsible to the principal. In addition, the agent may also be sued by the third party to the contract for fraud.

There are two caveats to these agency rules. First, the principal may honor—"ratify"—the contract, despite the agent's lack of authority. By honoring the contract, this so-called ratification binds the principal and the third party, and it relieves the agent from liability because the principal has granted the agent the de facto authority that had been lacking. This is known as "ratification authority." In the example, some university official with the appropriate authority over the use of university funds, such as a comptroller, would have to ratify the use of state funds for alcoholic beverages to relieve the dean from liability. Another example: if a student bought a computer using a university purchasing card without prior authorization, then the student is liable for the expense. But if the university uses the computer (or allows the student to use it), it has granted ratification authority, and the student is no longer liable. The university must pay the bill. Second, if the third party knew or ought to have known that the false agent was acting without authority or exceeding authority when the contract was made, the agent is not liable. Thus, if the vendor knew or suspected that the student did not have the appropriate authorization to buy a computer using a university purchasing card but sold it to him anyway, then the student is not liable. Technically, the vendor is liable. Realistically, in most situations like this, universities generally negotiate a settlement to preserve good community relations. In a best-case scenario (for the vendor, at least), the university would try to find nonrestricted funds (e.g., from an endowment) to pay the bill.

The significance of this second caveat—if the third party ought to have known that the agent lacked authority, then the agent is not liable—is well illustrated in a breach of contract dispute involving the University of Arizona, *Kaman Aerospace v. Arizona Board of Regents*.[1] This case hinged on a central precept of contract law: to be valid and enforceable, contracts (and their modifications) must be signed by someone in the institution who has authority to contractually bind the institution.[2] Conversely, contracts signed by somebody lacking authority to bind the institution are invalid and unenforceable. In that context, the University of Arizona president authorized only nine individuals (administrators) to execute written contracts on behalf of the university. And, by policy, that authority cannot be delegated further. Therefore, to be valid, any contract or contract modification must be signed by one of those nine university officials. Furthermore, Arizona law states that "persons dealing with public officers are bound, at their peril, to know the extent and limits of their power and that no right can be acquired except that predicated upon authorized acts of such officers."[3] That is, anybody doing business with the university is responsible for knowing which university officials have contract signing authority and which do not.

Within this setting, the University of Arizona entered into a "firm fixed price" contract worth $9 million with Kaman Aerospace to build a collimator for aligning telescope mirrors. The contract, which was signed by an authorized university official, contained a clause stating that "the proposal reflects a fixed price for the effort proposed. In the event that there is a modification to the work scope, a modified level of effort will be indicated in a revised scope of work to be agreed upon by the parties at the time of modification." Over a two-year period, there were eleven modifications to the contract, as university engineers changed, increased, and added work requirements exceeding those described in the original scope of work. As a result, the original terms and conditions of the contract were modified, with appropriately authorized signatures, raising the total cost to $12.8 million. But, as work continued, further design changes were made with the approval of university engineers. When Kaman submitted a bill ($6.25 million) for these additional changes, the university denied payment, claimed that these modifications to the scope of work were not approved by any university official with signing authority. At that point, Kaman stopped work on the project and filed a breach of contract lawsuit.

In its defense, the university claimed that "only a designated contracting officer of the State can bind the University" and that "Kaman has never alleged (and cannot allege) that any officially designated contracting officer ever assented to any agreement, written or otherwise, to pay Kaman more than the fixed price [$12.8 million]." Furthermore, even if additional changes to the design guidelines were documented in a written agreement prepared by the project engineers, the university was not obligated to pay for them because "no University contracting officer was ever involved in (let alone signed) the Design Guidelines [as they] were promulgated by the Steward engineers on the job site." Kaman countered: "Kaman is not saying that when these program people agreed on technical requirements, technical changes, that a price increase was automatically agreed to, automatically created. But we are saying that when technical changes were made [it] began a process that should have resulted in a contracts person ultimately agreeing on a contract modification." In other words, Kaman assumed erroneously that the engineers had the authority to approve design modifications and that, as a matter of procedure, appropriately authorized university officials would follow up and ratify agreements made by the engineers. This erroneous assumption proved to be a costly mistake. Citing Arizona state law requiring Kaman to know the scope of authority of any university official when entering an agreement, the court ruled against Kaman, denying its breach of contract claim; Kaman ought to have known that the university engineers lacked signing authority. Thus, without authorized signatures approving the additional design changes and costs, technically, there was no contract to breach.

This case clearly indicates the misunderstanding that can arise when individuals (agents) lacking authority enter into agreements binding the institution. Acting beyond the limited scope of authority can be just as disruptive as acting with no authority. The sin is the same in both situations: authority is exceeded. As a best practice, administrators and faculty members should be reminded periodically about the legal constraints on authority to enter agreements on behalf of the university.

During the course of routine administration, circumstances may encourage slipping beyond the limits of authority as an expediency. Unfortunately, that can have unpleasant consequences. An anecdote illustrates this point. In a remarkable earmark orchestrated by the state's senior Senator, Congress appropriated $50 million in funding for a new federal wind-energy research facility. The intent expressed in appropriations committee notes was that the facility would be operated by Flagship University, which would receive the $50 million for its construction. But there was a technical obstacle to overcome. Because it was not appropriated explicitly to Flagstaff, federal procurement regulations required the funding to be awarded through a competitive bid process. And, several other universities announced their intention to compete for this prize, despite congressional intent. Facing aggressive competition, Flagstaff's vice president for research realized the need for immediate expert help in Washington, D.C. A particularly distinguished consultant agreed to a contract for $80,000. However, according to university policies, the governing board must approve any consulting contract exceeding $50,000. Getting this approval usually took up to a month, if not longer, depending on when the next board meeting was held. The vice president faced a dilemma: wait for the board's approval and risk losing the facility or sign the contract without the board's approval, thus exceeding his authority. After weighing the two options, the vice president decided to "act now and ask forgiveness later by signing the contract without prior board approval."

At their next meeting, the board was asked formally to approve the contract retroactively. This did not please several members of the board who considered the violation of policy inexcusable. In their minds, the vice president had acted without authority, thus breaching his fiduciary duty. Indeed, they charged the vice president with deceitful insubordination and threatened dismissal. One board member advised menacingly that "you should hire an attorney." All in all, it was a very unpleasant altercation. At the end of a stormy session, the board approved the contract, while continuing to admonish the vice president for acting without authority. Incidentally, several months later, with the consultant's expert guidance, Flagstaff ultimately won the facility. But this did not mollify the angry board members.

Although the vice president willfully violated board bylaws and exceeded the limits of his authority, it could be argued reasonably that he fulfilled his duty of loyalty by acting in the institution's best interests. At least, when viewed retrospectively. Contrary to several board members' opinion, the vice president had acted in good faith. If the contract had been for services outside the scope of the university's permissible activities, a so-called *ultra vires* contract, the board could not ratify it; it would be voided, which could cause legal complications. However, the scope of the contract lay within the university's permissible activities (research), so the board had the authority to approve the contract. Therefore, the vice president's actions had not placed the institution at risk. But, as the governing board reminded the vice president, there is no reasonable excuse for exceeding authority.

With the benefit of hindsight, the vice president should have made an effort to inform the board informally, through a telephone call to the board secretary or chair, about the need for immediate action on the contract. At the very least, that might have lessened the board members' anger at this transgression. In situations like this, the administrator's mantra should always be "communicate, communicate, communicate."

APPARENT AUTHORITY

By simple definition, apparent authority means authority that is "seeming real or true, but not necessarily so."[4] Stated in agency law terms, the definition of apparent authority means exactly the same thing, but it sounds devilishly more complicated: "The principal, either knowingly or even mistakenly, permits the agent or others to assume that the agent possesses authority to carry out certain actions when such authority does not, in fact, exist. If other persons believe in good faith that such authority exists, the principal remains liable for the agent's actions and cannot rely on the defense that no actual authority was granted."[5] This pertains even if the principal and purported agent never discussed the arrangement. In other words, the principal gives the agent the appearance of having authority; this constitutes apparent authority. Providing an agent a particular job title or just allowing an agent to use company business cards or email address conveys apparent authority to an agent. For example, if a dean appoints an acting departmental chair, third parties are entitled to assume that this conveys authority to do the things ordinarily entrusted to a permanent chair, such as buying office computers. By virtue of the job title, the acting chair appears to have authority. If the acting chair does not have actual authority, third-party computer vendors will not be penalized even if the university maintains that an acting chair lacks the authority to buy office computers. To the vendors, the acting chair's authority reasonably seemed to be real and true, but that was not necessarily so. The authority was apparent by virtue of the title. Thus, the university remains responsible for acts done by the agent who was exercising apparent authority—who appeared to have authority.

Although its roots lie in commercial law, apparent authority manifests itself in other settings as well. For example, the doctrine of apparent authority arose following a misunderstanding between a student and the university in *Hannington v. Trustees of the University of Pennsylvania.*[6] In this case, a PhD student at the University of Pennsylvania, Steven Hannington, agreed to plan and organize a two-day conference on behalf of the University's Energy Management and Policy Program. In exchange, the university agreed to waive his tuition. Thus, Hannington stopped paying tuition. The dispute arose three years later when the university dismissed Hannington from the PhD program for failure to pay the three years of outstanding tuition. Hannington sued the university, alleging that there was an agreement for a complete waiver of all tuition and other fees related to his PhD candidacy. The university disagreed and countersued for the outstanding tuition, other fees, and interest. Before the case went to trial, attorneys for Hannington and the university negotiated, trying to reach a settlement. After six months of negotiations, Hannington's attorney informed the university and the court that a settlement had been reached; the university agreed to waive one year's tuition, and Hannington agreed to pay the remainder. Before the final paperwork was completed, however, Hannington changed his mind, refused to sign the agreement, fired his attorney, and asked the court to restore the case for trial.

The court refused to allow a trial, holding that Hannington's original attorney had the apparent authority to settle the dispute with the university and that it was, in fact, settled. In the court's opinion, "The doctrine of apparent authority permits a settlement agreement to be enforced where a third party [the university] reasonably believes that the principal's lawyer, the agent, has the authority to settle the case." This is so even if the lawyer does not have express authority to finalize the settlement. In this case, after six months of negotiating in good faith with Hannington's attorney, the university could reasonably presume that he had the authority (i.e., the apparent authority) to negotiate the settlement. If the attorney exceeded the scope of his express authority granted by Hannington, that would be a dispute between Hannington and his attorney, which should not affect the university.[7]

As demonstrated in *Hannington*, the appearance to outsiders that an agent has been given authority by the principal is central to cases of apparent authority. This critical point can be stressed via a counter example in a case involving two professors who relied on a department chair's apparent authority to offer them tenured faculty positions, *Johns Hopkins University v. Ritter*.[8] The two professors, Samuel Ritter and Rebecca Snider, were recruited from tenured positions at Cornell and Duke, respectively, to the department of pediatrics at Johns Hopkins University, where the departmental chair, Frank Oski, assured them that they would be hired at the full professor level with tenure. Although Dr. Oski told them explicitly that their appointments had to be approved by two faculty committees, the dean, and the governing board of trustees, Drs. Ritter and Snider assumed that this would be "just a matter of rubber stamping." Therefore, they resigned their positions at Cornell and Duke and began employment at Hopkins as "visiting" professors, pending formal appointments as full professors nine months later. Unfortunately, during the intervening period, the relationships between Drs. Ritter and Snider and their professional colleagues deteriorated badly. As one colleague complained, "in nine months they have alienated most of the physicians and administrators from whom they need support to succeed." Confronted with a litany of similar complaints, the dean decided not to pursue their formal appointments or to rehire them at the conclusion of their first-year contract.

Predictably, Drs. Ritter and Snider sued the university for breach of contract. In its defense, Johns Hopkins claimed that the employment contract did not include a commitment to a full professorship and tenure and that, even if such a commitment had been made, the person negotiating the contract for the university (Dr. Oski) had no authority to make it. The court ruled that "in the recruitment process, Dr. Oski had, indeed, promised the plaintiffs that they would be employed as full Professors, that they would initially be given the interim title of Visiting Professor, that the formal process for approving their appointments as full Professors would be started promptly, and that the end result was assured." Therefore, "the issue is not whether the evidence sufficed to support the plaintiffs' view of what was promised by Dr. Oski but whether, as a matter of law, Dr. Oski had the authority to promise what they claim he promised."

At the Johns Hopkins Medical School, the awarding of tenure requires approval by the medical advisory board and, ultimately, the governing board of trustees. But, according to the court, "There is . . . no evidence whatever that the Board of Trustees or the Advisory Board of the Medical Faculty ever authorized Dr. Oski to make a commitment on their behalf or even that Dr. Oski had ever sought such authority or discussed the matter with either body." The court continued:

> What, then, was the source of Dr. Oski's authority to bind the Advisory Board or the Board of Trustees to a "rubber stamp" procedure, to an abdication of their duties to make an objective and reasonable investigation and to exercise their honest judgment? It surely cannot be any notion of apparent authority. Apparent authority exists when the words or conduct of *the principal* [the Board of Trustees] cause the third party to believe that the principal consents to or has authorized the conduct of the agent. . . . As noted, there were no such words or conduct by anyone other than Dr. Oski in this case. There is no evidence that anyone at Hopkins in rank above Dr. Oski had even met Drs. Ritter and Snider or were aware of the negotiations prior to their conclusion, much less said or did anything to lead them to believe that Dr. Oski was authorized to promise tenure.

Thus, the court concluded that Dr. Oski had no authority—express or apparent—to make an effective commitment of tenure and that Drs. Ritter and Snider had no reasonable basis for believing that he did. Thus, Drs. Ritter and Snider lost the case. As a comment, the court noted: "The prevailing rule is that, when a tenure process is established in writing and is communicated to a prospective appointee, a subordinate official may not circumvent that process and bind the college."

ESTOPPEL

The court considered one final legal aspect of the *Hopkins* case, namely estoppel. The verb form "estop" derives from "stop up," "plug," "impede."[9] The noun form "estoppel" refers to a legal doctrine that precludes (stops) a person from denying the truth of a statement that he has previously asserted; it prevents a person from making conflicting testimonies that would materially change the outcome of a case or harm another person. Or, as the dictionary puts it: "the principle which precludes a person from asserting something contrary to what is implied by a previous action or statement of that person or by a previous pertinent judicial determination."[10] Thus, in *Hopkins*, an estoppel would have arisen if the university had somehow conveyed to Drs. Ritter and Snider that Dr. Oski actually had authority to offer tenured professorships but then later asserted that he did not when Drs. Ritter and Snider relied on that conveyance.

The court rejected that possibility of an estoppel.

> Like apparent authority, an agency by estoppel can arise only where the principal [the university], through words or conduct, represents that the agent [the dean] has authority to act and the third party [Drs. Ritter and Snider] *reasonably* relies on those representations. . . . In light of the written correspondence between Drs. Ritter and Oski on this very issue and the lack of any representation—written, oral, or by conduct—on the part of anyone on the Advisory Board or the Board of Trustees that the established written procedure for obtaining tenure would or could be effectively waived, it was clearly not reasonable, as a matter of law, for Drs. Ritter or Snider to believe that Dr. Oski had any authority whatever to bind Hopkins to a promise of tenure.

In other words, nobody at Johns Hopkins ever claimed that the dean could waive the required board approval of an offer of tenure. So, it was unreasonable for Drs. Ritter and Snider to rely on the assumption that he could. Thus, there was no estoppel. Reasonable reliance is the critical element in this situation.

Hypothetically, this case could have ended quite differently if the university had, indeed, given the impression that Dr. Oski possessed the authority to offer tenured professorships. Then, Dr. Ritter's and Dr. Snider's reliance on the dean's presumed authority, which ultimately proved to be quite detrimental to their careers, would have raised the legal concept of a specific type of estoppel known as promissory estoppel and the related concept of detrimental reliance. Their potential seriousness deserves more formal consideration.

PROMISSORY ESTOPPEL

Promissory estoppel arises when a contract-like promise is made but not kept. More specifically, this legal doctrine allows for enforcement of a promise despite the lack of a formal enforceable contract because one party has relied on the promise of the other and it would be unfair not to enforce the agreement. Stated differently, the doctrine of promissory estoppel prevents (estops) one person from reneging on a promise made to a second person if the second person has reasonably relied on that promise and acted upon it. As a matter of fairness, judges seek to identify and to remedy situations where promises or statements could lead to injustice. Therefore, to enforce a promise made by one person to another under the theory of promissory estoppel, the claimant normally has to prove three requirements: (1) there was a promise; (2) there was reasonable reliance on that promise that put the claimant in a position of detriment—that is, there was "detrimental reliance"; and (3) if the promise is not enforced, there will be an injustice.

Detrimental reliance is a key element of promissory estoppel. It derives conceptually from the Roman principle that "no one is allowed to go against the consequences of his own acts." Technically, detrimental reliance differs from promissory estoppel. An estoppel is a specific cause for action; "I want to recover on the basis of promissory estoppel—I relied to my detriment on a promise made to me." In contrast, detrimental reliance is not a cause for action unless it is in the context of a promissory estoppel; an individual cannot recover on simple detrimental reliance on something that has no promised outcome, such as a weather forecast, a stock-market hunch, or a horse-racing tip.

To understand promissory estoppel and detrimental reliance, it helps pedagogically to examine them in context. Since most court cases often have confounding legal issues, detrimental reliance will be illustrated initially in its simplest form via a hypothetical anecdote. At a time of budgetary turmoil due to an abrupt reduction in state support, Provost M. announced an emergency hiring freeze on all faculty and staff positions "until further notice." Thus, Provost M. was startled several weeks later when the head librarian submitted paperwork to hire a new reference librarian. In better times, this would be a routine appointment. But not now; it contravened the hiring freeze. So, the provost returned the paperwork without approval, adding the comment: "I'm sorry, but under the circumstances, you do not have the authority to make an offer."

About one month later, the provost's office received a letter from a lawyer demanding that the university honor its job offer to the candidate. As the attorney declaimed, the head librarian and the candidate had agreed on the terms of employment in a series of email exchanges. Therefore, the candidate had accepted the head librarian's offer in good faith and resigned from his previous institution. But the head librarian then rescinded the offer after the provost had not approved it. According to the attorney, there was a lot at stake, for the candidate would incur significant financial losses if the offer were not honored. These included the loss of future salary and pension benefits from the previous institution. Reflexively, the letter was forwarded to the chief legal counsel. In the provost's mind, the defense was simple: the head librarian lacked the authority to make the job offer and, therefore, had not tendered a binding formal commitment.

Unfortunately, the university's chief counsel didn't agree that it was so simple. As devil's advocate, the chief counsel argued that the candidate was unaware of the hiring freeze. Consequently, the candidate fully trusted the head librarian's authority to make the offer via the email exchanges. Relying on that apparent authority proved to be detrimental after the head librarian reneged, because the candidate was now without a job. In legal terms, this was a clear case of detrimental reliance. Moreover, the chief counsel explained that although there isn't a formal contract, the courts would probably invoke the doctrine of promissory estoppel because the candidate had relied detrimentally on the head librarian's presumed authority and it would be unfair not to enforce the agreement under these conditions.

Taking a closer look, was this really a compelling case of detrimental reliance warranting promissory estoppel? Yes. Each of the necessary conditions was clearly met in this anecdotal case. Indeed, it is a classic example of detrimental reliance when the employer makes a verbal offer of employment, the employee resigns from a current job in reliance on the offer, and then the employer withdraws the offer. As the chief counsel advised the provost, it doesn't necessarily matter if a formal offer letter has not been issued; an administrator with apparent authority, such as the head librarian, could make an informal offer that may be judged enforceable in the courts. Thus, the principle of promissory estoppel imposes a real-world limit to the provost's authority to control the hiring process.

In this case of detrimental reliance, the candidate might not recover future wages and benefits lost because the offer was rescinded but could probably recover some wages and benefits lost due to resignation from the previous employer—plus legal fees. Therefore, extending this hypothetical example, on the chief counsel's advice, the provost decided to honor the job offer. "After all," concluded the provost, "I don't know how much the courts might award in damages. It could be hundreds of thousands of dollars. But I do know how much the candidate will earn as a reference librarian. It's not that much, and at least the institution will get some return on its expenses." The issue could have been argued in court, but that would certainly become very expensive. As often occurs, the decision was to accept a settlement with known costs rather than enter into a prolonged contest with indeterminate costs.

Incidentally, the courts in different states have split on whether an offer of an "at-will" appointment can support a promissory estoppel claim. However, a common argument is that reliance on an at-will job offer could never be reasonable, because a promise to provide employment which is subject to termination at any time or for any reason does not provide any assurances about the employer's future conduct. The job offer could be terminated without cause at any time, even before the applicant starts work; if the employer could fire the employee after one minute on the job, the employer could presumably terminate a job offer before the employee's actual start date. Indeed, one Texas court has ruled that there "is no distinction between termination of employment before starting work and termination after employment has commenced."[11] It should be pointed out, however, that not all courts agree with this strong assertion and consider claims for promissory estoppel in situations like this. Usually, faculty members are not appointed at will, so this does not apply to them. However, most mid- and upper-level administrators are appointed at-will and may be affected by this caveat.

In the courts, detrimental reliance has arisen in scenarios involving contract-like arrangements concerning grades, degrees, and admissions. A textbook case arose in *Blank v. Board of Higher Education of the City of New York*.[12] The plaintiff, Errol Blank, was enrolled at Brooklyn College in a traditional course of study leading to the bachelor of arts (BA) degree. Because his goal was to attend law school, Blank took an interest in the college's professional option plan. It allows a student who needs fewer than thirty-two credits in electives to graduate and who has, in addition, completed one year as a full-time student in an approved law school, to be eligible for the BA degree "provided that the courses offered in fulfilment of the requirements for the degree, including courses completed in the law school, constitute, in the opinion of the Dean of the Faculty, an acceptable program for the BA degree." This program would enable Blank to begin law school in Syracuse before he had finished all of his coursework at Brooklyn and to use some of the law school courses to satisfy the BA requirements. But, before heading off to law school, Blank was advised that he would have to take two remaining psychology courses to satisfy degree requirements in his major, psychology, at Brooklyn. The psychology department head assured Blank that each of the courses could be taken without attending classes if the instructors agreed. They did, so Blank registered for the courses, arranged with the professors for the reading of the necessary material, and, after taking the examination required by each of them, passed each of the courses with a "B."

Two years later, after the relevant law school courses had been accepted under the professional option plan, Blank attended his graduation expecting to receive a BA from Brooklyn. However, he discovered that his name was not in the commencement program. Later, he learned that his degree was denied because he had not completed all course requirements—the two psychology courses—"in attendance." None of his administrative appeals was successful (he exhausted remedies), so Blank filed a lawsuit seeking conferral of the degree based on detrimental reliance.

The college argued that "only the dean of the faculty had the authority to determine a student's eligibility for the professional option plan and that the dean had not exercised such authority regarding the plaintiff. The college further argued that the dean had devised regulations concerning the professional option plan and that these regulations contained residence requirements that the student had not met."[13] According to Blank, he asked for assistance at the office of the dean of the faculty but was referred to the office of guidance and counselling. The court had no reason to doubt this assertion, concluding that this would appear to be standard procedure in an academic institution with more than ten thousand students.

Ultimately, the court ruled in Blank's favor. It surmised that "the chairman of the department of psychology and the two professors who taught the courses in question surely had authority to determine, as they did, the appropriate manner in which the courses should be taken by petitioner, within the published regulations. Petitioner acted in obvious reliance upon the counsel and advice of members of the staff of the college administration to whom he was referred and who were authorized to give him such counsel and advice." Furthermore, the court noted that "The dean of faculty may not escape the binding effect of the acts of his agents performed within the scope of their apparent authority, and the consequences that must equitably follow therefrom. Having given permission to take the subject courses in the manner prescribed, through his agents [the guidance counsellor, the Psychology department chair, and the two professors] . . . he cannot, in the circumstances, later assert that the courses should have been taken in another manner." Thus, all of the elements of an estoppel exist, including detrimental reliance. Blank had relied to his detriment on the apparent authority of college counselors and professors. Accordingly, since he had taken and passed the two required psychology courses, the court directed Brooklyn College to award the BA degree to Blank.

As *Blank* demonstrated, administrators must exercise caution when counseling students about unusual arrangements because of potential detrimental reliance resulting from misunderstandings A counter-example, *Grove v. Ohio State University*, further illustrates this need for caution in the context of admissions.[14] After his application for admission to the Ohio State University College of Veterinary Medicine had been rejected for a third time, an undergraduate student, Jack Grove, filed a lawsuit against the university claiming, among other things, detrimental reliance on promises made by members of the admissions committee. The first rejection was ostensibly because he lacked five quarter hours of elective courses. Afterward, a professor on the committee who had seemed quite encouraging during an admissions committee interview, Robert Hamlin, sent Grove a letter stating that: "If you can arrange to complete the above courses next year and wish to apply for the 1974 entering class, please let us know. We will then send you the necessary forms to reapply to the College of Veterinary Medicine." The next year, Grove's application was rejected again. Subsequently, Grove asked a member of the admissions committee, Walter Venske, why he was rejected and what corrective actions he might take. Dr. Venske told Grove that he should take additional courses in animal science to improve his chances for admission. However, he gave no indication that taking these courses would guarantee admission. So, following that advice, Grove applied unsuccessfully for a third time. This time the college gave no reasons for the rejection.

Under the doctrine of promissory estoppel, Grove claimed detrimental reliance. He relied to his detriment upon representations allegedly made during his first two interviews. Had these representations not been made, he would have abandoned hopes of a career in veterinary medicine and entered a different field. In fact, Grove ultimately went to law school.

The court ruled against Grove. It saw no promissory element in Professor Hamlin's letter. However, it did acknowledge a promissory element in Dr. Venzke's recommendation to take additional animal science courses after the second rejection. "Since Dr. Venzke was a member of the admissions committee, and since plaintiff was clearly approaching him to ascertain what was necessary to obtain the admission which he had only recently been denied, this Court concludes that Venzke could reasonably have expected his statements to induce plaintiff to take additional courses in animal science." However, the court dismissed that acknowledgment of promissory estoppel because Grove failed to establish that "injustice can be avoided only by enforcement of the promise." In fact, it added that Grove "utilized his Ohio State degree to gain an admission to the University of Dayton Law School. The additional courses which plaintiff took after Venzke's representation were included in that degree, and can hardly be considered detrimental." Consequently, the university prevailed. To exaggerate only slightly, this case makes the colloquial point that when fighting the university in court on academic issues: "you seldom win."

DELIBERATE EXCEEDANCE

Unfortunately, just like the driver who pays no attention to speed limits, some individuals pay little attention to the limits of their authority, knowingly exceeding them. Intentional disregard for the limits of authority can range from relatively benign transgressions to malicious criminal actions. At either extreme, it betrays disrespect for the organizational distribution of authority and, in some cases, the rule of law. As a core principle, of course, intentional disregard for the limits of authority must be stopped because of its disruption. Furthermore, flagrant disrespect for the limits of authority can also become very costly to an institution.

At the benign extreme, an individual may simply break the rules, hoping to "get away with it." This was illustrated earlier in the anecdote about the vice president who knowingly exceeded his authority to negotiate an $80,000 contract. A far more common transgression involves university parking regulations. The number of parking permits available for specific lots on campus is usually limited to ensure that each permit holder for a particular lot has a reasonable probability of finding a spot. Accordingly, a university parking permit authorizes the holder to park only in a particular lot on campus. However, for a variety of easily imagined reasons (such as making a delivery, picking up a package, or returning a library book), an individual may park deliberately in an unauthorized lot. This type of transgression may preclude a legitimate permit holder from finding a parking spot in that lot, so it cannot be tolerated. Thus, university policies call for issuing a parking ticket or even towing away the unauthorized vehicle.

At the malicious extreme, individuals may commit a crime by overstepping their authority. Unfortunately, universities are not exempt from instances of fraudulent accounting, theft, misuse of grant funds, and other illegal and unlawful acts that go beyond the limits of authority. In those situations, individuals may take advantage of apparent authority and commit the institution to some course of action beneficial to them. Once discovered, the cases are generally referred to legal counsel, for they usually involve criminal charges. At the very least, they violate the employees' duty of loyalty to the organization.

Deliberately exceeding the limits of authority may accompany insubordination. For example, an employee may not agree with a decision and then, "taking matters into his own hands," deliberately exceed his authority through actions designed to countermand the decision. Although laws may not be broken, these situations cannot be tolerated. Their disruptive and costly consequences can be analyzed further in an anecdote.

Several years ago, an enterprising dean at Flagship University, Dean B., prepared an application to the National Science Foundation (NSF) for a large, multimillion dollar engineering research center. These prestigious centers "promote partnerships among researchers in different disciplines and between industry and universities. They focus on integrated engineered systems and produce technological innovations that strengthen the competitive position of industry."[15] Thus, the proposal entailed the participation of numerous faculty members across the campus and at partnering universities and private businesses. The competition for an NSF engineering research center award is very stiff, so Dean B. dedicated considerable personal effort to help assemble a competitive proposal. It was a major undertaking, but it would certainly be worth the effort if the grant were funded. The center would bring in about $3 million per year for at least five years plus immeasurable personal and institutional prestige.

As part of the proposal, the NSF required the lead institution, Flagship University, to share in the cost of the center.[16] In this particular application, the cost-sharing requirement was $1 million. Among other considerations, this cost-sharing requirement ensured that the applicant institutions had a vested interest in the center. As a corollary, a wealthy institution could voluntarily promise cost-sharing contributions generously exceeding the required amount with the hope of persuading reviewers that it could provide a more supportive environment for an engineering research center. To eliminate this mercenary component from the review process, current NSF policy caps the maximum cost-sharing allowed, thus prohibiting voluntary cost-sharing above the required amount. Furthermore, details of the cost-sharing amounts are not made available to the proposal reviewers. However, at the time of Flagship's proposal, voluntary cost-sharing was unlimited, and the details were known to the reviewers. Therefore, ostensibly to strengthen the proposal, Dean B. wanted to volunteer very generous cost-sharing on behalf of the university.

Like most major research institutions, Flagship generally eschewed voluntary cost sharing. As a matter of prudent fiscal policy, the university would provide the required amount of cost sharing, but no more. Dean B. asked the vice president for research for an exception to this policy: "We need to commit at least $2 million in cost sharing just to be competitive." The vice president replied adamantly "No. The NSF requires $1 million, which I will add to your budget from institutional research funds. But as a matter of long-standing policy, Flagship does not commit voluntary cost sharing." Dejected, the dean retreated.

Several months later, Dean B. received the good news. Their application was successful; Flagship would receive an NSF engineering research center award. The news spread rapidly, and everybody was elated.

Then the vice president received the bad news. At a meeting with the vice president, Dean B. announced that the NSF now wanted confirmation of the university's $2 million in cost-sharing. The startled vice president exclaimed: "Two million? I said that the university would commit one million." With a slight shrug, Dean B. explained that "I had to commit $2 million for us to be competitive. And look; it worked. We won the center." The vice president could hardly enjoy the moment. The dean had deliberately disobeyed the vice president and had overstepped the limits of his authority by committing an additional $1 million in voluntary cost-sharing, thus insubordinately defying both the vice president's orders and the university's cost-sharing policies.

The vice president was in a quandary. Flagship University had won an unquestionably prestigious award. It would be foolish to turn it down just because of Dean B.'s insubordination; among other obvious considerations, that could weaken the university's chances of getting subsequent awards from NSF. The vice president decided to "make the most of it" and issued a press release congratulating the dean on this major accomplishment. However, a big issue hovered ominously in the vice president's thoughts: how to discipline the dean for such insubordination? Over the years, Dean B. had been very successful in building the institution's reputation and in attracting grants and gifts to the school. Few deans had matched this performance. Furthermore, the vice president wondered silently whether Dean B. had been right: maybe the extra $1 million made the difference between getting and not getting an award. That thought was quickly quashed. "That's not the point. I can't allow the dean to get away with this. If I let it go, the dean will just be encouraged to ignore the rules again and again."

With few other realistic disciplinary options, the vice president for research turned this personnel matter over to Provost M., who wrote a letter sternly rebuking Dean B. with a warning never to do that again. As further punishment, Provost M. insisted that the $1 million in extra, voluntary cost-sharing would be provided as a loan to the college budget. The college, and therefore the dean, would be required to pay it back to the provost, with 5 percent interest, out of the college's operating budget over a five-year period. Hopefully, that would discourage the dean from ever exceeding the limits of his authority again. When the dean was told about this financial arrangement, Provost M. detected what appeared to be a slight grin on the dean's face.

In the eyes of many observers, it appears that the dean insubordinately exceeded the limits of authority and got away with it. Provost M. had meted out a financial penalty to the college but not to the dean personally. To punish Dean B personally, following conventional progressive discipline, the dean was given a reprimand warning him not to exceed authority again. Realistically, however, Provost M. knew from past experience that this would have little effect on a powerful, successful dean. To say that "I'll put a letter in your file" would simply evoke an arrogant smirk. The only meaningful punishment for this particular infraction would be to fire the dean forthwith. However, the provost was understandably reluctant to dismiss an eminently successful dean such as Dean B. In these circumstances, the loss would not balance the gain. Of course, if the provost had been waiting for an excuse to fire the dean, this would be the ideal opportunity. But that was not the case this time. Thus, the many observers were basically right: the dean exceeded the limits of authority in this case, and the provost could do little about it.

The anecdote cannot end with that pessimistic, hopeless conclusion. Intentional flouting of the limits cannot be tolerated. Significantly in this case, the provost initiated progressive discipline with the reprimand and warning letter. If the errant dean exceeds the limits of authority again, for whatever reason, the provost should take a second step in progressive discipline, such as a brief (e.g., two weeks) suspension from the dean's position or reassignment from the dean's position to the faculty. The reassignment is comparable to firing the dean, which is inevitable if he continues to exceed the limits of authority intentionally.

A final technicality merits attention. How could the dean override the vice president for research and make the commitment? After all, the grant proposal was submitted formally by the Office of Sponsored Projects, which reports to the vice president for research. And, they require a letter from the vice president documenting any cost sharing. In this case, which is based on a real situation, human error was involved. The vice president's formal letter committing one million dollars was on file. Shortly before the submission deadline, however, the dean pushed through the change, claiming that a "last-minute decision had been made to increase the university's cost-sharing." Under pressure to meet the deadline, an inexperienced sponsored projects officer wrongly assumed that the dean had the apparent authority to change the vice president's commitment from one to two million dollars. In agency law terms, the dean (the agent) had falsely committed the principal (the university) to provide goods (two million dollars) to a third party (the principal investigator, via the NSF). The dean was a false agent.

Unlike this example, in an academic setting, most cases involving lack of authority or apparent authority do not involve malicious intentions on the part of university administrators. They arise primarily from misunderstandings about the actual limits of authority, with no intentions to deceive colleagues or students. For these reasons, most cases of misused or misunderstood authority in academia never end up in the courts. They are either tolerated or resolved "in-house." Nonetheless, these cases that never make it to the courts can have a disruptive impact on institutional administration, as the following situations illustrate.

UNINTENTIONAL MISTAKES DUE TO INEXPERIENCE

Commonly, unintentional transgressions occur due to inexperience. Limitations on an individual's authority may go unrecognized amid the blur of unfamiliar responsibilities and opportunities associated with a new job. Or, they may not be well understood due to inadequate preparation for the new job. A newcomer's mistakes in this regard are generally tolerated during the "honeymoon period," although tolerance can vanish abruptly if the mistake is not recognized by the offender.

In an academic setting, an enthusiastic rookie administrator may lose conscious awareness of the standard conventions of shared governance and single-handedly launch a new program or recruit a new faculty member without appropriate consultation. An anecdote illustrates the ease of over-stepping the limits of authority inadvertently. The case occurred shortly after Flagship University appointed a new vice president for research. Although he had been chair of the medical school's Stem Cell Research Laboratory for several years, this was his first senior administrative position. At the time of the appointment, the university's geosciences center, which reported to the vice president, was floundering. Its longtime director had stepped down two years earlier, and the search for a successor had not yielded a replacement. After studying the situation, the vice president concluded that a former class-mate and good friend, Professor R., would be an ideal director of the center. Professor R. was a distinguished geoscientist at a prominent East Coast uni-versity and a member of the National Academy of Sciences. Moreover, Pro-fessor R. was contemplating retirement and had expressed an eagerness to move to a warmer climate. Therefore, the vice president invited Professor R. to visit the center and suggest plans for improving its reputation. After an enjoyable dinner discussing Professor R.'s ideas, the vice president popped the question: "What would it take to entice you to accept the position as director of the geosciences center?" After a discussion about startup funds, remodeling research space, and resources to hire several new researchers, a deal was struck: "You're hired." A press release announcing the appointment was scheduled for a week later.

Shortly before the news release, the vice president met with the center faculty members to announce this joyous recruitment. But then, reality raised its unsightly head. Surprisingly, after the announcement, nobody smiled. In fact, the first question raised a disturbing point: "Why weren't we con-sulted?" And another: "Who were the other candidates?" The questioning ensued until the vice president clearly understood that there was little faculty support for this appointment, regardless of Professor R.'s stellar credentials. That evening the truth became evident: "What was I doing? I made a big mistake." Although unintentional, disregarding the standard consultation process was anathema to the university's academic heritage. Moreover, it went beyond the limits of authority, for it did not conform to university policy that mandates a consultative search process for administrative and faculty appointments at this level. But it was too late to turn back; the offer had been made and accepted. Furthermore, the vice president could not com-fortably apologize to the faculty members, because that would undermine Professor R.'s functional authority as the incoming center director. A mistake had been made unintentionally, and it could not be corrected. At the very least, the vice president had learned a lesson that would not soon be forgot-ten.

In this case, the novice vice president had simply overlooked the need to follow generic search procedures. This was not necessarily a deliberate attempt to circumvent the rules. It resulted most probably from the novelty of newfound power; suddenly the vice president had unaccustomed authority and had not yet learned to recognize its limits. This is analogous to the young automobile driver who has discovered the accelerator but not the brake pedal. The extent of tolerance for this kind of mistake depends, of course, on the setting. Medical schools, for example, have a much less developed tradition of faculty governance than colleges of arts and sciences. It would not necessarily be unusual for a medical school dean to appoint a clinical-center director with minimal faculty involvement. Nevertheless, regardless of the academic culture, the limits of authority must be learned, if not the "hard way" then through mentoring from a more experienced colleague.

Incidentally, had the vice president honored standard search procedures, consultation via a search committee comprised primarily of faculty members would carry the risk that the committee might put forth some other candidate instead of Professor R. That would leave two choices: reject their nomination or unhappily accept their recommendation. For the vice president, neither option is desirable. To minimize the chances of encountering this dilemma, the usual tactic is to request a list of three or four unranked nominees—all acceptable to the faculty members—from which the vice president will choose one, with the hope that Professor R. would be included in this larger pool. If none of them is acceptable, the vice president can ask the search committee for additional nominees. These are standard search and selection strategies in most institutions, and they should have been followed in this case.

PREMATURE ASSERTION OF AUTHORITY

Newly hired individuals may presume to have authority before the actual starting date of the new appointment. They may issue orders, policy statements, and so forth prematurely before having the requisite formal authority. Whether out of exuberance or less innocuous political maneuvering, this is inappropriate, for it undermines the incumbent's authority. Despite "lame-duck" status, the incumbent is still accountable for the responsibilities of the job. The premature directives may send conflicting and potentially confusing information to colleagues and subordinate employees. If something goes wrong as a result, the incumbent and not the newcomer will be held accountable.

The disruptive impact of premature authority can be demonstrated anecdotally. At the beginning of the academic year, the dean of Flagship University's Medical School announced that he would retire in ten months, on June

30 of the next year. Presumably, this would allow time for the search and selection of a successor, thus enabling a smooth transition in leadership. Fortunately, the search went smoothly and culminated in the recruitment of a successor, Dr. Q., in mid-April, with a start date of July 1. An eminent surgeon at a prestigious university, Dr. Q. had several years of experience as department chair and, importantly, director of his university's clinical practice plan. Since Flagship's clinical practice plan was not operating profitably, it was hoped that Dr. Q. (soon to be Dean Q.) could lead its reorganization.

Dr. Q. relished this opportunity. Indeed, shortly after the announcement of his appointment, Dr. Q. sent an email to all clinical faculty members outlining a detailed strategy for revamping the practice plan. This involved: merging or closing some clinics; revising faculty work assignments; changing salary incentives; and renegotiating hospital contracts. Moreover, he appointed a committee to begin implementation of these objectives. Predictably, the proposed changes spawned uncertainty, anxiety, and opposition from many quarters—affected faculty members, competing clinics, politicians, and many others. None of this troubled Dr. Q., who proceeded with directives to Flagship faculty members and staff.

However, all of this greatly troubled the incumbent dean. Amidst the confusion and consternation resulting from Dr. Q.'s aggressive email missives, clinical personnel morale dropped precipitously. The dean assured the department chairs, hospital executives, clinic directors, and others that no changes would take effect until Dr. Q.'s strategic plan had been well vetted and broadly endorsed. But, as a lame duck, his assurances received a lukewarm reception. The response was basically "Why should we listen to you? In several months, you'll be gone. We have to start building our relationships with Dr. Q. right now. Otherwise, it will be too late."

Consequently, the medical school and its affiliated clinics stalled in a holding pattern. The incumbent dean's authority was effectively neutralized as all attention now focused on the incoming successor. However, Dr. Q. did not yet have the formal authority to implement any planned changes. In fact, he didn't have the authority to begin the formal consultation process needed to gain acceptance of his plans. That would all have to wait until his official start date on July 1. In a sense, the school entered a state of Brownian motion; there was lots of activity, but it went nowhere.

As in this anecdotal case, when incoming administrators (such as Dr. Q.) assume authority prematurely, the incumbents face a dilemma. There are three fundamental options: simply ignore the problem ("I'm leaving soon, anyway"), ask the newcomer to stop ("wait until I'm gone"), or inform their supervisor ("the newcomer is making things difficult for me"). Like so many complex situations, there is no universally correct answer. However, the most probable reaction among seasoned administrators would be to ignore the problem. The difficult period would pass. The least effective reaction would be to inform the supervisor, who, presumably, would not want to confront a newly selected employee unless the premature actions cause demonstrably egregious complications.

SUMMARY

Axiomatically, formal authority cannot be exceeded. Therefore, an institution cannot exceed the authority granted to it in the originating document, such as a charter or statute. Likewise, individuals cannot act or make decisions unless the requisite authority has been delegated to them. In agency law, if an agent (e.g., a dean) acts without authority, the principal (e.g., the university), and the third party (e.g., a vendor) are not bound to each other; an agent acting without authority or exceeding its authority is liable for damages to the third party. Apparent authority arises when the principal gives an agent the appearance of having authority; providing an agent a particular job title or just allowing an agent to use company business cards or email address conveys apparent authority on an agent. If other persons believe in good faith that such authority exists, the principal remains liable for the agent's actions and cannot rely on the defense that no actual authority was granted. Estoppel refers to a legal doctrine that precludes persons from denying the truth of a statement that they had previously asserted. Promissory estoppel arises when a contract-like promise is made but not kept. It allows for enforcement of a promise despite the lack of a formal contract because one party has relied on the promise of the other and it would be unfair not to enforce the agreement. Detrimental reliance occurs when an individual relies to his detriment on a promise. Unintentionally exceeding authority usually occurs due to inexperience. Newly hired individuals may presume to have authority before the actual starting date of the new appointment, issuing orders, policy statements, and so forth prematurely before having the requisite formal authority. Whether out of exuberance or less innocuous political maneuvering, this is inappropriate, for it undermines the incumbent's authority.

NOTES

1. *Kaman Aerospace v. Arizona Board of Regents*, 171 P.3d 599 (Ariz. Ct. App., Div. II) (2007).

2. William A. Kaplin and Barbara A. Lee, *The Law of Higher Education*, 5th ed. (San Francisco: Jossey-Bass, 2013), 1882.

3. *Kaman Aerospace v. Arizona Board of Regents*.

4. "Oxford Dictionaries Online," Oxford University Press, http://oxforddictionaries.com/ ?attempted=true. (Accessed February 26, 2014).

5. The Free Dictionary, "Agency," *West's Encyclopedia of American Law* (2008), http:// legal-dictionary.thefreedictionary.com/agency. (Accessed February 14, 2014).

6. *Hannington v. Trustees of the University of Pennsylvania*, 809 A.2d 406 (2002).

7. South-Western CENGAGE Learning, "Third Party May Rely on Apparent Authority of Agent to Enter into Binding Contract," SW Legal Studies in Business, http://www.swlearning. com/blaw/cases/agency/0303_agency_01.html. (Accessed February 24, 2014).

8. *Johns Hopkins University v. Ritter*, 689 A.2d 91(Md. Ct. Spec. App.) (1996).

9. "Oxford Dictionaries Online."

10. Ibid.

11. *Talford v. Columbia Medical Center at Lancaster Subsidiary LP*, 198 S.W. 3d 462 (Tex. App.—Dallas, no pet.) (2006).

12. *Blank v. Board of Higher Education of the City of New York*, 273 N.Y.S. 2d 796 (N.Y. App. Div.) (1966).

13. William A. Kaplin and Barbara A. Lee, *The Law of Higher Education*, 4th ed. (San Francisco: Jossey-Bass, 2006), 209.

14. *Grove v. Ohio State University*, 424 F. Supp. 377 (S.D. Ohio) (1976).

15. National Science Foundation, "Engineering Research Centers," http://www.nsf.gov/funding/pgm_summ.jsp?pims_id=5502&org=ENG. (Accessed February 12, 2014).

16. "Mandatory Cost Sharing Requirements and Policies," http://www.nsf.gov/publications/pub_summ.jsp?WT.z_pims_id=5502&ods_key=nsf11537. (Accessed April 25, 2012).

Chapter Ten

Intrusive Management

QUESTIONS OF COMPETENCE: MICROMANAGEMENT

Effective administration requires well-recognized lines of authority that indicate clearly who's in charge. Ideally, in a perfect world, authority is delegated and that's that; the lines of authority are defined crisply. After authority has been transferred from one individual to another—from a superior to a subordinate—the superior entrusts the subordinate to manage the new responsibilities without interference. The subordinate is now clearly in charge of the delegated responsibility. Unfortunately, this idealized delegation can break down now and then, with the superior flouting the delegation and interfering with the subordinate's management. If the delegated authority has been usurped, conflicting orders and confusing responsibilities can disrupt even the most organized bureaucracy. Thus, when lines of authority become blurred, the question arises: "Who's in charge here?" It's bad when that is a good question.

A symptomatic breakdown occurs when the superior doubts an employee's competence. The root causes include mistrust, disrespect, emotional insecurity, and other factors that fall into a psychologist's domain. Logically, the question arises: "why did you delegate authority to somebody you don't trust?" Rational answers to this question may be quite elusive; they, too, may dwell in the psychologist's realm. Regardless of their origin, these doubts and their consequences may engender disruption of the managerial structure.

Micromanagement is a common corollary to questions of competence. Indeed, according to the *Wall Street Journal*, "Leadership experts say micromanagers—from small-business owners to managers in large organizations—share an unwillingness to trust subordinates."[1] Micromanagement is manifest as intrusive attention to activities that had been formally delegated to a subordinate. And, usually, this manifestation extends to ostensibly small details. All of this can be quite annoying to the affected employees and can erode morale. If the micromanager openly challenges the subordinate's authority with regularity, "who's in charge" becomes a good question that can potentially erode public confidence in an organization. In contrast, however, if the micromanager kibitzes "behind closed doors," so to speak, but leaves intact the subordinate's authority to announce and to enforce decisions, the disruption is generally contained. Although the subordinate's actual authority is compromised, the reporting lines remain intact to third-party observers, thus precluding major damage to the integrity of an organization.

Myriad publications, websites, and seminars offer advice on how to contend with a micromanaging supervisor. Tips range from documenting successes via a "paper trail" to being "super reliable."[2] These may prove effective on a case-by-case basis and certainly merit consideration by an individual affected by disruptive micromanagement. Ultimately, however, in many cases, remediation calls for replacement of the micromanaging superior or the mistrusted subordinate. Indeed, Rudolph Weingartner states this as a maxim of effective administration: "If the organizational chart is the right one, and micromanagement exists, either the supervisor or the supervised is the wrong person for the slot."[3] The extreme rule of conduct would entail elimination of the subordinate's position—let the micromanager handle the job.

OVERCAUTION

Micromanagement can occur subtly through overly cautious administration. This occurs when more than one level of the administration insists on thoroughly reviewing a decision before it is announced. For example, a supervisor insists on analyzing most or all of the data used by an employee to make a financial decision, regardless of the employee's delegated authority to make these decisions. In effect, the supervisor repeats the decision-making process. Although this extra level of review may be desirable or necessary in some situations, it can cause disruptive delays that may give the appearance of indecisiveness by the employee making the decision. An outsider might ask, "Why does it always take you so long to come up with these decisions?" Or, as Rudolph Weingartner puts it, "Such duplication of the decision-making process makes lavish use of time and personnel. Observers, though often not the participants, see the waste and wonder why they couldn't get it right in the first place."[4]

In addition to apparent indecisiveness, duplication of the decision-making process also obscures accountability and prompts reciprocal buck-passing. Again quoting Rudolph Weingartner, "Efforts on the lower level are likely to be slackened, since 'they' will make their own decision anyway. But because those higher 'theys' tacitly assume that the requisite deliberations had already taken place on the level below, their own efforts are very likely to cut corners as well."[5] He reduces this to a maxim: "Decisions obliged to be reached independently by more than one person or agency tend not to be attained responsibly by any of them."

Another example of subtle micromanagement due to overcaution occurs when higher-level authorities such as the governing board, the president, or the provost insist on previewing all communications concerning university interests prepared by lower-level administrators to ensure that they adhere accurately to university priorities. If there are deadlines for submitting materials, which is not unusual for congressional petitions or letters of support for a particular bill, shuttling documents around from one office to another for review consumes time and may cause delays that preclude getting the communication to Washington, D.C., in time to be relevant. Consequently, an institution will have sacrificed functional authority on an issue in favor of overcautious concerns about consistency of message. In this situation, complications in its own operating procedures impose constraints on institutional influence and raise concerns about indecision. Again, as an outsider might ask, "Why did it take the university so long to decide whether or not to support this legislation?"

Incidentally, in this context, insistence by higher-level administrators on previewing all decisions or communications concerning university interests may characterize mistrust of the lower-level administrators' abilities to handle the job. Indeed, as a form of micromanagement, it is diagnostic of a lack of confidence in their leadership skills. And it flouts the tenets of delegated authority. In these situations, the reasons for this untrusting micromanagement should be explored, for it undermines the university's overall administrative performance.[6]

ORGANIZATIONAL CHANGE UNDER NEW LEADERSHIP

New leadership often means new ways of doing business. Thus, when the banner above the door reads "Under new management," most observers anticipate some kind of change in how business is done—hopefully for the better. Of course, not everything changes, but something will probably be different.

How does new leadership bring about changes? The literature is replete with guidance on how to effect change within an organization, mainly because it is such a difficult challenge. Indeed, the University of California, Los Angeles, offers graduate degrees in organizational change within higher education.[7] Realistically, each case is different from the next, and there is no single "sure-fire" way to achieve change. One effective way is to replace personnel. Get rid of the "old guard" who may resist new ideas and bring in new employees with no ties to the old way of doing business. Theoretically, that purging method should work. However, despite the theoretical effectiveness of bringing in new employees to implement change, it isn't always desirable to dismiss employees who have invaluable technical expertise and experience. Indeed, the need to retain skilled employees, despite their resistance to change, imposes a very real limitation on a new leader's authority to bring about change. Consequently, another less disruptive way is to explain the new plans to the existing employees and then issue directives to put them into action. The expertise and experience are retained but redirected.

Even in the best of situations, new leadership may find it necessary to intervene directly to get things moving in the desired direction. Employees may balk at the implementation of a new plan or have difficulty adapting to new ways. The transition simply requires intrusive management. Thus, delegation of authority is suspended temporarily as new management steps in personally to reset business practices. This constitutes intrusive management that is undesirable, as always, but understandable by most unbiased bystanders. Employees who remain unresponsive to the changes imposed in these situations risk losing their jobs, no matter how much expertise and experience they have. As they say, "nobody is irreplaceable."

INTRUSION UNDER NEW LEADERSHIP

Newly appointed leaders inherit authority from their predecessors. Along with this, they also take over the associated responsibility and accountability for projects and initiatives inherited from the preceding administration. For that reason, new administrators usually take a close look at major projects begun prior to their arrival. After all, if something goes wrong, they now bear responsibility. These closer looks may intrude into lower levels of management, with consequential assaults on delegated authority. Indeed, authority may be wrested temporarily from a lower-level manager during this examination. These are generally necessary, justifiable, and publicly acceptable intrusions, but, unfortunately, they can inadvertently affect personal careers.

The wresting of authority can be illustrated by an anecdotal rendition of a new president's decision to reexamine a proposed site for Flagship University's new medical school campus. For several years prior to the new president's appointment, the preceding president had been looking for a new off-campus location for the cramped medical school and its affiliated clinics. This involved numerous discussions with members of the faculty, state legislators, the governor's office, the local hospitals, and other community leaders. Midway through this process, a new medical school dean was hired to lead this effort. The dean came with stellar credentials—department chair in an Ivy League medical school, chief-of-staff at a major university-affiliated hospital, definitive textbook author, and on and on. And, like many highly successful individuals with such an imposing résumé, the dean exuded powerful self-confidence.

The dean was charged with selecting the site and raising funds to build a new $300 million campus. With this charge came the requisite delegated authority. Admirably, the dean accomplished the mission within three years, obtaining consensus on a proposed site downtown and generating pledges for the $300 million. In the local community, this was a "big deal," because of the staggering economic implications: the new campus would become the kernel for a proposed biotechnology research park, a new cancer center, and various other health-related industries. The dean's already astral reputation soared, and invitations to speak at various economic-development forums rolled in.

About this time, the campus leadership changed; a new president was hired. Shortly after arriving on campus, the incoming president ordered a moratorium on all efforts to develop the new medical school site. Why? "I want to assure the public that the best possible site is chosen for this major addition to the community. Therefore, I'm appointing a task force headed by my chief of staff to evaluate all possibilities and to recommend the best location." With that statement, the new study was launched and previous plans were laid aside. Notably, the dean was not a member of the task force. Several months later, the president announced the results: the new site would be the same as that chosen by the dean. Only it wasn't expressed in those words. The announcement read: "I have conducted an exhaustive study of all possible locations, and I have decided that the downtown site serves the best interests of all constituents—the medical school, the hospitals, and the general public. Within the next several weeks, I'll commission an architect to design this new state-of-the-art health sciences center."

Notice that the president has now claimed "ownership" of the planned facility and, as a corollary, the dean's previous efforts have gone unacknowledged. From that point on, the president took public credit for the success of this project, thus eclipsing the dean's role. Indeed, the president (and not the dean) now received the invitations to speak about the new medical school campus at the various economic forums. The dean's previous efforts were basically forgotten. Stated differently, the new president wrested authority to select the new medical school location from the dean.

Notably, this was an informal rescission of the dean's delegated authority to choose the new medical school site, with no formal board action. The new president simply stepped in and took charge of this one-time, highly visible activity. Otherwise, the dean's authority remained intact. Technically, there was nothing that the dean could do about this. The limits of presidential authority were not exceeded, the dean was not deprived of a liberty or property interest, and the limits of public acceptance were not tested. In fact, many observers would agree that a second look at the site location served the public's best interest, especially considering the magnitude of the project. Moreover, it might also be agreed that excluding the dean in this second look ensured a "fresh set of unbiased eyes." Only a few perspicacious individuals inside and outside the university noticed the subtle shift in "ownership" from the dean to the new president.

Is there anything wrong with all of this? No. The new president could not be faulted for wanting to ensure that a project of this scope and importance was well planned. If something went wrong, the president would ultimately be held accountable. The dean's supporters might argue that as a matter of courtesy and respect, the dean's efforts should have received greater acknowledgment. After all, hadn't the dean garnered pledges for $300 million based on the earlier presumption of the downtown site? More cynical voices added that "this is all political theater by an ambitious, unscrupulous president who plans to run for governor in the next election." But, returning to the question about whether there was anything wrong here: the answer is no, nothing was technically wrong. The president acted well within the limits of authority and of acceptability by the governing board and the general public.

This anecdote illustrates how new leadership may take back specific aspects of delegated authority to accomplish a goal, such as change or validation of an inherited responsibility. And this is generally within most comfort zones. Indeed, it can be expected to occur to some extent throughout an organization. Recognizing this expectation, as a rule of thumb, the best tactic is obviously to cooperate with the new leadership as the limits of authority self-adjust to the new leader's priorities. Otherwise, the new boss may also justifiably move a recalcitrant employee out of the way.

INTRUSION BY OUTGOING LEADERSHIP

Influential outgoing administrators may intrude deliberately or inadvertently on the authority of their replacements. Ideally, they relinquish their position and authority to their successors and move into retirement or onto another job. However, in some cases, they remain with the institution in some other capacity, with the potential to intrude into their successor's authority. For example, in corporate governance, it is not uncommon for the former chief executive officer (CEO) and the current CEO (the president) to serve on the board of directors. The current CEO may also serve as board chair. Although the former CEO may have less formal authority than before, he may still have greater functional authority. Indeed, particularly influential former CEOs may cast a shadow over the newcomers. (Of course, the reverse may also occur.) The big temptation, notes one former CEO still on the board, "is to use one's power at the board and . . . run a sort of campaign against the chief executive . . . to try and make him more like you."[8] However, because this fairly common overlap is part of their culture, most corporations adapt to these inherent difficulties.

In academia, it is much less common for former presidents to continue in influential governance positions, such as serving on the board, especially in public institutions. However, it happens sometimes. A particularly high-profile example occurred at Boston University in 2003 when a highly influential CEO, John Silber, continued to serve the university, including sitting on the board, after stepping down as president. Ultimately, this caused difficulties for the board, resulting in a controversial decision to renege on hiring Dan Goldin as the university's ninth president.

To understand what went wrong in what one critic calls "the worst example of university management in the history of higher education,"[9] it helps to back up to 1971 when John Silber was appointed as the university's seventh president. For the next twenty-five years, Silber proved to be an effective president, although his strong-willed managerial style generated controversy. As reported in the *New York Times*, "Dr. Silber is regarded as a brilliant innovator and is widely credited with raising the university's profile and bringing in large sums of federal money for academic programs. But he is also known for running the university singlehandedly and for being confrontational with students and faculty."[10]

In 1996, Silber announced that he would resign the presidency. Before stepping down, he established a campus "task force on continuity," made up of professors, administrators, and trustees to "study ways to ensure the continuity and continued effectiveness of leadership."[11] The task force recommended that the board of trustees appoint Silber as the university's first chancellor—a position not defined in the trustee's charter.[12] In that capacity, the board granted Silber authority over critical university operations, such as long-range planning, venture-capital operations, and advising the president on hiring and tenure decisions. In addition, he retained his seat on the board.

The task force also recommended the appointment of Jon Westling, the university's provost for a dozen years, as president, and the board complied. This appointment raised some eyebrows, because Westling had been Silber's hand-picked successor and was hired to be president without an external search.[13] All in all, Mr. Silber was no longer president, but he still possessed considerable authority and commensurate power over the university's administration. In the words of the board head, Mr. Silber "has set the course that will take us into the next century, and we need his wisdom and experience as we navigate that course."[14]

Six years later, in 2002, Westling resigned the presidency. While keeping his position as chancellor, Silber stepped in as interim president, thus consolidating his authority. This time around, the board wanted a national search for the new president, and they asked Silber to coordinate this effort. Ostensibly, this was to be Silber's last official task for Boston University as chancellor, because he announced that "with the appointment of the new president, I would submit my resignation."[15] Typically, controversy once again surrounded Silber. Critics assailed his active participation in the selection of his successor: "Allowing a president to be involved in the selection of his or her successor almost ensures a disaster. . . . The president should not be an actor in any regard in the search process."[16]

Undaunted, Silber took control and recommended his choice for a successor, namely, Daniel Goldin. Notably, according to news reports, Silber circumvented the normal process by pushing Goldin as a candidate even before the search firm hired by the university had made its recommendations.[17] Although he had no prior experience in higher education, Goldin had sound managerial credentials hewn during his nine years as head of the National Aeronautics and Space Administration (NASA). The board followed Silber's recommendation and announced in August 2003 that Goldin would become the university's ninth president on November 1, 2003. Concurrently, according to the announcement, Silber would become president emeritus and would relinquish his seat on the board. In public statements, Silber announced that he was "honored" to be succeeded by Goldin. In turn, acknowledging Silber's iconic stature at Boston University, Goldin said that his goal would be to "develop a shared vision for the university."[18] It appeared that the university had achieved its goal of "continuity and continued effectiveness of leadership."

But then, things went sour as minds were changed. According to news reports, Goldin changed his mind about sharing his authority with Silber.[19] Indeed, in a letter to the board, Goldin said "There can only be one President."[20] To consolidate his authority, Goldin purportedly planned to fire numerous top administrators, including the provost, the chief financial officer, and several deans. According to the *Boston Globe*, he "developed what BU sources called a 'hit list' of campus officials whose loyalty he doubted because of their ties to outgoing leader John Silber and to several longtime BU trustees."[21] Amidst all of this, Silber's confidence in Goldin eroded, and he changed his mind about leaving the board.

Reportedly, Goldin "went berserk" at the news of this reversal of Silber's previous commitment to relinquish that last element of formal authority.[22] The discord was heightened in late October when the board voted "no confidence" in Goldin, reversing their unanimous decision to offer him the presidency. Then, on October 31, one day before he was scheduled to take office, the board announced that Goldin had resigned. He had changed his mind— or, perhaps more accurately, the board had changed his mind for him. In any event, the university agreed to pay Goldin $1.8 million in settlement costs.

This was an expensive reversal of a decision made five months earlier. And the costs could escalate. As one newspaper reported, "the about-face has raised questions about the university leadership, and it could imperil fund-raising and recruiting of administrators."[23]

How could the university make such a costly mistake? Not surprisingly, analyses abound. Most of them focus on an inevitable conflict between two strong individuals—Silber and Goldin—accustomed to the broad authority accorded long-serving top administrators. In behavioral terms, they were two alpha males vying for leadership, and one of them ultimately had to lose. From that angle, fault lies with Boston University for allowing Silber to retain his authority over university governance by remaining on the board of trustees. Members of the board allowed their allegiance to Silber, which had built up during his thirty-three-year tenure at the university, to overshadow good managerial practice. If the board had wanted Silber to retain even a share of presidential authority, they should have reappointed him to the position. As it was, Silber intruded into the new president's realm of authority. Giving him the benefit of any doubt, this intrusion was presumably inadvertent—at least, initially.

Putatively, time was also a factor. According to the *Chronicle of Higher Education*, the board acted hastily; they didn't allow sufficient time for careful vetting of Goldin's candidacy before offering him the job. "Boston's trustees were anxious to move the process along quickly. . . . [They] didn't want the search to go on for 'a month of Sundays.'"[24] The article continues: "But rushing the search was a 'huge mistake.' . . . It's worth the extra time at the beginning . . . to probe those challenges of personality and fit and management style. In most presidential searches, the board relies heavily on its search committee to identify potential problems. BU's search committee appears not to have fulfilled that duty." Arguably, however, more time spent vetting Goldin might not have altered the outcome. As NASA Administrator, he had been a highly visible public figure, and his strong personality was hardly a secret. Thus, more opinions about Goldin's suitability for the job may have been collected, but they may not have swayed the board's decision. After all, if Silber had been interested in further opinions about Goldin, he would not have advanced Goldin's candidacy before the executive search firm had completed its review process. And, Silber obviously exerted considerable influence over the board. In this case, the need for more time is open for debate. In contrast, the need for better judgment by the board members is much clearer—that is, through the lens of hindsight.

INTRUSION THROUGH FEAR OF RETRIBUTION

Administrators may intrude into their subordinate's realm of delegated authority by evoking fear inadvertently or deliberately. It is not uncommon for individuals to react to authority with fear—fear of retribution if orders are disobeyed, actions are not taken, fealty is not honored, or the boss is somehow displeased. In fact, fear of retribution is endemic to hierarchical structures where one individual possesses authority, and therefore power, over others. Of course, the extent of this fear depends on the individual; some kowtow timidly while others conform rebelliously. Regardless of the underlying psychology, fear of retribution motivates reactions tailored to please authority figures, ranging from obedient compliance with an order to decisions conforming to the boss's perceived wishes. Most administrators understand that their authority breeds fear of retaliation in many of their subordinates. Indeed, some exploit fear deliberately as a management tool; this is known as "management by fear."

Significantly, however, many administrators do not realize that the fear of retribution often extends beyond an administrative order to an administrative *wish*. In this instance, a wish may be little more than a suggested action or desired outcome, without the compelling force of an order. Even an innocent inquiry or "off-the-cuff" suggestion may inadvertently trigger fear of retribution if a concerned employee were to provide an unwelcome response. When told about this, a naïve administrator might reply: "Don't be ridiculous. I was just expressing an opinion, not giving an order." The rule of thumb, therefore, is not to think out loud, because for many subordinates, "your slightest wish is my command."

The inadvertent intrusion into a subordinate's realm of authority through provocation of fear by a seemingly innocuous inquiry can be illustrated in a hypothetical but quite realistic anecdote. It all started with a querulous young meteorology faculty member who disagreed with departmental colleagues about the impact of human activities on global warming. The disagreements became so acrimonious that the individual threatened to leave the university, claiming that the hostile intellectual climate stifled creative thinking. When told about the potential departure of the talented assistant professor, Provost M. asked the college dean if some other department might be a more suitable locus of appointment: "Let's just see if some department like chemistry would be interested in a promising meteorologist who's studying atmospheric greenhouse gases and so forth. That might be a good fit. If it is, we'll just transfer the appointment and salary money. If it's not, well . . . at least we tried." Thus, the dean relayed the inquiry to the chair of the chemistry department.

Accordingly, the chemistry chair passed the inquiry onto the departmental faculty members, who met to discuss it. The pros and cons were debated. In the beginning, the momentum turned against accepting the assistant professor, ostensibly because a meteorologist could not teach chemistry competently. Prior to a vote, however, a respected faculty member raised a troublesome issue: "Obviously the provost wants us to take this individual. What if we don't comply? I worry that we'll pay the price in the future." Another faculty member added: "I worry about that too. By not accepting this person, we're signaling that we don't need any new hires, so the provost won't allow us to fill the next vacancy." Several other colleagues expressed further worries about a wrathful provost. In reaction to the fear of retaliation, the momentum changed, and the department voted by a narrow margin to accept the transferred appointment.

At their next meeting, the dean perfunctorily told Provost M. about the transfer. Neither of them was aware of the departmental concerns about retaliation; they only knew the outcome. In fact, Provost M. hadn't even thought about the issue since the initial inquiry. It had quickly disappeared from consciousness—from the "radar screen"—as countless other items commanded the provost's attention. In contrast, the chemistry department faculty members recalled the episode vividly: "the provost forced us into taking this individual." For them, the fear of retaliation had blurred the limits of the provost's authority and seriously eroded their authority over faculty hiring.

Skeptics might question Provost M.'s apparent disinterest in the outcome of the inquiry. They could argue that the lack of attention was simply because the provost had prevailed; the chemistry department had capitulated by accepting the transfer. However, if the department had rejected the transfer, Provost M. might have reacted differently and, indeed, sought retribution at some time in the future. Any protestations by the provost to the contrary, such as "I'm not that kind of vengeful person," could be construed as disingenuous.

Apropos disingenuous, skeptics might add that Provost M.'s initial inquiry set up a no-win situation for the chemistry department. Even though it accepted the transfer as appeasement, the provost may deny some future request to hire a new faculty member because "I just gave the department an assistant professor; it's some other department's turn this time." In that sense, the inquiry also created a no-win situation for the provost, whose credibility and integrity will be maligned regardless of the outcome.

Could Provost M. have couched the inquiry in some fashion that would ameliorate fear of retribution? Probably not. Sure, the provost could have met personally with the chemistry department faculty members and reassured them that "there are no strings attached" to the deal. Realistically, however, this assurance would have marginal effect. It might allay some but most certainly not all fear of retaliation; the inherent tensions between the administration and the faculty members preclude assuagement. At best, the provost should recognize the underlying fear and its impact, communicate more clearly and directly, and, in the future, prove the paranoiac faculty members wrong by making personnel decisions irrespective of the transferred appointment.

LEGISLATIVE INTRUSION

The long arm of the legislature sometimes reaches down into public agencies and intrusively manipulates their operations. This occurs when a state legislature delegates authority to an agency but then overrides that delegation by mandating directly or indirectly certain actions by the agency. For example, in a public-university context, the state constitution or legislature may delegate full authority for managing a university to the governing board, which then delegates authority over all academic matters to the president, and on down the hierarchy, including shared governance with the faculty senate. Regardless of this delegation, however, the legislature may pass statutes or resolutions that require a specific academic action (typically pecuniary), with little regard for what the university administration and the faculty senate members think.

From their perspective, legislators view these incursions as an appropriate exercise of legislative authority. And, technically, they're correct. The legislature can pass whatever laws it desires as long as they're constitutional. However, from a university administrator's point of view, these incursions intrude into their realm of delegated authority. They represent legislative micromanagement. Usually, the two sides never see eye to eye on this point. However, the legislature always prevails, because it retains the option of rescinding all delegated authority.

These legislative intrusions into university administration often have political overtones. Usually they involve money for a particular legislative district one way or another. Common justifications are economic development and increased efficiency. For the same reason, namely the political overtones, the less benign intrusions are seldom successful. One legislative district's gain is generally another district's loss. So the intrusive legislation encounters a dense thicket of political and administrative resistance. Often it does not emerge intact.

The inherent mitigation of legislative intrusions by the dynamic political process is illustrated by a case in Hawaii. Like most state universities, the University of Hawaii (UH) is subject to occasional legislative intrusions. In the 1990s, for example, legislators in both the state House of Representatives and Senate introduced bills in three different sessions to move the College of Agriculture and Human Resources from the research-intensive Manoa campus (located in Honolulu on the island of Oahu) to the smaller baccalaureate

Hilo campus (located on the Big Island, Hawaii).[25] The transfer would include "All appropriations, records, equipment, machines, files, supplies, contracts, books, papers, documents, maps, and other personal property" in the college. Moreover, all grants, contracts, and other sources of revenue, including federal formula funding for applied agricultural research (such as Hatch Act funds) would also transfer. In other words, everything would move from one campus to another. The reason stated in the bills was innocuous: "The legislature believes that a transfer of the statewide agriculture extension service network to UH-Hilo will expand opportunities for a statewide role for UH-Hilo and better meet neighbor island extension needs with an expanded vision to include environmental resource management, sustainable community development, and distance education."[26] Significantly, the UH Manoa administration and faculty members were not consulted prior to submission of the bills, although they were certainly aware of this effort.

Beneath this bland justification, however, lay significant economic implications. No new operational money was appropriated for the transfer. Therefore, the college's state appropriated funding would be taken from UH Manoa's budget and given to UH Hilo. This infusion of many millions of dollars in new money and new jobs would significantly benefit Hilo's economy, which was struggling to recover from the demise of the local sugar industry. Proponents of the move also envisioned revitalization of the diversified agricultural industry consequent to relocation of the university's agricultural extension service to Hilo. In contrast, Honolulu's economy would suffer from the commensurate loss of these resources. The total impact approached $100 million, which is a lot of money at play in a small state. Thus, the political battle lines were drawn in dollar signs.

The proposed legislation then encountered the dense thicket of politics. After the first reading, the bills were referred to committees in both chambers. Political haggling motivated by the economic consequences caused the bills to die a quiet death that dooms many politically contentious bills. The Hilo delegation could not overcome the resistance set up by the much larger Honolulu delegation, so the proposed realignment was not to happen. As far as UH Manoa was concerned, the bills were not enacted, so, in a sense, "all's well that ends well." However, most significantly, politicians, and not academic administrators or faculty members, had decided the fate of the college.

Despite mitigation inherent to the political process, administrators cannot dismiss legislative intrusion, expecting it to bog down. They must aggressively confront the issues through testimony and the other political maneuvering. The procedures are usually well known in public and many private universities, and many institutions have staff members whose sole assignment is to manage these situations at both the state and the federal level. In states with a culture of frequent intrusions, high-level administrators of state agencies, including public universities, may devote considerable time and effort to lessen these distractions.[27] There is generally a cost: the large amount of staff and administrators' time spent on preparing materials required by the legislature, such as testimony supporting or opposing the proposed action, revised budget preparations, human resources' assessments, and so forth. And all of this detracts from other administrative concerns.

LEGISLATIVE LINE ITEMS

The legislature can modulate delegated authority through specific appropriations, such as line-item amounts for particular academic programs. In those cases, it matters little what the university administration or the faculty senate think about those programs; the legislature has trumped their authority by specifying how money is to be spent. In this way, persuasive individual legislators may direct university support to a favored program.

To avert situations like this, some benevolent state legislatures grant lump-sum budget authority to the public universities. In those states, the legislature appropriates the university's operating budget without instructions on how to spend the money. The governing board is delegated full authority over how the money is spent. For the university, this is clearly desirable. The phrase lump-sum is a bit misleading, however. This does not necessarily preclude separate legislation or joint resolutions by the legislature directing the university to fund specific programs at some specified level. Often, these mandates are not accompanied by additional funds to cover the added obligation. Thus, they are referred to as "unfunded mandates." They are anathema to university administrators, because the money to meet these mandates usually comes at the expense of other higher priority programs.

In this context, there is a technical difference between legislation and resolutions. Legislation, as law, requires university compliance. Technically, however, resolutions do not carry the full force of the law and do not necessarily require compliance. However, government agencies, including public universities, generally honor their intent, mainly to win the legislature's good will. Caveat: if a resolution is passed by only one legislative body (either the House or the Senate) but not by both, it is usually ignored. Also, unlike legislation, resolutions generally expire at the end of a legislative session.

Sometimes unfunded mandates derive indirectly from the political influence of individuals not in the legislature (i.e., private citizens) over the legislative process. In that context, a hypothetical but quite realistic example from Flagship University illustrates this route to legislative intrusion. The state legislature granted lump-sum budget authority to the university several years before the appointment of Provost M. This was a long sought-after change from the line-item budgets of the past, when the legislature effectively controlled how the university spent its funding. Thus, it came as a surprise to

Provost M. when the legislature passed a joint resolution mandating $400,000 in university support for the Cartography Center, which produced maps of the state's rivers and lakes, farm acreage in various crops (for example, corn and soy beans), wind farms, and so forth. This was an unfunded mandate, meaning that the provost would have to find the money somewhere in the academic budget to pay for the director's summer salary and for several staff members, including the director's spouse, who was a non-faculty researcher.

The origin of this resolution compounded the provost's consternation. After some investigation, the provost discovered that the center director was a long-time friend of the state legislature's house appropriations committee chairperson; they had grown up in the same small town. Thus, Provost M. surmised that the center director was involved in some way. It wasn't clear whether the director actively politicked the legislator for the funding, but the provost assumed that he had. As a result, the legislature had included a line item for the center in the university budget for many years. Because it was one of many line items, it had not attracted any particular attention. With the advent of lump-sum budgeting, the line item disappeared, but somebody had seen to it that the center's funding continued due to an unfunded resolution passed by both the house and the senate.

At first, the provost was inclined to ignore the mandate. After all, the university had lump-sum budget authority and was theoretically responsible for its own budget. Moreover, the Cartography Center was not central to the core academic mission. However, the university president sternly warned Provost M.: "Honor the resolution. If you don't, the legislature may react by restricting our lump-sum authority. It's not worth the risk."

Reluctantly, Provost M. informed the dean of arts and sciences that the college must allocate $400,000 in its budget to the Cartography Center, a unit within the college. The dean was furious. "Why should we have to pay for this? This is a university obligation." A heated discussion ensued, with comments like the provost's: "Why can't you control your director? If you were doing your job, we wouldn't have this problem." Ultimately, the heat subsided, and the provost agreed to split the cost with the dean. Neither the dean nor the provost was happy with the outcome; this was not a good day for either of them. But they realized that the compromise was in both of their best interests. The dean vowed to have a stern "heart to heart" with the director, and the provost intended to raise the topic once again with the president.

Some things don't change, and this is one of them. In general, the mandate conveyed in a legislature's resolution expires when the legislative session ends. However, in this particular case, the resolution was passed by the legislature the next year and has continued to be passed every year with predictable regularity. Only the amount changes—occasionally adjusted upward to account for inflation and pay raises. Both the dean and the provost grimace annually, pay the money, and move onto more pressing business that they can control. The dean had warned the director to stop politicking for the resolution "or else," but the warning fell on deaf ears. The director was otherwise quite effective and worth keeping on the job. In the provost's case, the follow-up conversation with the president also had gone nowhere.

The president reiterated the warning that failure to honor the resolution could trigger a backlash repeal or at least diminution of lump-sum budget authority. Could that really happen? Indeed it could—in part or in total. Many state universities have experienced rebukes from an irritated legislature, some real and some feigned. A seasoned CEO realizes that an occasional payoff, such as honoring an unfunded mandate or two—or three or four—outweighs the potential losses from a retraction of lump-sum budget authority. As they say, "pick your battles"; for the Flagship University president, this isn't one of them.

Could the dean or the provost have handled this differently? Yes. The most effective deterrent would be for the provost to push the full financial responsibility to the dean, and for the dean to push it further to the center director who was somehow instrumental in obtaining the recurring resolution. Thus, in that situation, the director would have to pay the full, mandated amount from the center's budget. Certainly, this would be a disincentive to continue pursuing the unfunded mandate. However, this aggressive response to the resolution carries the risk of a retaliatory, more restrictive resolution or piece of legislation in the next legislative session. The president's advice— "pick your battles"—rings true.

LEGISLATIVE INTENT

The intent of a law-making body, such as Congress or a state legislature, must be honored when interpreting a law. Sometimes, the intent is not written explicitly in the legislation, but it is usually documented in notes prepared during committee meetings and hearings. These legislative notes are frequently the primary record of legislative intent. Consequently, in many cases, it isn't sufficient to read the law as written. The accompanying notes must also be consulted to determine the true intent of the legislature. Indeed, in their efforts to carry out legislative intent when interpreting laws, the courts refer to the legislative notes whenever a statute contains ambiguities or fails to address some nuance. Failure to understand and to abide by the actual legislative intent of a law, including a budget appropriation, can have serious consequences that range from imperiled future funding to criminal charges.

As a rule of thumb, therefore, it is critically important to read the legislative notes accompanying a statute affecting the institution. Typically, in a university setting, this responsibility lies within the domain of the government relations officer or chief counsel. However, all senior-level administrators must be aware of this necessity. As a wise mentor stated, "ignore them at your peril."

The truth of that terse warning and its political implications can be illustrated in an anecdotal dispute over the allocation of funds at Flagship University. As a Land-Grant institution, Flagship University operated two major research farms, one near the main campus in a northern county and the other in a more rural southern county. Because of its location near the main campus, the northern farm had prospered and brought in considerably more research funding than the southern farm. Subtle tensions akin to jealousy had developed between the two farms over the years, resembling in many ways a more general tension between the urbane and rustic inhabitants of the northern and southern parts of the state, respectively. This subtle anxiety carried into the legislature, pitting the "city folks" versus the "country folks."

Although the legislature had granted Flagship University lump-sum budget authority many years ago, it routinely added line items and passed resolutions favoring specific academic programs. Thus, it came as no surprise to Provost M. when the legislature incorporated an extra $1 million line item specifically for "research on genetically modified corn varieties" into the university's annual budget. The provost included the additional $1 million in the allocation to the college of agriculture's dean, Dean H., and thought no more about it. Until a day about six months later, that is.

The day began with a telephone call from Regent L. The regent, who was a lawyer in a small town located about five miles from the southern farm, was mad—hopping mad. The cause of the anger came out in a staccato stream of invective. "I want you to fire Dean H. The legislature gave the college of agriculture $1 million to spend on the southern farm, but all of that money went up to the northern farm. That's against the law; I want the dean fired. And I want that money back down to the southern farm now. This kind of stuff has been going on too long." The harangue went on for another several minutes, with expletive-laden embellishments of the main point: fire the dean and send the $1 million to the southern farm. The conversation ended with the provost assuring Regent L. that the matter would be investigated promptly.

Early that afternoon, Dean H. was summoned to the provost's office. After relating the gist of the morning's telephone call from the regent, Provost M. said "explain yourself." Dean H. agreed that the full $1 million had been spent on research at the northern farm. When asked why the regent would assert that the money belonged to the southern farm, the dean replied that the law didn't specify which farm should receive the money. "The regent is just a bully playing politics, trying to get the money down south where it will help the local economy." After another few dismissive words on the topic, the dean got up, muttered "I've got more important things to think about," and left the room.

As the dean was leaving the office, Provost M. received another telephone call. This one was from state representative B., whose district included the southern farm. Representative B. was much calmer than Regent L., but the message was the same with one additional, important detail: the legislature intended explicitly for the full $1 million to be spent at the southern farm. "This is stated clearly in the legislative notes." After verifying this new information, Provost M. recognized the problem. Relying only on the wording of the legislation, the dean truly had not honored legislative intent. He had not read the legislative notes. Remembering the maxim "ignore them at your peril," Provost M. scheduled another meeting with Dean H. to point out the need to abide by legislative intent.

The dean was combative. "I know their intent; I don't have to read their notes. Representative B. just wants to put money in his home district, and Regent L., who lives there, is in cahoots. Both of them stand to benefit from the deal. But the northern farm is where the money would do the most good. We don't have any expertise in genetic engineering at the southern farm; they specialize in how to grow things in the soil, not sophisticated lab research. Sending the money down there for genetic engineering research would be like flushing it down the drain." Provost M. was not receptive to this argument; legislative intent must be honored. When ordered to transfer the $1 million from the northern to the southern farm budget, Dean H. stated bluntly that it was too late; the money had all been committed to the northern farm. The provost's irritation grew; "find a way to get $1 million to the southern farm within one week, or I'll take the money out of your next-year's budget and do it myself." The dean's parting comment laid the gauntlet: "you're wasting taxpayers' money."

During the ensuing week, both Regent L. and Representative B. contacted the provost several more times asking for a progress report. Regent L., in particular, was livid to learn that the issue hadn't been resolved already. At one point, the regent told the provost: "this is a racial issue, and you're part of the problem." That comment lingered in Provost M.'s thoughts all evening. Yes, the ethnic demography of the northern and the southern parts of the state were quite different, due in part to the large migrant farm worker population in the south. And that was reflected in the two farms' payrolls. The southern farm's crop development programs depended on this supply of low-paid labor, not high-paid laboratory scientists. Was the regent right? Was the legislative intent to bolster educational opportunities in modern genetic research and, therefore, higher salaries for inhabitants in the southern part of the state? If that were true, failure to honor that intent could be interpreted as a racist action. However, Provost M. pondered that it's one thing to read the legislative notes and quite another to read their minds.

To a degree, the provost sympathized with the dean's desire to maximize the academic return for the $1 million investment by sending it all to the northern farm. Genetic engineering research is very expensive, and the money would certainly defray some of those expenses. Nonetheless, a $1 million injection into the southern farm would pay for many new jobs and boost the local economy. To what extent should the university serve as a conduit for transferring state money into the local economy? That's not part of its academic mission. These conflicting thoughts whirled in the provost's head.

The deadline for Dean H. to transfer $1 million to the southern farm came and went without action. Provost M. concluded that Dean H. must be punished for this obstinacy and began planning the formal steps of progressive discipline. Before contacting the dean, however, the provost discussed these plans with the president, who had also been receiving irate telephone calls from Regent L. and Representative B. As Provost M. laid out plans for progressive discipline, the president interrupted and said decisively that this was insufficient to calm the storm. The dean must be fired now. "Next year's budget hearings are coming up, and I cannot face the members of the board and the legislature with this hanging over our head for another several months. It distracts from more important issues. And, it threatens our budgetary autonomy. Get this over with."

Submissively, Provost M. agreed to handle the situation that afternoon. The dean was an at-will appointment serving "at the pleasure of the provost," so the termination process should be uncomplicated. To facilitate the dean's return to the faculty, the provost would offer a one-year paid leave of absence and $100,000 in discretionary funds to reestablish a research program. Following the old adage to "give good news in your office and bad news in theirs," Provost M. went over to the dean's office and delivered the formal termination letter. Dean H. read the letter, took a deep breath, looked up defiantly, and snarled "You're a miserable failure as provost." The appointment of an interim dean was announced the next day, and $1 million was transferred promptly from the northern to the southern farm's budget.

This story has multiple critical lessons to be learned. First, always read the legislative notes to ascertain legislative intent. Second, don't flout the legislative intent. The potential risks far outweigh the gain. And third, don't dawdle when a decision needs to be made. When confronted with a clear case of insubordination and little likelihood that Dean H. would abide by legislative intent, Provost M. put off decisive action to rectify the situation. It took the president's insistence on swift dismissal to conclude this unfortunate episode.

GUBERNATORIAL INTRUSION

Governors have the authority and the responsibility to carry out the laws of the state and have the forces to ensure that this gets done. In short, governors are powerful people. Through the electoral process, they are vested with the supreme executive power of their state. As in California, they have the authority to "assign and reorganize functions among executive officers and agencies and their employees, other than elective officers and agencies administered by elective officers."[28] Furthermore, "The Governor is commander in chief of a militia that shall be provided by statute. The Governor may call it forth to execute the law."[29] And, the governor even has some authority over life and death through the power to "grant a reprieve, pardon, and commutation, after sentence, except in case of impeachment."[30]

Most governors use this immense power judiciously to manage the affairs of state. They delegate authority, which migrates down into the labyrinthine bureaucracy until it comes to rest at a level commensurate with the responsibility for some aspect of state government. Driver's licenses, prisons, state universities: the governor bears responsibility for them all, but they generally function fairly smoothly under this system of delegated authority. Moreover, public "watchdogs" keep a vigilant eye on the workings of government to monitor the responsible use of gubernatorial power.

Nonetheless, an obtrusive governor may occasionally reach beyond the limits of authority. His or her hand may extend into the bureaucracy to guide some managerial action or decision. Like other managerial intrusions, these gubernatorial incursions may range from the benign to the scandalously malignant. Indeed, stories abound about gubernatorial misuse of authority, and several prominent governors have gone to jail for crimes such as "wire fraud, attempted extortion, soliciting bribes, conspiracy to commit extortion and conspiracy to solicit and accept bribes."[31]

A governor's willingness to exert power depends highly on public opinion. If a particular expression of authority would likely arouse opposing public opinion and a consequent loss of votes, a governor would most probably think carefully about its use. The influence may come indirectly. For example, if some gubernatorial action compromised a university's accreditation, the accrediting association's reaction would most probably incite public opinion unfavorable for the governor. Likewise, if the governor provoked some academic organization's sanction or censure, this would probably inflame public opinion. These potentially negative outcomes modulate a governor's use of authority.

The influence of these various modulating factors can be illustrated in context anecdotally. In the normal course of events one morning, Provost M. received a disturbing telephone call. As the chief academic officer at the state's Flagship University, the provost was accustomed to inquiries and even demands from members of the public. That's part of the job at a public institution. But this call was different. It was from the state's duly elected chief executive officer, Governor K. The conversation was short and to the point: "Provost M., I want you to close the social sciences policy institute. It has been publishing too many articles that disagree with the core values of this state." After a short pause, the provost answered: "With all due respect, I don't have the authority to close the institute unilaterally. Only the governing board has the authority to close an institute, and according to their policy, this is an academic issue that would require consultation with the faculty senate. I'm sure that the senate would hesitate to flout the principles of academic freedom in this case."

Governor K. was not easily dissuaded. "Perhaps you don't realize that the state constitution, which was ratified by the people, authorizes me to appoint members of the governing board, who, in turn, appoint your boss, the president. So I have the authority to order the institute's closure. Now do it promptly." The trepidatious provost replied: "I understand. But I cannot act beyond the limits of my authority." Provost M. has defied the governor. Common wisdom would posit that the provost will soon be looking for another job and that the institute will be closed.

Does the governor really have the legal authority to dictate the provost's actions? Not directly. The university was established by the legislature, with full authority over its operations granted to the governing board. In some states, the governor is an ex officio member of the board. But even then, he is only a single member and does not speak for the board as a whole. However, the governor has the authority to appoint the other members of the board, so realistically, a thread of power wends its way from the governor via the governing board to the president to the provost. So, at least in this state, the governor may wield power in this situation without transgressing the limits of gubernatorial authority.

But, realistically, the governor would encounter difficulties getting away with this intrusion into university governance. For starters, the university's accreditation would be at risk. While the accreditors cannot readily dispute Governor K.'s order to close the social sciences policy institute on legal grounds, they can declare the institution noncompliant with its accreditation standards because of the governor's interference in university governance, which they would consider an abuse of power. Certainly, a politically savvy governor would not want to be held responsible for jeopardizing the university's accreditation. Thus, the accreditors, a third party, would impose realistic limitations on the governor's power. The AAUP might also join the fray by sanctioning and censuring the university for failure to comply with its standards on governance and academic freedom, respectively. And blame for the sanction and censure would fall on the governor. In addition, there would undoubtedly be a chorus of protests from the institute's allies both on and off campus. These usually draw attention from the news media, which could embroil the governor in a damaging public relations battle. At the end of the day, the governor could prevail but at a political cost. Like everybody else, even powerful governors have to pick their battles.

With these limitations, a cautious governor would most probably follow a less confrontational pathway to closure. Informally, he would instruct members of the board to close the institute because of its "offensive politics." Pressure from board members could force the president to order the provost to begin the formal process for institute closure. In this scenario, the provost would appoint a task force to evaluate the institute. Properly done, in consultation with the faculty senate, membership would be chosen carefully to ensure a broad spectrum of academic and political viewpoints; the task force recommendations—whatever they may be—must be credible. The institute's fate would then depend on their recommendations, which would be transmitted via the provost and the president to the board for their final decision. Technically, the board would be under no obligation to honor the task force recommendations; they could ignore or "reinterpret" any findings that were disagreeable to the governor. Unless there was sound evidence that the task force membership was "rigged" or that their analysis was seriously flawed for one reason or another, the case could be closed without drawing adverse attention from the accrediting association, AAUP, and so forth. Due process would have been followed.

What would motivate the governor to intrude in the university's academic affairs? When elected, Governor K. took on the responsibility to represent the electorate's interests in governmental matters. The governor assumed that this meant oversight of the public university, especially since it consumes a large chunk of the state's budget. With that responsibility, the governor was given the requisite authority, which in this state means control over appointments to the university's governing board. From Governor K.'s point of view, the governor is, therefore, accountable to the electorate if the university's social sciences policy institute promulgates ideas abhorrent to many of the state's citizens. Therefore, it seems well within the limits of gubernatorial authority to demand closure of the institute. Furthermore, why fuss with the governing board when it's much easier just to call the provost directly and order the job done. That leapfrogging, of course, flouts the chain of command.

By the way, did Provost M. learn anything about authority from the conversation with Governor K.? Not yet. However, the moment may come when another truth becomes apparent: the Governor's initial demand may have been deflected, but his formal authority remains intact, as does the power associated with it. As Justin Longenecker comments in his textbook on management, "Subordinate power should not render managers impotent."[32] Sooner or later, Provost M. may be fired for disobeying the order. It may happen quickly. The governor may request the governing board to order the president to fire the provost and then close the institute while they're at it. The provost's only lifeline in this situation would be any negative attention from the ensuing press coverage, lawsuits, accreditation difficulties, and other collateral damage from groups that did not accept the governor's authority in this case. Politicians avoid this kind of publicity like cats avoid water. Or it may happen slowly. Because of the governor's displeasure, the board, via the president, may gradually erode the provost's authority until the message is clear: it's time to go.

GOVERNING BOARD INTRUSION: SPECIAL FAVORS

Fundamentally, members of the governing board should not intrude into administrative operations of the university except under the most compelling circumstances. Indeed, as stated in the AGB *Statement on Board Responsibility for Institutional Governance*: "boards should exercise restraint in matters of administration. And . . . individual board members [should] avoid even the perception of any personal agendas or special interests. Board members and governing boards should not be seen as advocates for their appointing authorities or for certain segments among their constituents or the electorate; regardless of how they were selected or elected as board members, their commitment should clearly be to the welfare of the institution or system as a whole."[33] In this statement, the AGB affirms the fiduciary responsibilities of the board and its individual members.

Nonetheless, occasionally a member of the governing board will ask the university administration for a special favor. Often these constitute political favors. In contrast to personal favors, political favors involve money more often than not. However, in a university setting, the beneficiary is often not a single individual but a larger group such as an entire community. Of course, the person making the request may benefit indirectly, but the main objective is to bolster a local condition (usually the economy) in one way or another. Furthermore, these favors are characteristically legal; no laws are broken in granting the favor. The exceptions to this would be if an individual were to receive direct financial payment as part of the favor. That kind of situation would most probably violate state ethics laws.

Although the university is under no obligation to honor these intrusive requests, sometimes it is in the university's best interest to grant these favors despite their inappropriateness. An anecdotal example illustrates a minor intrusive request for a political favor. A governing board member, Regent G., urged Provost M. to make a $100,000 grant to the university's agricultural extension agent in a far northern county to study the local deer population. Not coincidentally, the regent had a hunting cabin in that county. Provost M.

agreed to relay the request to the university's research committee for consideration during the next scheduled competition for intramural research funding. Cutting the conversation short, Regent G. said "thanks" and hung up. Later that day, the university president was on the phone. "Just honor Regent G.s request. Forget the research committee." There was to be no further discussion; the money was to be awarded promptly to the grateful extension agent.

The issue here is a simple political favor. There was no corrupt intent. The money could not go into the extension agent's pocket; university spending regulations prevented that. It must be spent on graduate student salaries, supplies, and travel. As an avid deer hunter from an equally avid deer-hunting county, Regent G. was interested ostensibly in little more than maintaining a viable and productive herd for the hunting season. The local community benefited from the boost to the economy provided by visiting hunters, and one or two graduate students received a subsistence-level stipend studying white-tailed deer habitat. Like many of the county's inhabitants, Regent G. saw little problem with this request. After all, the taxpayers were entitled to some return on their investment in the state university.

The regent's request clearly exceeded the limits of an individual board member's authority. Moreover, the case could probably be made that it threatened the institution's accreditation—albeit in a very small way. So, why would a regent dare pose such a request, clearly violating the board's ethical standards precluding them from interfering with the university's administration? Furthermore, why would the president yield so quickly to a single board member?

The answer to the first question is pretty straightforward. From Regent G.'s perspective, taking occasional advantage of the authority inherent to being a member of the governing board was a reasonable perquisite for serving on the governing board. The answer to the second question is also fairly straightforward. The president's acquiescence was a matter of political expediency. Presumably, the president needed Regent G.'s political support for other higher-priority items. In that context, it would be better to lose this battle over $100,000 than to risk losing a subsequent battle over a $10 million tuition increase. Furthermore, nobody seemed to care very much about this minor intrusion; the amount of money was fairly small, and there were no glaring legal violations or improprieties. So, the president decided: "Let it go. Politically, this is a small price to pay for Regent G.'s support."

However, another anecdote illustrates a more aggressive request from a governing board member that cuts deeper into the university administration's authority. At the time, the university was in the midst of a budget crisis. Consequently, Provost M. had asked each college dean to make sizeable budgetary cuts. The law school dean responded by eliminating a legal clinic in a neighboring county, thus saving $400,000 annually. The clinic was quite popular. It provided pro bono legal advice to individuals who could not otherwise afford a lawyer and a modest boost to the local economy; in addition to a full-time secretary, three local attorneys and four law students were employed part time. Nonetheless, the clinic was peripheral to the school's core academic mission, and the $400,000 budget could be used to offset other cuts on the main campus. Therefore, the law school dean ordered the clinic's closure. The lease was canceled, and all employees were issued termination notices.

Unfortunately for the provost, this law clinic was in Regent R.'s hometown. The regent was furious at the announced closure. This fury was manifest in a telephone call to Provost M., when Regent R. demanded restoration of the $400,000 needed to run the legal clinic. The provost replied that the law school dean makes those decisions. "In this case, the cut was necessary for budgetary reasons." The regent was unmoved: "I don't care about the dean. You're the provost, and I told you to restore the $400,000. The county needs that clinic. Don't you understand what I said?" Provost M. answered that: "As a matter of principle, I cannot tell the dean how to manage the law school's budget, especially in these tight times. That is the dean's responsibility."

Regent R. was not happy with that reply, so this was not the last word on the subject. The regent called the law school dean, demanding restoration of the law clinic. According to Regent R., "The university has a moral obligation to keep this clinic open." The dean's response was predictable: "My budget was cut by eighteen percent. What am I supposed to do? Print money? Talk to the provost about it." That triggered several more calls from Regent R. to Provost M. repeating the order: restore the $400,000 so the clinic can re-open. Each time, Provost M. had the same answer: "That's the dean's decision, not mine." Ultimately, an exasperated Regent R. recognized the stalemate and stopped calling.

Meanwhile, Provost M. recounted the saga to the university president, who relayed it to the board chair. What transpired between the board chair and Regent R. behind closed doors remains unknown, but Regent R.'s term on the governing board expired later that year and, unusually, was not renewed. Presumably, the governor concluded that Regent R.'s actions compromised the board's integrity. Incidentally, there was no further discussion with the provost about the $400,000, and the clinic remained closed.

Was Regent R. wrong in making this request? Yes. But, in his opinion, he had the same right as any other county resident to express displeasure at closure of the legal clinic; he expressed a legitimate concern about the underprivileged clientele of the university's law clinic, and there's nothing wrong with that. Moreover, its closure didn't have an ostensible personal financial impact on him as a regent. True: maybe some of Regent R.'s friends or distant relatives lost their jobs when the clinic closed. Plus the loss of

$400,000 in the local economy may have impacted the regent's business efforts. But that was not readily evident. Nonetheless, Regent R. clearly crossed the limits of authority when ordering the dean and the provost to restore funding for the clinic. He (and Regent G. in the previous example) violated two basic tenets of governing board ethics: restraint in administrative matters and fiduciary responsibility.

For Regent R., the more effective strategy would have been to raise the awareness of fellow board members about the consequences of this particular closure in a more general discussion of the university's budget situation. It is unlikely that the board as a whole would interfere with the dean's actions, but at least this would have brought the issue to a higher level that might have had a chance, no matter how small, of garnering some support. Regent R. may have learned this lesson but, unfortunately, was not destined to have another opportunity to apply it.

SUMMARY

When a supervisor flouts the delegation of authority and interferes with a subordinate's management, this constitutes micromanagement. It often indicates questions about the subordinate's competence. Micromanagement can also occur subtly via overly cautious administration, when more than one level of the administration insists on thoroughly reviewing a decision before it is announced. Authority may be wrested temporarily from a lower-level manager if new leaders find it necessary to intervene directly to get things moving in the desired direction. They also usually take a close look at major projects begun prior to their arrival, because if something goes wrong, they now bear responsibility. Outgoing administrators may intrude in their successors' authority if they remain with the institution in some other governance capacity. Administrators may intrude into their subordinate's realm of authority because of the subordinate's fear of retribution if the boss is somehow displeased. This fear often extends beyond an administrative order to an administrative wish, which may be little more than a suggested action, an innocent inquiry, or "off-the-cuff" suggestion without the compelling force of an order. In public universities, a state legislature may pass statutes or resolutions that require a specific academic action, regardless of what the university administration thinks. The legislature may also modulate delegated authority through line-item appropriations or unfunded mandates for particular academic programs. Sometimes, legislative intentions are not incorporated into the final piece of legislation; they are documented as "legislative notes," which should always be checked for legislative intent. An obtrusive governor may occasionally reach into the bureaucracy to guide some managerial action or decision, although they are usually subject to intense public scrutiny. Occasionally, an influential individual such as a member of the governing board will ask the university administration for a special favor. Although the university is under no obligation to honor these intrusive requests, sometimes it is in the university's best interest to grant the favor.

NOTES

1. Cari Tuna, "Micromanagers Miss Bull's-Eye," *Wall Street Journal* (2008), http://online.wsj.com/article/SB122566866580091589.html. (Accessed December 26, 2012).

2. Simon North, "How to Manage a Micromanager," *Forbes* (2012), http://www.forbes.com/sites/deborahljacobs/2012/05/07/how-to-manage-a-micromanager/. (Accessed July 26, 2014).

3. Rudolph H. Weingartner, *Fitting Form to Function: A Primer on the Organization of Academic Institutions*, 2nd ed. (Lanham, MD: Rowman and Littlefield, 2011), 25.

4. Ibid., 70.

5. Ibid.

6. Dean O. Smith, *Managing the Research University* (New York: Oxford University Press, 2011), 29.

7. University of California Los Angeles, "Higher Education and Organizational Change," http://gseis.ucla.edu/education/academic-programs/higher-education-organizational-change/. (Accessed July 17, 2014).

8. Jay W. Lorsch and Andy Zelleke, "Should the CEO Be the Chairman?," *MIT Sloan Management Review* (2005), http://sloanreview.mit.edu/article/should-the-ceo-be-the-chairman/. (Accessed June 27, 2014).

9. Sara Rimer, "Boston U. Pays Leader to Quit before Starting," *New York Times* (2003), http://www.forbes.com/sites/deborahljacobs/2012/05/07/how-to-manage-a-micromanager/. (Accessed July 17, 2014).

10. "Turmoil at the Top at Boston University," *New York Times* (2003), http://www.nytimes.com/2003/10/28/us/turmoil-at-the-top-at-boston-university.html?src=pm. (Accessed July 17, 2014).

11. Courtney Leatherman, "Silber Leaves Boston U. Presidency to Become Its Chancellor," *Chronicle of Higher Education*, April 12, 1996.

12. Trustees of Boston University, "Charter, Statutes and by-Laws: Acts of 1869, Chapter 322," (1869), http://www.bu.edu/trustees/boardoftrustees/charter/. (Accessed July 17, 2014).

13. Megan Rooney and Julianne Basinger, "Silber's Shadow Looms over Boston U. Search," *Chronicle of Higher Education*, December 6, 2002.

14. Courtney Leatherman, "Silber Leaves Boston U. Presidency to Become Its Chancellor," *Chronicle of Higher Education*, April 12, 1996.

15. Megan Rooney and Julianne Basinger, "Silber's Shadow Looms over Boston U. Search," *Chronicle of Higher Education*, December 6, 2002.

16. Thomas Bartlett, "How Not to Choose a President," *Chronicle of Higher Education*, November 14, 2003.

17. Ibid.

18. Jamilah Evelyn, "Boston University's Trustees Waffle on Giving Presidency to Former NASA Chief," *Chronicle of Higher Education*, November 7, 2003.

19. Ibid.

20. Marcella Bombardieri, "BU Revokes Offer to Goldin; Severance Said to Be $1.8m Interim Chief Is Dean of Medical School," *Boston Globe* (2003), https://secure.pqarchiver.com/boston/access/435383891.html?FMT=ABS&FMTS=ABS:FT&type=current&date=Nov+1%2C+2003&author=Marcella+Bombardieri%2C+Globe+Staff&pub=Boston+Globe&edition=&startpage=A.1&desc=BU+REVOKES+OFFER+TO+GOLDIN%3B+SEVERANCE+SAID+TO+BE+%241.8M+INTERIM+CHIEF+IS+DEAN+OF+MEDICAL+SCHOOL. (Accessed July 17, 2014).

21. Marcella Bombardieri and Patrick Healy, "Goldin's 'Hit List' Stunned Trustees," ibid., http://www.boston.com/news/local/articles/2003/11/02/goldins_hit_list_stunned_trustees/. (Accessed July 17, 2014).

22. Ibid.

23. Rimer, "Boston U. Pays Leader to Quit before Starting."

24. Bartlett, "How Not to Choose a President."

25. State of Hawaii House of Representatives Eighteenth Legislature, "Relating to the University of Hawaii, H. B. 3314," (1996); State of Hawaii House of Representatives Nineteenth Session, "Relating to the University of Hawaii H. B. 554," (1997); State of Hawaii Senate Nineteenth Legislature, "Relating to the University of Hawaii, S. B. 660," (1997); State of Hawaii House of Representatives Twentieth Legislature, "Relating to the University of Hawaii H. B. 1395," (1999).; State of Hawaii Senate Twentieth Legislature, "Relating to the University of Hawaii S. B. 1442," (1999).

26. State of Hawaii House of Representatives Twentieth Legislature, "Relating to the University of Hawaii H. B. 1395."

27. Smith, *Managing the Research University*, 26–27.

28. California constitution, "Article 5, § 6," (1868).

29. "Article 5, § 7," (1868).

30. "Article 5, § 8," (1868).

31. Monica Davey and Emma G. Fitzsimmons, "Jury Finds Blagojevich Guilty of Corruption," *New York Times* (2011), http://www.nytimes.com/2011/06/28/us/28blagojevich.html. (Accessed March 20, 2012).

32. Justin G. Longenecker, *Principles of Management and Organizational Behavior*, Fourth ed. (Columbus, OH: Charles E. Merrill Publishing, 1964), 222.

33. Association of Governing Boards of Universities and Colleges, "AGB Statement on Board Responsibility for Institutional Governance," (2010), http://agb.org/news/2010-03/statement-board-responsibility-institutional-governance. (Accessed June 30, 2014).

Chapter Eleven

Resisting Authority

DISOBEYING ORDERS

On occasion, an employee may refuse to comply with the employer's directions. Refusal to obey orders amounts to defiance of authority, which, by definition, constitutes insubordination. Often these three terms are used synonymously. For example, according to the *Oxford Dictionary*, insubordination means "defiance of authority; refusal to obey orders."[1] Thus, resistance to authority by disobeying orders constitutes insubordination.

Understandably, disobeying orders—resistance to authority—cannot be tolerated in any organization. Employees are expected to follow directives issued by their employer or face dismissal. Therefore, when overt disobedience occurs, an employer usually responds very quickly to correct the situation. And that usually involves firing the defiant employee: "If you won't do it, then I'll find somebody who will." This reaction to flagrant disobedience is generally to be anticipated, for few defenses exculpate refusal to perform a task included in the job description.

Of course, special situations may arise when employers excuse disobeying an order for one reason or another. For example, they may be sympathetic to the employee's reasons for disobedience. An anecdote illustrates this kind of situation. Shortly before the beginning of the fall semester, the dean of the College of Arts and Sciences was called to meet with the university's president. The conversation was straight to the point. A professor in the college had given the starting quarterback for the varsity football team a failing grade (an F) in a summer-school history course, thus making him ineligible for the forthcoming season. According to the president, "The athletic director has asked me to change the grade. And, several members of the Board of Regents have also asked me how this could happen. I want you to take care of this and get back to me this afternoon." Shocked, the dean replied, "This is an unacceptable assault on the university's academic integrity." But, after calming down, acquiesced: "Okay, I'll look into the matter." The president nodded and said "I understand. Thank you."

Later that morning, the dean met with the department chair and the professor, who were defiantly angry, to ask for details on the case. Although the dean never ordered them directly to change the grade, there was little doubt about his intentions. The chair declared promptly: "You can tell the president that we will not change the grade, no matter what. The kid was routinely late to class and flunked the final exam." That afternoon, the dean returned to the president and relayed the chair's message: "They won't change the grade, and I don't blame them. If you want the grade changed, you had better do it yourself." Rebuffed, the president turned away while thanking the dean for at least looking into the matter.

In the end, the president changed the student's grade from an F to an Incomplete (I), thus restoring his eligibility for the fall semester. Neither the dean nor the chair was informed formally about this change, but they surmised as much when they saw him play in the first game of the season. The topic was never raised again by the president.

In this case, both the chair and the dean were disobedient. Neither of them agreed to change the grade, despite the obvious wishes of their superiors. They had clearly defied authority, exposing themselves to disciplinary actions. Lawyers might argue in court that they were never issued a direct order to change the grade, so how could they be insubordinate? But this case was not going to court, because the dean and presumably the president (who also came from the professoriate) were sympathetic to the reasons for refusal to obey. Incidentally, in the court of public opinion, the president might be judged harshly for changing the grade from an F to an I. But, as the president knows, most football fans, including many influential alumni and donors, probably would have done the same thing.

Insubordination is not always blatant. For example, it becomes less clear-cut if an order is issued by an individual who is misusing authority. In that situation, refusal to obey may be appropriate. For example, if a dean asks an office assistant to go pick up his or her laundry, a refusal is in order. Even if it could be argued that the dean's time could be spent more profitably on pressing university matters than on going to the cleaners. Likewise, if a department chair asks an assistant professor to babysit his or her children every Monday afternoon, a refusal may be appropriate. This request could be construed as a misuse of authority, because of the chair's power advantage over the assistant professor. Depending on the circumstances, of course, refusal to obey would not constitute insubordination per se.

On occasion, disobedience can be very difficult to detect. An order is not obeyed, indicative of insubordination, but the actual disobedient act cannot be pinpointed with certainty. These situations can be quite perplexing for an administrator. Without clear evidence of disobedience or, for that matter, any indication of intended disobedience, the uncertainty may reduce to the feeling that "something's not right," with only marginal hope of discovering the exact cause.

The subtlety and irony of uncertain disobedience in a self-protective context can be illustrated by an anecdotal case involving Professor T. in the Economics Department at Flagship University. It began when the chair sent an email informing the eminent professor, who was a particularly distinguished scholar, about next semester's teaching load: "The provost told the dean that some senior members of the economics faculty, including you, are not teaching enough students to satisfy university requirements. You have taught only one course per semester for the past two years, and the enrollment has never exceeded five students each time. Therefore, I am assigning Economics 101 to you for next semester. With enrollment projected at 150 undergraduate students, this assignment should bring you into compliance." Markedly, the memo was copied to the dean. Professor T. fulminated against the assignment, replying irately to the chair (but not the dean): "Economics 101 is a freshman-level course that any of our junior faculty members can teach. However, I am uniquely qualified to teach my graduate-level course on Keynesian economics. It would be a disservice to our graduate students if we deprived them of my advanced course on this important topic by relegating me to such an introductory course." The chair and Professor T. jousted in several more rounds of email exchanges about the assignment, with the chair sending copies to the dean each time. Ultimately, the chair prevailed; Professor T. obediently stopped short of insubordination and reluctantly accepted the assigned task.

But the issue wasn't dead just yet. While cogitating on the thread of emails, Professor T. noticed that the chair had copied the dean each time. Why? Having served as the departmental chair for several years in the past, Professor T. knew that the authority to make all departmental teaching assignments is delegated to the chair; neither the provost nor the dean is involved in departmental teaching matters at this level. In fact, thought the professor, "they seldom pay even the slightest attention to them. Why would they care about my assignment?" Therefore, out of piqued curiosity, Professor T. wrote an email asking the chair why the dean was copied: "Did the dean request to be copied on all teaching assignments? Or just mine?" The chair quickly replied: "No, the dean had not requested to be copied. I wanted to let the dean know that I was trying to work through the situation that had been raised during the annual review of the department." On reading this reply, the professor thought wryly, "you're afraid of the dean, and now you're just covering your back." By inference, the chair feared a reprimand from the dean if this particular assignment were not carried out.

On further reflection of the situation, Professor T. came up with an intriguing hypothesis: by copying the dean in the emails, the chair had ceded the authority delegated by the dean to make teaching assignments. If that were true, then the professor might legitimately contest the assignment directly to the dean, without involving the chair. Normally, a dean would not interfere with a chair's teaching assignment, except in the most unusual situations. However, with little to lose, the intrepid professor decided to test this hypothesis by appealing the assignment to the dean. Lo and behold: the dean agreed to meet with Professor T. and, after hearing the rationale for the appeal (ceded authority) and the argument against the assignment (misaligned expertise), agreed with the professor. Professor T. would not be teaching Economics 101 after all.

The chair was astounded by the dean's reversal of Professor T.'s teaching assignment. He could not understand the logic behind the decision. In a conversation with the dean, the chair simply repeated that: "He agreed to teach it. This is not right." With resignation, the chair sent Professor T. a brusque email announcing the reversal; the dean was not copied this time.

Professor T. had successfully disobeyed the chair without overt insubordination. In fact, acknowledging the chair's authority, the professor initially acquiesced to the assignment. In that respect, he was not disobedient. However, by including the dean in the process via the email copies, the chair opened the door for the professor's "end run" to the dean outside the chain of command, without appearing to be insubordinate. Fortunately for Professor T., the dean agreed that the chair had tacitly surrendered not only the delegated authority to make this particular teaching assignment but also the power to enforce the assignment. It goes beyond that. The chair also forfeited functional authority, manifest as a loss of respect as a strong leader by Professor T. and, most probably, the dean as well.

This case also illustrates the risks of "covering your back" behavior. There was no technical need for the chair to copy the dean on the emails—certainly not in this context where authority had been clearly delegated. Nonetheless, timorous individuals may derive comfort from the benefits of self-protective measures, such as copying the dean in emails to formidable faculty members. Sometimes, the "cover your back" approach may be desirable and perhaps necessary for one reason or another. Nonetheless, it generally imposes unnecessary limits on authority; formal authority may become less effective, and functional authority will most probably suffer. As they say, "authority not used is authority wasted." And that can restrain administrative effectiveness.

PASSIVE RESISTANCE

Passive resistance constitutes a form of insubordination. It ranges from overt to remarkably subtle. Overt passive resistance, manifest as nonviolent opposition to authority, occurs primarily in political settings. For example, civil disobedience involves refusal to obey government commands without resorting to violence or active measures of opposition. Pragmatically, the goal is to force concessions from the government without necessarily rejecting its legitimacy. Often these sought-after concessions include limits on the government's authority. Over the ages, civil disobedience has effectively provoked meaningful political and social changes in numerous settings, including the nationalist movement in India and the civil rights movement in the United States. These two examples were spearheaded by Mohandas Gandhi and Martin Luther King Jr., respectively, and their names are indelibly associated with the social consequences that can come from passive resistance.

In the political realm, passive resistance depends in part on public awareness of defiant disobedience. Consequently, mass demonstrations, road blockages, building occupations, and so forth are carried out in the full view of cameras held by supporters as well as government officials. The more publicity is generated, the better.

On a much smaller, more subtle scale, passive resistance pervades the administrative realm as well. In principle, it occurs for the same reason: disagreement with administration policies or rules. Unlike large-scale civil disobedience, however, administrative passive resistance is usually difficult to detect. Indeed, its indiscernibility is a characteristic trait in an administrative setting. Orders are given and acknowledged, but somehow they're not obeyed. Nothing gets done. Aggravatingly, there may be a considerable time lag before the failure to obey orders is noticed by the administrator who issued them. Even more aggravating, it may be deceptively difficult to fathom why nothing got done. In the face of passive resistance, formal authority remains intact—the boss is still the boss—but its acceptance is denied. Its legitimacy is challenged imperceptibly.

Because of its invisibility, passive resistance in the workplace can disrupt effective management insidiously. Moreover, this practice is not confined to a particular segment of the organizational ladder. Indeed, most experienced administrators throughout the organization have sharply honed skills in passive resistance, with particular expertise in maintaining its invisibility. Small, hardly discernible snags of resistance retard the flow of managerial initiatives, with more or less impact depending on the situation. In this way, imperceptible but very constraining limits are imposed on authority.

DELIBERATE PROCRASTINATION

A cardinal method of passive resistance, deliberate procrastination extends beyond slow reaction to an administrative directive or situation. It occurs predominantly when an employee simply does not agree with an administrative directive. Fearful of expressing dissatisfaction or disagreement with the administrator, an employee may intentionally disobey by not honoring the directive in the least visible way possible, usually through simple procrastination. The logic would be "if I wait long enough, the boss will lose interest in this situation or move onto another position." Carefully done, this deliberate "slow down" can severely limit the administrator's authority in this particular situation. In fact, its significance as a prime tool for subterfuge can hardly be overstated. Like a small plumbing leak, intentional procrastination can go undetected for months and months, slowly eroding the managerial infrastructure.

How can management avert passive resistance via deliberate procrastination? The best antidote is prior consultation with those affected by a directive. This answer emanates from the fundamental reciprocity tenet of authority: "the decision as to whether an order has authority or not lies with the persons to whom it is addressed, and does not reside in 'persons of authority' or those who issue the orders."[2] In other words, authority is reciprocal.[3] Stated contextually, it may be fruitless to issue a directive that predictably will evoke passive resistance. Thus, an administrator must gauge acceptance of a directive before giving it. This generally involves a priori consultation with those affected by the directive and those who are expected to execute the directive. In some cases, the simple courtesy of consultation ameliorates resistance, while in others it identifies contentious issues that breed resistance and must be resolved before issuing the directive. Of course, the extent of consultation depends on the specific situation.

Anecdotal accounts of deliberate procrastination abound in academia. Some are amusing, but most are disturbing, mainly because of their disruption. Furthermore, many of them could have been avoided by preceding consultation. This important point—the need for consultation—can be illustrated anecdotally in an academic context. As the new students were moving into their rooms at the onset of the fall semester, the provost went into the dormitories to greet them and their parents. Amidst the commotion, the provost noticed that the carpets were dirty and torn; tears were mended with gray duct tape. Furthermore, the walls were dirty; they had been cleaned, but the paint was old and dull. Simply put, these buildings needed new carpeting and a fresh paint job. Money was not a deterrent, because the university had a sizeable reserve account for these purposes.

Therefore, at the next staff meeting, the provost complained about the shabby conditions and instructed the dean of students, who was responsible for the dorms, to arrange for these repairs over the semester break in late December. The dean nodded in apparent affirmation. As a follow-up a month later, the provost asked the dean whether the contracts had been signed. The dean replied "No, not yet. Purchasing is working on them." As the semester came to an end, the contracts had not yet been finalized, so the work could not be done during the holiday break. Annoyed, the provost asked for an explanation. According to the dean, "The last time we had the dorms painted, the initial contracts were contested on a technical point by one of the potential vendors. So purchasing is being extra cautious in writing these contract specifications before issuing the advertisement seeking bids. And that takes time. It will be another several weeks before the advertisement for bids can be sent out."

Several weeks later, the contracts still had not been finalized due to some other technicality. At that point, the provost instructed the dean to provide a specific plan for getting the repairs done, including a timetable, within two weeks. Compliantly, the dean submitted a plan on time. According to the timeline, contracts should be issued within one month. Disappointingly, the repairs could not begin until summer, when the dorms were vacant, but they should be completed by August. Although this seemed like a long time to wait, the provost accepted the plan, thinking that at least, something will now get done before the fall semester begins. The contracts were, in fact, issued on schedule in late spring. But, by mid-summer, work had not yet begun. When asked why, the dean replied in a matter-of-fact fashion: "summer is the busiest season for the construction industry. The contractors are having scheduling difficulties. But they should have those resolved shortly." With controlled irritation at this obfuscation, the disappointed provost chastised the dean for allowing this project to drag into the busy summer; "I expected you to do a better job of shepherding these contracts through the system. There's no reason why this should have taken so long." Meanwhile, another incoming cohort of students would encounter the same torn carpets and dull walls in the fall.

Out of exasperation, the provost asked the chief financial officer to investigate the situation. "Why is this taking so long?" The explanation proved to be fairly simple. As a routine matter, the dormitories were scheduled for new carpets and fresh paint every five years. The next scheduled refurbishment was next summer—nine months from now, or twenty-one months after the provost's initial order to have it done last December. Ostensibly, the dean hoped to stall until the repairs could be made at the regularly scheduled time period, namely next summer. With that news, the provost realized the futility of pursuing the issue with the dean, relented, and said no more about the proposed project. New carpets and fresh paint would come sooner or later, at their appointed time. The dean's procrastination saw to that.

Three questions arise immediately. First, why didn't the provost consult with the dean before issuing the maintenance order? That common-sense managerial task would have provided the dean an opportunity to explain the scheduled maintenance cycle. As it was, the provost indirectly chastised the dean for the shabby conditions and usurped the dean's authority to make the necessary improvements without incorporating him into the decision-making process. Certainly, the provost acted within his authority, and the dean must comply. However, failure to consult with the dean before issuing the directive was a managerial mistake. It was a cardinal error that the provost hoped not to repeat—at least not very often.

Second, why didn't the dean just provide a straightforward explanation for delaying the repairs? Why resort to passive resistance? The true answer may never be known without psychological insights. However, one possibility may be the dean's innate fear of confronting an authority figure, namely the provost. Another possibility may stem from the provost's intrusion into authority that had been delegated to the dean; this micromanagement may have triggered resentment, which became manifest as passive resistance. Regardless, the dean erred by his reticence. Some critics might comment: "How could somebody rise to the dean's position without knowing the importance of speaking up in situations like this?" There are no satisfying replies to this comment; but, situations like this do occur, and the best that can be said is that "we all have our strengths and weaknesses."

Third, why didn't the provost begin disciplinary measures when it appeared that the dean was not meeting expectations? A particularly stern administrator might have taken disciplinary action when it first appeared that the directive was not being honored promptly. However, perhaps naively, the provost found the dean's explanations frustrating but credible. The university's bidding and procurement process is notoriously slow, and the low-bid contractors are sometimes unreliable. Furthermore, the provost was quite pleased with all other aspects of the dean's job performance. Nonetheless, critics could justifiably fault the provost for not holding the dean accountable in this case. But what would be an appropriate disciplinary action? Probably the most effective would be a formal letter expressing disappointment in the dean's handling of this assignment and a less-than-average increase during the next cycle of pay raises. In fairness to the dean, however, given the vaguely plausible explanations for the delays, most human resource officers would probably counsel that this one isolated transgression did not warrant formal disciplinary action—just a tough verbal rebuke.

DUPLICITY

By its nature, deliberate passive resistance is duplicitous. A directive is ac-knowledged but not honored. The employee may acknowledge the directive by saying "yes," implying "Yes, I'll do what you said." Without any further explanation, the administrator may reasonably assume that the directive will be carried out dutifully. But, the word "yes" doesn't necessarily mean "yes, I'll *do* what you said." Instead, it may mean "yes, I *heard* what you said." Meanwhile, the employee silently questions the directive and decides disin-genuously not to follow through. This duplicity may not be intentional, but it cannot be denied.

Duplicity may derive from a conflict between authority and loyalty. An employee's obligation to honor a directive may clash with loyalty to some other cause. The simple solution is passive resistance—procrastination with the hope that the conflict will somehow resolve itself over time. If this divergence between authority and loyalty occurs frequently, of course, the employee should not remain on the job; he or she cannot be trusted. But if it occurs very rarely, then it may be tolerable, depending on the specific situa-tion.

Duplicitous passive resistance due to conflicting obligations to authority and to loyalty can be illustrated anecdotally. At one time, Flagship Univer-sity had both a School of Government and a College of Social Sciences. Responding to the governing board's call for greater efficiency, a faculty committee recommended merging the school into the college. Therefore, the president assigned the task to the provost. From the beginning, faculty mem-bers in the college were generally supportive, because they envisioned a stronger, more comprehensive academic unit. In contrast, faculty members in the school unanimously opposed the merger, because they foresaw an ero-sion of their autonomy. Furthermore, their animosity focused on the college dean who had been openly encouraging the merger. Sensing this animosity, to facilitate the merger process, the college dean agreed to retire—to "get out of the way." Taking advantage of this opportunity, Provost M. appointed the School of Government dean to serve simultaneously as interim dean of the College of Social Sciences. Presumably, serving as dean of both units at the same time would catalyze the merger. The government dean agreed to this joint assignment and vowed to get the job done.

After one month, Provost M. asked the dean about progress towards the merger. In reply, the dean said that "I'm working on it. This is tricky, as you can imagine." The provost agreed; it would be tricky. Another month passed, and the provost asked for another verbal progress report. Again, the response was, "I'm working on it." This became the template exchange for the follow-ing six months: "I'm working on it." Then, serendipitously, Provost M. met a former colleague who mentioned that the dean was questioning School of

Government alumni about the wisdom of the merger. The colleague added: "In my opinion, he's undermining the merger." The next day, the provost confronted the dean with this allegation. In defense, the dean replied that "There's a lot of resistance to this merger. I have to convince skeptical alumni, and I need to know their opinions. It's not easy." Although the dean did not refute the allegation, the provost agreed apprehensively: "I understand that it's not easy. But I trust that you'll bring a merger plan within the next two months." The dean nodded affirmatively. After the meeting, Provost M. called numerous colleagues, asking delicately what they knew about the proposed merger. The feedback was disturbing; the dean had, indeed, been questioning the wisdom of the merger in private and, in one conversation, had reportedly joked about "doing nothing" to move it along.

After informing the president about this apparent betrayal, Provost M. confronted the dean with the new allegations. Instead of mounting a defense, the dean simply offered to retire; the offer was accepted without hesitation. Wrestling with anger management, the provost terminated the meeting. Afterward, the introspection began: "Now what will I do? After nine months, we've accomplished nothing." In fact, it was worse than nothing. The former dean had sown the seeds of dissent and now, as a retiree, actively opposed the merger in public with remarkable effectiveness. The governing board's support for the merger had waned considerably during this time, perhaps as a result of the former dean's campaign against it. Discouraged but undaunted, Provost M. appointed another interim dean to oversee both the School of Government and the College of Social Sciences. But the momentum was lost. Within a year, the provost accepted defeat and launched a national search for a new dean of Social Sciences. Nine months later, a second search was begun, this time for a new dean of the School of Government. The merger wasn't going to happen.

For the next several months, Provost M. thought off and on about all of this. "I trusted the dean. Why didn't I see this coming?" Like a jilted lover, the provost could only feel betrayal. There were no exculpatory explanations of what had transpired. And none can be invented. This was plain and simple duplicitous passive resistance. In the provost's opinion, the dean was like a snake in the grass: unseen and treacherous. Several colleagues offered no sympathy. They told Provost M. that "you deserved to be jilted. Anybody could have seen this coming. You were very naïve in trusting an individual with such a long history with the school to orchestrate its merger; somebody with no previous affiliation should have been entrusted to this task." The provost's opinion of the dean was unmoved by that rebuke; the dean was guilty of duplicitous betrayal.

However, there are two sides to this story. The dean clearly disagreed with the proposed merger. That should have been no surprise, because the dean had been affiliated with the school for many years. That is where his loyalty lay. But shouldn't the dean have confessed this bias up front? From the dean's perspective, not necessarily. *Carpe diem.* Here was the chance to protect the school against the whims of seemingly unappreciative members of the faculty and the higher administration. Wasn't there a question of loyalty to the university as a whole? Yes, but in this case, the dean's loyalty was clearly dedicated to the smaller unit—the school—and not the whole institution. That should not have been a surprise either. Deans are hired to do one thing: promote their college or school. And that is exactly what this dean did. In the process of passive resistance, the dean had singlehandedly neutralized the authority of the governing board, the president, the provost, and the faculty committees who had recommended the merger to manage this aspect of the university's organization.

STRATEGIC PROCRASTINATION

Procrastination isn't always a bad thing. Sometimes it serves a useful purpose by providing a strategic delay between one action and another. A common example on a small scale is to defer accepting or returning a telephone call until background information about the caller or specific issue has been obtained. Many individuals routinely screen telephone calls professionally and personally for this strategic reason: to gain the time needed to prepare for the call. And that is usually good, especially in the managerial realm. Surprises, misunderstandings, and mistakes can be avoided when the recipient is prepared to speak with the caller. Procrastination strategies can also give the delaying parties time to expand their power base to increase their chances of prevailing once a final decision is rendered. In other words, they "buy time" to mobilize additional support.

Beneficial procrastination is such a commonplace strategic practice that illustrative examples are easily imagined. A typical scenario might involve a news reporter calling a vice president for research for comments on a recently published scientific study on some topic. As usual, the administrative assistant answers the incoming call, says that the vice president is currently unavailable, asks what topic the reporter wants to talk about, and says that the vice president will return the call promptly. The assistant then informs the vice president about the call and the topic. Before returning the call, the vice president can do some "homework" on the topic. This is good, of course, because the vice president can then respond knowledgeably and more authoritatively to the reporter's questions. From that viewpoint, strategic procrastination has beneficially enhanced the vice president's functional authority.

Is there a downside to this kind of strategic procrastination? Perhaps in some situations. Continuing the example, if the reporter has a deadline, the vice president's procrastination may preclude inclusion of his or her remarks in the reporter's story. An opportunity for potentially good publicity will have been lost. Nitpickers might consider it insincere for the administrative assistant to claim that the vice president is "currently unavailable" if, in fact, he or she could answer the telephone at that time. However, it might also be argued that the vice president is "unavailable" if he or she is not yet prepared to respond to the reporter's questions. All in all, despite occasional negative consequences, strategic procrastination can serve a beneficial function in efficient management.

ADMINISTRATIVE RESISTANCE: LAME DUCKS

Passive resistance also sets in after employees announce their intention to step down—voluntarily or involuntarily. They become a "lame duck." From that moment on, managerial decisions will be scrutinized by colleagues. They will be looking for any parting favors for old friends or allies, biased decisions, financial improprieties, and other last-minute perfidious deals in otherwise routine financial and personnel decisions. Impeccable behavior and performance in the past does not shield against this close scrutiny. Insulting as this inspection may appear to be, most experienced employees understand the rationale and accept its inevitability. Basically, those remaining on the job have a fiduciary responsibility to monitor institutional assets.

The scrutiny may not be immediately apparent to the lame duck. It may become noticeable only after orders are issued but not implemented within the time-frame remaining on the job. Also, it may not be readily obvious who is actually screening these orders. In a well-functioning bureaucracy, experienced employees up and down the chain of command seem reflexively to take a close look at the lame duck's managerial actions. Unless a directive must be implemented promptly, they may be inclined simply to "sit on" it until the lame duck's replacement has been hired. This constitutes administrative procrastination. And it is generally accepted informally as a reasonable strategy during the transition from a departing manager to his or her replacement.

Parenthetically, the true reason for "sitting on" an order during this transition period may have nothing to do with managerial acumen. Employees down the chain of command may procrastinate because they're concerned about retribution if they approve an order that is then criticized by the new boss. Fundamentally, they don't want to risk losing their job or getting a pay raise because they approved an order issued by an outgoing manager who won't be around to defend them.

The dynamics of this surrender of authority to administrative resistance can be illustrated by an anecdote. Although Provost M. had experienced this lame duck scrutiny during previous job transitions, it was particularly noticeable after he announced his intention to step down from the position at Flagship University. Although the announcement was issued six months before the provost's actual departure date, administrative procrastination began immediately. The first indications occurred when the president told Provost M. to suspend ongoing searches for two deans. According to the president, "The best candidates won't come unless they know who their new boss will be." Untold, but certainly communicated, was also the conventional practice of allowing the successor to appoint his or her own managerial team. The provost understood the rationale and didn't need further explanation; the searches would be suspended until a new provost had been hired. And that search had not yet begun. Disappointed members of the search committees suggested that they should at least continue their efforts until they had identified a short list of three or four finalists because several top-notch candidates might not be available later. Their disappointment was compounded when the president rejected that suggestion and said that the new provost would have the opportunity to revise the job descriptions and expectations of the new deans. In other words, the search committee members—if they were retained by the new provost—may be confronted with the need to start from the beginning all over again. Administrative procrastination had begun.

Further indications materialized with increasing regularity. Two months earlier, Provost M. had set aside $500,000 in the budget to install new seating in the performing arts theater but had not gotten around to issuing a formal award notice to the theater director. Now a lame duck, the provost hastened to send an official award notice that authorized expenditure of the funds. A short time later, the theater director asked the provost if the award was forthcoming. Surprised, Provost M. replied: "I signed the award document a while ago; you should have gotten it by now. I'll have my administrative assistant look into this." The news was discouraging. Yes, the award document had been sent to the accounting office for processing—setting up an account and so forth. But it might as well have entered a black hole, for it never emerged from the accounting office. The award was sitting on a clerk's desk, and, according to the assistant, was on indefinite hold. Provost M. comprehended what that meant: the award would not be issued until a new provost had endorsed it. As other expenditures were deferred, the provost gradually realized the futility of making any significant personnel decisions or financial transactions. Administrative resistance would relegate them to what the lame duck provost now called "the black hole." In his waning days on the job, the provost had become ineffectual.

In situations like this, surrender of authority precedes surrender of the position. Of course, there are no formalities involved. Theoretically, the lame duck incumbent retains full authority inherent to the position; job descriptions and delegations are not changed. However, functional limitations to this authority are imposed as the institution enters a period of transition. And, these more restrictive limits are enforced via administrative procrastination. This practice, which follows an unwritten code, is standard in nearly all organizations. Managerial flow may become somewhat retarded as decisions are deferred. That is a downside to administrative procrastination. Nevertheless, the upside is that the incoming manager has greater flexibility to align priorities with his or her own, thus reducing the chances of disruptive turbulence in the managerial flow. This is a sizeable advantage to administrative procrastination during times of transition. That explains why it is a commonly accepted aspect of organizational behavior.

There can be collateral consequences to this kind of administrative resistance. The outgoing employee (the lame duck) may have made commitments, and the intended recipients may take actions predicated on timely processing of the commitments. This could result in embarrassing, confusing, and potentially costly complications. Therefore, the lame duck employee must communicate any perceived changes in normally expected administrative timelines to affected colleagues.

INCOMPETENCE

Incompetence can be an unintentional method of resisting authority. Indeed, a surefire way to disrupt administrative efficiency and thwart decision making is to submit assignments laden with errors. The list of aggravating mistakes is long: arithmetic mistakes, misspellings, inattention to details, failure to follow directions, incoherent writing, and so on. Unfortunately, for the most part, errors must be corrected, and that takes time and effort, thus stalling progress toward completion of an assignment. Stated differently, errors impose a drag on administrative flow.

Simplistically, errors fall into three vaguely defined classifications. The most benign are the occasional slip-ups, such as a typographical error, a misplaced decimal point, a forgotten email attachment, and the like. For the most part, they are easy to correct and readily forgiven—that is, if they occur infrequently. Less benign are the failures to overlook important details. Examples include oversights (part of a report is missing or out of date), inconsistencies (two sections in a report contradict each other), nonsensical statements (the data don't support the conclusion), and numerous other aggravating situations. This kind of error can be fixed, but the correction may take a disruptive amount of time. If an individual commits errors like this very often, his or her competence comes into question, and forgiveness becomes problematic. The most malignant errors, with few exceptions, involve failure to follow directions. This might occur, for example, if architectural plans for a new facility did not meet building codes, or, less egregious but potentially very damaging, an important deadline is missed because of confusion about the due date. Errors of this type can be quite costly and difficult to forgive. Furthermore, they raise serious concerns about competency.

Irrespective of error type, time spent correcting the situation comes at the expense of smooth administration. From another viewpoint, errors constrain an administrator's authority. A directive is given well within the limits of authority, but it is not implemented properly—at least not initially. The errors impose de facto limits on authority. Of course, an administrator will customarily replace employees who consistently make mistakes. But challenges arise if the error-prone individual has compensatory value, such as special skills or institutional memory. As always, the details of every situation dictate the solution.

The disruptive effects of incompetence can be placed in an illustrative context. Flagship University's multidisciplinary Center for Alternative Energy, which reported to the vice president for research, had just undergone its regularly scheduled five-year performance review. The evaluation committee's report, which was addressed to the vice president and copied to the provost, praised the Center's training programs but questioned its research efforts. Specifically, the committee commented that: "The Center has an unfocused research mission. Although individual investigators are conducting research in their own separate disciplines, they are not addressing any common themes. Consequently, there is little justification for a Center; the whole is not greater than the sum of its parts." Because the state legislature and the governor had mandated university research into alternative sources of energy, the vice president felt compelled to preserve the center.

Furthermore, the state had solicited proposals for multimillion-dollar institutional multidisciplinary research grants to study alternative energy sources. This one-time initiative would accept applications within a two-year time period. The vice president was convinced that the center could submit a competitive application for these funds if it were to coordinate the research projects of its various members. Therefore, he ordered the center director to prepare a strategic plan that identified no more than three core research areas that the individual investigators would concentrate on. Restating the review committee's admonishing words, "bring the center's research efforts into focus." Importantly, the plan was to include detailed proposals describing research on one of the three core topics from each investigator and time lines for implementation. It was due in nine months, which would allow plenty of time to prepare a proposal.

The director submitted the strategic plan exactly nine months later. It was impressive on the outside, but the vice president soon discovered that it was vacuous on the inside. Three core topics had been identified, as instructed, but few of the detailed research proposals were related to these core areas. Instead, the proposals were for the investigators' ongoing research in their own discipline. To the disappointed vice president, it looked as if they had simply "cut and pasted" existing proposals into the strategic plan without any attempt to address the center's core themes. In other words, they hadn't followed directions. There was no focus. So, the director was told to revise the strategic plan in accordance with the original order: include research proposals that focus on one of the three core topics. The director asked for and got another nine months to correct the plan. The revised plan arrived on the due date nine months later. It contained a new, well-written section describing the center's training activities, but, to the vice president's dismay, the research proposals differed little from the first version. There was no coordination to the individual research projects. For a second time, the director had not followed directions.

In consternation, the vice president mulled dismissal of the center director but decided that a change in leadership would probably delay completion of a proper strategic plan even longer. The university would probably miss the proposal deadline altogether. Instead, the vice president convened a meeting with all center researchers and the director. After explaining carefully what was expected in the plan, the vice president granted the director, whose competence was now in question, three months to submit a second revision. Unlike the previous submissions, the re-revised plan arrived one month overdue, after four months. It was marginally better; about half of the investigators had modified their existing research efforts to address one of the three core areas as instructed. The vice president was dissatisfied, however, because the center's efforts in these areas appeared dilute. With only about half the researchers involved, the center didn't look as if it had a critical mass in any of its core areas. But twenty-two months had now passed without a satisfactory strategic plan, and further delays would seriously imperil a timely application for state funds. Consequently, the vice president accepted the marginal strategic plan and assembled a small group of center faculty members to prepare hastily the grant application under the leadership of a trusted associate vice president.

In subsequent discussions with the provost, the vice president vented frustration and disappointment with the center and, more acutely, its director. They agreed that the director should be dismissed because of incompetence; that conclusion was inescapable. But when? They argued amicably about the timing. In the provost's opinion, "you should have replaced the director right after the review committee's negative evaluation of the center. The handwriting was on the wall, and you didn't read it." In rebuttal, the vice president noted that the director was an experienced administrator and accomplished researcher; "who would have thought that somebody with those credentials couldn't follow directions?" Looking forward, they also agreed that an immediate change in leadership might signal instability within the center and jeopardize its chances of winning state funding in the grant competition. So, the vice president decided to wait (i.e., to procrastinate) another nine months until after the results of the competition were announced. Regardless of the outcome, a new director would be chosen at that time. Without referring to incompetence, the rationale would be simply "to select innovative new leadership." And, the newly appointed director's first task would be to prepare a new strategic plan that focused the center's research efforts.

As an afterthought, the vice president meditated on the director's failure to produce an acceptable strategic plan. Surely, this wasn't such a difficult or onerous task. Was it disinterest in the center, lack of confidence in its members, laziness? Or, could it even have been intentional for some unfathomable reason? There were no obvious answers to these questions. With the benefit of hindsight, one thing was certain, however: the director should have been dismissed promptly after the committee's pejorative review. In the vice president's words, "The provost was right. I shouldn't have put off making the change. Live and learn."

DECISION-MAKING DELAY

Delaying the decision-making process constitutes an effective tactic for resisting authority and maintaining the status quo. It is employed routinely by individuals who do not want changes made. If they are part of the decision-making process but do not want change, they deliberately slow down the process through various procedural delays. If they are not involved in designing the process, then they can deliberately delay it by stalling before becoming involved. The ultimate goal is to blunt the momentum for change.

There are several common delaying tactics. One is to insist on a drawn-out process of public review, including extensive hearings and lengthy opportunities for public comment on publications of draft and final decisions. This method occurs regularly in academic settings, especially in the context of shared governance. For example, faculty senates can be notoriously slow and deliberate when reviewing an unpopular administrative proposal. A second tactic is to take legal action which is structured to be as time-consuming as possible. Motions are filed at the last possible moment and all possible delays and appeals are requested. Just threatening legal action can sometimes introduce hesitation in a decision-making process.

Strategic delays are often used by individuals who do not have the power to win directly in court or through legislative action. Rather than waste their resources on a fight they cannot win, they use delaying tactics to frustrate their opponent—similar to a Senate filibuster. Modifying an example provided by Brad Spangler in an essay on decision-making delay:[4] A city government was considering the approval of a new university physical plant. Although the plant would be on university-owned property, residents of the neighborhood near the proposed site were opposed to the idea, but they didn't have the political clout to stop it. So they decided to delay the deci-sion-making process by asking for a variety of site assessments, insisting on a long string of public meetings, and bringing a lawsuit which they knew they couldn't win, but it delayed the process even further. Their goal was to delay the decision long enough for the university to become frustrated and give up. At the same time, they also hoped to gain enough community sup-port that local decision makers would decide to refuse the necessary permits for political reasons if the university pursued its quest. If they succeed, the opponents will have effectively modulated the university's authority over the use of its own resources.

Delaying tactics that disrupt a decision-making process can be countered be setting deadlines for reaching a decision. Without deadlines, an opposing party may delay a decision indefinitely. Thus, as a general rule, deadlines must be established a priori, with the stipulation that consultation or negotia-tion will be terminated at that time. A related strategy is to emphasize the cost of delay. Setting a deadline can have a related effect on the perception of costs. Though in some cases time limits present the same pressures to both sides, it is often the case that a deadline may be asymmetrical, meaning that the costs of delay are higher for one side than the other. As Brad Spangler points out, "Thus, it is possible to force a settlement if you can convince your opponent that you have unlimited time to spend on the issue (indefinite delay) and that their costs will be affected. If the cost of a long delay is too high for them, they are likely to give in and come to an agreement."[5]

The costs of delay can be manipulated.[6] One method is to increase the costs of not reaching an agreement. In an academic dispute over workload reporting requirements with the faculty senate, the administration might in-crease the cost of delay by threatening imposition of even less acceptable alternative requirements if a settlement is not reached about the issue at hand. A second method is to form an alliance with outsiders. That is, increase the costs of delay by involving other parties in the process who can somehow influence the outcome. For example, the administration's cost of delaying resolution of a staff employees' labor dispute will be increased greatly if teaching assistants honor a picket line. A third, commonly used method is to manipulate the decision-making schedule in order to take advantage of time constraints. In universities, for example, summer breaks can always exert time pressure on any lengthy deliberations by the faculty members. The administration may delay the discussion of a contentious topic until well into the academic calendar, with the hope of gaining an advantage near the end of the session.

Incidentally, decision-making delays are not always intentional. They can occur unintentionally when individuals are confronted with too much infor-mation, thus requiring too much thinking about the problem. Decisions are delayed, and managerial progress slows down. In the extreme, too much information, or synonymously too many options, cannot only obfuscate the situation but also lead to "analysis paralysis"—an inability to make a decision.

The phrase "analysis paralysis" has entered the modern colloquial lexicon probably because it rings true in many people's minds. But, exactly what does it mean? According to the dictionary, "Analysis paralysis is an informal phrase applied to when the opportunity cost of decision analysis exceeds the benefits."[7] Or, in much simpler terms, it is "A condition of not being able to decide on a matter when there is no clear cut best option. It leads to an ever longer period of gathering more information in the hope that more information will guide the decision maker to an option that is clearly better."[8] In these situations, it becomes increasingly more difficult to make a decision as more and more information is gathered. In the extreme, it manifests itself as resistance to authority, failure to follow a directive. Understandably, inability to make a decision under these conditions neutralizes an employee's effectiveness.

FAILURE TO GIVE INFORMATION

Failure to give information is a disconcerting act of resistance that can stifle effective administration. This occurs when employees, including administrators, withhold information that they have the authority to release. A major reason is that they fear retribution if they suspect that their supervisor might not approve of divulgence. Although these apprehensive employees may have the authority to disclose information, fear provokes reticence. And this uncommunicativeness stifles the smooth flow of management, for decisions dependent on the desired information must be deferred until it has been obtained.

Theoretically, reluctance to divulge information translates into reluctance to exercise discretion, which is a prime feature of authority. In that context, James D. Thompson has noted bluntly that "Individuals exercise discretion whenever they believe it is to their advantage to do so and seek to evade discretion on other occasions."[9] Stated differently, individuals will withhold information if this serves their perceived advantage. Thompson extends this notion: "the individual will seek the most favorable results he perceives to be available, and under some circumstances, these results come by evasion of discretion. . . . The more serious the individual believes the consequences of error to be, the more he will seek to evade discretion. Under these circumstances, pains are taken to seek and develop substitutes for judgment. Consequences of error may fall on others."[10] In these situations, the individual abrogates authority.

An administrator may unwarily provoke reluctance to exercise discretion among most or all of the employees within his or her realm of authority. The underlying reasons may vary, but they commonly reduce to the employees' fear of reproach if they somehow displease the boss by giving out nonroutine information.

An anecdote illustrates this point. Shortly after the congressional elections in 2010, the incoming Republican majority in the House of Representatives declared a moratorium on earmarks—special appropriations directed by a particular member of Congress to benefit his or her constituents. This cessation in earmarked appropriations would have a significant impact on Flagship University's research enterprise, because the university usually received about $40 million in research funding annually via that route.

The discontinuation of politically charged earmarks aroused widespread public interest and, therefore, coverage by the news media. In that context, one newspaper reporter left a telephone message asking Professor T., current chair of the faculty senate, to comment on the moratorium's impact on Flagship's research efforts.

To frame an answer before returning the call, the curious professor asked the director of sponsored research, who administered incoming research awards from all sources, how much earmarked funding the university had received in the previous year. Surprisingly, the director claimed not to know the answer and referred Professor T. to his boss, the vice president for research, who maintained those data. But, the vice president was unavailable that afternoon. According to the administrative assistant, that didn't matter because the associate vice president for research, who handled federal relations, could answer the question just as well. When asked, however, the associate vice president professed not to know how much research funding was attributable to earmarks and recommended asking the director of sponsored research. Then, the associate vice president added guardedly: "why do you want to know?" Sensing suspicion in the question, Professor T. explained that the information was simply to help craft a meaningful answer for the newspaper reporter. At that, the associate vice president closed the conversation with an apology for not being able to help.

Frustrated, the professor returned to the director of sponsored research, who again pleaded ignorance and asserted that the associate vice president for research surely knew the answer. Irritated at this classic "run around" where nobody knew anything, Professor T. (an economist) decided personally to search the federal budget for the information, since it seemed unavailable from university sources.

Later that day, Professor T. received a terse email from the vice president for research. "I understand that a reporter is asking you about earmarks. Given the complexities of the federal budget process, I prefer to handle all communications about earmarks with reporters. Please refer them to my office, since you are not authorized to comment on behalf of the university in these matters." Astonished, the professor replied hastily that "As an economist by profession, I certainly understand the federal budget process. And as the faculty senate chair, I am indeed authorized to comment on university matters. Nonetheless, I shall refer the reporter to you." After angrily tapping the "send" key, Professor T. called the reporter and said simply that questions about earmarks should be addressed to the vice president for research, who represented the university in these issues.

Professor T. stewed on the reason why neither the director of sponsored research nor the associate vice president for research willingly would provide information about the university's earmarked funding. It most certainly wasn't because of ignorance. Both individuals reported directly to the vice president for research and presumably knew the extent of university earmarks. "After all," thought the professor, "If they don't know, who does know? That's their job." Were there defensible reasons for such tight control over communications about this particular issue, namely earmarks? Debatably. According to some critics, including the AAU, earmarks are anathema "because they circumvent a competitive, peer-reviewed process and subsequent accountability."[11] Since Flagship University was a member of that prestigious organization, revelation of its earmarked funding might prove embarrassing. Nevertheless, there was surely no point in trying to conceal the data; they were available to the general public as part of the federal budget. Moreover, members of Congress unabashedly publicize earmarks that they garner for their constituents. There must be some other reason for this reluctance to divulge information.

The answer to one other question clarified the situation. Why had the associate vice president so promptly told the vice president about the inquiry, which was nothing more than an innocuous request for information from an academic leader, the chair of the faculty senate? The stern tone of the vice president's email provided insight into the reason. It revealed a strong, controlling personality. Professor T. concluded that fear underlay the director's and the associate vice president's reticence, or in other words, their evasion of discretion. Communicating information about earmarked funding lay well within the limits of their formal authority, but they feared reprisal if they were to subvert their boss's dominance over the topic. Furthermore, what if the news report were somehow unflattering because of information they had given Professor T.? Realistically, the vice president's staff members imposed restrictive limits to their own authority by dint of fear. Professor T. surmised that fear of reprisal was not specific to this one issue. It was probably far more pervasive in the office of the vice president for research and, for that matter, right up the hierarchy of the upper administration. Maybe the vice president for research also operated in a presidential climate of fear. As they say, "leaders set the tone at the top."

FAILURE TO REPORT INFORMATION

Failure to report information, especially if it is required by law, also constitutes an act of resistance to authority. The two actions—giving and reporting information—differ technically and legally. Giving means to "freely transfer the possession of something to someone" whereas reporting means to "give a spoken or written account of something that one has observed, heard, done, or investigated."[12] Those last four verbs ("observed," "heard," "done," "investigated") comprise the difference; they imply that experiences are reported. Extending the pedantry a bit farther, giving generally connotes free-will transfer of information, while reporting often connotes obligatory transfer of information. Furthermore, failure to report information can disrupt administration much more seriously than failure to give information. In fact, it can have adverse legal consequences.

Why can failure to report information be so disruptive? There are two answers to this question. The first answer to this question comes circuitously. Within any complex organization, it is a truism that problems exist. They may be inefficiencies in the decision-making process, querulous personnel relations, or other troublesome aspects of the enterprise that impede optimal performance. Consequently, to achieve smooth administrative flow, these impediments must be resolved. Unfortunately, administrators may be unaware of troubles down in the organizational hierarchy. In contrast, employees working close to the locus of these difficulties may have unique knowledge about them. Ideally, these employees report problems to their supervisors who, in turn, find a solution to them. However, as Mary Walton pointed out, in many settings "people are afraid to point out problems for fear they will start an argument, or worse, be blamed for the problem."[13] As Sophocles said long ago, "no man cares to hear ill news."[14] Thus, the problems continue to disrupt performance because they have not been reported to the administrators with the authority to resolve them.

The second answer is far more obvious. Failure to report information can also be disruptive from a legal perspective. According to the law, some information must be reported to higher authorities. Of course, the courts may require disclosures of one sort or another, such as financial information during a divorce hearing. Within academe, most university honor codes require reporting of cheating observed in the classroom. For example, at the University of California, Los Angeles, "When a student is suspected to be involved in academic dishonesty, the Academic Senate requires that the instructor report the allegation to the Dean of Students' Office."[15] In 1990, the federal government passed the so-called Clery Act, which requires all institutions of higher education participating in the federal student financial aid program to disclose information about crime on their campuses and in the surrounding communities.[16]

In addition, state laws require reporting of any indications of child abuse to the appropriate authorities, such as the police. In Pennsylvania, for example, the law reads:

> A person who, in the course of employment, occupation or practice of a profession, comes into contact with children shall report or cause a report to be made [to the county children and youth social service agency or the Commonwealth Department of Public Welfare] . . . when the person has reasonable cause to suspect, on the basis of medical, professional or other training and experience, that a child under the care, supervision, guidance or training of that person or of an agency, institution, organization or other entity with which that person is affiliated is a victim of child abuse, including child abuse by an individual who is not a perpetrator. [17]

In many fewer words, an individual who witnesses child abuse must report the incident to an agency with the authority to intercede. Failure to report information covered by these federal and state reporting requirements can have serious consequences.

A tragically disruptive case of failure to report information occurred at Pennsylvania State University (Penn State), *Commonwealth of Pennsylvania v. Sandusky*.[18] It all centered around former Penn State assistant football coach Jerry Sandusky, who was indicted in 2011 by a grand jury on forty-five counts of sexually molesting ten boys on or near the university campus, going back to 1994.[19] According to the indictment, university police first learned about the abuses from a victim's mother in 1998. Following a lengthy joint investigation by the police and the Pennsylvania Department of Public Welfare, the county District Attorney decided that there would be no criminal charges, and that case was closed. Coincidentally, Sandusky retired from coaching in 1999, although he retained emeritus access to university athletic facilities. But the abuses continued. In 2000, a university janitor observed Sandusky performing oral sex with a young boy and reported the incident to his supervisor. However, no formal report to the proper legal authorities was made, and, again, no actions were taken. Then, in 2002, a graduate student witnessed another sexual episode in the locker-room showers and promptly informed head football coach Joe Paterno that he had seen Sandusky "fondling or doing something of a sexual nature to a young boy."[20] Paterno relayed the information to his boss, Athletic Director Tim Curley. About a week later, the student was called to a meeting with Curley and Senior Vice President for Finance and Business Gary Schultz, where he again reported what he had observed. To deter further abuses on campus, Sandusky's keys to the locker room were taken away. Subsequently, Curley and Schultz reported the incident to Penn State president Graham Spanier, who approved the handling of the matter—take away the keys. However, none of these individuals—Paterno, Curley, Schultz, and Spanier—informed any law enforcement authority, the Commonwealth of Pennsylvania Department of Public Welfare, or appropriate county child protective services agency about Sandusky's actions. Curiously, Schultz did not inform the university police, who reported to him.

The turning point occurred in 2008, when the mother of a high school freshman told high school officials that Sandusky had engaged in inappropriate sexual conduct with her son at the school. The high school officials contacted the police, and in 2009, Pennsylvania's attorney general launched an investigation. This culminated with the 2011 indictment and criminal complaint against Sandusky for alleged sexual abuse over a fifteen-year period.[21] In December 2011, Sandusky was arrested on fifty counts of sexually abusing ten boys.[22] At the trial, he was found guilty on forty-five counts of sexual abuse of ten boys and will probably spend the rest of his life in prison.[23]

Significantly, the grand jury also indicted Curley and Schultz for perjury and failing to report the sexual abuse incidents to the proper state or law enforcement authorities. They now await trial.[24] Ironically, perjury is a third-degree felony, punishable by up to seven years in prison, whereas failure to report child abuse is only a misdemeanor, punishable by up to one year in prison, like a traffic ticket.

The failure to report information had further consequences. On November 9, 2011, the board of trustees fired both Paterno and President Spanier, citing failure of leadership in both cases.[25] According to news reports, "Their departures reflect the seriousness and widespread concern that neither man alerted Pennsylvania law enforcement when Sandusky's on-campus sexual abuse of a minor was brought to their attention."[26] At the time, no formal charges were brought against either man, however. Three months after Penn State's board of trustees fired him, Paterno died from lung cancer that was diagnosed just days after his abrupt dismissal. President Spanier remained at Penn State as a tenured faculty member.

However, President Spanier was indicted subsequent to an independent investigation into the case commissioned by the board and conducted by former FBI director Louis Freeh. The Freeh investigation released emails indicating that president Spanier was, indeed, aware of Sandusky's sexual abuse of young boys as early as 1998, despite his previous denials to the grand jury.[27] Moreover, Spanier intentionally withheld information about the case from the board of trustees. According to the investigation report, when Curley and Schultz were charged, President Spanier told his staff he would tell the board "nothing more than what we said publicly." Based on evidence released by the Freeh report, a grand jury indicted former president Spanier on charges of perjury, child endangerment, obstruction, failure to report and conspiracy to commit all of those counts.[28] This case is pending trial.

President Spanier's reluctance to inform the board of trustees demonstrates the tensions inherent to the delegation of authority by the governing board to the president. According to the Freeh report, when one senior administrator suggested an independent investigation into the matter, President Spanier expressed concern that the board would acquire oversight powers in the crisis that could never be revoked. His chief counsel commented that if "we do this, we will never get rid of this group in some shape or form. The board will then think that they should have such a group."[29] Clearly, he did not want to grant any managerial leeway to members of the board; the delegation of authority by the board to the president was absolute. And, in this respect, many members of the board were quite loyal to the president. They might claim that "we appointed him president. Now let him do his job." That is not an unreasonable approach to take. Until things go wrong, that is. Then, as in this case, the governing board cannot escape culpability. As the Penn State trustees admitted, "as members of the University community, we all feel a personal sadness, disappointment and indeed, anger, over the failures of our leadership. The Board of Trustees, as the group that has paramount accountability for overseeing and ensuring the proper functioning and governance of the University, accepts full responsibility for the failures cited in the Freeh Report."[30]

Inevitably, the university questioned why its senior administrators failed to report Sandusky's alleged sexual abuse of boys on campus to the proper authorities. As reported in the Spanier indictment, when asked why they remained silent, Curley, Schultz, and other Penn State officials "all provided similar responses. They said that Graham Spanier was a controlling President who did not easily brook contrary advice or anything he might view as disloyalty."[31] A particularly harsh critic commenting on the collective silence: "When people stand by the unethical actions of their subordinates, they own that unethical action. Their silence suggests that their only problem with the unethical action is that it was detected. We should hold executives accountable for the actions of their employees when all evidence suggests that the organization tolerated unethical behavior."[32] Certainly the media and members of the general public offered their opinions. They range from the university's insular propensity to deal with problems "in house" to its protective support for the football program.[33] The latter explanation has generated a national debate over the inordinate influence of athletics on college priorities. In the aftermath, there have been congressional and NCAA hearings on universities' abilities to monitor their football programs.[34] Significantly, NCAA president Mark Emmert portrayed the Penn State scandal in terms of power: "What does this say about the power of the enthusiasm that we may have for any one sport or any one program? Can we structure organizational cultures where we love and revere and enjoy our athletic teams but at the same time keep them in proper perspective?"[35] Rhetorically, is the power so great that it limits institutional reaction to sexual abuse?

Reducing the issue to a matter of power *ipso facto* introduces the element of fear. In this situation, that means fear of retaliation for aggravating the vaunted Penn State football program. One individual familiar with the case commented on an undercurrent of fear: "I clearly could have imagined an institution behaving the way it did. . . . While there are a lot of good people, they're afraid to stand up and speak out on things."[36] As alluded to by NCAA president Emmert, this fear of provocation must have permeated the university's uppermost levels of management.

But, fear of whom? The university president? The football coach? Neither; in fact, by inference they were subject to the same fear as their subordinates. Contextually, the source of fear extends beyond single individuals with authority. It originates from a football ethos that transcends one person. From that perspective, it resembles fear of a supernatural being—an omnipresent god, so to speak. In this instance, it took a disgraceful scandal to overcome the cohesive forces of the football legacy. Penn State is not alone in this respect. Other universities with major football programs have had scandals within the past decade or so: Ohio State University, University of Miami, University of Colorado, University of Southern California, and on and on. The aura surrounding big-time college football imposes limits on the president's authority; he or she risks retaliation sooner or later from one source or another when opposing the athletic program's hegemony. That is a very real fear.

SUMMARY

Resistance to authority by disobeying orders constitutes insubordination. As a fundamental principle, insubordination—resistance to authority—cannot be tolerated in any organization. Of course, if an order is issued by an individual who lacks the requisite authority, refusal may be appropriate. Passive resistance is a form of insubordination. Unlike large-scale civil disobedience, administrative passive resistance is usually difficult to detect. Resisting authority through deliberate procrastination can occur when an employee disagrees with administrative policies or rules. The best antidote is prior consultation with those affected by a directive. By its nature, deliberate passive resistance is duplicitous. Duplicity may derive from a conflict between authority and loyalty. Sometimes, procrastination can serve a useful purpose by providing a strategic delay between one action and another. Passive resistance also sets in after employees announce their intention to step down; their managerial decisions will be scrutinized by colleagues, who may be inclined simply to "sit on" an order until the lame duck's replacement has been hired.

Incompetence can be an unintentional method of resisting authority because of time delays spent correcting the situation. Individuals who do not want changes made may delay the decision-making process or stall before becoming involved. Strategic delays are often used by individuals who do not have the power to win directly in court or through legislative action. Decision-making delays are not always intentional. They can occur unintentionally when an individual is confronted with too much information. Failure to give information is a disconcerting act of resistance that can stifle effective administration. This occurs when employees, including administrators, withhold information that they have the authority to release. Failure to report information, especially if it is required by law, also constitutes an act of resistance to authority. This can be quite disruptive, especially if it violates the law.

NOTES

1. "Oxford Dictionaries Online," Oxford University Press, http://oxforddictionaries.com/?attempted=true. (Accessed July 17, 2014).

2. Chester I. Barnard, *Functions of the Executive* (Cambridge, MA: Harvard University Press, 1938), 163.

3. Kenneth P. Mortimer and T. R. McConnell, *Sharing Authority Effectively* (San Francisco: Jossey-Bass, 1978), 17.

4. Brad Spangler, "Decision-Making Delay," ed. Guy Burgess and Heidi Burgess, *Beyond Intractability* (Boulder, CO: Conflict Information Consortium, University of Colorado, Boulder, 2003), http://www.beyondintractability.org/essay/delay. (Accessed March 10, 2014).

5. Ibid.

6. Roy J. Lewicki, Bruce Barry, and David M. Saunders, *Negotiation* (New York: McGraw Hill/Inwin, 2003), 89.

7. "Merriam Webster Dictionary," Merriam-Webster, Incorporated, http://www.merriam-webster.com/dictionary/. (Accessed February 7, 2011).

8. Jargon Database.com, "Analysis Paralysis," http://www.jargondatabase.com/Category/Other/Pop-Culture-Jargon/Analysis-Paralysis. (Accessed November 10, 2011).

9. James D. Thompson, *Organizations in Action* (New York: McGraw-Hill, 1967), 118.

10. Ibid., 120–21.

11. Dean O. Smith, *Managing the Research University* (New York: Oxford University Press, 2011), 78–79.

12. "Oxford Dictionaries Online." (Accessed April 24, 2012).

13. Mary Walton, *The Deming Management Method* (New York: Putnam, 1986), 72.

14. Sophocles, "Antigone," (1912), http://ancienthistory.about.com/library/bl/bl_text_sophocles_antigone.htm. (Accessed April 24, 2012).

15. Los Angeles University of California, "Student Guide to Academic Integrity," http://www.studentgroups.ucla.edu/dos/students/integrity/. (Accessed February 16, 2012).

16. *Jeanne Clery Disclosure of Campus Security Policy and Campus Crime Statistics Act (Clery Act)*, 20 U.S.C. § 1092(F) (1990).

17. Commonwealth of Pennsylvania, "Persons Required to Report Suspected Child Abuse," *Child Protective Services Law, § 6311 (a)* (2009).

18. *Commonwealth of Pennsylvania v. Sandusky*, 2013 PA Super 264 J-A24001- (2013).

19. Police Criminal Complaint Number G07-1146135 November 4 2011 Commonwealth of Pennsylvania vs. Gerald Arthur Sandusky Magisterial District Number 49-2-01, (2011), http://www.co.centre.pa.us/media/#p11. (Accessed February 15, 2012).

20. Ibid.

21. Ibid.

22. Commonwealth of Pennsylvania, "Arrest Warrant Complaint No. G071146135 December 7, 2011 Commonwealth of Pennsylvania v. Jerry A. Sandusky. Mag. Dist. No. Mdj-49-3-02," (2011), http://www.co.centre.pa.us/media/#p11 (Accessed February 16, 2011); Mark Viera, "Sandusky Arrested on Charges Involving Two New Accusers," *New York Times* (2011), http://www.nytimes.com/2011/12/08/sports/ncaafootball/sandusky-arrested-on-new-sexual-abuse-charges.html. (Accessed February 16, 2012).

23. *Commonwealth of Pennsylvania v. Sandusky.*

24. Brenda Medina, "How Penn State's Sex-Abuse Scandal Unfolded," *Chronicle of Higher Education* (2011), http://chronicle.com/article/How-Penn-States-Sex-Abuse/129767/ (Accessed February 16, 2012).

25. Pennsylvania State University, "Report of the Board of Trustees Concerning Nov. 9 Decisions," *Penn State Live: The University's Official News Source* (2012), http://live.psu.edu/story/58341#rss49. (Accessed February 17, 2012).

26. Michele Goodwin, "Paterno and Spanier Out, but Tragedy Remains at Penn State," *Chronicle of Higher Education* (2011), http://chronicle.com/blogs/brainstorm/paterno-and-spanier-out-but-tragedy-remains-at-penn-state/41187. (Accessed February 16, 2012).

27. Freeh Sporkin and Sullivan LLP, "Report of the Special Investigative Counsel Regarding the Actions of the Pennsylvania State University Related to the Child Sexual Abuse Committed by Gerald A. Sandusky," (2012), http://thefreehreportonpsu.com/. (Accessed July 13, 2012).

28. "Spanier Indictment: Presentment of the Grand Jury," (2012), http://www.attorneygeneral.gov/uploadedFiles/Press/spanier-schultz-curley_presentment-11-1-12.pdf. (Accessed March 17, 2014).

29. "Report of the Special Investigative Counsel Regarding the Actions of the Pennsylvania State University Related to the Child Sexual Abuse Committed by Gerald A. Sandusky." 29.

30. Karen B. Peetz, "Letter to the Alumni from Chairman Peetz - July 18, 2012," (2012), http://www.psu.edu/trustees/chairmanlettertoalumnijuly182012.html. (Accessed July 20, 2012).

31. "Spanier Indictment: Presentment of the Grand Jury". (Accessed March 17, 2014).

32. Tom Bartlett, "Penn State, Motivated Blindness, and the Dark Side of Loyalty," *Chronicle of Higher Education* (2011), http://chronicle.com/blogs/percolator/penn-state-motivated-blindness-and-the-dark-side-of-loyalty/27932?sid=at&utm_source=at&utm_medium=en (Accessed February 21, 2012).

33. Libby Sander and Jack Stripling, "An Insular Penn State Stayed Silent," *Chronicle of Higher Education*, http://chronicle.com/article/An-Insular-Penn-State-Stayed/129713/. (Accessed February 17, 2012).

34. Lynn Sweet, "Sandusky Sex Abuse Scandal: Rush Calls for NCAA Hearing," *Chicago Sun-Times* (2011), http://blogs.suntimes.com/sweet/2011/11/penn_state_sandusky_sex_scanda.html. (Accessed February 21, 2012).

35. Libby Sander, "Emmert Says Penn State Scandal, a 'Cautionary Tale,' Could Trigger NCAA Sanctions," *Chronicle of Higher Education* (2011), http://chronicle.com/blogs/players/emmert-calls-penn-state-scandal-a-cautionary-tale-for-big-time-sports-programs/29230. (Accessed February 21, 2012).

36. Brad Wolverton, "An Icon Falls, and a President with Him," *Chronicle of Higher Education*, http://chronicle.com/article/An-Icon-Fallsa-President/129766/. (Accessed February 16, 2012).

Chapter Twelve

Terminations

FIRING PERSONNEL

Just as hiring personnel is a primary managerial responsibility, firing personnel is also a primary responsibility. Indeed, the two responsibilities are complementary. To repeat former Chairman of the Federal Reserve Paul Volcker's comment about governing boards: "The board's inescapable and prime responsibility is hiring and firing the CEO."[1] And that obligation reverberates down into the organizational hierarchy. Thus, a priori, administrators have delegated authority to hire and fire their staff members.

In principle, the firing process repeats the hiring process. It is general practice to inform the next-higher authority about intentions to fire a subordinate, which constitutes an implicit request for approval. This is particularly the rule if the original appointment required higher-level approval. For example, if the president must approve the provost's hiring of a dean, then the president must approve the provost's firing of a dean. That is, the firing process follows the same pathway as the hiring process.

Incidentally, the terms "fired" and "laid off" differ technically. Employees are fired when their personal performance is unsatisfactory or if they do not comply with institutional standards. Under these circumstances, there is no expectation of being rehired at a future date. Employees are laid off when an institution undergoes restructuring or downsizing because of insufficient funds. A typical situation might occur when a grant or contract expires. Theoretically, the layoff has nothing to do with the employee's personal performance. It may be temporary, with the expectation that the employee may be rehired when funding is restored.

Few people relish the task of informing somebody that they have been fired—or laid off, for that matter. Nonetheless, effective administration re-

quires the replacement of incompetent or unwanted employees, and somebody has to deliver the unwelcome message: "You're fired!" Nobody wants
to hear these words. In fact, few people probably hear exactly those two
words, but they may hear a less abrasive phrase that means the same thing,
such as: "your services are no longer required." Nobody wants to hear these
words either. Regardless of the context, a fundamental question must be
answered: "What are the limits of authority when firing somebody?"

The limits of authority depend on the nature of the appointment. In that
context, there are three contractual conditions that determine how an employee can be fired: collective-bargaining agreements, contractual termination
clauses, and "at-will" agreements. And the procedures vary somewhat between these conditions.

COLLECTIVE-BARGAINING AGREEMENTS

Due process lies at the core of collective-bargaining agreements, which contain quite detailed procedures for terminating union members. The collective-bargaining agreement between the University of Hawaii and its faculty
union offers an illustrative template.[2] The termination process begins when
an administrative official (such as a dean) informs the employee (and the
union) of the reasons for dismissal—the first step in due process. If the
employee contests the charges, the university and the union jointly establish
a committee to investigate the reasons for termination. If the committee
concludes that the charges have substance, the termination procedure continues to the next step: the employee may file a formal grievance based on the
premise that a termination notice constitutes an alleged violation of the union
contract. Formally, the grievance is evaluated by an impartial representative
of the university president. This is often a senior staff member of the human
resources department. If the grievance does not favor the employee, he or she
may file an appeal that goes to arbitration. Ultimately, the arbitrator's decision is final.

On the one hand, this is a long, tortuous process that tests the most patient
soul. Consequently, administrators shy away from any but the most compelling cases calling for the firing of a union member. From a union member's
perspective, that is the way it should be. On the other hand, this is a relatively
simple process to follow, since the guidelines are so clearly defined in collective-bargaining agreements (i.e., the contracts). Moreover, the process is
highly regulated by both state and federal labor-relations laws. Thus, there is
generally little ambiguity to the overall procedure. That is a distinct administrative advantage of collective bargaining. (Of course, there are disadvantages as well.)

Significantly, as de facto representatives of "management," senior executives are excluded from union coverage and its guarantee of due process. In a university setting, the excluded group includes deans, vice presidents, and higher officials in the organizational hierarchy. Therefore, collective-bargaining agreements provide no guidance for the termination of excluded managerial employees. Nor do they provide any protection for members of management. They're "on their own."

CONTRACTUAL TERMINATION CLAUSES

The process for firing nonunionized employees, including faculty members and administrators, depends on whether an employment contract with a termination clause is involved. The procedural clause may be addressed explicitly in the employment contract, or it may be contained in an employee handbook or other institutional policy document that serves as a de facto contract between the employee and the university. In either case, the process can range from the simple to the complex.

At the simple end of the scale, rudimentary due process applies. This can be limited to timely notification of pending dismissal, description of the reasons, and provision for a hearing on the matter. There need not be the opportunity for an appeal.

Faculty members with limited-term contracts, such as individuals on probation for tenure, visiting and adjunct faculty, lecturers, and temporary part-time instructors, have a property right to continued employment during the life of their contract. Therefore, in most institutions, they have at minimum the right to rudimentary due process if they are subject to dismissal during the period of their employment contract. Generally, they do not have a property right to renewal of a contract. So, constitutional due process protections generally do not apply to the nonrenewal of a faculty member's contract, unless, for example, proper notice is not provided.[3] Nonetheless, the AAUP guidelines recommend somewhat more than the minimal due process in cases of nonrenewal: "the administration should provide the faculty member with adequate notice of non-reappointment with, upon request, a written explanation for the decision, and the opportunity to appeal the decision to a faculty body on grounds that the decision was based upon an impermissible consideration or inadequate consideration."[4]

At the complex end of the scale, tenured faculty members at most universities have the right to due process based on AAUP guidelines for dismissal proceedings.[5] These guidelines adapt legal due process to an academic setting, providing for more rigorous academic due process that "entails more than the legal barebones procedural requirements described above" (referring to the rudimentary due process).[6] As AAUP Associate Secretary Louis Joughin states: "Basically academic due process is a system of procedures designed to produce the best possible judgments in those personnel problems of higher education which may yield a serious adverse decision about a teacher."[7]

Roughly like the collective-bargaining procedures, AAUP-recommended academic due process encompasses the following steps: a statement of charges in "reasonable particularity"; an opportunity for a hearing before a faculty hearing body; the right of counsel if desired; the right to present evidence and to cross-examine; a record of the hearing; and an opportunity for consideration of the case by the governing board.[8] The last component implicitly acknowledges that the final decision rests with the governing board, which has the option of requesting reconsideration by the hearing body if new evidence or objections arise. (Recall the general rule: if the governing board approved the hiring, it must approve the firing.) Although there is no formal grievance step in the AAUP procedure, as in a union contract, this is nevertheless a relatively stressful process that discourages all but the most convincing cases for firing an individual. And, these convincing cases often end up in courts of law where they are ultimately decided.

In nearly all terminations, the human resources department monitors compliance with federal laws and internal policies. Importantly, the human resources employees do not make the decisions; that authority resides in the line managers, such as the provost or the division director. Thus, the human resources personnel provide technical advice based on what they're told are the facts of the case.

TERMINATION "FOR CAUSE"

The termination clauses in most executive-level and faculty member contracts address two fundamental situations: "for good reason" and "for cause." The first, dismissal for "good reason," occurs in the corporate world when a company changes ownership, and, consequently, the employees' authority and responsibilities are materially diminished. In these cases, the employer pays all outstanding obligations and, typically, severance pay (e.g., full salary for a year). Termination "for good reason" is seldom good news, but it is usually considered benign and not conducive to litigation. "Good reason" usually doesn't apply to a university setting except when there is major organizational restructuring such as eliminating a department or closing a campus.

The second feature addressed in most executive-level and faculty member contracts is termination "for cause." In this context, "cause" means that the employee misbehaved in some way. According to these contracts, the employer may dismiss the employee at any time "for cause." Outstanding wages and other obligations are paid, but no more. Stated succinctly, the employee is fired. In a bad-case scenario, to avert possible retaliation (such as theft, property damage, or threats to other employees), the terminated employee's office keys are confiscated, locks are changed, and all personal items are handed over by security agents at the building's front door.

Importantly, regardless of the circumstances, employers must maintain confidentiality about termination proceedings at all times, as the terminated employee has an expected right to privacy. In general, employers may discuss business-related matters concerning the employee, such as job performance, disciplinary actions, and the reason for termination, confidentially with other individuals on a strict "need-to-know" basis. However, they should not discuss these matters with individuals who do not have a "need-to-know," such as former coworkers; this opens the door to potential defamation and invasion of privacy legal claims. Furthermore, the discharged employee should not be disparaged in front of other employees. As a best practice, when asked why a person was fired, the appropriate answer is simply that "this is a personnel matter, and I can't talk about it."

In nearly all cases of termination of a faculty member for cause, within both the institution and the courts, academic due process proceeds with deliberate attention to the professional impact on the employee's academic reputation. As one court opined: "[t]he serious consequences of a 'just cause' dismissal are one reason why university regulations prescribe a rigorous process when accusations . . . are made."[9] Furthermore, if an employment contract is ambiguous about a procedural issue, it is often interpreted by the courts according to academic custom. As noted in *Greene v. Howard University*, "Contracts are written, and are to be read, by reference to the norms of conduct and expectations founded upon them. This is especially true of contracts in and among a community of scholars, which is what a university is. The readings of the market place are not invariably apt in this noncommercial context."[10] Thus, terminations of faculty members for cause generally proceed with slow deliberation, as the process wends its way through the institution and the courts.

Within academia, there are four generally accepted causes for termination of nontenured and tenured faculty members. In table 12.1, they are listed along with their fundamental transgressions and various examples drawn from court cases.[11]

INCOMPETENCE

Incompetence arises as a cause for dismissal when a faculty member simply cannot perform the basic elements of the job. An extensive list of professional incompetencies was documented in the case of *Riggin v. Board of Trustees*

Table 12.1. Causes for Faculty Termination

Cause	Transgression	Examples
Incompetence	Inability to perform	Poor teaching Not preparing for class Poor relations with students Sloppy or undocumented research
Insubordination	Unwillingness to perform	Refusal to teach assigned courses Refusal to develop assigned new courses Refusal to participate in departmental affairs Refusal to keep office hours Refusal to submit required research reports
Breaches of academic integrity	Failure to meet expected standards of veracity and honor	Plagiarism Research misconduct Misrepresenting academic credentials Awarding grades higher or lower than earned Exploiting students
Moral turpitude	Reprehensible personal conduct	Criminal behavior Immoral behavior Possession of child pornography

of Ball State University, which involved the firing of a tenured professor, Richard Riggin.[12] According to the board of trustees, Professor Riggins was unfit to perform in the classroom (after twenty-two years) for ten reasons:

1. Dr. Riggin is an ineffective teacher, in that he:

(a) Spends an excessive amount of time on nonpertinent matters;

(b) Fails to cover the basic course materials which students are expected to learn from his classes, as described in the catalog or course syllabi; and

(c) Demonstrates lack of adequate preparation and lack of organization in lectures.

2. Dr. Riggin has frequently failed to meet classes as scheduled, at the prescribed hour or for the prescribed length of time.

3. Dr. Riggin does not observe regular office hours, in violation of the published College of Business policy that faculty members are to have a minimum of ten (10) hours per week of scheduled office hours.

4. Dr. Riggin fails to carry out his responsibilities with respect to:

(a) Cooperating with faculty colleagues on matters such as teaching assignments and class scheduling;

(b) Responding in an appropriate and timely fashion to communications from within his Department and College;

(c) Participating in departmental, collegiate and university affairs; [and]

(d) Engaging in research and scholarly activities.

5. Dr. Riggin has been informed repeatedly of these problems and has refused to take corrective steps, and, subsequently, has even refused to discuss them with the Department Head and/or Dean.

In short, the board "threw the book at him."

After exhausting all preliminary procedures available within the university, which included a hearing before an ad hoc committee that ultimately recommended his discharge and a review of that hearing by the board of trustees, Professor Riggin's employment was terminated. He challenged that decision, claiming that his First Amendment rights to equal protection and free speech had been violated. The court disagreed, ruling in favor of the board, thus upholding Professor Riggin's dismissal.

The courts have ruled that the employer has broad powers in determining what determines an employee's ability to perform his or her job. Indeed, the cause may not be related directly to professional competence. This is exemplified in a 1977 case, *Gaylord v. Tacoma School District No. 10*, where the Supreme Court of Washington upheld the dismissal of a teacher, James Gaylord, by the Tacoma school district's board of education on the basis of his admission to two individuals that he was homosexual. [13] Although his teaching performance had been excellent, the court reasoned that it was possible that the teacher no longer would be able to perform adequately in the classroom if public knowledge of his homosexual conduct led to notoriety and gossip. In the words of the court, "After Gaylord's homosexual status became publicly known, it would and did impair his teaching efficiency. A teacher's efficiency is determined by his relationship with his students, their parents, the school administration, and fellow teachers. If Gaylord had not been discharged after he became known as a homosexual, the result would be fear, confusion, suspicion, parental concern, and pressure on the administration by students, parents, and other teachers." In other words, "public knowledge of James Gaylord's status as homosexual would impair the optimum atmosphere in the classroom and is cause for dismissal." Thus, the court ruled in favor of the school district and against Gaylord.

According to this ruling, an employee can be fired for cause if his or her job performance is affected adversely by some action or circumstance. In this case, the cause was the negative impact on Gaylord's ability to teach judging from at least one complaint by a student and opposition from several professional colleagues. Importantly, Mr. Gaylord did not commit an immoral or illegal act; there was no moral turpitude. His dismissal was upheld because, in the eyes of the board, his ability to teach—to perform his job competently—was affected adversely. The fact that the governing board has such broad powers to determine sufficient cause means that administrators and educators can be dismissed from their duties regardless of any laws that make their actions legal; perceived impairment of an employee's efficiency to perform his or her job can provide sufficient cause for termination. Therefore, as a practical matter, it must be remembered that any actions or public statements that could potentially hinder teaching proficiency may have unfavorable consequences.

INSUBORDINATION

Insubordination, defined commonly as the refusal to obey orders, is a fairly straightforward cause for dismissal.[14] For the most part, employees in all walks of life understand this basic fact: when an employee explicitly refuses to obey orders, dismissal is the usual outcome. Indeed, it is a well-established and accepted belief that employees, including executive-level administrators, have a duty to obey all reasonable directives of the employer. Even if an order is given in bad faith, an employee may still have an obligation to follow it, with an opportunity to file a grievance after the fact. The law is clear on that basic principle of authority. For example, the California Labor Code states that "An employee shall substantially comply with all the directions of his employer concerning the service on which he is engaged, except where such obedience is impossible or unlawful, or would impose new and unreasonable burdens upon the employee."[15]

Therefore, when an employee refuses to comply with the employer's directions, this defiance of authority constitutes insubordination. The factual scenarios may differ, but the common element is the willful or intentional failure to obey a lawful and reasonable request of a supervisor. Stated more formally, this requires that: "(1) a direct or implied order . . . was issued to an employee, (2) the employee received and understood the order and (3) the employee refused to obey the order either through a statement of refusal or nonperformance."[16] The actual refusal elevates insubordination above disrespectful insolence, although in some situations, the two are closely aligned. Indeed, some legal scholars adhere to a broader definition of insubordination that subsumes insolence and rude or disruptive behavior: "Insubordination encompasses all varieties of unwillingness or conscious failure to perform one's job, ranging from dereliction to defiance to disruptive behavior."[17]

In the legal lexicon, insubordination has a broader definition. According to *Black's Law Dictionary*, insubordination "means to have a lack of respect or the refusing to obey orders of a person in authority."[18] In that framework, it means more than failure to obey the request of a supervisor; it also means an action that shows disrespect or harassment toward a supervisor. The State of California expands on this broader definition by including four categories in its definition of insubordination:[19]

1. Disobeying an employer's order or instruction.

2. Exceeding authority.
3. Disputing or ridiculing authority.
4. Using vulgar or profane language toward the supervisor.

By these criteria, an employee is, of course, insubordinate if he "refuses, without justification, to comply with the lawful and reasonable orders of the employer or the employer's representative" or "commits an act which exceeds the authority either expressly granted by the employer or impliedly created by failure of the employer to object to a particular course of conduct." Those two categories conform to the standard definition of insubordination. But these criteria go beyond that by adding disrespectful verbal or written comments to the definition. An employee is insubordinate if he: "makes a statement or remark, which is not the result of an error in judgment, under the circumstances which damage or tend to damage the employer's interest" or "addresses vulgar, profane, insulting, obscene, derogatory, or offensive language of a vile nature toward the employer or the employer's representative when such remarks are unjustified under the circumstances, and not within the normal exchange and customary good-natured banter between the employer or the employer's representative and the employee."[20]

These guidelines expand the definition of insubordination to encompass standards of behavior that an employer can reasonably expect from an employee. Consequently, employees are considered insubordinate if they intentionally disregard the employer's interest and willfully violate these standards of behavior. That is, insubordinate employees disrespect the employer's authority. And, because this can be so disruptive, it is generally a cause for termination. Quite simply, it undermines the administration's authority and ability to lead an institution effectively.

Although academics enjoy broad freedoms, they, too, must respect their employers and abide by their directions. As stated by the courts in *Chitwood v. Feaster*, "A college has a right to expect a teacher to follow instructions and to work cooperatively and harmoniously with the head of the department. If one cannot or does not, if one undertakes to seize the authority and prerogatives of the department head, he does not immunize himself against loss of his position simply because his noncooperation and aggressive conduct are verbalized."[21] Consequently, a faculty member cannot refuse to meet some departmental obligation without risking dismissal.

In academia, insubordination has many dimensions. A typical example might occur when a professor refuses to teach an assigned course. Assuming that the course lies within the professor's area of expertise (in many smaller institutions, that area may be quite expansive), the refusal constitutes insubordination and a clear-cut basis for disciplinary action. Tenure, incidentally, is irrelevant in these situations. Tenured faculty members have been lawfully terminated for refusing to teach assigned classes, develop assigned new courses, attend mandatory faculty workshops, participate in required commencement exercises, adhere to university grading policies, submit required grant or contract reports, cover base course material as stipulated in a syllabus, keep office hours for advising students, participate in departmental affairs, and serve on committees. [22] And, by inference, nontenured personnel can be terminated for these reasons as well. In each of these cases, the insubordinate faculty member failed to comply with the terms of employment.

Charges of insubordination may derive from disagreements about the limits of free speech. In general, they involve an institution's accusation of insubordination, countered by an employee's charge of infringement of First Amendment rights. At stake in the context of insubordination is the right of a public employee, such as an administrator or a faculty member, to criticize a superior. Is this criticism protected by the First Amendment or is it insubordination? The Supreme Court laid the foundational guidelines for answering this question in *Pickering*. [23] To be protected by the First Amendment, the criticism must be of public importance and it must not cause a disruptive impact between the employee and a proximate supervisor. Unless both of these criteria are met, the charges of insubordination generally prevail. This was exemplified in *Roseman*, where an associate professor did not explicitly refuse to obey orders, but the court ruled that her criticism of her supervisor constituted an insubordinate attitude. [24] Furthermore, the balance between free speech and insubordination shifted dramatically toward the employer following *Garcetti*, which ruled that speech "pursuant to official duties" is not protected by the First Amendment and can be the subject of employer disciplinary actions. [25] Thus, in that context, free speech that disrupts close working relationships or the basic functioning of a public university can be construed as insubordination and, therefore, grounds for dismissal. In private universities, there are usually similar limitations on freedom of speech.

In some states, insubordination may legally require a showing of more than one single instance of disobedience. For example, the Mississippi Supreme Court has defined insubordination as a "constant or continuing intentional refusal to obey a direct or implied order, reasonable in nature, and given by and with proper authority." [26] In other words, an isolated case of resistance may not necessarily constitute insubordination, but repeated cases will. Restated in more general terms, to be a cause for termination, insubordination usually requires cumulative acts with prior reprimands or warnings. Thus, according to the State of California misconduct code, "if an employee is discharged after an act of disobedience of an employer's reasonable order and that act is not of itself misconduct but is part of a prior pattern of cumulative acts of insubordinate conduct, the employer must have given prior reprimands or warnings for the acts in the prior pattern in order for the ultimate discharge to be for misconduct." [27] As a rule of thumb, these prior warnings should be in writing to establish a formal record. However, a single act without prior reprimands or warnings can be considered insubordinate if the act is substantially detrimental to the employer's interest.

BREACHES OF ACADEMIC INTEGRITY

Breaches of academic integrity, synonymous with academic misconduct, occur when an individual does not adhere to commonly held ethical standards of honesty and integrity. At most institutions, this fundamental expectation is stated explicitly in some document, such as a faculty or student handbook. At Stanford, for example, the faculty handbook contains explicit language: "In order to maintain the integrity of its teaching and research and to preserve academic freedom, Stanford University demands high standards of professional conduct from its faculty. In the case of a serious violation of these standards, a faculty member may face disciplinary charges."[28] Similarly, the student handbook states: "Students at Stanford are expected to show both within and without the University such respect for order, morality, personal honor and the rights of others as is demanded of good citizens. Failure to do this will be sufficient cause for removal from the University."[29]

Dismissals of tenured faculty members for academic misconduct occur infrequently. Also, they may be subject to political pressure, drawing various opposing and supporting constituencies into the fray, especially in public institutions. For these two reasons, faculty-member dismissals often attract public attention. A particularly infamous example occurred when the University of Colorado fired a tenured professor, Ward Churchill, for academic misconduct, including plagiarism, fabrication, and falsification (*Churchill v. University of Colorado at Boulder*).[30] The case originated on September 12, 2001, in the aftermath of the September 11 terrorist attack on the World Trade Center, when Churchill wrote an essay, "Some People Push Back: On the Justice of Roosting Chickens."[31] In that essay, Churchill argued that American foreign policies provoked the attacks and questioned the innocence of some of the victims, characterizing them as part of the infrastructure of an imperialist government and as "little Eichmanns." This comparison referred to Adolf Eichmann, a Nazi officer and convicted war criminal for his role as the primary planner of the Holocaust. The essay received little attention until January 2005, when Churchill was invited to speak at Hamilton College in New York. In preparation for his visit, the college's newspaper discovered the essay and publicized its controversial content. The essay was subsequently picked up by national media outlets and quickly mushroomed into a national controversy.

In response to the loud public outcry condemning Churchill's essay, the university's board of regents held a special meeting, where they voted unanimously to authorize the creation of an ad hoc panel to investigate Churchill's academic works, with the apparent goal of establishing cause to fire him. This vote, incidentally, contradicted the board's policy stating that faculty members "should not be subjected to direct or indirect pressures or interference from within the university, and the university will resist to the utmost such pressures or interference when exerted from without."[32] Nonetheless, after approximately two months, the panel concluded that the essay's content did not engender imminent violence or unduly interfere with university operations, constituted protected free speech, and therefore could not serve as the grounds for dismissal of a tenured employee "for cause."

During this preliminary inquiry, however, the panel received several complaints that Churchill had engaged in repeated instances of academic misconduct in his published scholarly writings. In response to those complaints, the university launched a formal investigation of Churchill for nine alleged instances of academic misconduct. Following meticulous due process involving several investigative committees, the university ultimately concluded that Churchill had committed "three acts of evidentiary fabrication by ghostwriting and self-citation, two acts of evidentiary fabrication, two acts of plagiarism, and one act of falsification in his academic writings." After further reviews, in 2007 the board ultimately terminated Churchill's employment, describing his conduct as falling below the minimum standards of professional integrity and academic honesty. Churchill promptly filed a lawsuit, claiming that the university had initiated an investigation into his academic integrity and terminated his employment in retaliation for his controversial but constitutionally protected free speech, namely the essay. As a remedy, he asked for reinstatement of his tenured position and "front pay"—that is, reimbursement for all salary not paid during the investigation and trial.

In trial court, a jury ruled in Churchill's favor, stating that "His employment was terminated in retaliation for his free speech." Furthermore, the jury concluded that the university had not "shown by a preponderance of the evidence that [Churchill] would have been dismissed for other reasons." However, the jury found that Churchill suffered no actual economic or noneconomic damages and awarded him nominal damages in the amount of one dollar.

This was a short-lived victory for Churchill. After the verdict, the university claimed "absolute immunity" against a lawsuit aimed at the board of regents' termination decision because it was a "quasi-judicial" action. Absolute immunity shields against lawsuits a public official's conduct that violates a plaintiff's constitutional rights even if that conduct was malicious. It is available to a narrow class of public officials whose special functions or constitutional status requires complete protection from a lawsuit, such as judges and magistrates. The university argued that the board of regents was in this protected class because its investigation of Churchill was akin to a judicial process; that is, it was "quasi-judicial." Thus, by their argument, absolute immunity would shield the board members (public officials) termination actions (conduct) that violated Churchill's (plaintiff) freedom of speech (constitutional rights) even if that termination was malicious. The court agreed with this argument, declared absolute immunity, and vacated the jury's verdict, including the one-dollar award. Moreover, in this context, the court ruled that "even if equitable remedies were legally permissible in this case, the reinstatement would be inappropriate given that Churchill's relationship with the University was irreparably damaged." The court reasoned further that reinstatement would likely result in undue interference with the academic process, thus harming "the integrity of the University, its faculty, and its students given the fact that Churchill committed numerous instances of academic dishonesty in his scholarship."

In justifying its rulings, the trial court rejected the jury verdict in Churchill's favor, reasoning that it merely meant that the university failed to prove by a preponderance of evidence that he would have been terminated for reasons other than his protected speech in the essay. "Just because the University used the discovery of Churchill's academic misconduct as a pretext for its violation of his constitutional rights, the trial court reasoned, does not make the findings condemning his lack of academic integrity any less meritorious." The case ended in 2013 with Churchill's termination when his appeal to the Colorado Supreme Court was unsuccessful.

Because of the underlying political implications, this case ignited a firestorm of controversy that still smolders. The university's investigative committee on misconduct presaged this attention in the introduction to their report: "Professor Churchill repeatedly suggested to the Committee that he was targeted for investigation in a discriminatory manner due in part to his controversial left-wing views, but the Committee notes that public figures who choose to speak out on controversial matters of public concern naturally attract more controversy and attention to their background and work than scholars quietly writing about more esoteric matters that are not the subject of political debate."[33] During the proceedings, various academic groups, including the venerable ACE, National Association of Independent Colleges and Universities, American Association of State Colleges and Universities, and AAU filed an amicus brief supporting the university's claim of absolute immunity, arguing that it protects universities against repeated claims by dissatisfied faculty members and upholds the courts' deference to universities in making academic judgments.[34] Some website blogs added vitriolic criticism of Churchill.[35] In contrast, the equally venerable American Civil Liberties Union, AAUP, and National Coalition against Censorship filed an amicus brief opposing absolute immunity for the board of regents, arguing that it was inappropriate in this case, and supporting the jury verdict in favor of Churchill's First Amendment rights. Likewise, the National Lawyers

Guild filed two separate briefs in support of Churchill, asserting that "academic freedom, a central component of the First Amendment and essential to a thriving democracy, is imperiled when state university officials succumb to political pressure to fire a tenured professor over constitutionally protected statements."[36] Amidst all of this wrangling, the political controversy allegedly cost the university president, Elizabeth Hoffman, her job when she refused a demand from Colorado Governor Bill Owens to fire Churchill promptly in 2005, shortly after revelation of the "little Eichmann" essay.[37] (Who has the power in this kind of situation? Clearly, the governor.) The arguments pro and con over Churchill's dismissal continue in various web blogs, most of them with strong political overtones. All of this demonstrates the sometimes contentious and tumultuous impact when a university fires a tenured professor—especially in a politically-charged context. It also demonstrates, once again, how effectively the doctrines of immunity protect public university administrators within the legal system. As in this case, the core issues may never be addressed.

In addition to institutional policies, the federal government imposes regulatory compliance with ethical standards of integrity in research on all recipients of federal grants and contracts.[38] Technically, it holds the institution accountable for any violations by its employees. However, the institution will undoubtedly pass this accountability down to the transgressing investigator. Indeed, faculty members and administrators have lost their jobs—they were fired, resigned, or retired—for flouting federal standards for ethical behavior.

These cases involving alleged violations of federal regulations seldom reach the courts. They are usually investigated so rigorously by the university and the federal government that there is little defense against the charges. Usually, the university investigates misconduct allegations initially. If it concludes that misconduct has occurred, it informs any federal agencies that had funded the researcher. The agencies then launch their own independent investigation. If they also conclude that misconduct has occurred, they order appropriate sanctions against the researcher—independent of any university sanctions. One notable example involved famed Harvard professor Marc Hauser. After his students accused him of reporting faulty data, Harvard administrators seized some of Professor Hauser's files and launched an in-house investigation. At that time, Professor Hauser was placed on a one-year's leave of absence and, subsequently, was not allowed to teach a scheduled course. Harvard's investigation found that Professor Hauser had, indeed, committed eight cases of scientific fraud. By law, the university informed the Department of Health and Human Services, which also investigated the allegations and concluded that misconduct had occurred in six cases. According to the Department's Office of Research Integrity (ORI), Dr. Hauser had fabricated data, manipulated results in multiple experiments, and described how studies were conducted in factually incorrect ways.[39] The ORI sanctions were that Professor Hauser: exclude himself from serving as an advisor to the U.S. Public Health Service; agree to have his work supervised if it is supported by federal funding; and have any institution employing him vouch for the validity of any research supported by federal grants. Disgraced professionally, Professor Hauser resigned his faculty position at Harvard rather than wait for further university disciplinary actions. Faced with the extensive evidence implicating scientific misconduct, it is extremely doubtful that a lawsuit would gain any traction. In the absence of any major procedural or legal errors, the courts would most probably defer to the university and federal judgments.

MORAL TURPITUDE

Moral turpitude refers to an "offense or a crime that is illegal but also shows a person's baseness and depravity."[40] Crimes involving moral turpitude entail reprehensible behavior and, in a broad sense, immoral conduct that violates the prevailing ethical standards of the community at the time. The AAUP transposes this definition to the academic setting: "The standard is not that the moral sensibilities of persons in the particular community have been affronted. The standard is behavior that would evoke condemnation by the academic community generally."[41] Within academia, immoral behavior tends to cover acts of sexual misconduct, sexual harassment, and dishonesty, such as plagiarism, which set a bad example for students. Indirectly, this refined definition links moral turpitude with a faculty member's ability to teach. Apropos this linkage, the courts have ruled that immorality "is sufficient cause only where the record shows harm to pupils, faculty, or the school itself."[42] That is, there must be evidence showing that the behavior impairs the teacher's effectiveness in the classroom.[43]

In that context, classroom effectiveness is a broad phrase that covers not only pedagogy but also professional stature. In *Corstvet v. Boger*, for example, a tenured professor at Oklahoma State University (OSU) was fired for moral turpitude after he was caught soliciting sex in the men's rooms of the Student Union Building.[44] Although he "was considered a very good teacher with excellent research capabilities," the court noted that "The sole issue is not simply whether the incident affected his teaching ability." It affirmed the university's contention that Professor Corstvet's "conduct constitutes moral turpitude and exhibits a pattern unfit . . . for a . . . faculty member"; it was "grossly unbecoming and unfit behavior" for an OSU professor. In other words, the act of moral turpitude compromised Professor Corstvet's stature in the community and, by inference, his effectiveness in the classroom. This resembles the conclusion in *Gaylord*.

Moral turpitude extends beyond the walls of academia into society at large. Egregious criminal behavior unrelated to a faculty member's academic appointment, for example, can be a cause for dismissal. In 1979, a tenured professor, Makram Samaan, pleaded guilty to charges of billing fraud in his private clinical psychology consulting practice. Because of this conviction, he was fired from his university job after an internal review by a faculty committee of the evidence. Subsequently, Dr. Samaan filed a lawsuit, *Samaan v. Trustees of the California State University and Colleges*, claiming that his dismissal violated his rights to due process.[45] The courts disagreed and affirmed the university's actions in terminating him.

Sexual harassment of students or colleagues may not constitute moral turpitude definitionally, but it certainly constitutes offensive behavior that may be cause for dismissal. Harassment depends on the local mores and circumstances. Comments of a sexual nature may be acceptable in one culture but not another. Nonetheless, some harassment situations are readily apparent: for example, fondling or blatant sexual overtures. Moreover, there are numerous court cases affirming faculty dismissals because they offered good grades for sexual favors.[46] Others are less obvious: for example, an offer of special help in a course over lunch or dinner. Commonly, if an individual claims to be the victim of harassment, the institutional practice is to respect the claim and to take corrective measures, such as a reprimand to the offender, reassignment of one or both of the parties, and other disciplinary actions.

Perhaps the most common moral dilemma involves consensual sexual relationships between faculty members and students. In academia, as in all other workplaces, these kinds of relationships arise. Indeed, they are inevitable. Because of the complexity of faculty—student relationships, explicit regulations and dogmatic policies are not always feasible. In fact, specific policies prohibiting or even discouraging romantic relationships are inherently difficult to enforce. Nonetheless, these relationships are generally frowned upon if the faculty member is the student's instructor, supervisor, or advisor.

The best practice is to develop an institutional policy for managing (not prohibiting) faculty—student romances. For example, the University of Wisconsin–Madison's policy states that: "The university presumes that the ability to make objective decisions is compromised if there is a romantic and/or sexual relationship between two individuals who have a reporting or evaluative relationship. The power differential may not only obscure objectivity but may influence perceptions of consensuality. Therefore, the individual with the power or status advantage is required to report the relationship to his or her supervisor to ensure that the conflict of interest is removed."[47] This policy applies to the following situations:

- "One member of a couple supervises the other or teaches in an academic program in which the other member is enrolled.
- One member of a couple will vote on or substantially influence the other's salary, job contract, promotion, or other condition of employment.
- One member of a couple is the other's instructor or grader in a course or degree program, or is in a position to influence the other's academic progress."

The fundamental power imbalance between the faculty member and the student lies at the core of these situations. Fortunately, educational institutions recognize this imbalance and, like the University of Wisconsin–Madison, have internal procedures for investigating troublesome cases. The Wisconsin policy of removing the inherent conflict of interest—that is, of managing the relationship—provides a good working model. Managing a consensual romantic relationship is fairly straightforward. The basic rule is to mitigate the power imbalance. For example, if a faculty advisor enters into a romantic relationship with his or her graduate student, the student must choose another advisor. Or, if a department chair enters into a romantic relationship with another department member, somebody besides the chair (such as an associate chair or a dean) must determine pay raises, promotions, and so forth for the romantic partner. If a professor becomes involved with a student in a class, a mitigation strategy will depend on the available options. At best, another teacher in the class will oversee all grading of the student's efforts. At worst, the student may have to drop the class. Except in egregious cases, the resolution of a romantic relationship stops short of dismissal.

WRONGFUL TERMINATION

Legally, "wrongful termination" occurs when an employer has dismissed an employee in violation of the employee's legal rights. It is also called "wrongful discharge." To be "wrongful," one or more legal rights specified in the employment contract or in federal antidiscrimination laws must have been violated. It is not enough for the employee to simply show that he or she was treated unfairly. It may also be wrongful if the employer has not followed its own termination procedures documented in an employee handbook or similar policy statement. Note that the absence of a formal contract of employment does not preclude wrongful dismissal when a de facto contract exists by virtue of the employment relationship. Terms of an implied contract may include obligations and rights outlined in an employee handbook.

Wrongful termination difficulties arise if the employee disputes the events that constitute "cause" in the employer's eyes. These disputes can easily transform into a lawsuit for breach of contract. The terminated employee could assert that his or her actions did not meet the criteria specifying "for cause" and, therefore, the employer had no defensible reason to terminate the employment. These lawsuits usually fall under the aegis of case law (based on precedence rather than statute or regulation) and are endemically costly and time-consuming for both parties.

Because of the uncertain outcome, expense, and publicity of trials, universities will often try to settle termination disputes out of court. Regardless of the strength of their case, universities usually prefer these settlements; they bring matters to a conclusion, and very importantly, minimize unwanted, potentially embarrassing publicity. They are sometimes called "nuisance settlements." Often they oblige the university to pay the fired employee what appears to be an exorbitant sum of money—perhaps in the millions of dollars. Although such large payments may seem outrageous to members of the public, the amount is most probably less than the anticipated costs if the case were to go to court.

ALTERNATIVE DISPUTE RESOLUTION

Out-of-court settlements, which do not necessarily come easily, usually involve some means of formal alternative dispute resolution. In fact, because dismissals for cause seldom generate good will between the parties involved, making any kind of negotiation difficult, many employment contracts explicitly require attempts to resolve these disputes through alternative dispute resolution before taking them to the courts. In some jurisdictions, including all federal agencies, alternative dispute resolution is a required precursor to consideration before the courts.[48] Agreements reached in this way are enforceable. If an agreement cannot be reached, both parties retain the option of further litigation.

The most common type of alternative dispute resolution involves formal mediation. Most civil—but not criminal—employment and contract disputes can be resolved through mediation. This involves a third party, a neutral mediator, who is trained to help people discuss their differences. In principle, the mediator does not decide who is right or wrong or issue a decision. Instead, the mediator helps the parties work out their own solutions to problems. According to the EEOC, "One of the greatest benefits of mediation is that it allows people to resolve the charge in a friendly way and in ways that meet their own unique needs. Also, a charge can be resolved faster through mediation. While it takes less than 3 months on average to resolve a charge through mediation, it can take 6 months or longer for a charge to be investigated. Mediation is fair, efficient and can help the parties avoid a lengthy investigation and litigation."[49] While some observers may question the assertion that charges are resolved "in a friendly way," few would disagree about the practical advantages of this mediation process.

Professional mediators generally adhere to a structured discussion between the disputing parties. After the mediator explains the rules, each party is invited to explain without interruption the source of the dispute, any adverse consequences, and how to resolve it. Following this, the parties discuss the issues jointly and then in a private caucus with the mediator. Following the caucuses, the parties come back together for direct, joint negotiations. If an agreement is reached, the mediator prepares a written agreement that serves as a legally binding contract. If no agreement is reached, the parties may agree to binding arbitration or going to court.

The dynamics leading up to mediation are illustrated in a mediated employment dispute that occurred in 2004 when the University of Hawaii dismissed its president, Evan Dobelle, "for cause." When it hired Dobelle, the university offered him a lucrative seven-year contract. Importantly, the contract contained termination clauses. If Dobelle were terminated without cause, he would receive full payment of the amount due for the remainder of the seven-year contract. In contrast, if Dobelle were fired "for cause," the university had to pay only the outstanding salary up to the termination date. According to the contract, "cause" meant "Conviction for a felony offense; A determination by doctors that the president is mentally unstable or otherwise unable to perform the duties of his office; Conduct of the president that (a) constitutes moral turpitude, (b) brings public disrespect and contempt or ridicule upon the university, and (c) proven in a court of law, would constitute grounds for criminal conviction of the president or civil liability of the university."[50] In short, the president would have to commit a criminal or immoral act or become mentally unbalanced to be fired "for cause."

Shortly after his appointment, Dobelle's relationship with the board began to deteriorate. Although his first-year evaluation by the board was favorable, Dobelle received a highly publicized negative second-year evaluation that contained pejoratives such as "arrogance," "disrespectful," "cronyism," "lavish spending," and "condescending."[51] Things went from bad to worse. According to newspaper accounts posted shortly before Dobelle's scheduled third-year evaluation, "The regents have been publicly feuding with Dobelle since a closed-door meeting in September when the regents gave him a negative second-year evaluation. Dobelle . . . refused to accept the goals and performance expectations that the regents set for him."[52]

The festering relationship came to a head when the board fired Dobelle "for cause" in June 2004. In their announcement, the board did not reveal the basis of "for cause."[53] Regardless, termination "for cause" had major financial implications, because the university did not have to pay Dobelle any further salary or other severance benefits. In contrast, had the university terminated Dobelle *without* cause, it would have been obligated to pay Dobelle the entire remaining salary of his seven-year contract plus other benefits that would have totaled $2.3 million in severance pay.[54] Moreover, the university would have to continue paying Dobelle indefinitely as a tenured professor (albeit at a more modest professor's salary). Thus, the university certainly had a financial motivation to terminate "for cause." Not surprisingly, Dobelle threatened to file a lawsuit contesting the "for cause" termination.

Rather than entering a prolonged legal struggle, the university agreed to mediation. A settlement was reached.[55] Dobelle agreed to resign the presidency and his tenured faculty position. In return, the university agreed to rescind its "for cause" declaration, thus retracting its assertion of misfeasance by Dobelle, and to pay a settlement of $1.6 million in cash, plus all legal costs, two years of salary as a nontenured researcher, and the remaining payments on Dobelle's $2 million life insurance policy. In addition, Dobelle would become vested in the state pension plan. The total cost to the university, including its own $1 million in legal fees, was about $3.3 million.[56]

Pundits might question why the university would agree to such an expensive settlement. Indeed, it would have been less expensive simply to buy out the remainder of the seven-year presidential contract and pay the incentive fund. Under those conditions, however, Dobelle would remain at the university as a tenured professor, earning a professor's salary doing what professors do: teaching, research, and service, for an indefinite time and, therefore, at an indefinite cost to the university. Assumedly, the university had prepared cost projections, including legal fees, of the various termination options and realized a priori the likelihood of very expensive litigation. Did the university miscalculate, or did it include other nonfinancial factors in its projections? This remains unknown. Most probably, human nature also played a role here. As in the caricature of a bitter divorce, perhaps neither party really cared to be on the same campus with the other, regardless of the immediate financial consequences of the split. As momentum to terminate Dobelle generated by several regents grew, the board as a whole may have coalesced around the notion of firing him "for cause," and this positive feedback increased the momentum. This energy may have blurred the image posed by a realistic financial projection.

Furthermore, pundits may argue that the university dropped the "for cause" claim too readily. Unfortunately, the robustness of the board's case remains a mystery, because it never divulged the basis of the "for cause" claim. According to the mediation settlement, "the Board recognized at the time that it was obligated to apprise Dr. Dobelle of the basis of its 'for cause' decision, to allow him the opportunity to respond, and to reconsider their decision thereafter if warranted. This is the reason why the grounds for Dr. Dobelle's termination were not made public at the time. During the mediation process, Dr. Dobelle was apprised of the basis for the Board's 'for cause' termination, and Dr. Dobelle was given the opportunity to respond to the issues raised."[57] According to the mediation settlement, there were "several misunderstandings as the result of misinformation," and there were two sides to the dispute. Regardless of the strength of their case, the university faced the prospects of a long, expensive legal battle if they were to persist in the termination "for cause." From a public relations perspective, this would incur negative publicity that has an incalculable opportunity cost. Clearly, the university decided to settle the case and move on. And that was a wise decision from an administrative perspective.

Observers also might ask why the university didn't try to negotiate a mediated termination in the first place, rather than to precipitate an ugly, public dispute. A peaceful solution to a dysfunctional relationship would certainly have been more akin to the norm. Presumably, this rare action—threatening litigation—manifested how deeply and quickly the relationship between Dobelle and the board had eroded. In that sense, both parties failed to recognize the adverse consequences of their querulous interactions leading up to the mediation. At best, they reached an agreement that brought this unfortunate episode to a mutually agreeable conclusion, but only after numerous media reports that were devoured and savored by a news-hungry public. Going their separate ways, the University of Hawaii went on to celebrate its one hundredth anniversary three years later under a new president, and Evan Dobelle went on to become president at another college.

AT-WILL AGREEMENTS

To mitigate the firing process, many employers, including state agencies, appoint personnel with "at-will" agreements. These employment agreements are of an indefinite duration and can be terminated by either the employer or the employee at any time for any reason—that is, with or without cause. As defined by the State Bar of Georgia, "Employment at will means that in the absence of a written contract of employment for a defined duration, an employer can terminate an employee for good cause, bad cause or no cause at all, so long as it is not an illegal cause."[58] What causes might be illegal? Those that violate EEO laws (based on race, color, religion, sex, or national origin), the ADA (based on a physical disability that does not impair the ability to do a job), or the Occupational Safety and Health Act of 1970 (based on a request for a safety inspection of the workplace).

In general, if there is no formal contract, employment is de facto at-will. Likewise, if there is a contract, but it doesn't contain language specifying termination procedures, then employment is by default at-will. In principle, at-will arrangements provide advantages and disadvantages for both employer and employee. Obviously, the employer benefits because incompetent or undesirable employees can be terminated quickly and easily. Conversely, an employee can quit on the drop of a hat in response to unfavorable working conditions or a better job offer. Historically, this was an antidote to servitude against an employee's will.

Importantly, termination of an at-will appointee does not require due process. Some employers may, nonetheless, choose to afford due process, but that is at their discretion. At Colorado State University, for example, "with respect to termination of employment [of at-will appointees] . . . any due process required shall be provided administratively in such manner as may be determined by the President and vice presidents of the University."[59]

The terms of an at-will appointment can surprise an employee who assumes that a contract necessarily implies the right to due process; it does not. Thus, some employers require new employees to read and sign an agreement indicating that they understand the terms of an at-will arrangement. For example, at the University of Southern California, an employee must certify that "I understand that my employment and compensation are at-will and therefore can be terminated with or without cause, at any time without prior notice, at my option or the University's option. . . . I understand that this at-will employment relationship may not be modified by any oral or implied agreement, and that no employee handbook, nor any course of conduct, practice, policy, award, promotion, performance evaluation, transfer, or length of service can modify this at-will relationship."[60] Furthermore, most organizations have similar language defining their at-will hiring policies embedded within their standard operating policies and procedures.

Within university and corporate settings, nearly all staff and administrative employees have at-will appointments; the few exceptions usually include the chief executive, academic, operating, and financial officers as well as the football and basketball coaches. There are two other major classes of employees exempted from at-will arrangements: those covered by collective bargaining agreements and tenured faculty members. In these cases, stereotypic collective bargaining agreements and governing-board policies, respectively, contain specific termination guidelines that trump otherwise generic at-will policies. Historically, faculty members have enjoyed an unusually protective procedural bulwark against termination to ensure the long-held rights of academic freedom.

Parenthetically, in some states, the employer does not have to tell employees why they are being fired. Pragmatically, not telling them would be a mistake; it compounds any bad feelings and reinforces any thoughts about filing a lawsuit against the employer. If the employer questions the employee about some aspect of his or her job performance that may become a cause for termination—a so-called investigatory interview—the employee has the right to legal representation. This is known as the "Weingarten rights." Significantly, the employer isn't required to inform the employee about the Weingarten rights. It's up to the employee to know these rights to representation.

As a general rule for survival, it is always good to assume and to insist on the right to legal representation.

PROGRESSIVE DISCIPLINE

Despite the apparent permissiveness of at-will appointments, most institutions impose an orderly sequence of corrective actions before terminating an employee whose performance has been unsatisfactory. At minimum, this may involve little more than a second-level review of a pending dismissal by human resources personnel to ensure that federal antidiscrimination laws will not be broken. More likely than not, however, institutional policies call for what is known as "progressive discipline." Synonyms include positive discipline systems, positive improvement plans, and corrective action procedures. These terms all refer to a system of escalating responses to unsatisfactory job performance. Rather than fire an employee summarily following a first or minor infraction, the employer enacts a series of escalating responses intended to correct the negative performance. The rationale is that the institution's disciplinary actions should be proportional to the severity of the problem.

Progressive discipline typically involves three stages: an initial verbal warning, accompanied by a written warning, reassignment or suspension, and finally termination. Of course, the specific details of each stage will depend on factors such as the severity of the underperformance, the employee's work history, and other contextual issues. In most situations, the human resources office becomes involved in developing the specific wording of the verbal and written warnings and any other documentation. It is important to heed their advice because of the potential for subsequent grievances by the employee.

An anecdote illustrates the application of progressive discipline and two possible outcomes. Shortly after accepting the position, Provost M. faced a daunting agenda of unfamiliar academic tasks. Noticeably, one colleague inherited from the predecessor's administration, associate provost McP., continually stepped forward to offer guidance and much-needed help on the thornier issues. Provost M. appreciatively accepted this offer and for the next several months assigned various projects to the willing associate.

As time passed, Provost M. began to detect a stasis in the office's workflow. Quite simply, things weren't getting done. A cursory inspection one afternoon promptly revealed that associate provost McP. was the bottleneck. Indeed, not a single assignment had been completed; in fact, many had not been acted upon at all. It was as if work was disappearing into a huge void, never to reappear again. The associate provost had already left for the day, so

Provost M. would have to wait until the following morning to say something about this intolerable situation.

Before speaking with the associate provost, Provost M. consulted with the director of human resources. The director recommended progressive discipline. Therefore, with guidance from the office of human resources, Provost M. met with associate provost McP. and explained that all assignments are expected to be completed in a timely manner; failure to meet these expectations could lead to disciplinary actions. Furthermore, Provost M. said that two current assignments must be finished by no later than 5 p.m. next Friday. The conversation was pleasant and low-key, and associate provost McP. agreed to "do better." Despite this gentle warning, subsequent assignments still were not completed on schedule, including the two due "next Friday." Thus, with further guidance from human resources, Provost M. followed up three months later with a written letter documenting what assignments remained undone, explaining once again the expectation that they should be completed in a timely manner, and setting a timeline for completing future assignments. Furthermore, the letter contained an explicit warning that failure to abide by these expectations may lead to discharge. Again, the conversation was amicable, and associate provost McP. agreed to work harder to meet deadlines. But after another three months, associate provost McP.'s performance still had not improved. Therefore, it was time for the third stage of progressive discipline: reassignment to a position with different, less time-sensitive responsibilities at a small branch campus located on the other side of town. Associate provost McP. was not happy, and stormed out of the office announcing: "I quit! But you can't get rid of me that easily." Although somewhat shaken by the outburst, Provost M. felt relief that the problem had finally been resolved.

As it turned out, the problem was not quite resolved. Shortly later, former associate provost McP. filed a wrongful termination suit against the university based on "constructive discharge," another legal issue that modifies authority.

CONSTRUCTIVE DISCHARGE

"Constructive discharge occurs generally when working conditions are so intolerable as to amount to a firing, despite a lack of a formal termination notice."[61] According to the Supreme Court, constructive discharge requires that the plaintiff "must show that the abusive working environment became so intolerable that her resignation qualified as a fitting response."[62] Although that court ruling applied to a sexual harassment case, it also applies when "the plaintiff quits in reasonable response to an employer-sanctioned adverse action officially changing her employment status or situation, for example, a humiliating demotion, extreme cut in pay, or transfer to a position in which she would face unbearable working conditions."

The origin of constructive discharge goes back to the formative stages of the organized labor movement in the United States. Specifically, the National Labor Relations Act, which was designed to increase employee rights in the workplace, prohibits employers from "discrimination in regard to hire or tenure of employment or any term or condition of employment to encourage or discourage membership in any labor organization."[63] In other words, employers may not terminate employees just because they support membership in a union. Soon after passage of this law (in 1935), the NLRB realized that an employer could circumvent it by imposing threatening work conditions that forced an employee to quit. Consequently, the NLRB (through the courts) developed the constructive discharge doctrine to protect employees against an employer's attempt to force their resignation by creating intolerable working conditions. Various court decisions have elaborated on this concept, but the basic tenet remains intact.

In the preceding anecdote, former associate provost McP. claimed that the reassignment constituted placement in a position with "unbearable working conditions." Using the Supreme Court ruling as a guide, the university's defense rested on three assertions. First, the university had followed its policies (progressive discipline) for resolving the underlying unsatisfactory performance issue. Second, the plaintiff (McP.) had not complained to the university beforehand that the reassignment posed an unbearable working condition, thus precluding the university from any remedial action. And third, reasonable employees might not agree that the reassignment created such intolerable working conditions that abruptly quitting was a reasonable response. The attorneys were confident that the university would prevail, although they acknowledged the uncertainty inherent to any court proceeding. Before the case went to court, however, the university agreed to a settlement that awarded former associate provost McP. the equivalent of one year's salary (plus fringe benefits) and attorney fees in return for dropping the case; the total amount was about $250,000.

Why would the university settle for so much money when they had what appeared to be a solid defense? The university attorneys predicted that the legal costs of going to court would exceed this settlement. Plus, it would attract undesirable attention that might alienate potential donors and legislators, which could ultimately be much costlier in the long run. Basically, this was a "nuisance settlement," with the university paying associate provost McP. purely for economic reasons and not because of responsibility.

The entire episode with associate provost McP. illustrates the sometimes puzzling aspects of employee discipline and termination. The provost had followed the recommended procedures of progressive discipline but somehow, in the process, had exposed the university to a constructive discharge lawsuit, which ultimately cost $250,000 to settle. What went wrong? The answer is that nothing clearly went wrong. The progressive discipline was well orchestrated and achieved the desired goal. Of course, the courts decide each case on its own merits. Nonetheless, reasonable observers would probably agree that the transfer to another campus located in the same city was not "unbearable." Furthermore, there was no "humiliating" change in title or pay. Therefore, McP. was not denied a liberty interest. Importantly, Provost M. didn't have an obvious "hidden agenda" of forcing associate provost McP. to resign when making the reassignment, which seriously eroded the argument for constructive discharge. Indeed, if there was any "hidden agenda," it might have been the associate provost's intention to claim constructive discharge, regardless of the merit of the case, knowing that the university would probably settle out of court. This kind of behavior is difficult to defend against.

SUBSTANCE ABUSE

Terminating employees with substance-abuse problems poses special administrative considerations. For example, alcoholism and drug addiction are considered diseases and, therefore, alcoholics and drug addicts are considered individuals with disabilities subject to protection by the ADA and the Family Medical Leave Act (FMLA).[64] Therefore, federal laws dictate the conditions for terminating these employees, thus limiting employer discretion. Furthermore, several states (e.g., Minnesota) protect employees from being fired for poor performance due to alcoholism without reasonable accommodation.[65]

Legally, the ADA requires an employer to reasonably accommodate employees who can demonstrate that they are "substantially limited in a major life activity." Therefore, if employees can show that their excessive and uncontrollable drinking or drug addiction prevents them from performing the tasks of their employment, then the employer may be obligated to provide some accommodation that allows them to keep their job. According to the ADA, this does not require the employer to alter the essential functions of the job to accommodate them. Most commonly, granting an employee a leave of absence to undergo formal rehabilitation for alcohol or drug addiction constitutes a sufficient and reasonable accommodation. Accordingly, the FMLA prohibits an employer from terminating an employee for extended absences taken in order to obtain treatment for substance abuse. Thus, if an employee is attempting to access professional help in combating alcoholism, for example, an employer must allow the absence. However, the ADA does not require the employer to tolerate relapse or consistent refusal to obtain help when given an appropriate opportunity for rehabilitation.

Incidentally, the ADA distinguishes the use of a substance from addiction to a substance. "Addiction is a disability, and addicts are individuals with disabilities protected by the Act. The protection, however, does not extend to actions based on the illegal use of the substance. In other words, an addict cannot use the fact of his or her addiction as a defense to an action based on illegal use of drugs." The intent here is to protect addicts as long as they are not using drugs.

Importantly, the ADA does not require an employer to tolerate alcoholism or the use of illegal drugs at the workplace. Indeed, it grants an employer the right to terminate an employee who is under the influence of alcohol or drugs on the job. The ADA is quite explicit in this, stating that the employer may:

- prohibit the illegal use of alcohol or illegal drugs at the workplace by all employees
- require that employees shall not be under the influence of alcohol or be engaging in the illegal use of drugs at the workplace
- hold an employee who is an alcoholic or engages in the illegal use of drugs to the same qualification standards for employment or job performance and behavior as other employees

Thus, employees may be fired without accommodation for rehabilitation if they show up "under the influence" on the job or if any unsatisfactory performance or behavior is related to their alcoholism or drug use. However, it is common to use progressive discipline, beginning with a formal letter advising the employee of unacceptable behavior (ranging from disruption to smelling of alcohol) and the requirement for rehabilitation (using paid sick leave) before returning to work. The employer may even pay for the costs of rehabilitation. If an employer offers appropriate accommodation to an alcoholic employee, for example, and problems with the employee's alcohol abuse and resulting performance persist, then an employer can rightfully terminate the employee. In this context, by the way, a "functional alcoholic" is not protected by the ADA if the employer has policies banning the use of alcohol on the job or showing up for work under the influence of alcohol.

The ADA and FMLA requirements are meant to encourage individuals who are suffering from substance abuse to seek the treatment they need without worrying about being fired for seeking professional help. Nonetheless, despite the social virtue of this approach, some employers (including university administrators) tend to shy away from this direct approach to employee substance abuse because it entails a significant investment of both administrative effort and money—in another word, hassle. For example, it is often difficult to persuade other employees to testify against an alleged alcoholic. So, to evade ADA accommodation requirements, administrators may look for ways to fire a substance abuser, such as an alcoholic, for some reason other than alcoholism, such as failure to meet classes, hold office hours, attend required faculty meetings, use profanity in the classroom. Alcoholism may be the root cause, but it is not mentioned in the termination action. With patience, this indirect termination strategy usually works. However, it subverts the good intentions of the law, and, for that reason, should not be condoned.

In this and all other aspects of administration in higher education, the ultimate goal is to "do the right thing." Nothing less is expected from the conscience of society.

SUMMARY

Just as hiring personnel is a primary managerial responsibility, firing personnel is also a primary responsibility. Due process lies at the core of collective bargaining agreements. The process for firing nonunionized employees depends on whether an employment contract with a termination clause is involved. Faculty members with limited-term contracts have the right to rudimentary due process if they are subject to dismissal. Tenured faculty members at most universities have the right to extensive due process based on AAUP guidelines. The termination clauses in most executive-level and faculty-member contracts address termination "for cause," meaning that the employee misbehaved in some way. There are four generally accepted causes for termination of faculty members: incompetence, insubordination, breaches of academic integrity, and moral turpitude. Although academics enjoy broad freedoms, they must abide by their employer's directions or risk disciplinary action. "Wrongful termination" occurs when an employer has dismissed an employee in violation of the employee's legal rights. Often, universities try to settle termination disputes out-of-court through some form of alternative dispute resolution. To mitigate the firing process, many employers appoint personnel with "at-will" agreements. These employment agreements can be terminated by either the employer or the employee at any time for any reason. Rather than fire an employee following a first infraction, most employers enact progressive discipline, a series of escalating responses intended to correct the negative performance. Constructive discharge occurs when working conditions are so intolerable that they amount to a firing, despite the lack of a formal termination notice. If employees can show that substance abuse use affects job performance adversely, then the employer may be obligated to provide some accommodation that allows them to keep their job. However, an employer is not required to tolerate substance abuse at the workplace.

NOTES

1. Paul Volcker, quoted in William G. Bowen, *The Board Book: An Insider's Guide for Directors and Trustees* (New York: W. W. Norton, 2008), 46–47.

2. University of Hawaii Professional Assembly (UHPA) and the University of Hawaii Board of Regents (UH-BOR), "Disciplinary Actions," in *July 2009–June 2015 Agreement between the University of Hawaii Professional Assembly (UHPA) and the University of Hawaii Board of Regents (UH-BOR)* (2011).

3. Donna R. Euben, "Termination and Discipline," *Faculty Termination & Disciplinary Issues* (2004), http://www.aaup.org/issues/appointments-promotions-discipline%C2%A0/termination-discipline-2004. (Accessed January 20, 2014).

4. American Association of University Professors, "1958 Statement on Procedural Standards in Faculty Dismissal Proceedings," (1990), http://www.aaup.org/report/1958-statement-procedural-standards-faculty-dismissal-proceedings. (Accessed January 20, 2014).

5. Ibid.

6. Euben, "Termination and Discipline."

7. Louis Joughin, "Academic Due Process," *Law and Contemporary Problems* 28, no. Summer (1963): 576.

8. American Association of University Professors, "1958 Statement on Procedural Standards in Faculty Dismissal Proceedings"; Euben, "Termination and Discipline."

9. *Yao v. Board of Regents of University of Wisconsin System*, 649 N.W. 2d 356 (2002).

10. *Greene v. Howard University*, 412 F.2d 1128 (1969).

11. Steven G. Poskanzer, *Higher Education Law: The Faculty* (Baltimore: Johns Hopkins University Press, 2002), 208–26.

12. *Riggin v. Board of Trustees of Ball State University*, 489 N.E.2d 616 (1986).

13. *Gaylord v. Tacoma School District No. 10*, 88 Wn. 2d 286, 559 P. 1340, *cert denied,* 46 U.S.L.W. 3220 (1977).

14. "Oxford Dictionaries Online," Oxford University Press, http://oxforddictionaries.com/?attempted=true. (Accessed July 28, 2014).

15. California Labor Code §2856 (2013).

16. Keisha-Ann G. Gray, "Defiant and Disrespectful," *Legal Clinic* (2011), http://www.hreonline.com/HRE/view/story.jhtml?id=533342732. (Accessed August 15, 2013).

17. Poskanzer, *Higher Education Law: The Faculty*, 209–10.

18. "Black's Law Dictionary Free Online Legal Dictionary," http://thelawdictionary.org/. (Accessed July 17, 2014).

19. State of California Employee Development Department, "Misconduct MC 255," http://www.edd.ca.gov/uibdg/Misconduct_MC_255.htm. (Accessed March 10, 2014).

20. Ibid.

21. *Chitwood v. Feaster*, 468 F.2d 359 (1972).

22. Poskanzer, *Higher Education Law: The Faculty*, 210.

23. *Pickering v. Board of Education*, 391 U.S. 563 (1968).

24. *Roseman v. Indiana University*, 520 F. 2d 1364 (3rd Cir. 1975); cert. denied, 424 U.S. 921 (1975).

25. *Garcetti v. Ceballos*, 547 U.S. 410 (2006).

26. *Sims v. Board of Trustees*, 414 So. 2d 437 (Miss.) (1982).

27. State of California Employee Development Department, "Misconduct MC 255." (Accessed March 11, 2014).

28. Stanford University, "Statement on Faculty Discipline, § 4.3.A(1)," *Faculty Handbook* (2007), http://facultyhandbook.stanford.edu/ch4.html#g. (Accessed November 12, 2013).

29. "Academic Honesty and Dishonesty," *Stanford Teaching Commons*, https://teachingcommons.stanford.edu/resources/teaching-resources/how-evaluate-students/academic-honesty-and-dishonesty. (Accessed November 12, 2013).

30. *Churchill v. University of Colorado at Boulder*, 2012 CO 54 No. 11SC25 (2012).

31. Ward Churchill, "Some People Push Back: On the Justice of Roosting Chickens," (2011), http://www.kersplebedeb.com/mystuff/s11/churchill.html. (Accessed June 23, 2014).

32. University of Colorado Board of Regents, "Faculty Responsibility §5.D.2," *Regents Laws*, http://www.cu.edu/regents/article-5-faculty. (Accessed June 25, 2014).

33. University of Colorado at Boulder, "Report of the Investigative Committee of the Standing Committee on Research Misconduct at the University of Colorado at Boulder Concerning Allegations of Academic Misconduct against Professor Ward Churchill," (2006), https://portfolio.du.edu/downloadItem/141202. (Accessed June 25, 2014).

34. State of Colorado Supreme Court, "*Amici Curiae* Brief of American Council on Education, National Association of Independent Colleges and Universities, American Association of State Colleges and Universities, and Association of American Universities," (2012), http://www.acenet.edu/news-room/Documents/Amicus-Brief-Submitted-to-the-Colorado-Supreme-Court-in-Ward-Churchill-v-the-University-of-Colorado.pdf. (Accessed June 23, 2014).

35. Bill O'Reilly, "The Demise of Ward Churchill," http://www.creators.com/opinion/bill-oreilly/the-demise-of-ward-churchill.html. (Accessed June 23, 2014).

36. National Lawyers Guild, "*Amicus Curiae*," https://www.nlg.org/publications/amicuscuriae. (Accessed June 23, 2014).

37. Oliver Uytterbrouck, "UNM Presidential Candidate Won't Bend to Political Wills," *Albuquerque Journal* (2011), http://www.abqjournal.com/74257/news/unm-presidential-candidate-wont-bend-to-political-wills.html. (Accessed June 23, 2014).

38. Dean O. Smith, *Managing the Research University* (New York: Oxford University Press, 2011), 145–68.

39. Office of Research Integrity, "Case Summary: Hauser, Marc," *Federal Register* 77, no. 173 (2012): 54917–19.

40. "Black's Law Dictionary Free Online Legal Dictionary." (Accessed November 18, 2013).

41. American Association of University Professors, "Statement of Principles on Academic Freedom and Tenure," (1940), http://www.aaup.org/AAUP/pubsres/policydocs/contents/1940statement.htm. (Accessed November 18, 2013).

42. *Reinhardt v. Board of Education*, 19 Ill. App.3d 481 (1974).

43. Nathan L. Essex, *School Law and the Public Schools: A Practical Guide for Education Leaders* (Needham Heights, MA: Allyn and Bacon, 1999), 185.

44. *Corstvet v. Boger*, 757 F. 2d 223, 227 (10th Cir.) (1985).

45. *Samaan v. Trustees of the California State University and Colleges* 150 Cal.App.3d 646 (1983).

46. Poskanzer, *Higher Education Law: The Faculty*, 220–26.

47. University of Wisconsin–Madison, "Consensual Relationship Policy," http://www.ohr.wisc.edu/polproced/uppp/1505.html. (Accessed November 25, 2013).

48. United States Equal Employment Opportunity Commission, "Mediation," http://www.eeoc.gov/employees/mediation.cfm. (Accessed April 25, 2012).

49. Ibid.

50. Craig Gima, "UH Regents Considering Whether to Fire Dobelle," *Honolulu Star Bulletin* (2004), http://archives.starbulletin.com/2004/06/13/news/index1.html. (Accessed April 21, 2011).

51. University of Hawaii Board of Regents, "University of Hawaii Board of Regents' Annual Evaluation of President Evan S. Dobelle," (2003), http://ilind.net/misc%20/dobelle_eval.pdf. (Accessed April 22, 2011).

52. Craig Gima, "Dobelle Fired," *Honolulu Star Bulletin* (2004), http://archives.starbulletin.com/2004/06/16/news/story1.html. (Accessed April 22, 2011).

53. University of Hawaii System, "UH Board of Regents Terminates President Dobelle," (2004), http://www.hawaii.edu/news/article.php?aId=819. (Accessed April 22, 2011).

54. Gima, "UH Regents Considering Whether to Fire Dobelle."

55. University of Hawaii Board of Regents, "Statement of the Board of Regents of the University of Hawaii, Dr. Evan S. Dobelle, and Mediator Warren Price," *Honoluluadvertiser.com* (2004), http://the.honoluluadvertiser.com/article/2004/Jul/29/br/statement.html. (Accessed April 25, 2011).

56. Ray Daysog, "Legal Fees to Cost UH $1M," *Honolulu Star Bulletin* (2004), http://archives.starbulletin.com/2004/09/24/news/index2.html. (Accessed April 23, 2011); Vicki Vi-

otti, "Dobelle Legal Costs Hit $1M," *Honoluluadvertiser.com* (2004), http://the.honoluluadvertiser.com/article/2004/Sep/25/ln/ln17a.html. (Accessed April 23, 2011).

57. University of Hawaii Board of Regents, "Statement of the Board of Regents of the University of Hawaii, Dr. Evan S. Dobelle, and Mediator Warren Price," *Honoluluadvertiser.com*, http://the.honoluluadvertiser.com/article/2004/Jul/29/br/statement.html.

58. State Bar of Georgia, "What Georgia Employers Need to Know," http://sos.georgia.gov/firststop/georgia_employers.htm. (Accessed June 4, 2013).

59. Colorado State University, "Provision of Due Process to Grievants, § K.8.2," *Academic Faculty and Administrative Professionals Manual* (2010), http://www.facultyandstaff.colostate.edu/ugo/UGO9-AtWillEmployees0410.pdf. (Accessed June 3, 2013).

60. University of Southern California, "At-Will Employment Agreement," (2000), http://policies.usc.edu/emp_forms.html. (Accessed May 24, 2011).

61. "Constructive Discharge Law and Legal Definition," *USLegal* (2011), http://definitions.uslegal.com/c/constructive-discharge/. (Accessed June 1, 2011).

62. *Pennsylvania State Police v. Suders*, 542 U.S. 129 (2004).

63. *National Labor Relations Act*, 29 U.S.C. § 158(a)(3) (2010).

64. *Americans with Disabilities Act*, 28 C.F.R. § 35.131, (2010). *Family and Medical Leave Act*, 29 C.F.R. § 825.119, (1993).

65. *Minnesota Human Rights Act*, § 363A.03.36(2), (2013).

Subject Index

Case Index

339

About the Author

Dean O. Smith has been a professor of physiology for thirty-eight years at the University of Wisconsin–Madison, University of Hawaii, and Texas Tech University. For twenty-two of those years, he was in higher administration as an associate vice president for research, a vice president for research, an executive vice chancellor, and a system senior vice president. Over the years, he has published 135 scientific articles and a definitive book on university research management. He is now professor emeritus at the University of Hawaii.